CASE CLOSED™

VOLUME 12

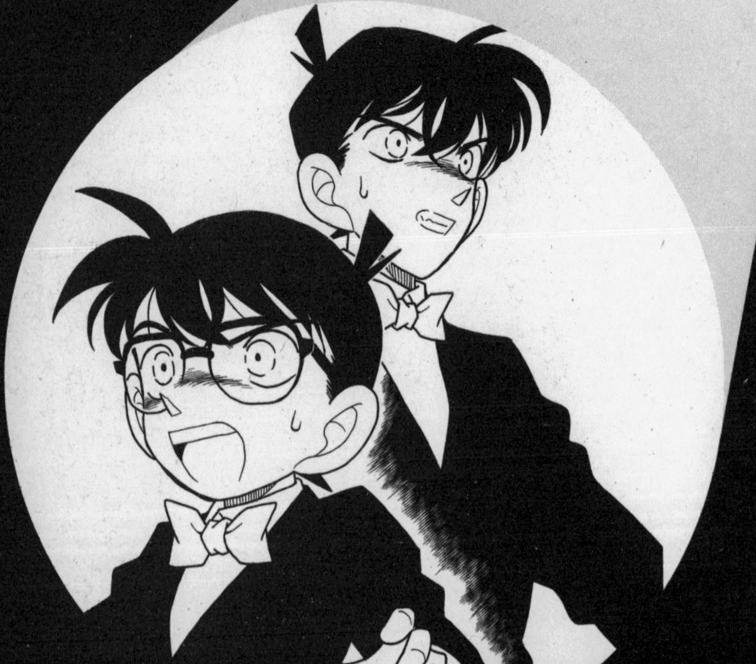

Gosho Aoyama

Case Briefing:

Subject: Jimmy Kudo, a.k.a. Conan Edogawa
Occupation: High School Student/Detective
Special Skills: Analytical thinking and deductive reasoning, Soccer
Equipment: Bow Tie Voice Transmitter, Super Sneakers,
                    Homing Glasses, Stretchy Suspenders

The subject is hot on the trail of a pair of suspicious men in black when he is attacked from behind and administered a strange substance which physically transforms him into a first grader. When the subject confides in the eccentric inventor Dr. Agasa, they decide to keep the subject's true identity a secret for the safety of everyone around him. Assuming the new identity of first-grader Conan Edogawa, the subject continues to assist the police force on their most baffling cases. The only problem is that most crime-solving professionals won't take a little kid's advice!

Table of Contents

ONFIDEN

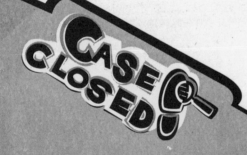

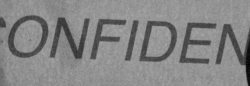

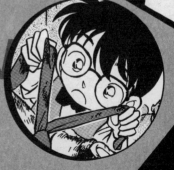

CASE CLOSED
Volume 12 • VIZ Media Edition
GOSHO AOYAMA

Translation & English Adaptation
Naoko Amemiya

Touch-up & Lettering
Walden Wong

Cover & Graphics Design
Andrea Rice

Editor
Urian Brown

Managing Editor **Annette Roman**

Director of Production **Noboru Watanabe**

Vice President of Publishing **Alvin Lu**

Sr. Director of Acquisitions **Rika Inouye**

Vice President of Sales & Marketing **Liza Coppola**

Publisher **Hyoe Narita**

© 1994 Gosho AOYAMA/Shogakukan Inc.
First published by Shogakukan Inc. in Japan as "Meitantei Conan."
New and adapted artwork and text © 2006 VIZ Media, LLC.
All rights reserved.
The stories, characters and incidents mentioned in this publication are entirely fictional.

No portion of this book may be reproduced or transmitted in any form or by any means without written
permission from the copyright holders.

store.viz.com

Printed in the U.S.A.
Published by VIZ Media, LLC
P.O. Box 77010
San Francisco, CA 94107

10 9 8 7 6 5 4 3 2 1
First printing, July 2006

www.viz.com

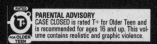

FILE 1: DOCTOR AGASA'S TREASURE CHEST

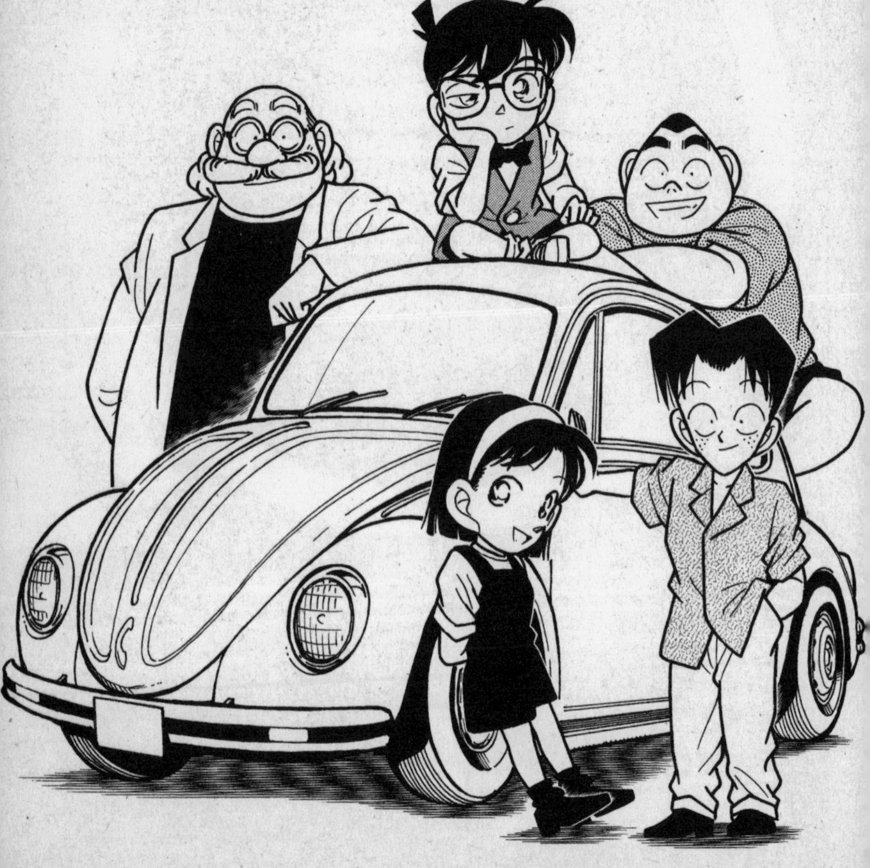

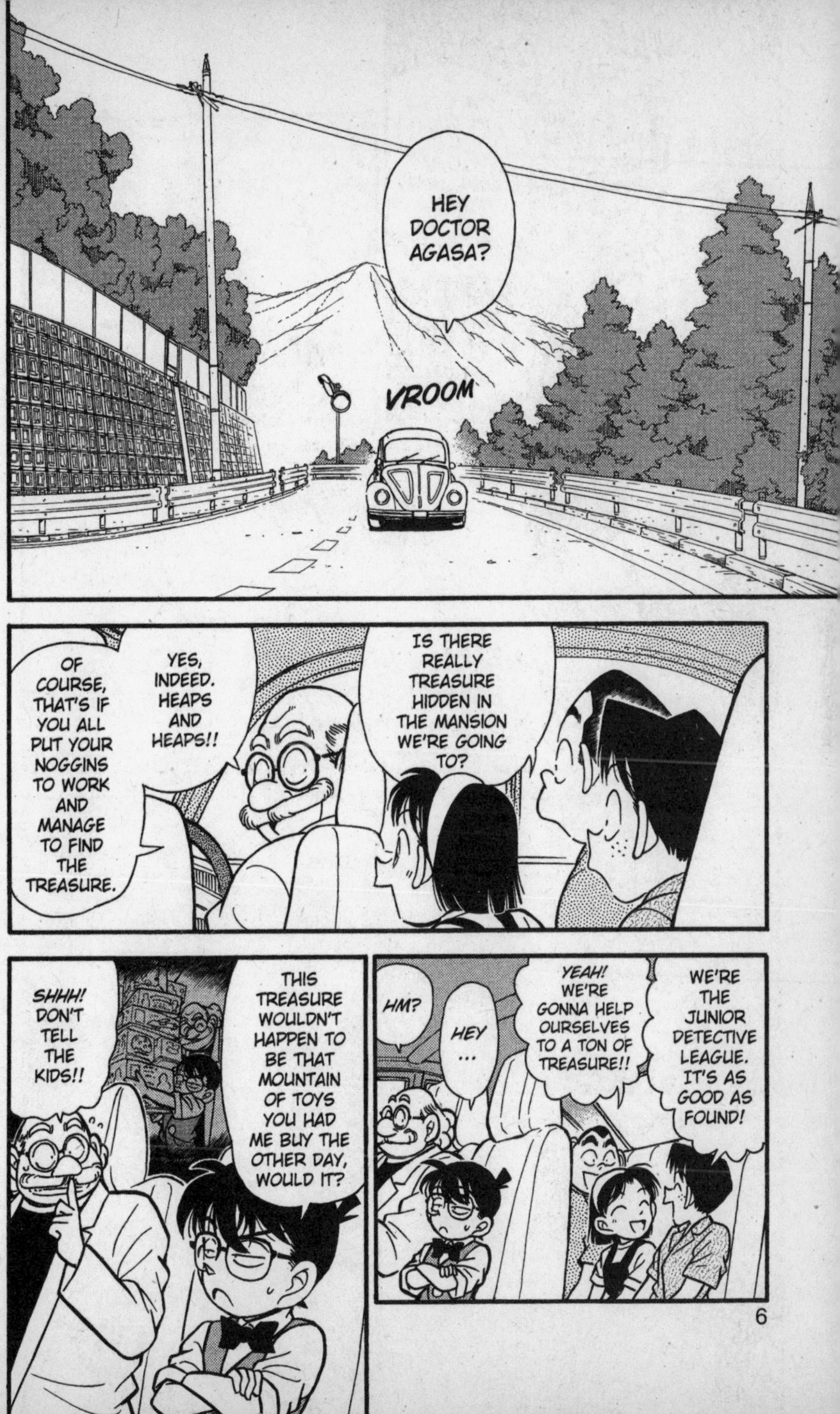
HEY DOCTOR AGASA?
VROOM
IS THERE REALLY TREASURE HIDDEN IN THE MANSION WE'RE GOING TO?
YES, INDEED. HEAPS AND HEAPS!!
OF COURSE, THAT'S IF YOU ALL PUT YOUR NOGGINS TO WORK AND MANAGE TO FIND THE TREASURE.
WE'RE THE JUNIOR DETECTIVE LEAGUE. IT'S AS GOOD AS FOUND!
YEAH! WE'RE GONNA HELP OURSELVES TO A TON OF TREASURE!!
HEY ...
HM?
THIS TREASURE WOULDN'T HAPPEN TO BE THAT MOUNTAIN OF TOYS YOU HAD ME BUY THE OTHER DAY, WOULD IT?
SHHH! DON'T TELL THE KIDS!!

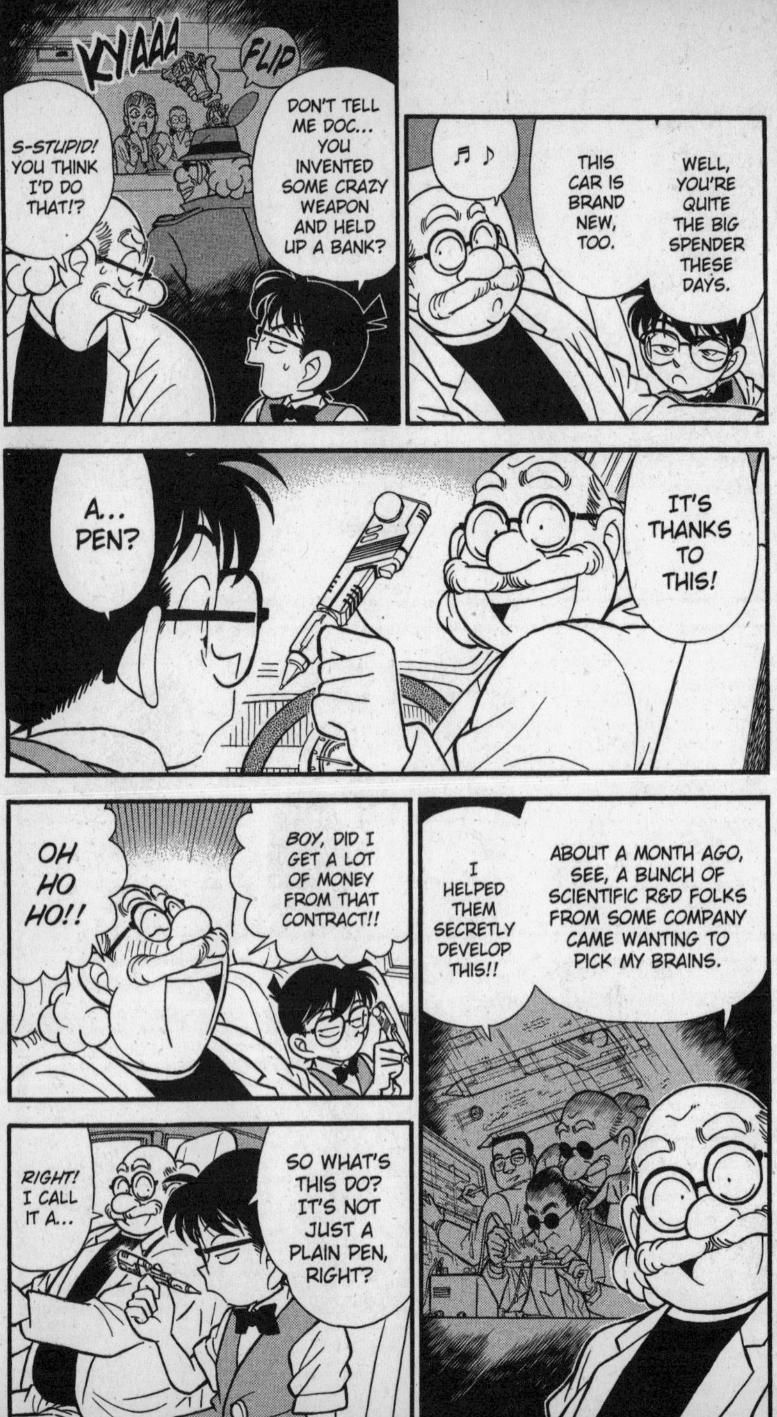

WELL, YOU'RE QUITE THE BIG SPENDER THESE DAYS.
THIS CAR IS BRAND NEW, TOO.
♬ ♪
FLIP
DON'T TELL ME DOC... YOU INVENTED SOME CRAZY WEAPON AND HELD UP A BANK?
KYAAA
S-STUPID! YOU THINK I'D DO THAT!?
IT'S THANKS TO THIS!
A... PEN?
ABOUT A MONTH AGO, SEE, A BUNCH OF SCIENTIFIC R&D FOLKS FROM SOME COMPANY CAME WANTING TO PICK MY BRAINS.
I HELPED THEM SECRETLY DEVELOP THIS!!
BOY, DID I GET A LOT OF MONEY FROM THAT CONTRACT!!
OH HO HO!!
SO WHAT'S THIS DO? IT'S NOT JUST A PLAIN PEN, RIGHT?
RIGHT! I CALL IT A...

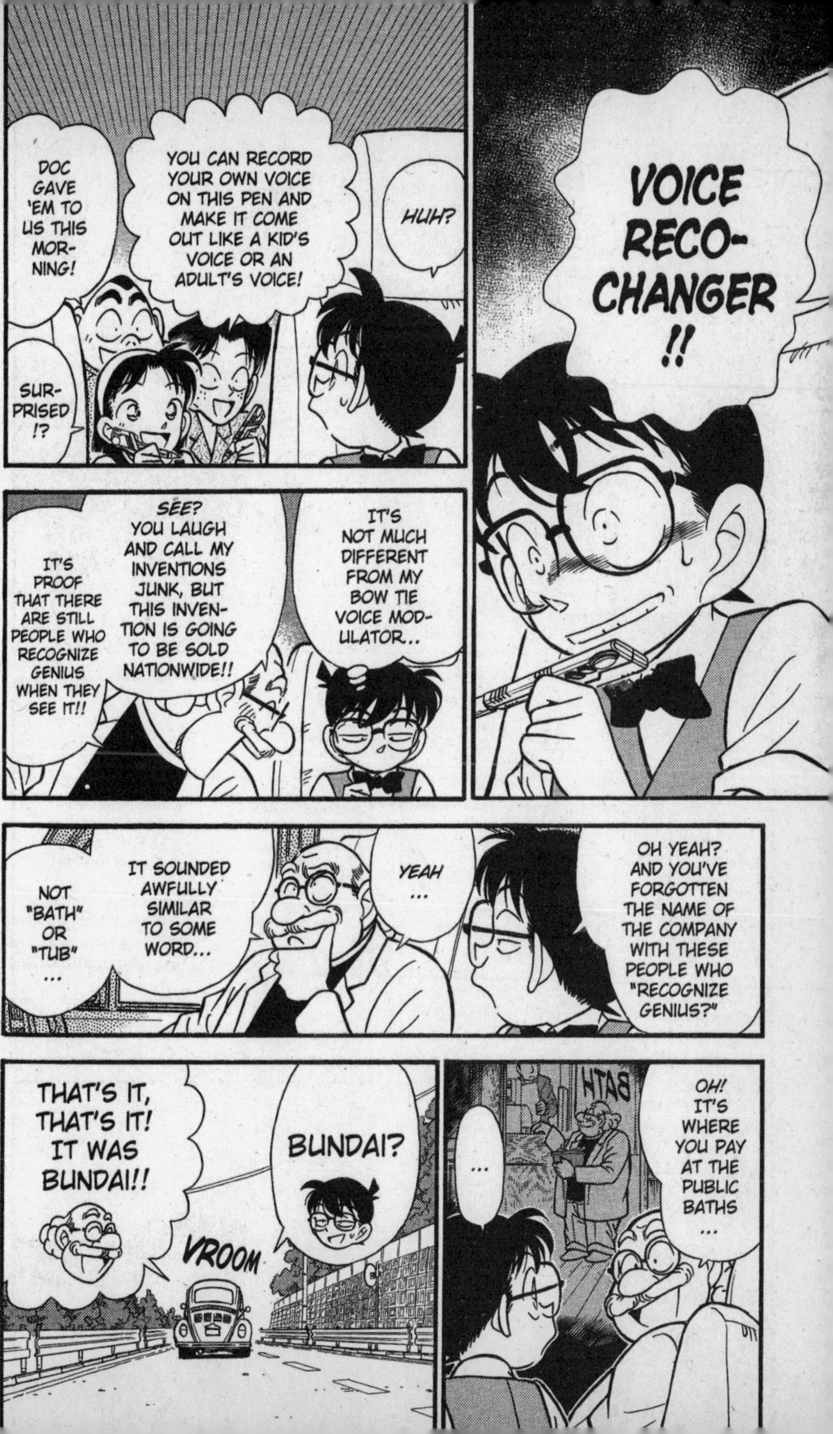

DOC GAVE 'EM TO US THIS MOR-NING!
SUR-PRISED!?
YOU CAN RECORD YOUR OWN VOICE ON THIS PEN AND MAKE IT COME OUT LIKE A KID'S VOICE OR AN ADULT'S VOICE!
HUH?
VOICE RECO-CHANGER!!
IT'S PROOF THAT THERE ARE STILL PEOPLE WHO RECOGNIZE GENIUS WHEN THEY SEE IT!!
SEE? YOU LAUGH AND CALL MY INVENTIONS JUNK, BUT THIS INVEN-TION IS GOING TO BE SOLD NATIONWIDE!!
IT'S NOT MUCH DIFFERENT FROM MY BOW TIE VOICE MOD-ULATOR...
NOT "BATH" OR "TUB" ...
IT SOUNDED AWFULLY SIMILAR TO SOME WORD...
YEAH ...
OH YEAH? AND YOU'VE FORGOTTEN THE NAME OF THE COMPANY WITH THESE PEOPLE WHO "RECOGNIZE GENIUS?"
THAT'S IT, THAT'S IT! IT WAS BUNDAI!!
BUNDAI?
VROOM
BATH
...
OH! IT'S WHERE YOU PAY AT THE PUBLIC BATHS ...

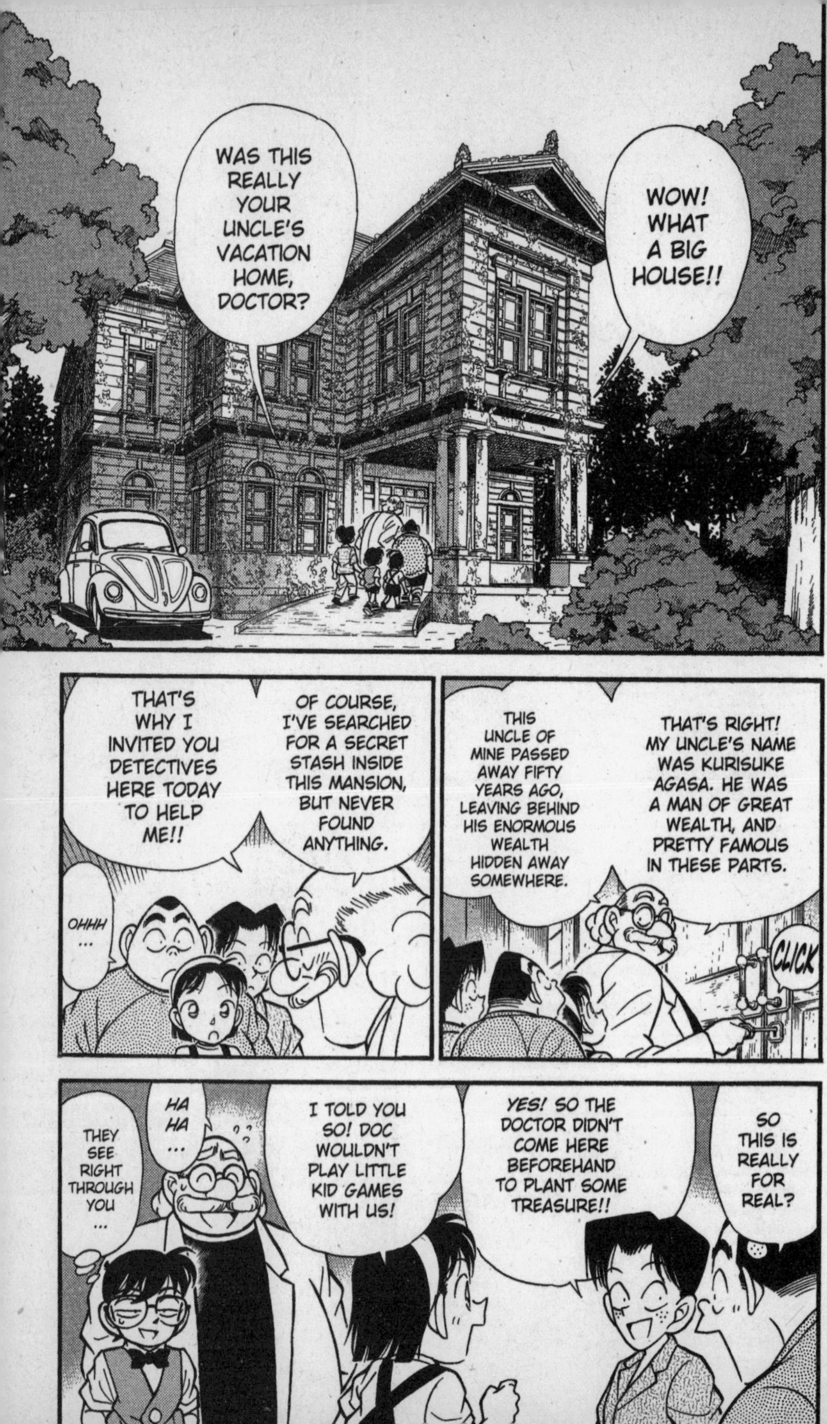
WOW! WHAT A BIG HOUSE!!
WAS THIS REALLY YOUR UNCLE'S VACATION HOME, DOCTOR?
THAT'S RIGHT! MY UNCLE'S NAME WAS KURISUKE AGASA. HE WAS A MAN OF GREAT WEALTH, AND PRETTY FAMOUS IN THESE PARTS.
CLICK
THIS UNCLE OF MINE PASSED AWAY FIFTY YEARS AGO, LEAVING BEHIND HIS ENORMOUS WEALTH HIDDEN AWAY SOMEWHERE.
OF COURSE, I'VE SEARCHED FOR A SECRET STASH INSIDE THIS MANSION, BUT NEVER FOUND ANYTHING.
THAT'S WHY I INVITED YOU DETECTIVES HERE TODAY TO HELP ME!!
OHHH ...
SO THIS IS REALLY FOR REAL?
YES! SO THE DOCTOR DIDN'T COME HERE BEFOREHAND TO PLANT SOME TREASURE!!
I TOLD YOU SO! DOC WOULDN'T PLAY LITTLE KID GAMES WITH US!
HA HA ...
THEY SEE RIGHT THROUGH YOU ...

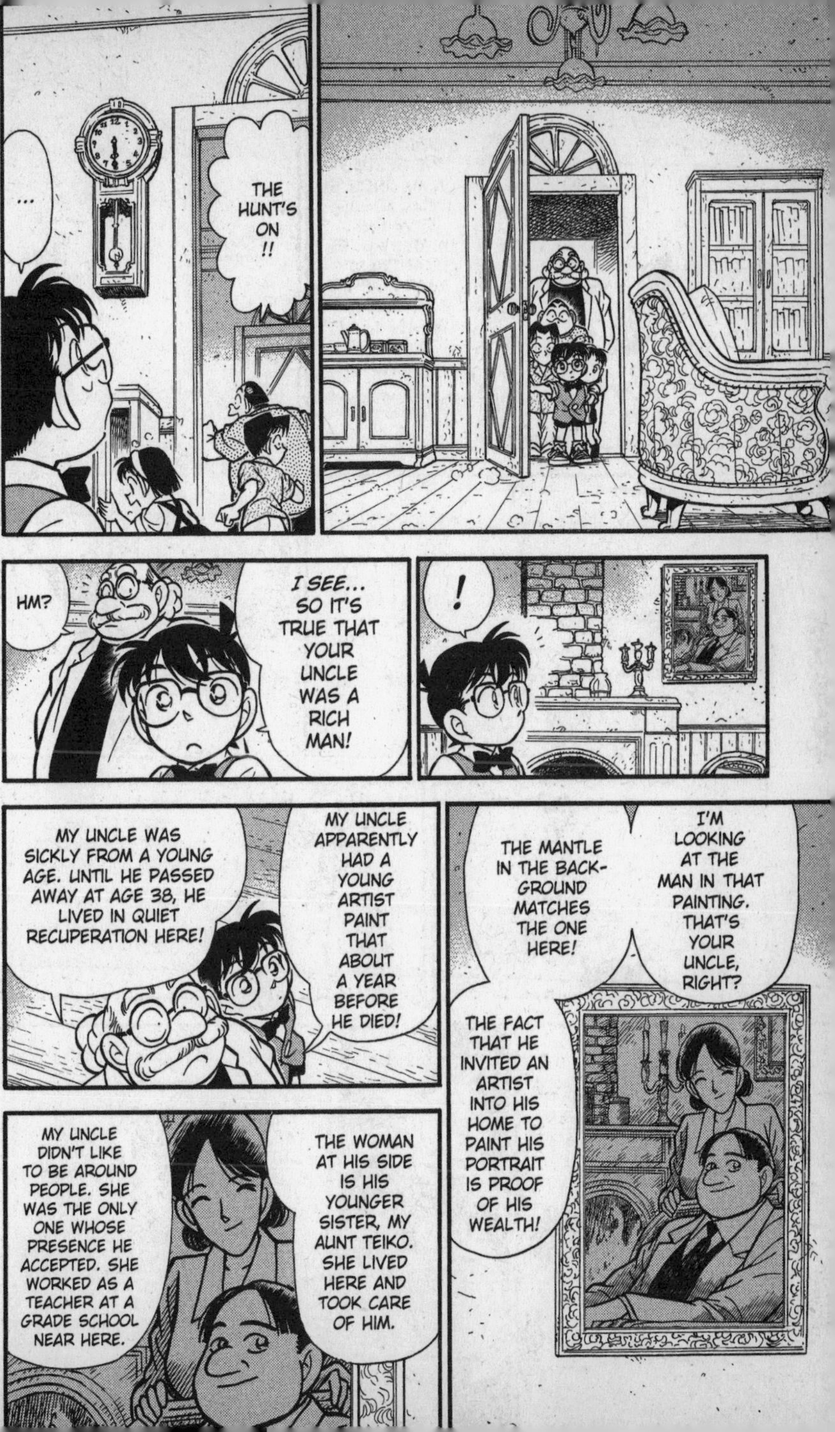
THE HUNT'S ON !!
...
!
I SEE... SO IT'S TRUE THAT YOUR UNCLE WAS A RICH MAN!
HM?
I'M LOOKING AT THE MAN IN THAT PAINTING. THAT'S YOUR UNCLE, RIGHT?
THE MANTLE IN THE BACK-GROUND MATCHES THE ONE HERE!
THE FACT THAT HE INVITED AN ARTIST INTO HIS HOME TO PAINT HIS PORTRAIT IS PROOF OF HIS WEALTH!
MY UNCLE APPARENTLY HAD A YOUNG ARTIST PAINT THAT ABOUT A YEAR BEFORE HE DIED!
MY UNCLE WAS SICKLY FROM A YOUNG AGE. UNTIL HE PASSED AWAY AT AGE 38, HE LIVED IN QUIET RECUPERATION HERE!
THE WOMAN AT HIS SIDE IS HIS YOUNGER SISTER, MY AUNT TEIKO. SHE LIVED HERE AND TOOK CARE OF HIM.
MY UNCLE DIDN'T LIKE TO BE AROUND PEOPLE. SHE WAS THE ONLY ONE WHOSE PRESENCE HE ACCEPTED. SHE WORKED AS A TEACHER AT A GRADE SCHOOL NEAR HERE.

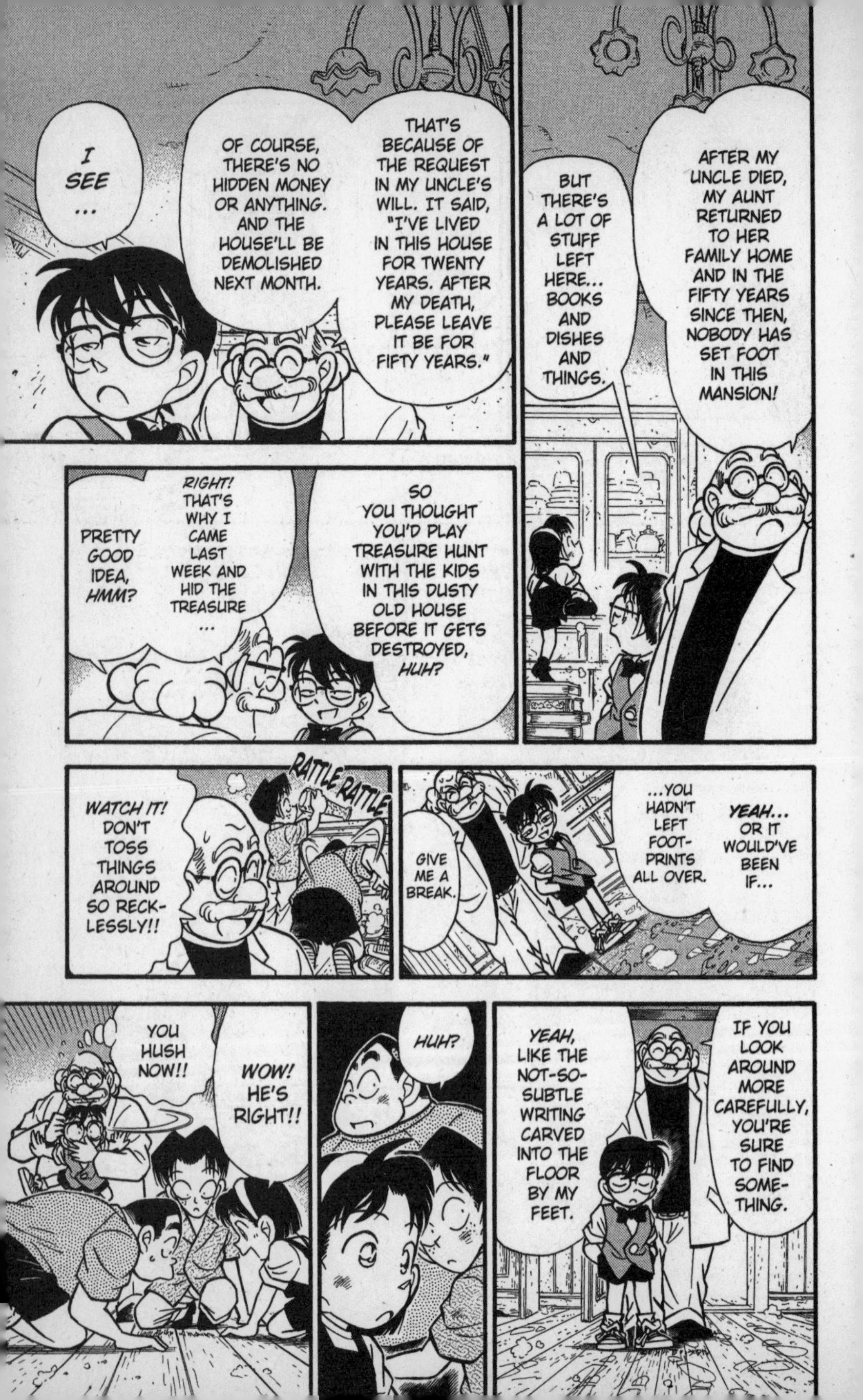
AFTER MY UNCLE DIED, MY AUNT RETURNED TO HER FAMILY HOME AND IN THE FIFTY YEARS SINCE THEN, NOBODY HAS SET FOOT IN THIS MANSION!
BUT THERE'S A LOT OF STUFF LEFT HERE... BOOKS AND DISHES AND THINGS.
THAT'S BECAUSE OF THE REQUEST IN MY UNCLE'S WILL. IT SAID, "I'VE LIVED IN THIS HOUSE FOR TWENTY YEARS. AFTER MY DEATH, PLEASE LEAVE IT BE FOR FIFTY YEARS."
OF COURSE, THERE'S NO HIDDEN MONEY OR ANYTHING. AND THE HOUSE'LL BE DEMOLISHED NEXT MONTH.
I SEE...
SO YOU THOUGHT YOU'D PLAY TREASURE HUNT WITH THE KIDS IN THIS DUSTY OLD HOUSE BEFORE IT GETS DESTROYED, HUH?
RIGHT! THAT'S WHY I CAME LAST WEEK AND HID THE TREASURE...
PRETTY GOOD IDEA, HMM?
YEAH... OR IT WOULD'VE BEEN IF...
...YOU HADN'T LEFT FOOT-PRINTS ALL OVER.
GIVE ME A BREAK.
RATTLE RATTLE
WATCH IT! DON'T TOSS THINGS AROUND SO RECK-LESSLY!!
IF YOU LOOK AROUND MORE CAREFULLY, YOU'RE SURE TO FIND SOME-THING.
YEAH, LIKE THE NOT-SO-SUBTLE WRITING CARVED INTO THE FLOOR BY MY FEET.
HUH?
WOW! HE'S RIGHT!!
YOU HUSH NOW!!

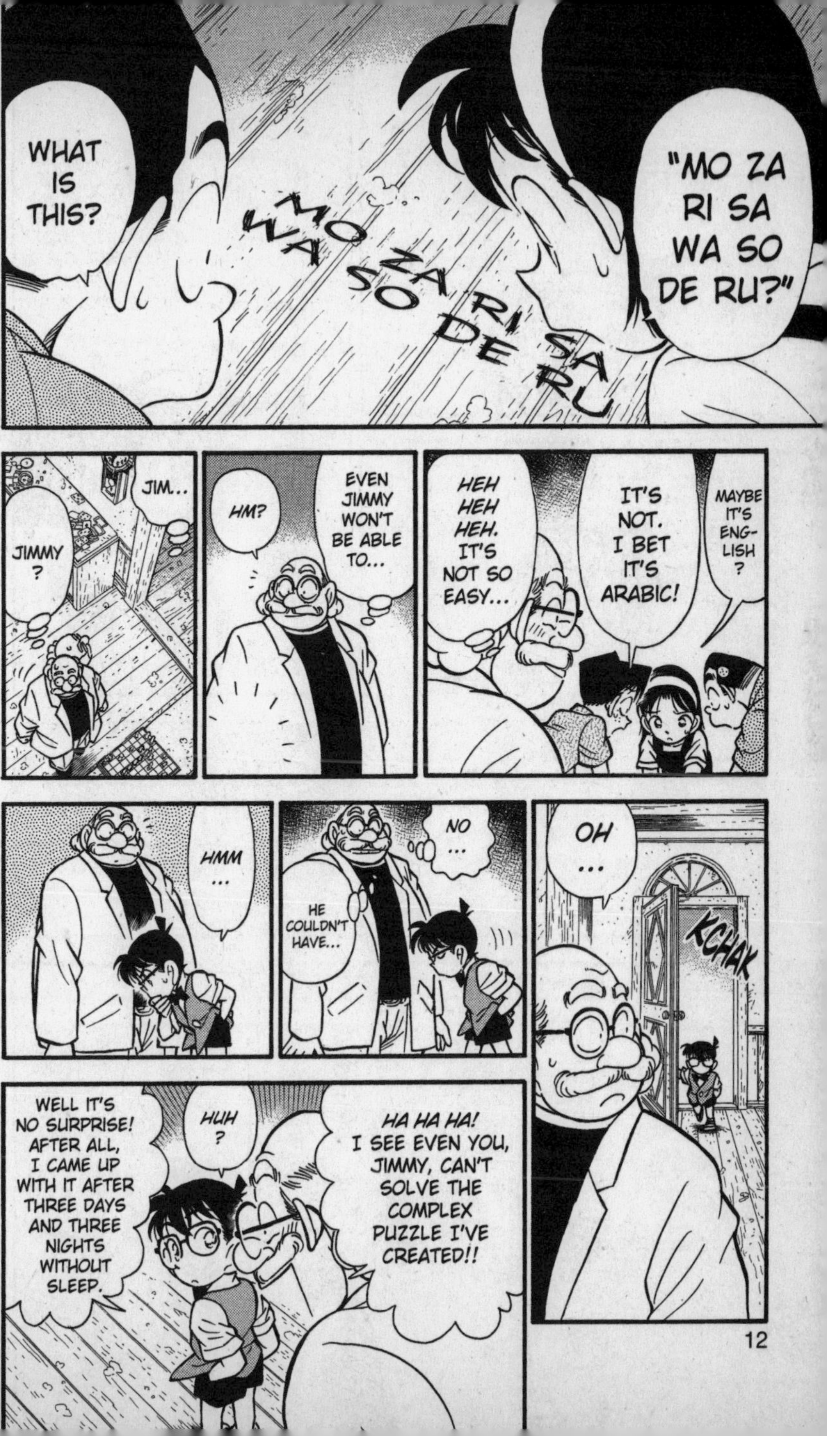
WHAT IS THIS?
"MO ZA RI SA WA SO DE RU?"
MO ZA RI SA WA SO DE RU
JIM...
JIMMY ?
HM?
EVEN JIMMY WON'T BE ABLE TO...
MAYBE IT'S ENGLISH ?
IT'S NOT. I BET IT'S ARABIC!
HEH HEH HEH. IT'S NOT SO EASY...
HMM ...
NO ...
HE COULDN'T HAVE...
OH ...
KCHAK
HA HA HA! I SEE EVEN YOU, JIMMY, CAN'T SOLVE THE COMPLEX PUZZLE I'VE CREATED!!
HUH ?
WELL IT'S NO SURPRISE! AFTER ALL, I CAME UP WITH IT AFTER THREE DAYS AND THREE NIGHTS WITHOUT SLEEP.

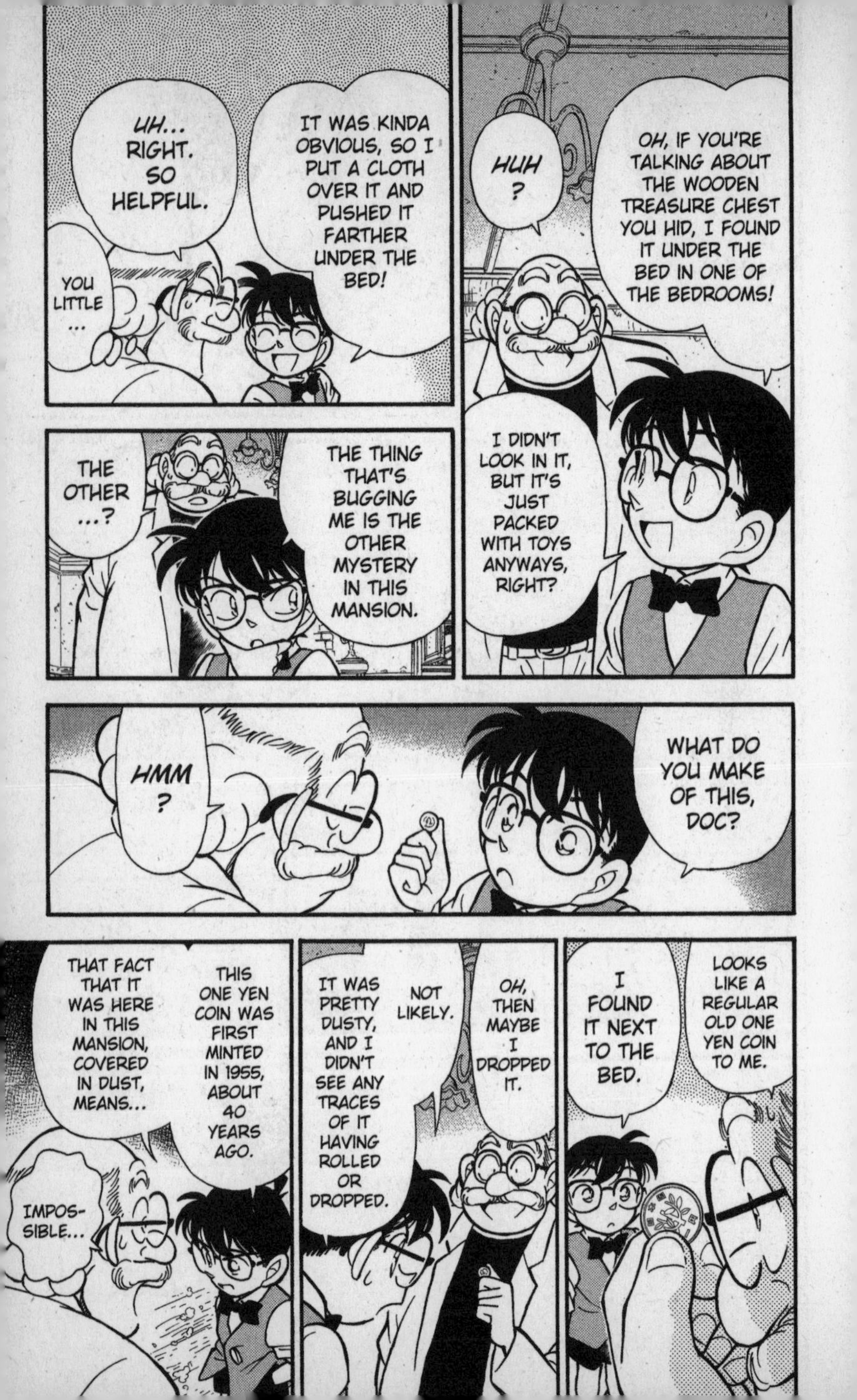
OH, IF YOU'RE TALKING ABOUT THE WOODEN TREASURE CHEST YOU HID, I FOUND IT UNDER THE BED IN ONE OF THE BEDROOMS!
HUH?
I DIDN'T LOOK IN IT, BUT IT'S JUST PACKED WITH TOYS ANYWAYS, RIGHT?
IT WAS KINDA OBVIOUS, SO I PUT A CLOTH OVER IT AND PUSHED IT FARTHER UNDER THE BED!
UH... RIGHT. SO HELPFUL.
YOU LITTLE...
THE THING THAT'S BUGGING ME IS THE OTHER MYSTERY IN THIS MANSION.
THE OTHER...?
WHAT DO YOU MAKE OF THIS, DOC?
HMM?
LOOKS LIKE A REGULAR OLD ONE YEN COIN TO ME.
I FOUND IT NEXT TO THE BED.
OH, THEN MAYBE I DROPPED IT.
NOT LIKELY.
IT WAS PRETTY DUSTY, AND I DIDN'T SEE ANY TRACES OF IT HAVING ROLLED OR DROPPED.
THIS ONE YEN COIN WAS FIRST MINTED IN 1955, ABOUT 40 YEARS AGO.
THAT FACT THAT IT WAS HERE IN THIS MANSION, COVERED IN DUST, MEANS...
IMPOSSIBLE...

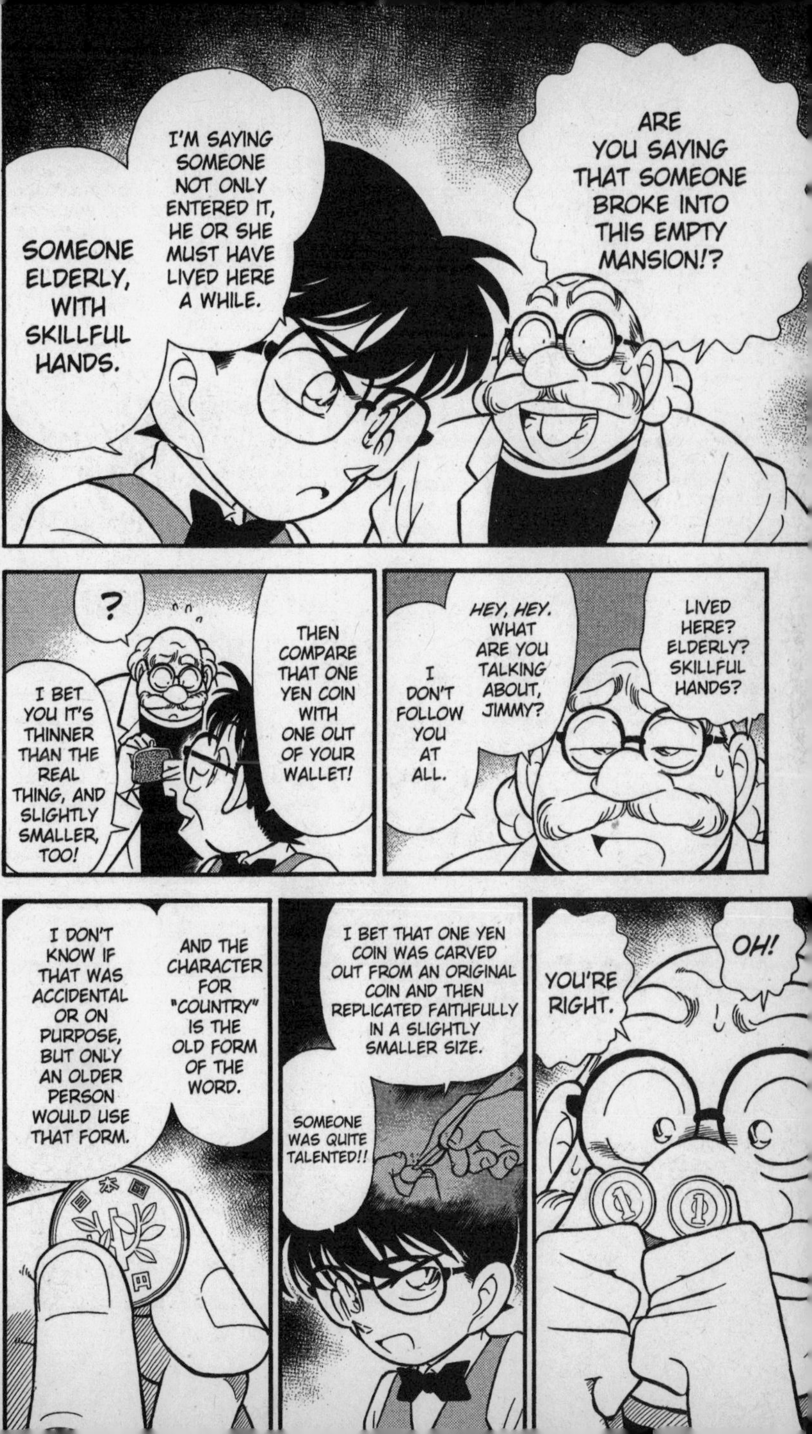
ARE YOU SAYING THAT SOMEONE BROKE INTO THIS EMPTY MANSION!?
I'M SAYING SOMEONE NOT ONLY ENTERED IT, HE OR SHE MUST HAVE LIVED HERE A WHILE.
SOMEONE ELDERLY, WITH SKILLFUL HANDS.
LIVED HERE? ELDERLY? SKILLFUL HANDS?
HEY, HEY. WHAT ARE YOU TALKING ABOUT, JIMMY?
I DON'T FOLLOW YOU AT ALL.
THEN COMPARE THAT ONE YEN COIN WITH ONE OUT OF YOUR WALLET!
?
I BET YOU IT'S THINNER THAN THE REAL THING, AND SLIGHTLY SMALLER, TOO!
OH!
YOU'RE RIGHT.
I BET THAT ONE YEN COIN WAS CARVED OUT FROM AN ORIGINAL COIN AND THEN REPLICATED FAITHFULLY IN A SLIGHTLY SMALLER SIZE.
SOMEONE WAS QUITE TALENTED!!
AND THE CHARACTER FOR "COUNTRY" IS THE OLD FORM OF THE WORD.
I DON'T KNOW IF THAT WAS ACCIDENTAL OR ON PURPOSE, BUT ONLY AN OLDER PERSON WOULD USE THAT FORM.

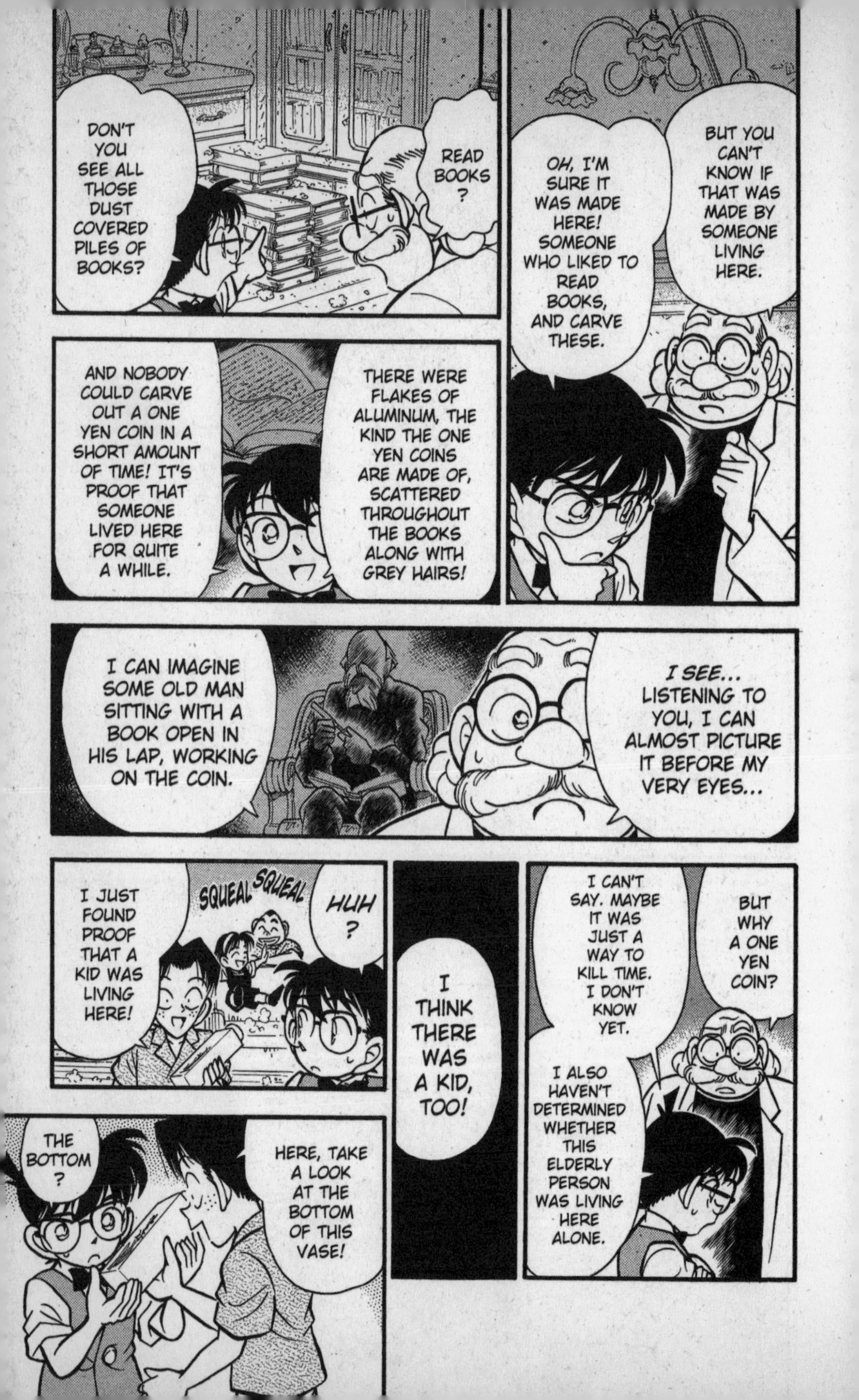
BUT YOU CAN'T KNOW IF THAT WAS MADE BY SOMEONE LIVING HERE.
OH, I'M SURE IT WAS MADE HERE! SOMEONE WHO LIKED TO READ BOOKS, AND CARVE THESE.
READ BOOKS?
DON'T YOU SEE ALL THOSE DUST COVERED PILES OF BOOKS?
THERE WERE FLAKES OF ALUMINUM, THE KIND THE ONE YEN COINS ARE MADE OF, SCATTERED THROUGHOUT THE BOOKS ALONG WITH GREY HAIRS!
AND NOBODY COULD CARVE OUT A ONE YEN COIN IN A SHORT AMOUNT OF TIME! IT'S PROOF THAT SOMEONE LIVED HERE FOR QUITE A WHILE.
I SEE... LISTENING TO YOU, I CAN ALMOST PICTURE IT BEFORE MY VERY EYES...
I CAN IMAGINE SOME OLD MAN SITTING WITH A BOOK OPEN IN HIS LAP, WORKING ON THE COIN.
BUT WHY A ONE YEN COIN?
I CAN'T SAY. MAYBE IT WAS JUST A WAY TO KILL TIME. I DON'T KNOW YET.
I ALSO HAVEN'T DETERMINED WHETHER THIS ELDERLY PERSON WAS LIVING HERE ALONE.
I THINK THERE WAS A KID, TOO!
HUH?
SQUEAL SQUEAL
I JUST FOUND PROOF THAT A KID WAS LIVING HERE!
HERE, TAKE A LOOK AT THE BOTTOM OF THIS VASE!
THE BOTTOM?

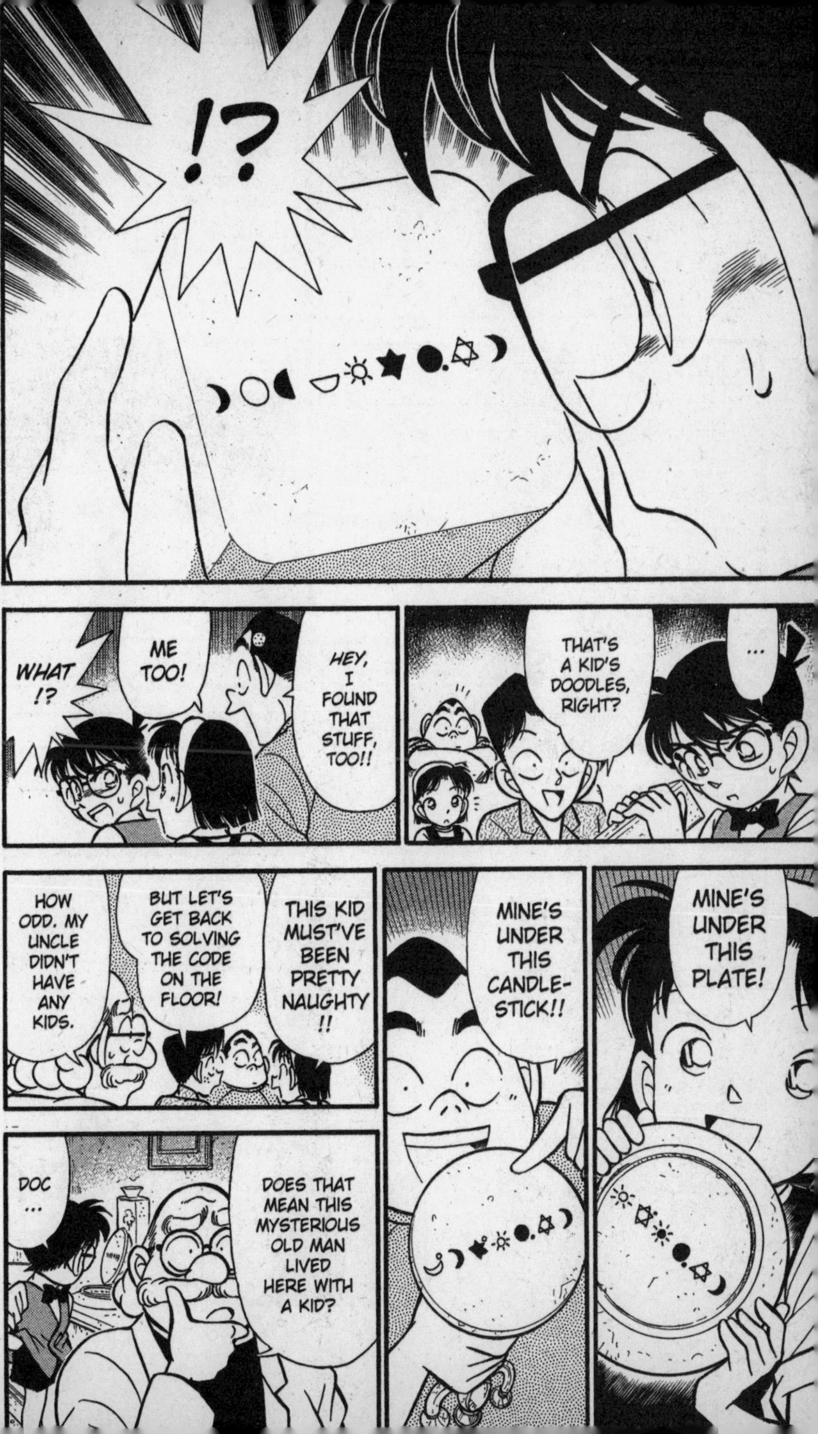
!?
...
THAT'S A KID'S DOODLES, RIGHT?
HEY, I FOUND THAT STUFF, TOO!!
ME TOO!
WHAT!?
MINE'S UNDER THIS PLATE!
MINE'S UNDER THIS CANDLE-STICK!!
THIS KID MUST'VE BEEN PRETTY NAUGHTY!!
BUT LET'S GET BACK TO SOLVING THE CODE ON THE FLOOR!
HOW ODD. MY UNCLE DIDN'T HAVE ANY KIDS.
DOES THAT MEAN THIS MYSTERIOUS OLD MAN LIVED HERE WITH A KID?
DOC...

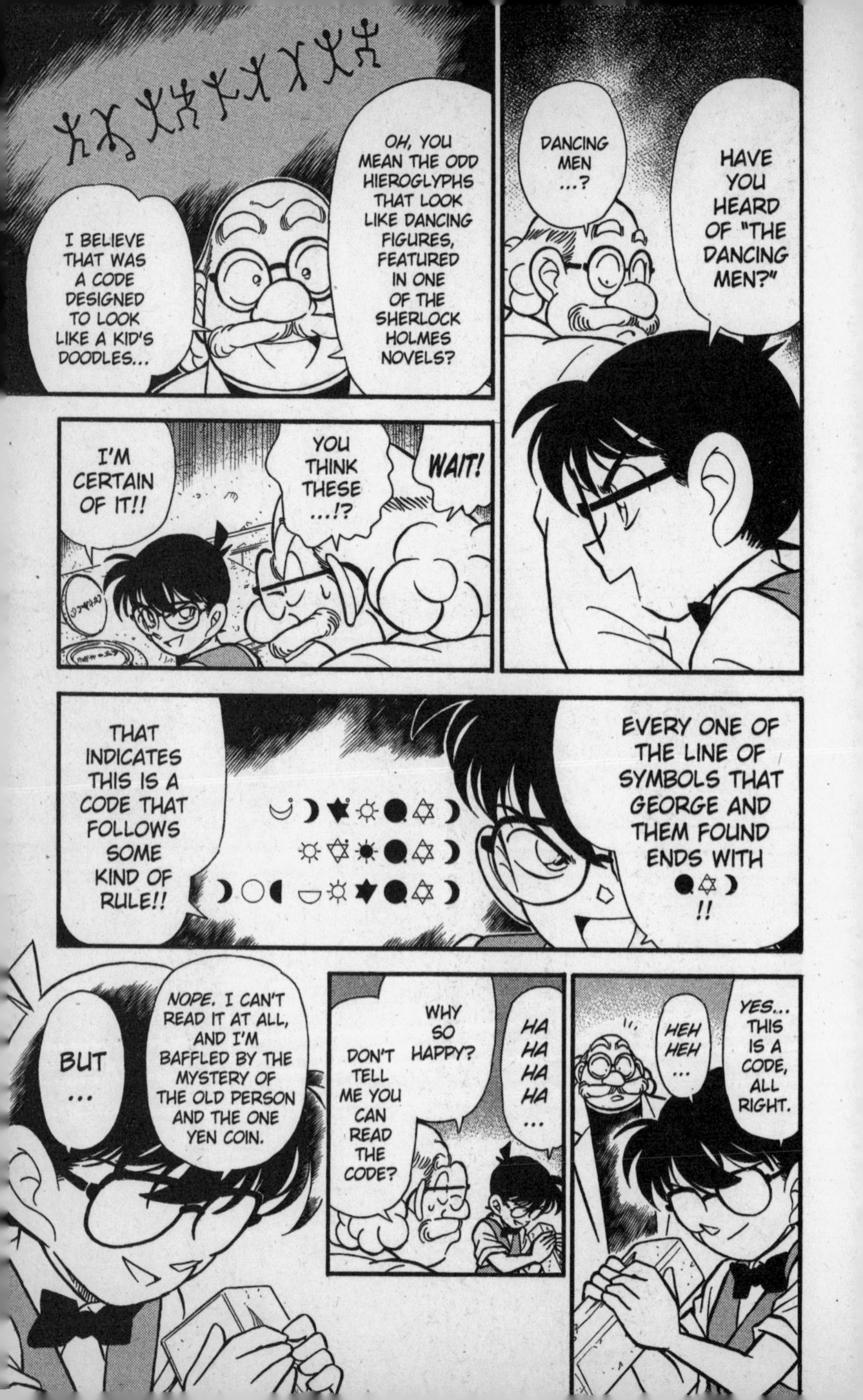

HAVE YOU HEARD OF "THE DANCING MEN?"
DANCING MEN ...?
OH, YOU MEAN THE ODD HIEROGLYPHS THAT LOOK LIKE DANCING FIGURES, FEATURED IN ONE OF THE SHERLOCK HOLMES NOVELS?
I BELIEVE THAT WAS A CODE DESIGNED TO LOOK LIKE A KID'S DOODLES...
WAIT!
YOU THINK THESE ...!?
I'M CERTAIN OF IT!!
EVERY ONE OF THE LINE OF SYMBOLS THAT GEORGE AND THEM FOUND ENDS WITH
!!
THAT INDICATES THIS IS A CODE THAT FOLLOWS SOME KIND OF RULE!!
YES... THIS IS A CODE, ALL RIGHT.
HEH HEH ...
HA HA HA HA ...
WHY SO HAPPY?
DON'T TELL ME YOU CAN READ THE CODE?
NOPE. I CAN'T READ IT AT ALL, AND I'M BAFFLED BY THE MYSTERY OF THE OLD PERSON AND THE ONE YEN COIN.
BUT ...

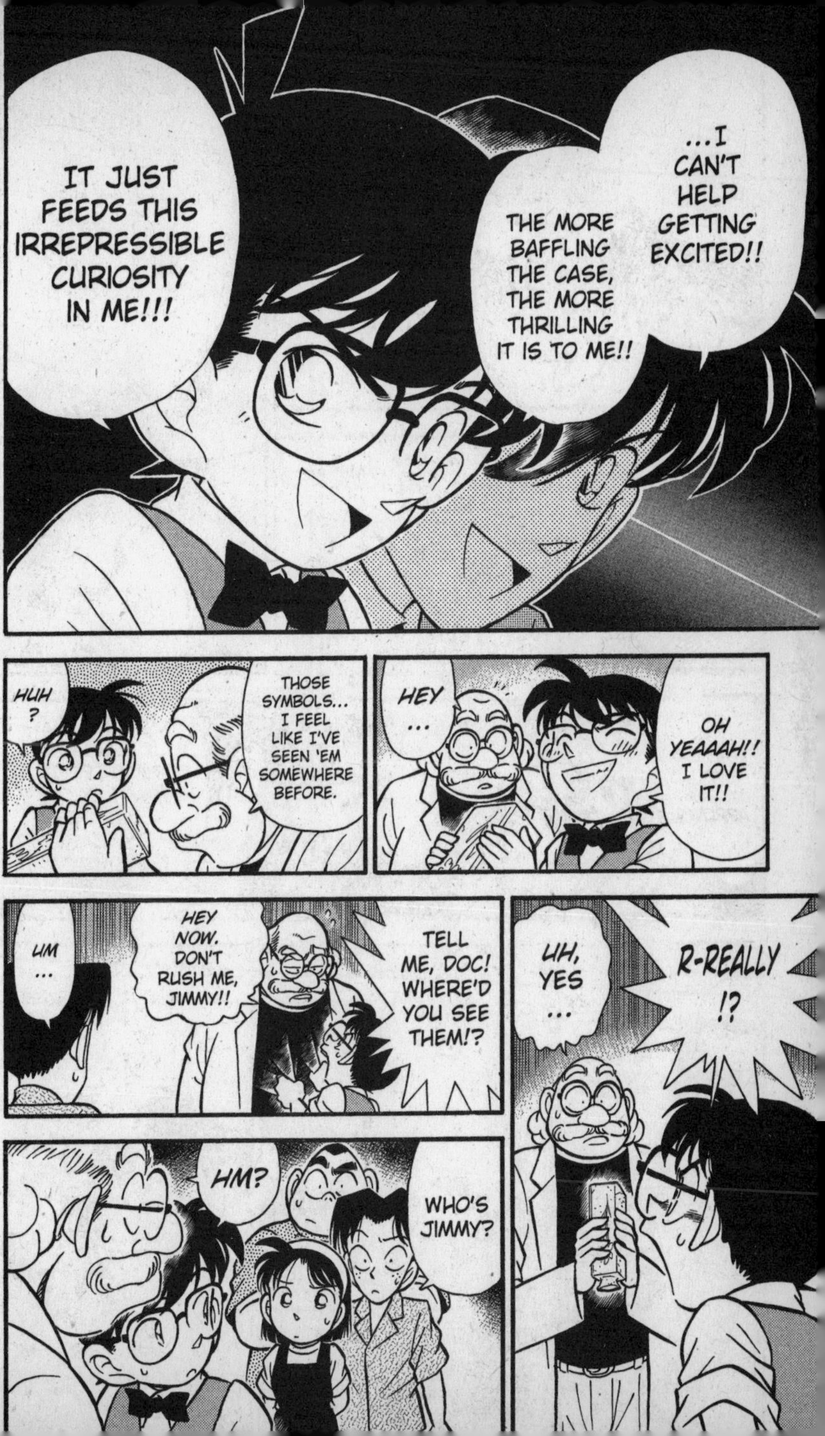

THE MORE BAFFLING THE CASE, THE MORE THRILLING IT IS TO ME!!
...I CAN'T HELP GETTING EXCITED!!
IT JUST FEEDS THIS IRREPRESSIBLE CURIOSITY IN ME!!!
OH YEAAAH!! I LOVE IT!!
HEY ...
THOSE SYMBOLS... I FEEL LIKE I'VE SEEN 'EM SOMEWHERE BEFORE.
HUH ?
R-REALLY !?
UH, YES ...
TELL ME, DOC! WHERE'D YOU SEE THEM!?
HEY NOW. DON'T RUSH ME, JIMMY!!
UM ...
WHO'S JIMMY?
HM?

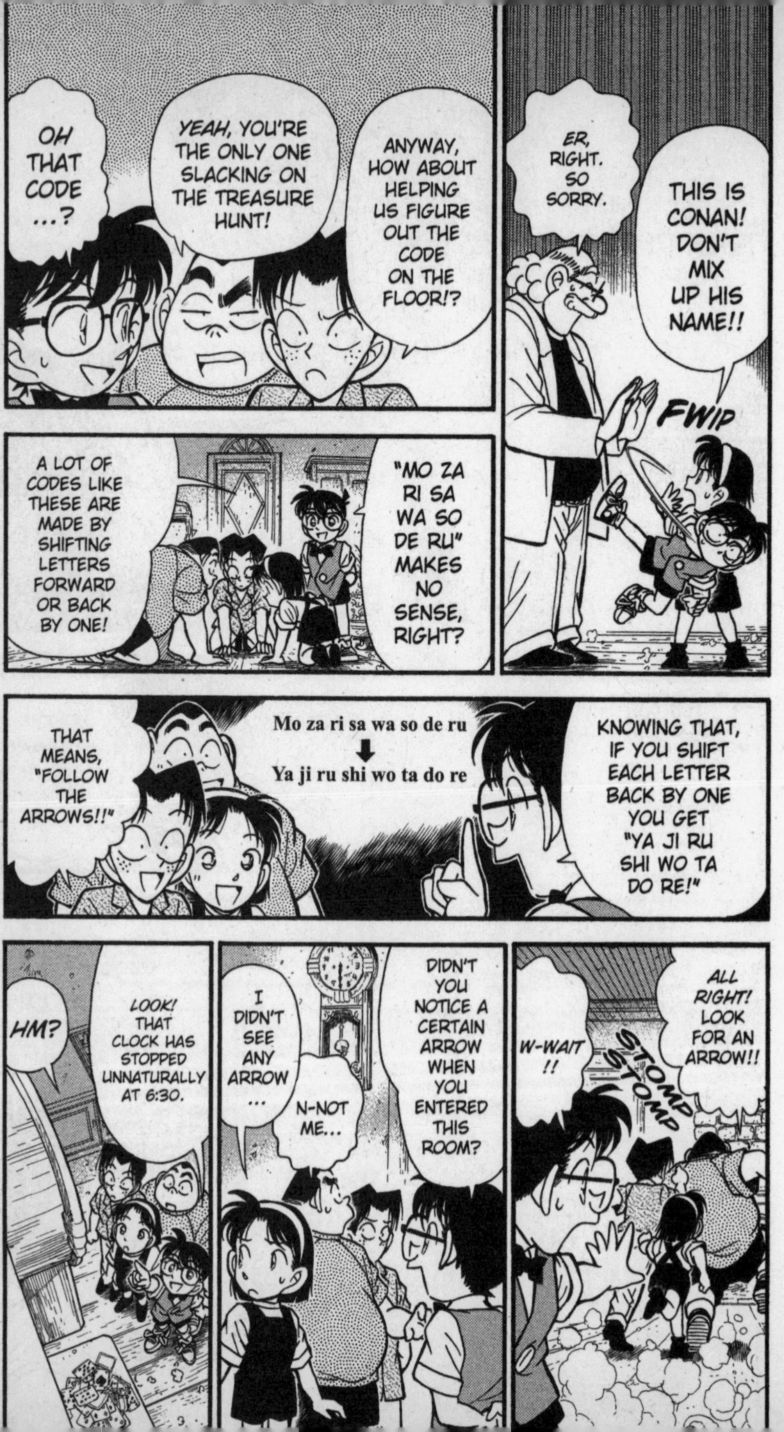

OH THAT CODE ...?
YEAH, YOU'RE THE ONLY ONE SLACKING ON THE TREASURE HUNT!
ANYWAY, HOW ABOUT HELPING US FIGURE OUT THE CODE ON THE FLOOR!?
THIS IS CONAN! DON'T MIX UP HIS NAME!!
ER, RIGHT. SO SORRY.
FWIP
A LOT OF CODES LIKE THESE ARE MADE BY SHIFTING LETTERS FORWARD OR BACK BY ONE!
"MO ZA RI SA WA SO DE RU" MAKES NO SENSE, RIGHT?
KNOWING THAT, IF YOU SHIFT EACH LETTER BACK BY ONE YOU GET "YA JI RU SHI WO TA DO RE!"
Mo za ri sa wa so de ru
Ya ji ru shi wo ta do re
THAT MEANS, "FOLLOW THE ARROWS!!"
ALL RIGHT! LOOK FOR AN ARROW!!
STOMP STOMP
W-WAIT !!
DIDN'T YOU NOTICE A CERTAIN ARROW WHEN YOU ENTERED THIS ROOM?
N-NOT ME...
I DIDN'T SEE ANY ARROW ...
LOOK! THAT CLOCK HAS STOPPED UNNATURALLY AT 6:30.
HM?

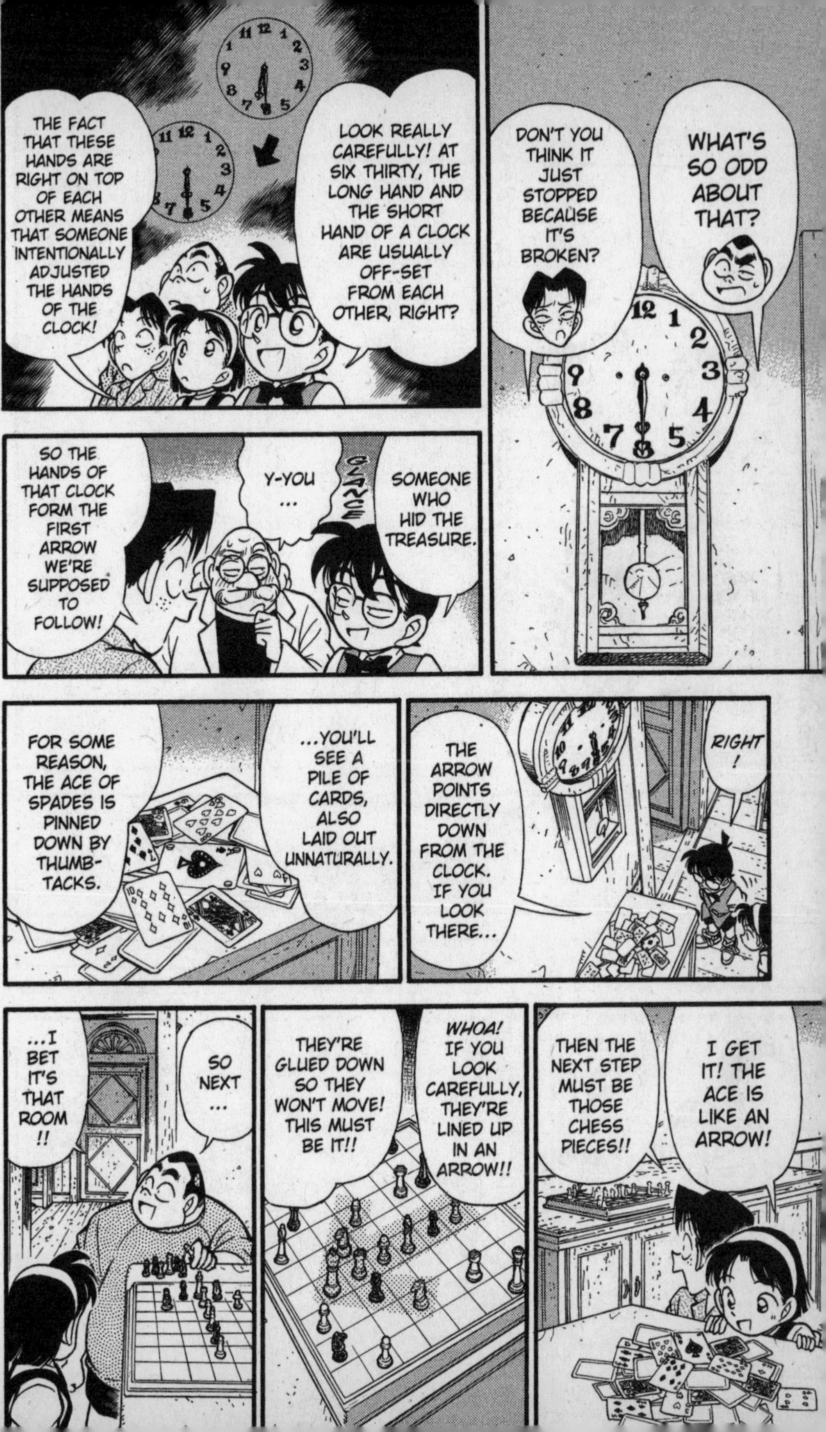
WHAT'S SO ODD ABOUT THAT?
DON'T YOU THINK IT JUST STOPPED BECAUSE IT'S BROKEN?
LOOK REALLY CAREFULLY! AT SIX THIRTY, THE LONG HAND AND THE SHORT HAND OF A CLOCK ARE USUALLY OFF-SET FROM EACH OTHER, RIGHT?
THE FACT THAT THESE HANDS ARE RIGHT ON TOP OF EACH OTHER MEANS THAT SOMEONE INTENTIONALLY ADJUSTED THE HANDS OF THE CLOCK!
SOMEONE WHO HID THE TREASURE.
GLANCE
Y-YOU ...
SO THE HANDS OF THAT CLOCK FORM THE FIRST ARROW WE'RE SUPPOSED TO FOLLOW!
RIGHT!
THE ARROW POINTS DIRECTLY DOWN FROM THE CLOCK. IF YOU LOOK THERE...
...YOU'LL SEE A PILE OF CARDS, ALSO LAID OUT UNNATURALLY.
FOR SOME REASON, THE ACE OF SPADES IS PINNED DOWN BY THUMB-TACKS.
I GET IT! THE ACE IS LIKE AN ARROW!
THEN THE NEXT STEP MUST BE THOSE CHESS PIECES!!
WHOA! IF YOU LOOK CAREFULLY, THEY'RE LINED UP IN AN ARROW!!
THEY'RE GLUED DOWN SO THEY WON'T MOVE! THIS MUST BE IT!!
SO NEXT ...
...I BET IT'S THAT ROOM!!

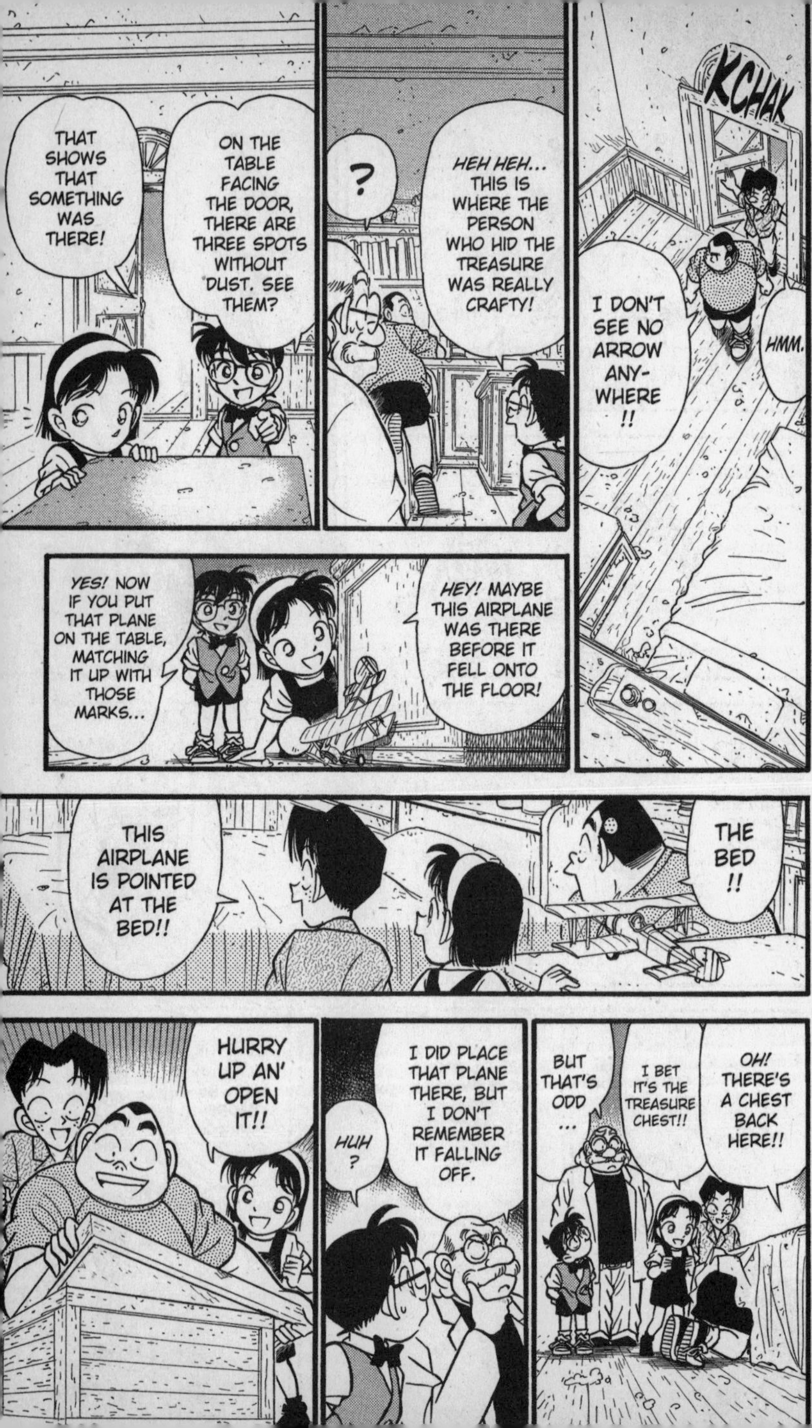
KCHAK
HMM.
I DON'T SEE NO ARROW ANYWHERE !!
HEH HEH... THIS IS WHERE THE PERSON WHO HID THE TREASURE WAS REALLY CRAFTY!
?
ON THE TABLE FACING THE DOOR, THERE ARE THREE SPOTS WITHOUT DUST. SEE THEM?
THAT SHOWS THAT SOMETHING WAS THERE!
HEY! MAYBE THIS AIRPLANE WAS THERE BEFORE IT FELL ONTO THE FLOOR!
YES! NOW IF YOU PUT THAT PLANE ON THE TABLE, MATCHING IT UP WITH THOSE MARKS...
THIS AIRPLANE IS POINTED AT THE BED!!
THE BED !!
OH! THERE'S A CHEST BACK HERE!!
I BET IT'S THE TREASURE CHEST!!
BUT THAT'S ODD ...
I DID PLACE THAT PLANE THERE, BUT I DON'T REMEMBER IT FALLING OFF.
HUH ?
HURRY UP AN' OPEN IT!!

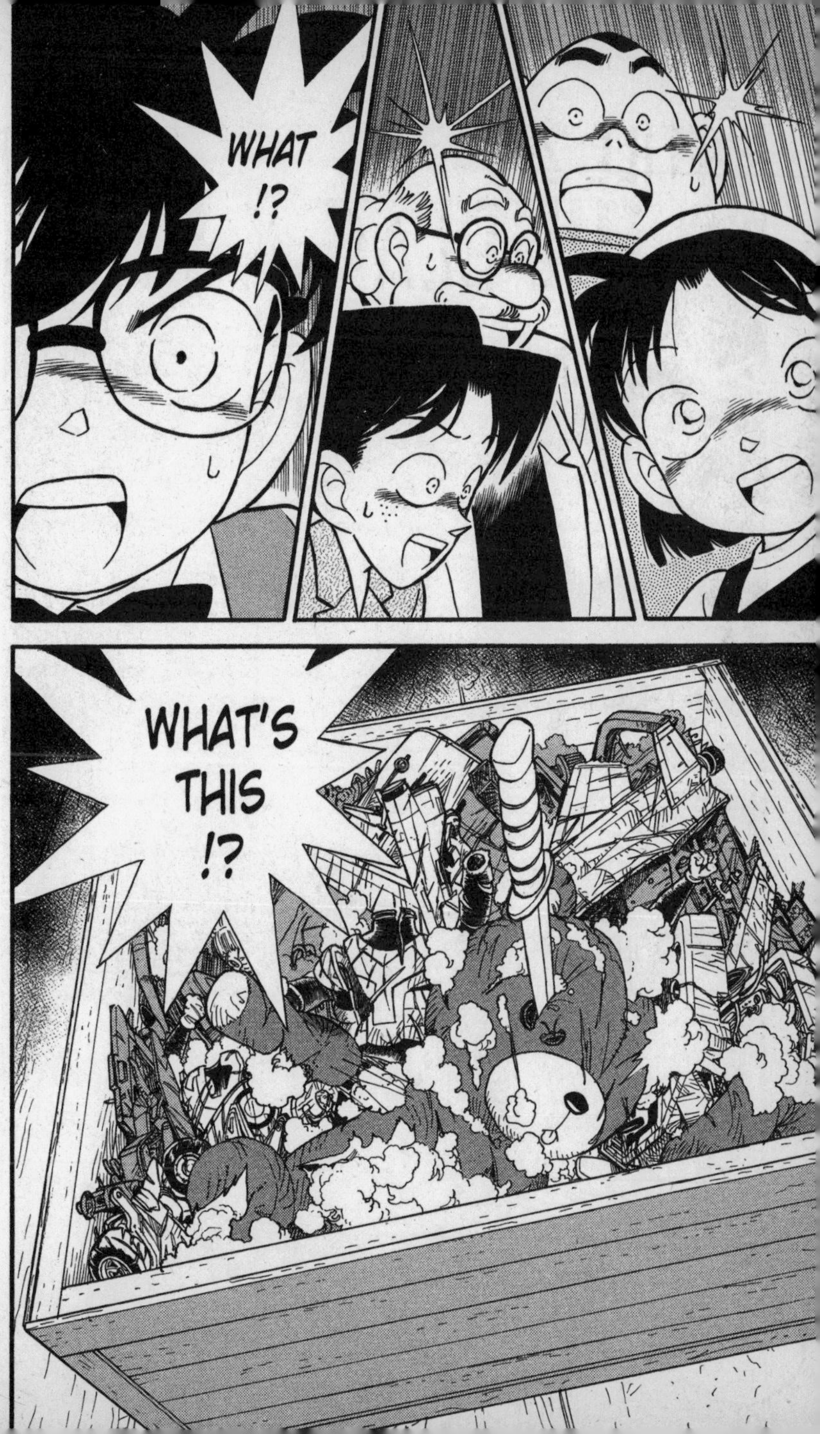
WHAT !?
WHAT'S THIS !?

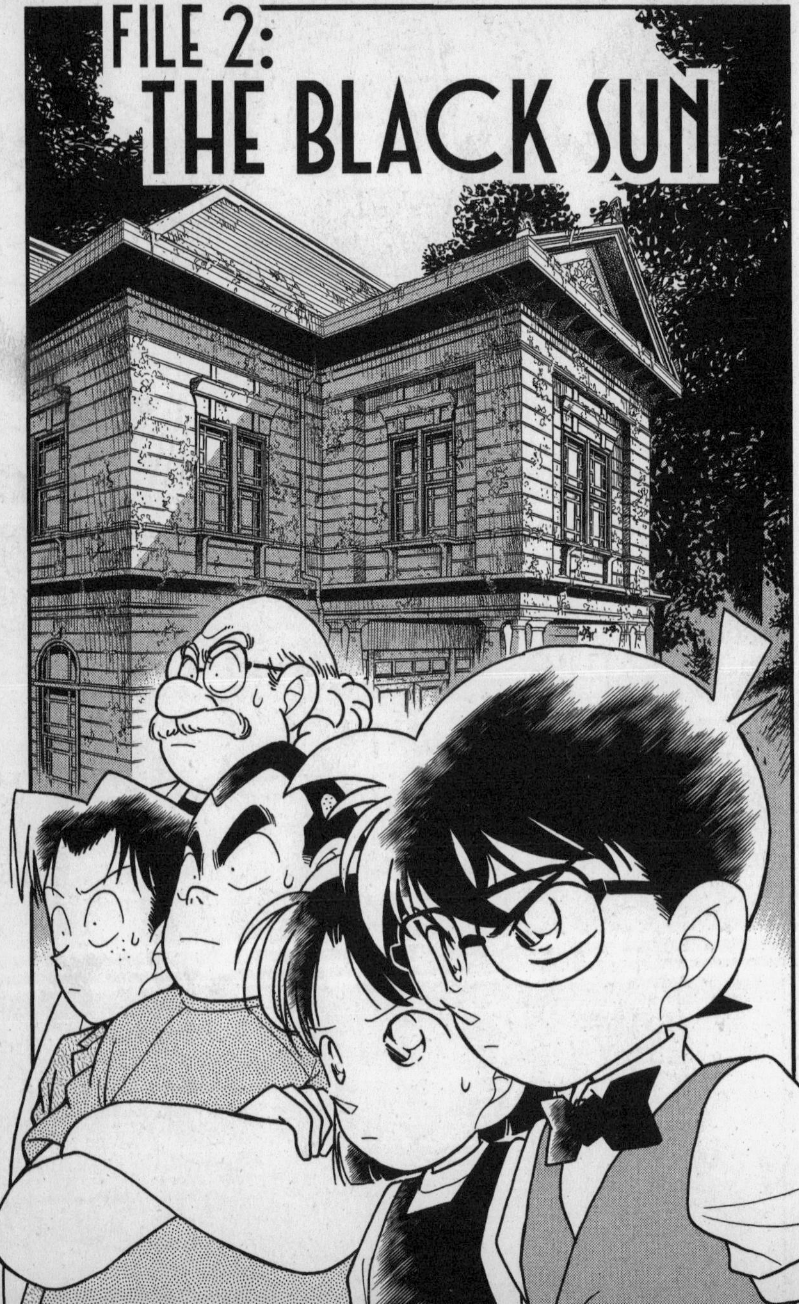
FILE 2:
THE BLACK SUN

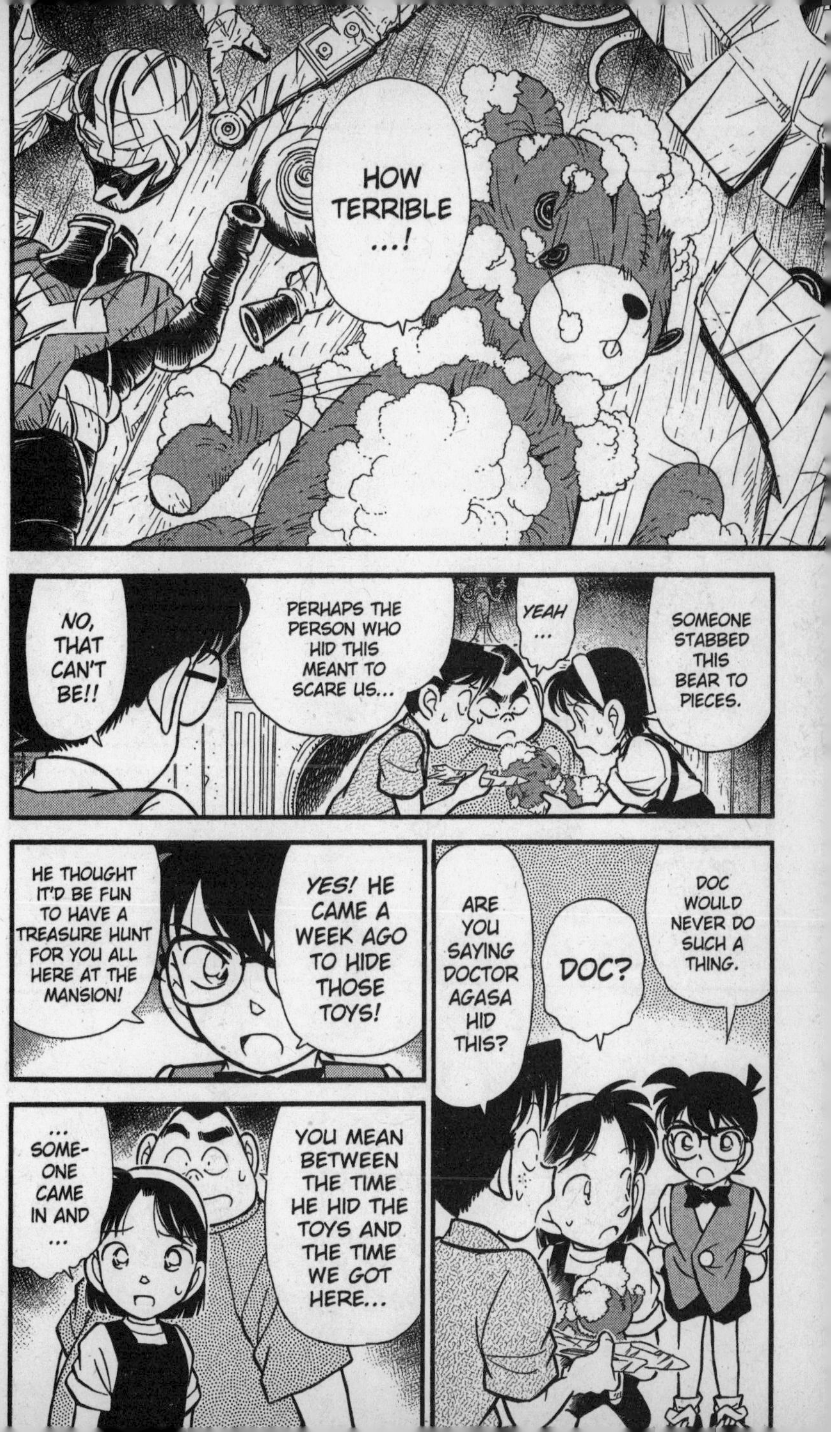
HOW TERRIBLE ...!
SOMEONE STABBED THIS BEAR TO PIECES.
YEAH ...
PERHAPS THE PERSON WHO HID THIS MEANT TO SCARE US...
NO, THAT CAN'T BE!!
DOC WOULD NEVER DO SUCH A THING.
DOC?
ARE YOU SAYING DOCTOR AGASA HID THIS?
YES! HE CAME A WEEK AGO TO HIDE THOSE TOYS!
HE THOUGHT IT'D BE FUN TO HAVE A TREASURE HUNT FOR YOU ALL HERE AT THE MANSION!
YOU MEAN BETWEEN THE TIME HE HID THE TOYS AND THE TIME WE GOT HERE...
... SOME-ONE CAME IN AND ...

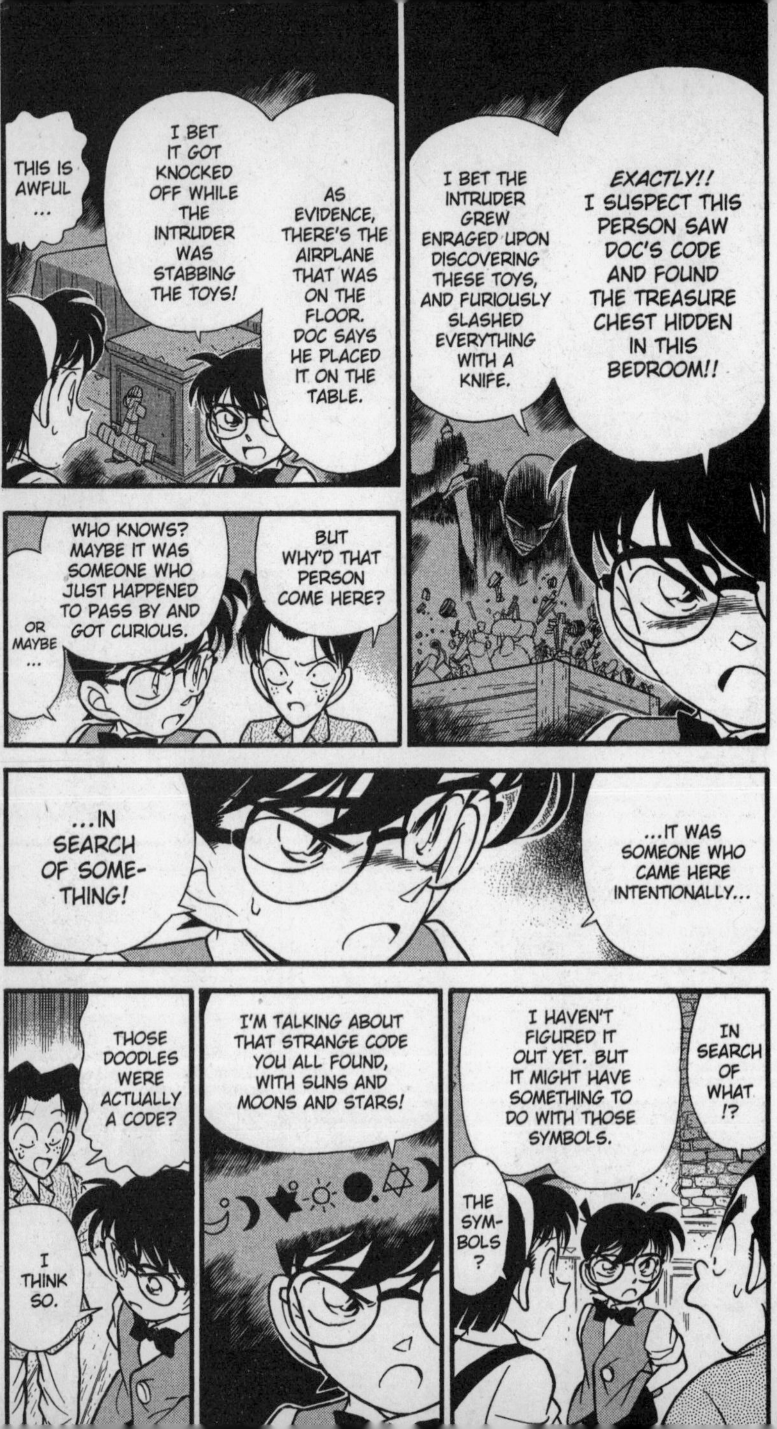
EXACTLY!! I SUSPECT THIS PERSON SAW DOC'S CODE AND FOUND THE TREASURE CHEST HIDDEN IN THIS BEDROOM!!
I BET THE INTRUDER GREW ENRAGED UPON DISCOVERING THESE TOYS, AND FURIOUSLY SLASHED EVERYTHING WITH A KNIFE.
AS EVIDENCE, THERE'S THE AIRPLANE THAT WAS ON THE FLOOR. DOC SAYS HE PLACED IT ON THE TABLE.
I BET IT GOT KNOCKED OFF WHILE THE INTRUDER WAS STABBING THE TOYS!
THIS IS AWFUL ...
BUT WHY'D THAT PERSON COME HERE?
WHO KNOWS? MAYBE IT WAS SOMEONE WHO JUST HAPPENED TO PASS BY AND GOT CURIOUS.
OR MAYBE ...
...IT WAS SOMEONE WHO CAME HERE INTENTIONALLY...
...IN SEARCH OF SOME-THING!
IN SEARCH OF WHAT!?
I HAVEN'T FIGURED IT OUT YET. BUT IT MIGHT HAVE SOMETHING TO DO WITH THOSE SYMBOLS.
THE SYM-BOLS?
I'M TALKING ABOUT THAT STRANGE CODE YOU ALL FOUND, WITH SUNS AND MOONS AND STARS!
THOSE DOODLES WERE ACTUALLY A CODE?
I THINK SO.

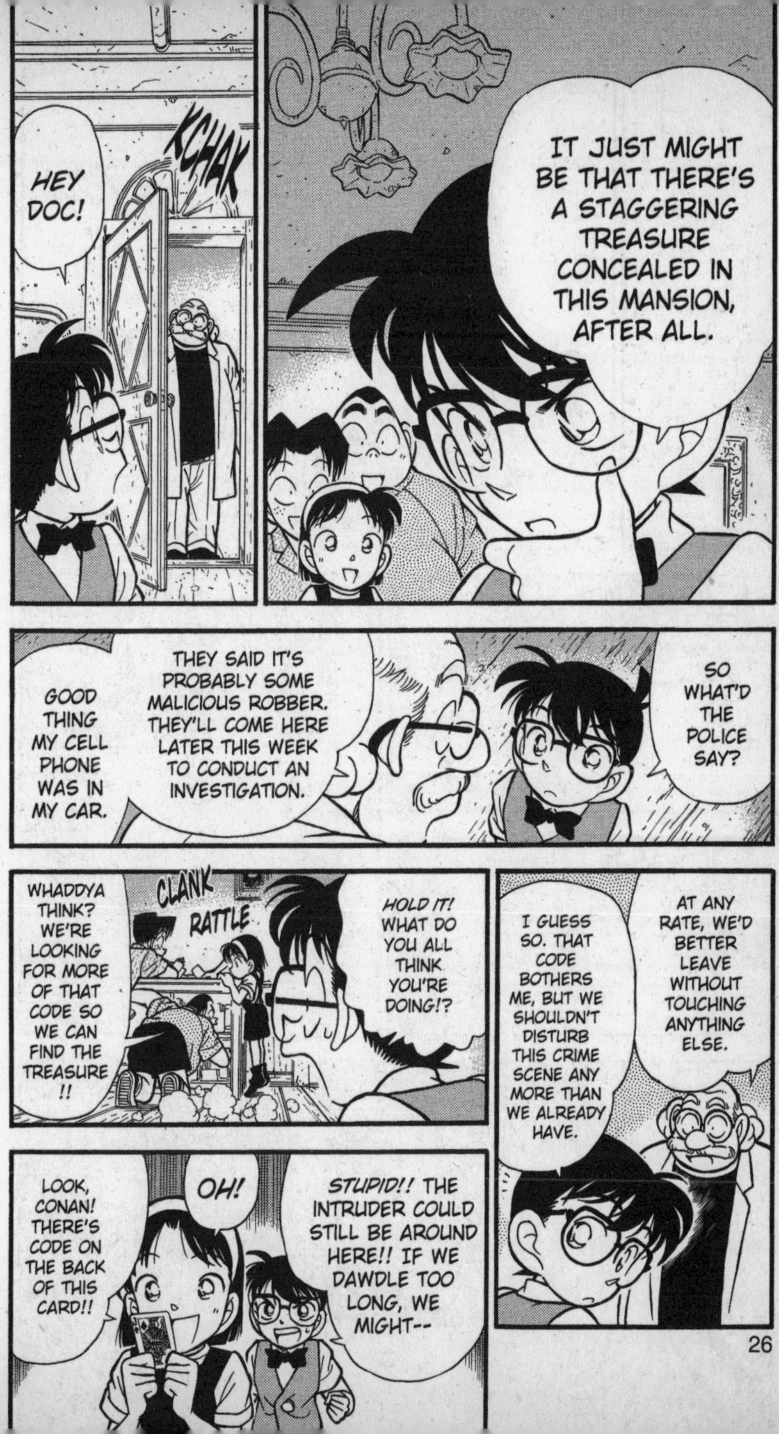
KCHAK
HEY DOC!
IT JUST MIGHT BE THAT THERE'S A STAGGERING TREASURE CONCEALED IN THIS MANSION, AFTER ALL.
GOOD THING MY CELL PHONE WAS IN MY CAR.
SO WHAT'D THE POLICE SAY?
THEY SAID IT'S PROBABLY SOME MALICIOUS ROBBER. THEY'LL COME HERE LATER THIS WEEK TO CONDUCT AN INVESTIGATION.
CLANK
RATTLE
HOLD IT! WHAT DO YOU ALL THINK YOU'RE DOING!?
WHADDYA THINK? WE'RE LOOKING FOR MORE OF THAT CODE SO WE CAN FIND THE TREASURE !!
AT ANY RATE, WE'D BETTER LEAVE WITHOUT TOUCHING ANYTHING ELSE.
I GUESS SO. THAT CODE BOTHERS ME, BUT WE SHOULDN'T DISTURB THIS CRIME SCENE ANY MORE THAN WE ALREADY HAVE.
LOOK, CONAN! THERE'S CODE ON THE BACK OF THIS CARD!!
OH!
STUPID!! THE INTRUDER COULD STILL BE AROUND HERE!! IF WE DAWDLE TOO LONG, WE MIGHT--

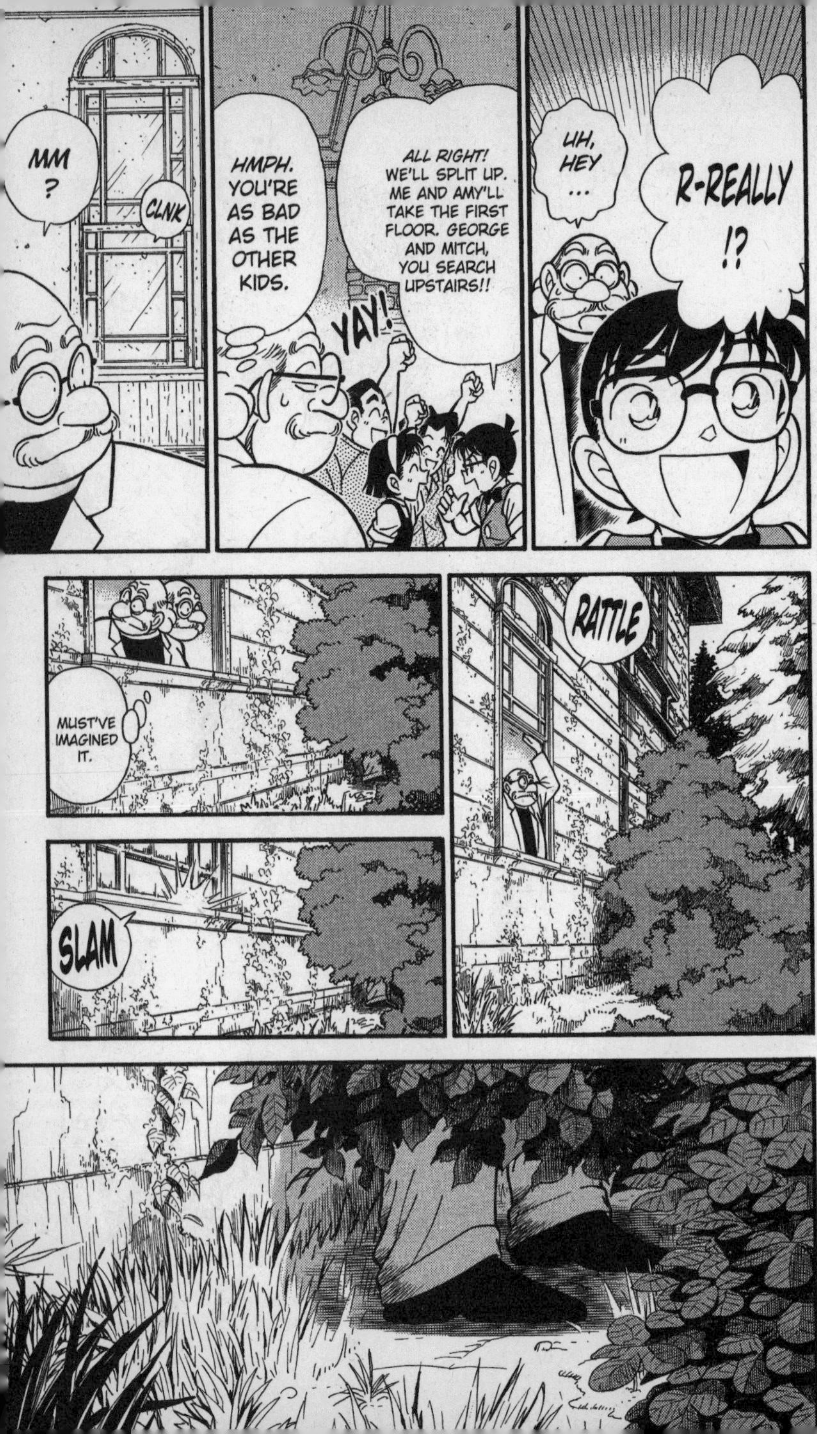
MM ?
CLNK
HMPH. YOU'RE AS BAD AS THE OTHER KIDS.
ALL RIGHT! WE'LL SPLIT UP. ME AND AMY'LL TAKE THE FIRST FLOOR. GEORGE AND MITCH, YOU SEARCH UPSTAIRS!!
YAY!
UH, HEY ...
R-REALLY !?
MUST'VE IMAGINED IT.
RATTLE
SLAM

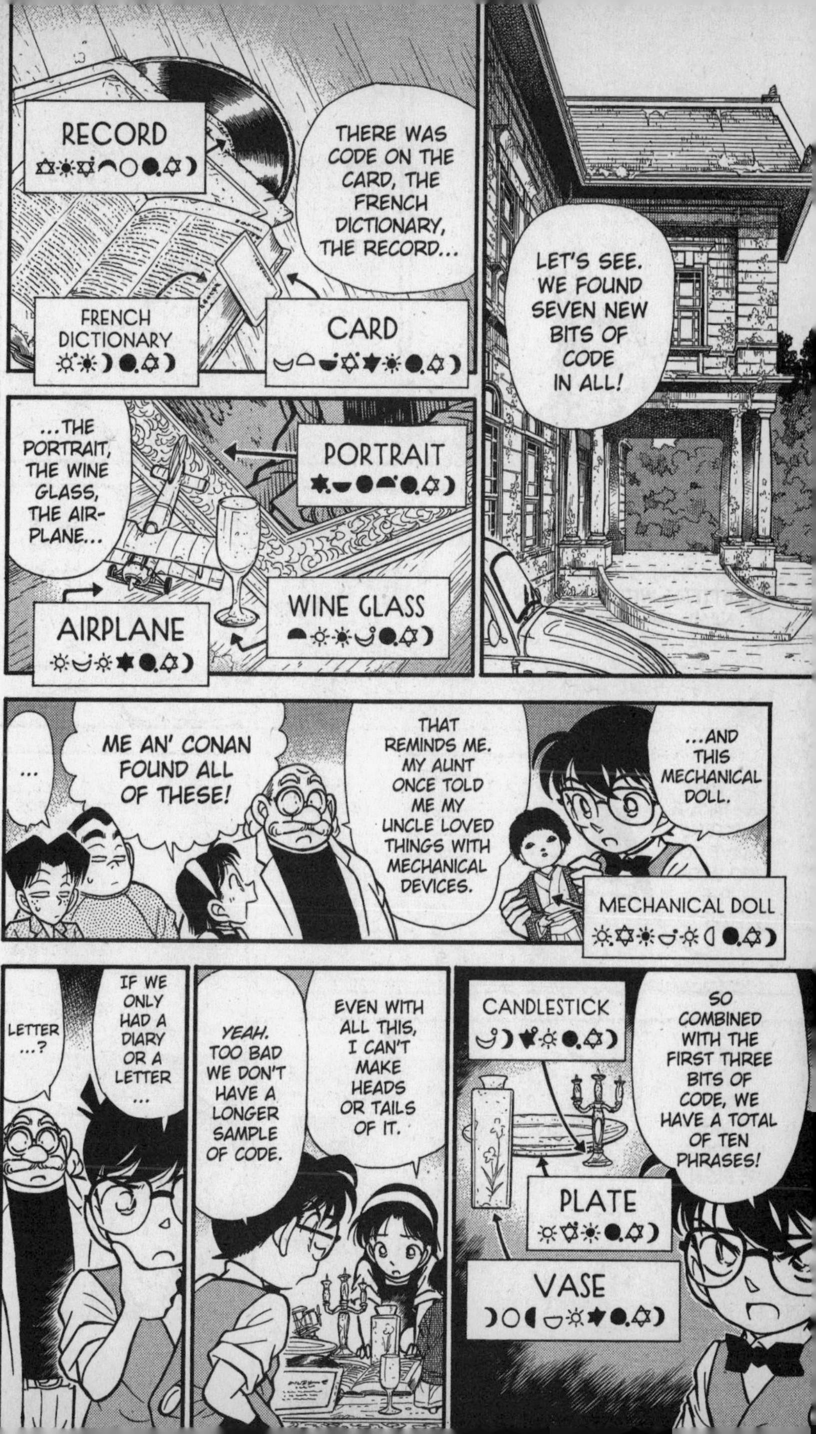
LET'S SEE. WE FOUND SEVEN NEW BITS OF CODE IN ALL!
THERE WAS CODE ON THE CARD, THE FRENCH DICTIONARY, THE RECORD...
RECORD
FRENCH DICTIONARY
CARD
PORTRAIT
...THE PORTRAIT, THE WINE GLASS, THE AIR-PLANE...
WINE GLASS
AIRPLANE
...AND THIS MECHANICAL DOLL.
MECHANICAL DOLL
THAT REMINDS ME. MY AUNT ONCE TOLD ME MY UNCLE LOVED THINGS WITH MECHANICAL DEVICES.
ME AN' CONAN FOUND ALL OF THESE!
...
SO COMBINED WITH THE FIRST THREE BITS OF CODE, WE HAVE A TOTAL OF TEN PHRASES!
CANDLESTICK
PLATE
VASE
EVEN WITH ALL THIS, I CAN'T MAKE HEADS OR TAILS OF IT.
YEAH. TOO BAD WE DON'T HAVE A LONGER SAMPLE OF CODE.
IF WE ONLY HAD A DIARY OR A LETTER ...
LETTER ...?

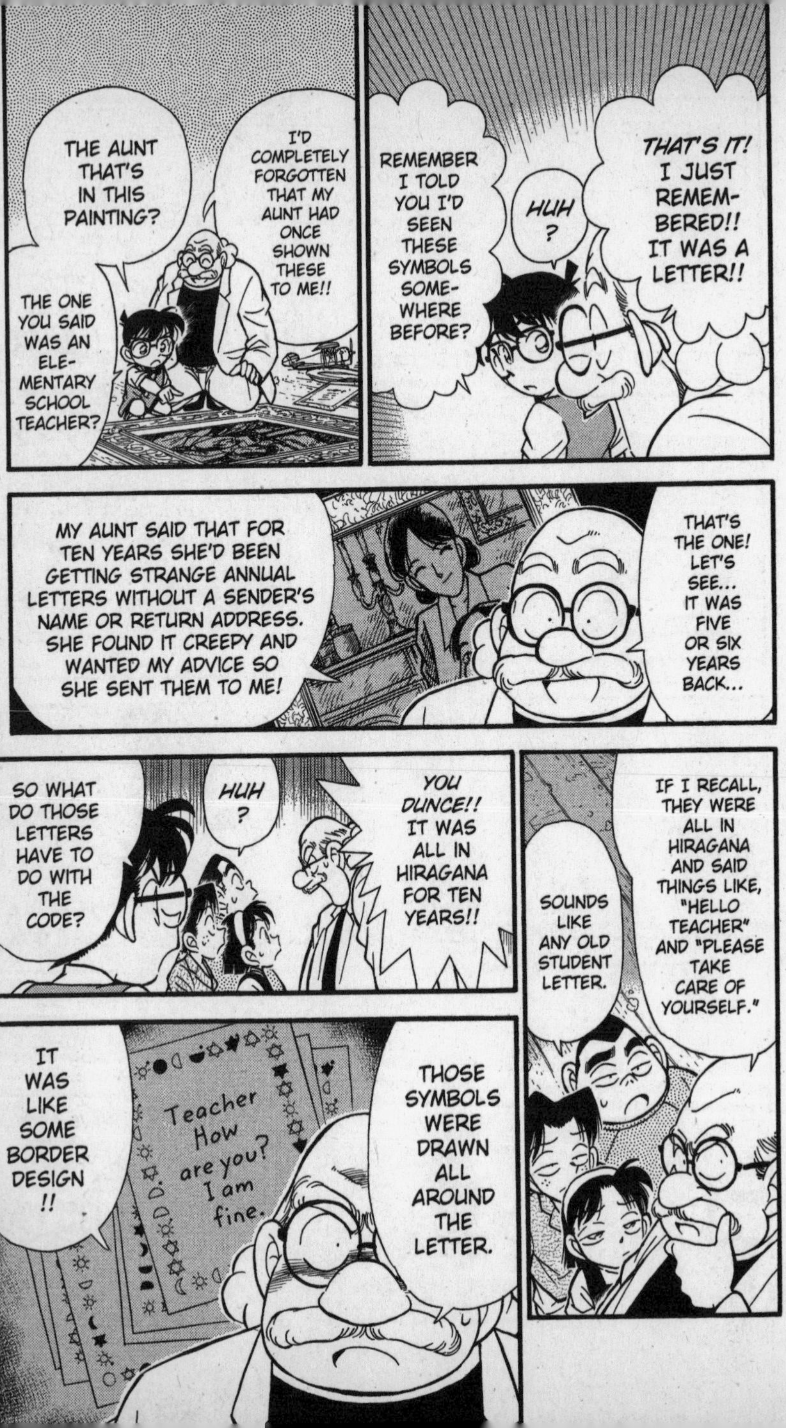
THE AUNT THAT'S IN THIS PAINTING?
THE ONE YOU SAID WAS AN ELE-MENTARY SCHOOL TEACHER?
I'D COMPLETELY FORGOTTEN THAT MY AUNT HAD ONCE SHOWN THESE TO ME!!
REMEMBER I TOLD YOU I'D SEEN THESE SYMBOLS SOME-WHERE BEFORE?
HUH?
THAT'S IT! I JUST REMEM-BERED!! IT WAS A LETTER!!
MY AUNT SAID THAT FOR TEN YEARS SHE'D BEEN GETTING STRANGE ANNUAL LETTERS WITHOUT A SENDER'S NAME OR RETURN ADDRESS. SHE FOUND IT CREEPY AND WANTED MY ADVICE SO SHE SENT THEM TO ME!
THAT'S THE ONE! LET'S SEE... IT WAS FIVE OR SIX YEARS BACK...
SO WHAT DO THOSE LETTERS HAVE TO DO WITH THE CODE?
HUH?
YOU DUNCE!! IT WAS ALL IN HIRAGANA FOR TEN YEARS!!
IF I RECALL, THEY WERE ALL IN HIRAGANA AND SAID THINGS LIKE, "HELLO TEACHER" AND "PLEASE TAKE CARE OF YOURSELF."
SOUNDS LIKE ANY OLD STUDENT LETTER.
IT WAS LIKE SOME BORDER DESIGN!!
Teacher How are you? I am fine.
THOSE SYMBOLS WERE DRAWN ALL AROUND THE LETTER.

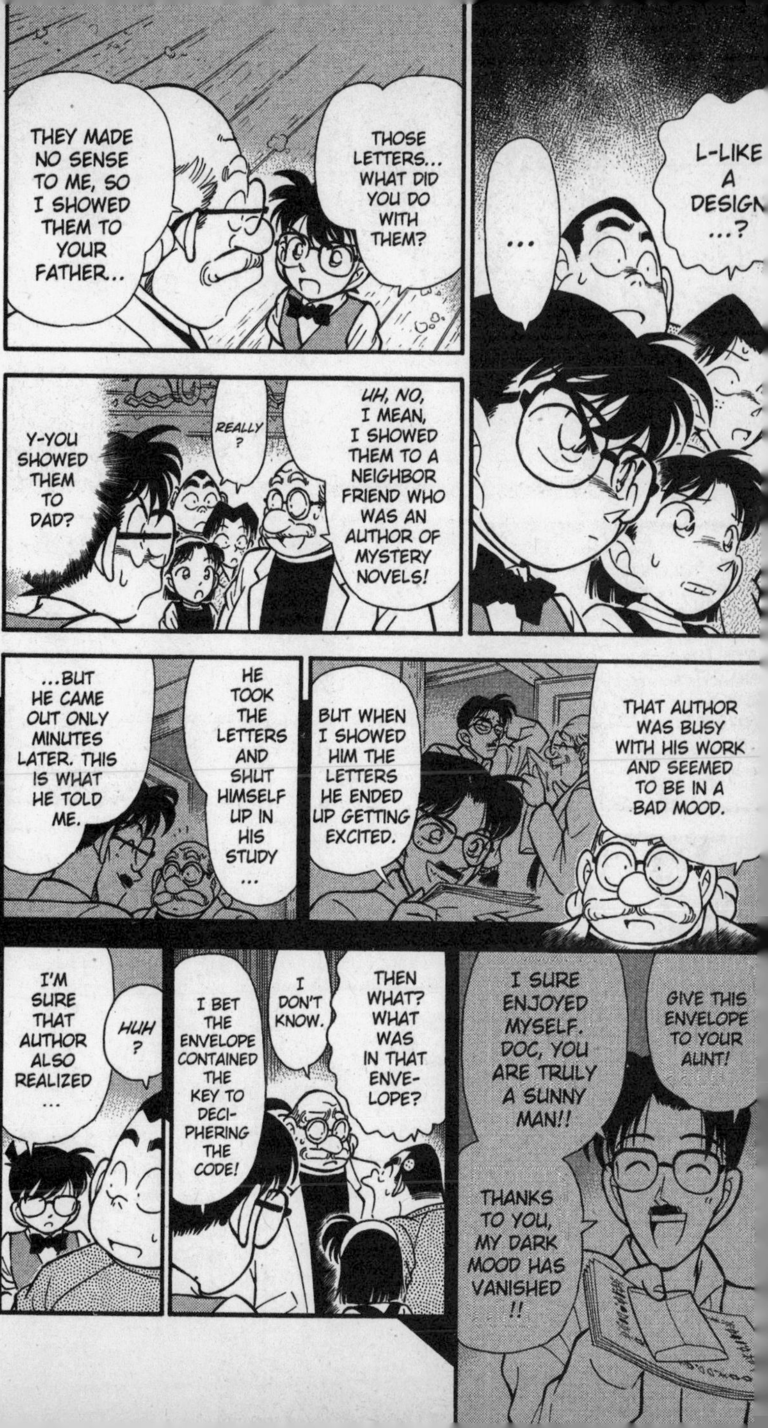

L-LIKE A DESIGN...?
...
THOSE LETTERS... WHAT DID YOU DO WITH THEM?
THEY MADE NO SENSE TO ME, SO I SHOWED THEM TO YOUR FATHER...
UH, NO, I MEAN, I SHOWED THEM TO A NEIGHBOR FRIEND WHO WAS AN AUTHOR OF MYSTERY NOVELS!
REALLY?
Y-YOU SHOWED THEM TO DAD?
THAT AUTHOR WAS BUSY WITH HIS WORK AND SEEMED TO BE IN A BAD MOOD.
BUT WHEN I SHOWED HIM THE LETTERS HE ENDED UP GETTING EXCITED.
HE TOOK THE LETTERS AND SHUT HIMSELF UP IN HIS STUDY...
...BUT HE CAME OUT ONLY MINUTES LATER. THIS IS WHAT HE TOLD ME.
GIVE THIS ENVELOPE TO YOUR AUNT!
I SURE ENJOYED MYSELF. DOC, YOU ARE TRULY A SUNNY MAN!!
THANKS TO YOU, MY DARK MOOD HAS VANISHED!!
THEN WHAT? WHAT WAS IN THAT ENVE-LOPE?
I DON'T KNOW.
I BET THE ENVELOPE CONTAINED THE KEY TO DECI-PHERING THE CODE!
HUH?
I'M SURE THAT AUTHOR ALSO REALIZED...

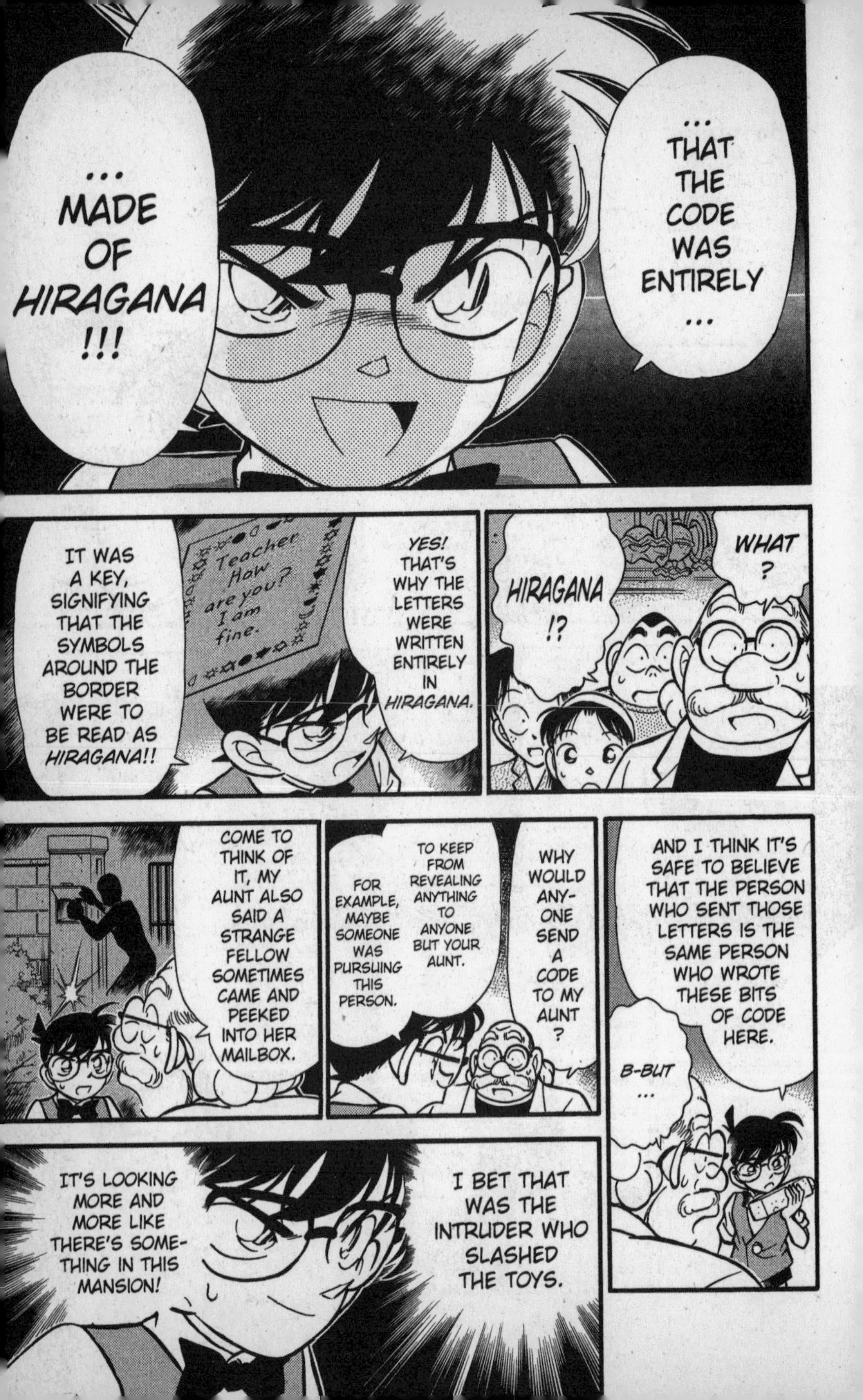
... THAT THE CODE WAS ENTIRELY ...
... MADE OF HIRAGANA !!!
WHAT ?
HIRAGANA !?
YES! THAT'S WHY THE LETTERS WERE WRITTEN ENTIRELY IN HIRAGANA.
Teacher How are you? I am fine.
IT WAS A KEY, SIGNIFYING THAT THE SYMBOLS AROUND THE BORDER WERE TO BE READ AS HIRAGANA!!
AND I THINK IT'S SAFE TO BELIEVE THAT THE PERSON WHO SENT THOSE LETTERS IS THE SAME PERSON WHO WROTE THESE BITS OF CODE HERE.
B-BUT ...
WHY WOULD ANY-ONE SEND A CODE TO MY AUNT ?
TO KEEP FROM REVEALING ANYTHING TO ANYONE BUT YOUR AUNT.
FOR EXAMPLE, MAYBE SOMEONE WAS PURSUING THIS PERSON.
COME TO THINK OF IT, MY AUNT ALSO SAID A STRANGE FELLOW SOMETIMES CAME AND PEEKED INTO HER MAILBOX.
I BET THAT WAS THE INTRUDER WHO SLASHED THE TOYS.
IT'S LOOKING MORE AND MORE LIKE THERE'S SOME-THING IN THIS MANSION!

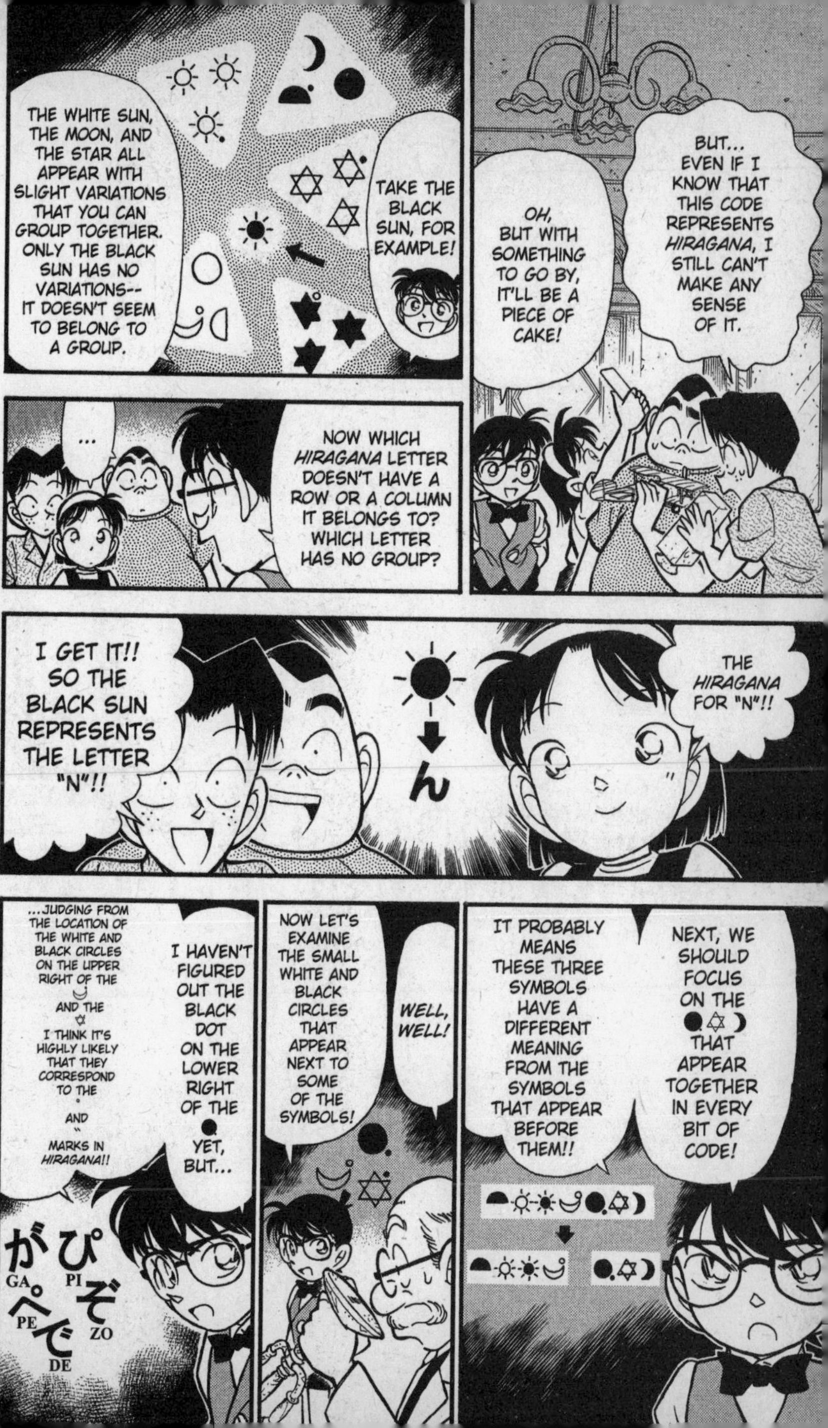
BUT... EVEN IF I KNOW THAT THIS CODE REPRESENTS HIRAGANA, I STILL CAN'T MAKE ANY SENSE OF IT.
OH, BUT WITH SOMETHING TO GO BY, IT'LL BE A PIECE OF CAKE!
TAKE THE BLACK SUN, FOR EXAMPLE!
THE WHITE SUN, THE MOON, AND THE STAR ALL APPEAR WITH SLIGHT VARIATIONS THAT YOU CAN GROUP TOGETHER. ONLY THE BLACK SUN HAS NO VARIATIONS-- IT DOESN'T SEEM TO BELONG TO A GROUP.
NOW WHICH HIRAGANA LETTER DOESN'T HAVE A ROW OR A COLUMN IT BELONGS TO? WHICH LETTER HAS NO GROUP?
...
THE HIRAGANA FOR "N"!!
ん
I GET IT!! SO THE BLACK SUN REPRESENTS THE LETTER "N"!!
NEXT, WE SHOULD FOCUS ON THE THAT APPEAR TOGETHER IN EVERY BIT OF CODE!
IT PROBABLY MEANS THESE THREE SYMBOLS HAVE A DIFFERENT MEANING FROM THE SYMBOLS THAT APPEAR BEFORE THEM!!
WELL, WELL!
NOW LET'S EXAMINE THE SMALL WHITE AND BLACK CIRCLES THAT APPEAR NEXT TO SOME OF THE SYMBOLS!
I HAVEN'T FIGURED OUT THE BLACK DOT ON THE LOWER RIGHT OF THE YET, BUT...
...JUDGING FROM THE LOCATION OF THE WHITE AND BLACK CIRCLES ON THE UPPER RIGHT OF THE AND THE I THINK IT'S HIGHLY LIKELY THAT THEY CORRESPOND TO THE ° AND ゛ MARKS IN HIRAGANA!!
が GA
ぴ PI
ぺ PE
ぞ ZO
で DE

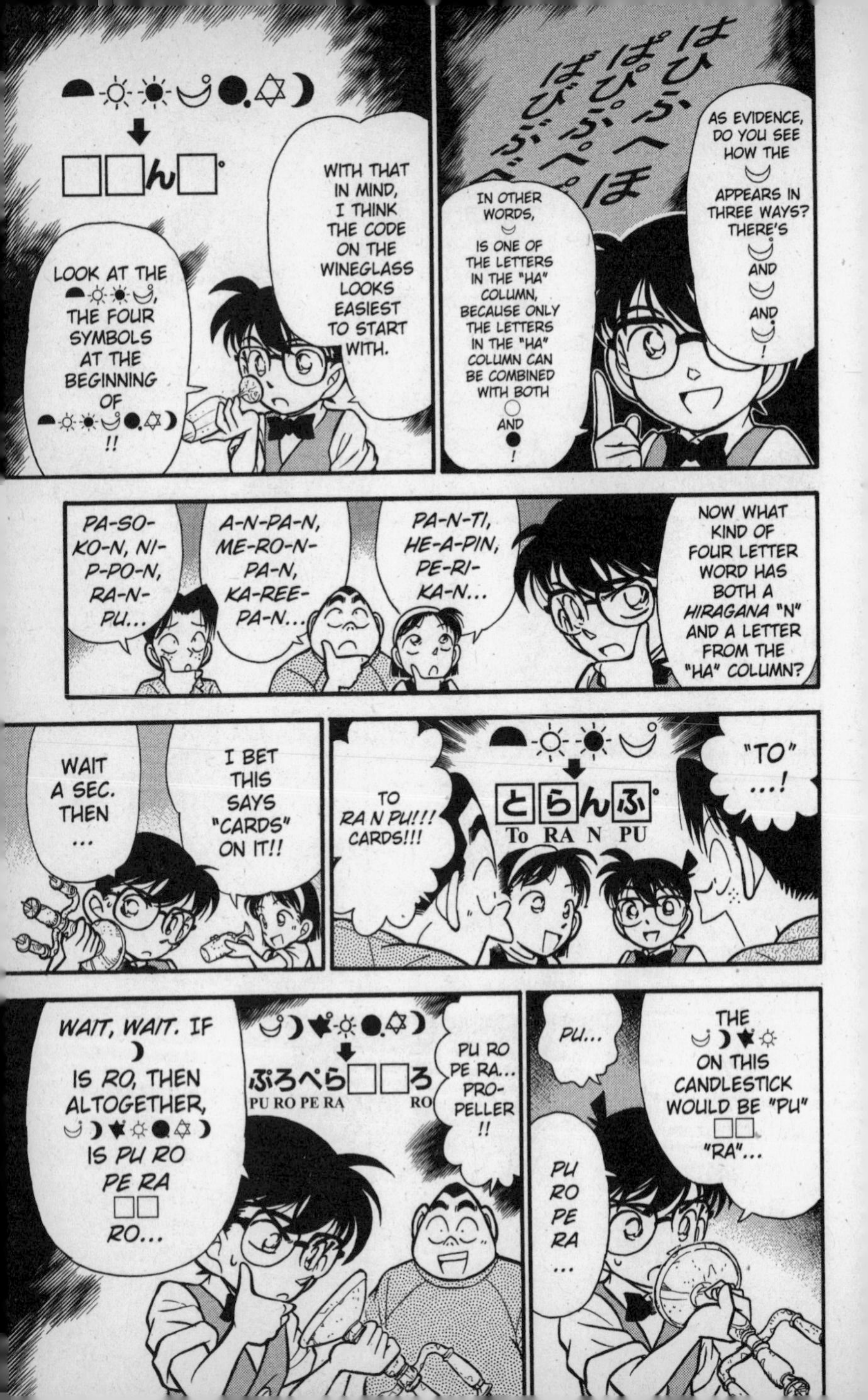
はひふへほ
ぱぴぷぺ
ばびぶ
AS EVIDENCE, DO YOU SEE HOW THE APPEARS IN THREE WAYS? THERE'S AND AND !
IN OTHER WORDS, IS ONE OF THE LETTERS IN THE "HA" COLUMN, BECAUSE ONLY THE LETTERS IN THE "HA" COLUMN CAN BE COMBINED WITH BOTH AND !
ん
WITH THAT IN MIND, I THINK THE CODE ON THE WINEGLASS LOOKS EASIEST TO START WITH.
LOOK AT THE, THE FOUR SYMBOLS AT THE BEGINNING OF !!
NOW WHAT KIND OF FOUR LETTER WORD HAS BOTH A HIRAGANA "N" AND A LETTER FROM THE "HA" COLUMN?
PA-N-TI, HE-A-PIN, PE-RI-KA-N...
A-N-PA-N, ME-RO-N-PA-N, KA-REE-PA-N...
PA-SO-KO-N, NI-P-PO-N, RA-N-PU...
"TO" ...!
とらんぷ
To RA N PU
TO RA N PU!!! CARDS!!!
I BET THIS SAYS "CARDS" ON IT!!
WAIT A SEC. THEN ...
THE ON THIS CANDLESTICK WOULD BE "PU" "RA"...
PU...
PU RO PE RA ...
PU RO PE RA... PRO-PELLER !!
ぷろぺら ろ
PU RO PE RA RO
WAIT, WAIT. IF IS RO, THEN ALTOGETHER, IS PU RO PE RA RO...

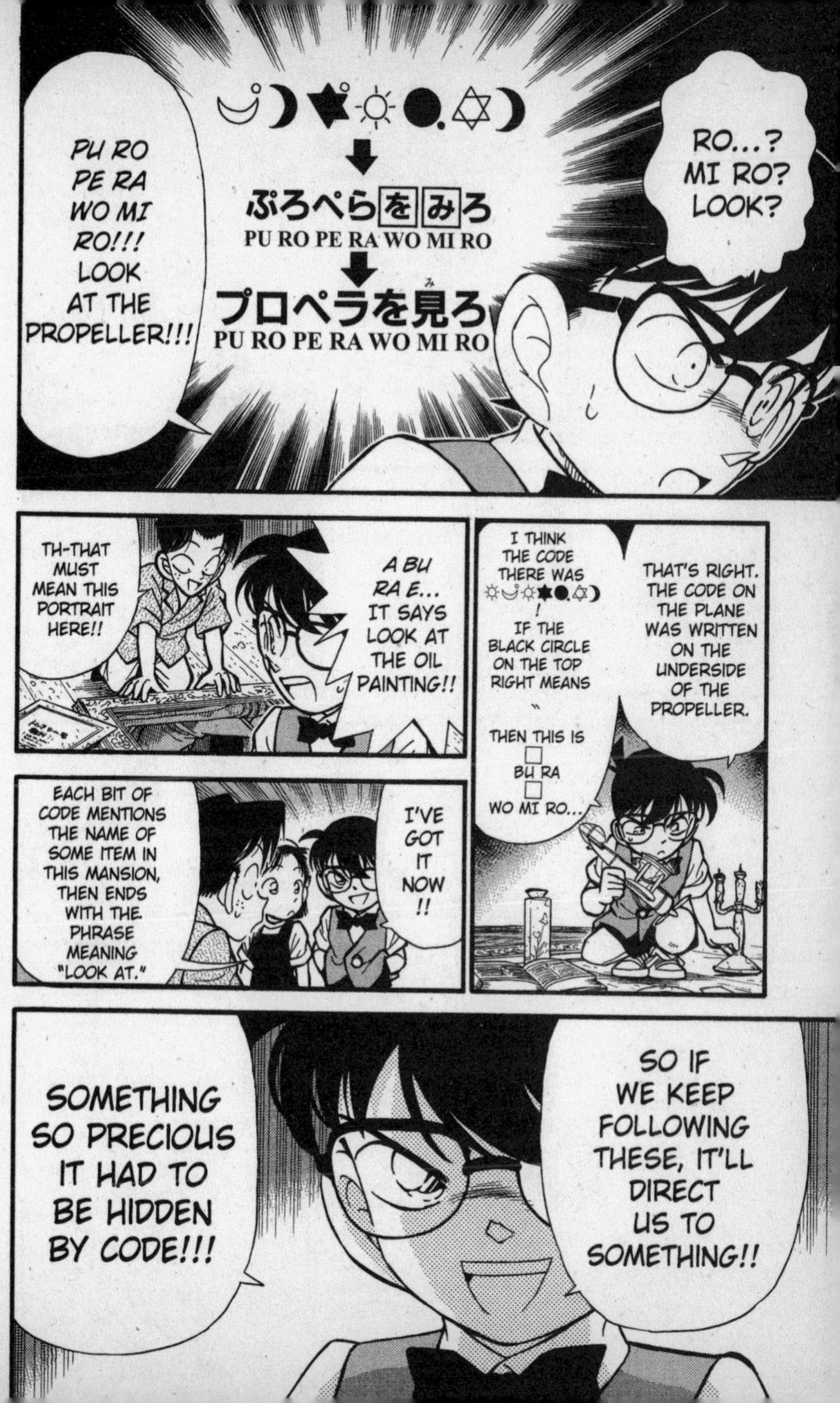
RO...? MI RO? LOOK?
ぷろぺらをみろ
PU RO PE RA WO MI RO
プロペラを見ろ
PU RO PE RA WO MI RO
PU RO PE RA WO MI RO!!! LOOK AT THE PROPELLER!!!
THAT'S RIGHT. THE CODE ON THE PLANE WAS WRITTEN ON THE UNDERSIDE OF THE PROPELLER.
I THINK THE CODE THERE WAS ! IF THE BLACK CIRCLE ON THE TOP RIGHT MEANS " THEN THIS IS BU RA WO MI RO...
A BU RA E... IT SAYS LOOK AT THE OIL PAINTING!!
TH-THAT MUST MEAN THIS PORTRAIT HERE!!
I'VE GOT IT NOW!!
EACH BIT OF CODE MENTIONS THE NAME OF SOME ITEM IN THIS MANSION, THEN ENDS WITH THE PHRASE MEANING "LOOK AT."
SO IF WE KEEP FOLLOWING THESE, IT'LL DIRECT US TO SOMETHING!!
SOMETHING SO PRECIOUS IT HAD TO BE HIDDEN BY CODE!!!

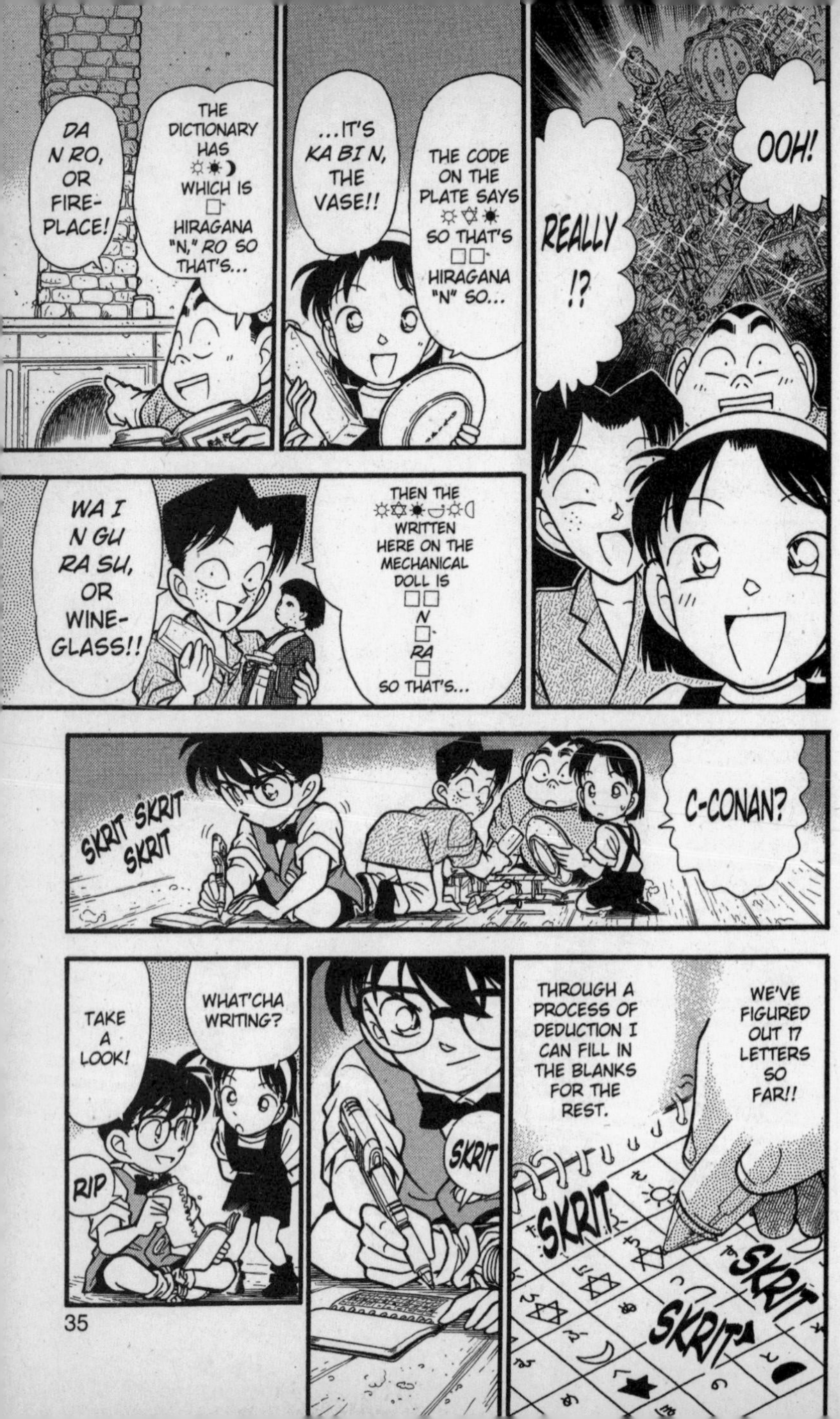
OOH!
REALLY!?
THE CODE ON THE PLATE SAYS ☼✡✹ SO THAT'S □□ HIRAGANA "N" SO...
...IT'S KA BI N, THE VASE!!
THE DICTIONARY HAS ☼✹☽ WHICH IS □ HIRAGANA "N," RO SO THAT'S...
DA N RO, OR FIRE-PLACE!
THEN THE ☼✡✹◡☼◖ WRITTEN HERE ON THE MECHANICAL DOLL IS □□ N □ RA □ SO THAT'S...
WA I N GU RA SU, OR WINE-GLASS!!
C-CONAN?
SKRIT SKRIT SKRIT
WE'VE FIGURED OUT 17 LETTERS SO FAR!!
THROUGH A PROCESS OF DEDUCTION I CAN FILL IN THE BLANKS FOR THE REST.
SKRIT
SKRIT
SKRIT
SKRIT
SKRIT
WHAT'CHA WRITING?
TAKE A LOOK!
RIP

HERE'S THE KEY TO DECIPHERING THE CODE!!
GREAT !!
AS YOU CAN SEE, ☼✡○✶● REPRESENT THE HIRAGANA ROWS OF AIUEO!!
DO YOU NOTICE HOW EACH SYMBOL VARIES ACROSS THE ROW FOLLOWING THE SAME RULE?
TAKE THE ☼ AND THE ✡ AND THE ✶ FOR EXAMPLE. STARTING AT THE TOP, THE POINTY PART THAT IS MISSING ROTATES CLOCKWISE.
○ AND ● ALSO HAS MISSING PARTS THAT ROTATE CLOCKWISE.
AND THE MYSTERIOUS BLACK DOT AT THE BOTTOM RIGHT OF SOME SYMBOLS ...
... IS AN ADDITIONAL MARK THAT'S USED WHEN THERE AREN'T ANY MORE VARIATIONS LEFT!
HMM, INDEED ...
SO NOW IF WE USE THIS CHART TO READ ALL THE PIECES OF CODE ...
SKRIT
SKRIT
SKRIT

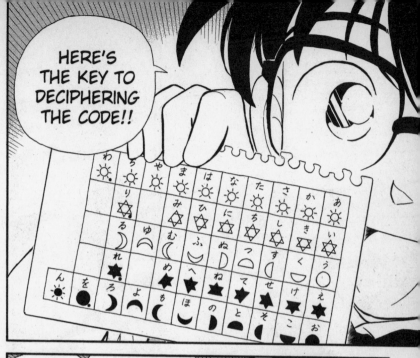

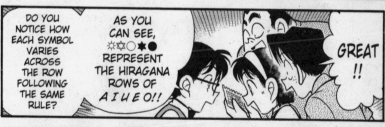

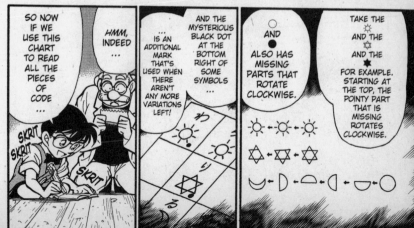

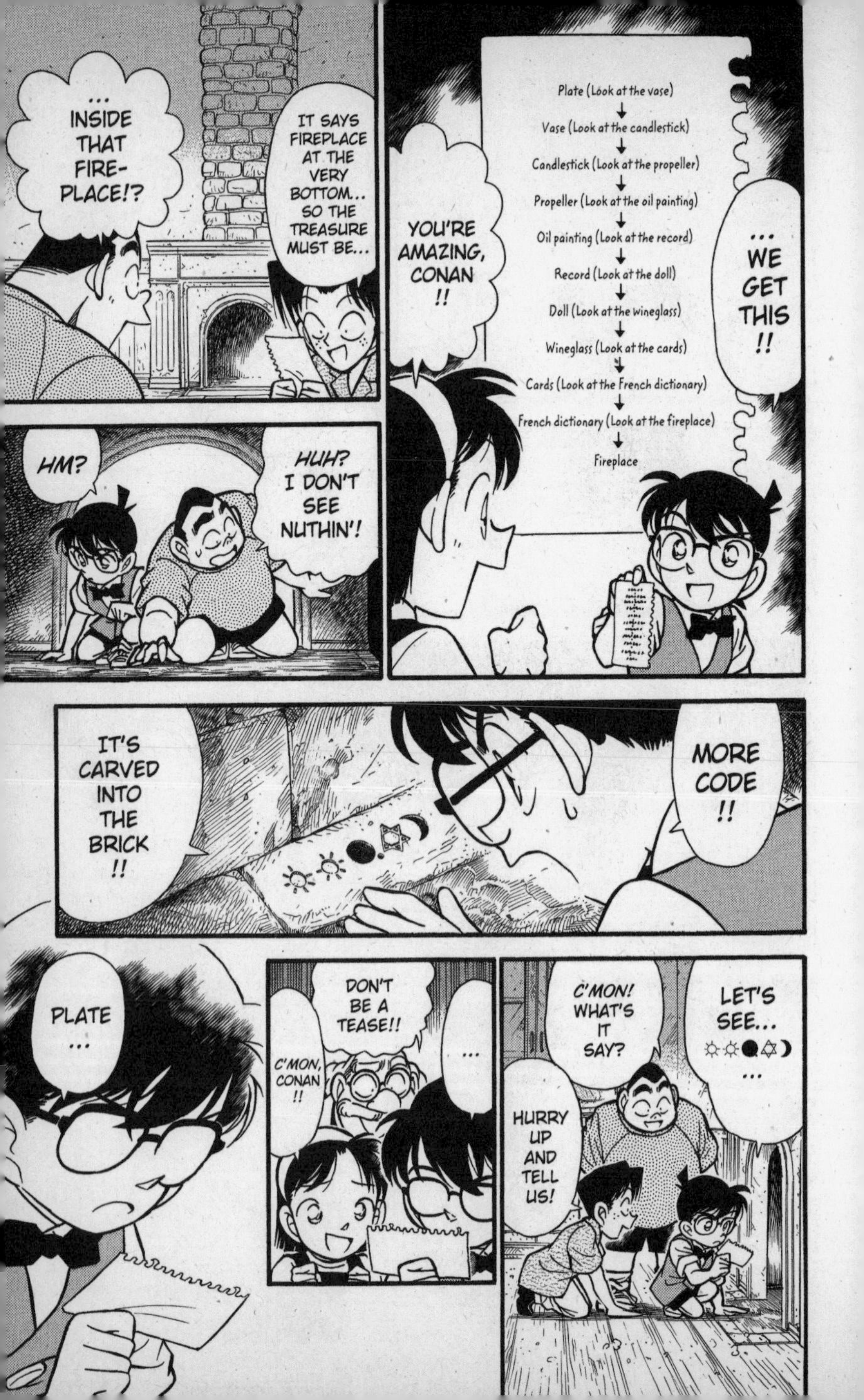

Plate (Look at the vase)
Vase (Look at the candlestick)
Candlestick (Look at the propeller)
Propeller (Look at the oil painting)
Oil painting (Look at the record)
Record (Look at the doll)
Doll (Look at the wineglass)
Wineglass (Look at the cards)
Cards (Look at the French dictionary)
French dictionary (Look at the fireplace)
Fireplace
YOU'RE AMAZING, CONAN !!
... WE GET THIS !!
IT SAYS FIREPLACE AT THE VERY BOTTOM... SO THE TREASURE MUST BE...
... INSIDE THAT FIRE-PLACE!?
HM?
HUH? I DON'T SEE NUTHIN'!
IT'S CARVED INTO THE BRICK !!
MORE CODE !!
LET'S SEE... ☼☼●✡☽ ...
C'MON! WHAT'S IT SAY?
HURRY UP AND TELL US!
DON'T BE A TEASE!!
C'MON, CONAN !!
...
PLATE ...

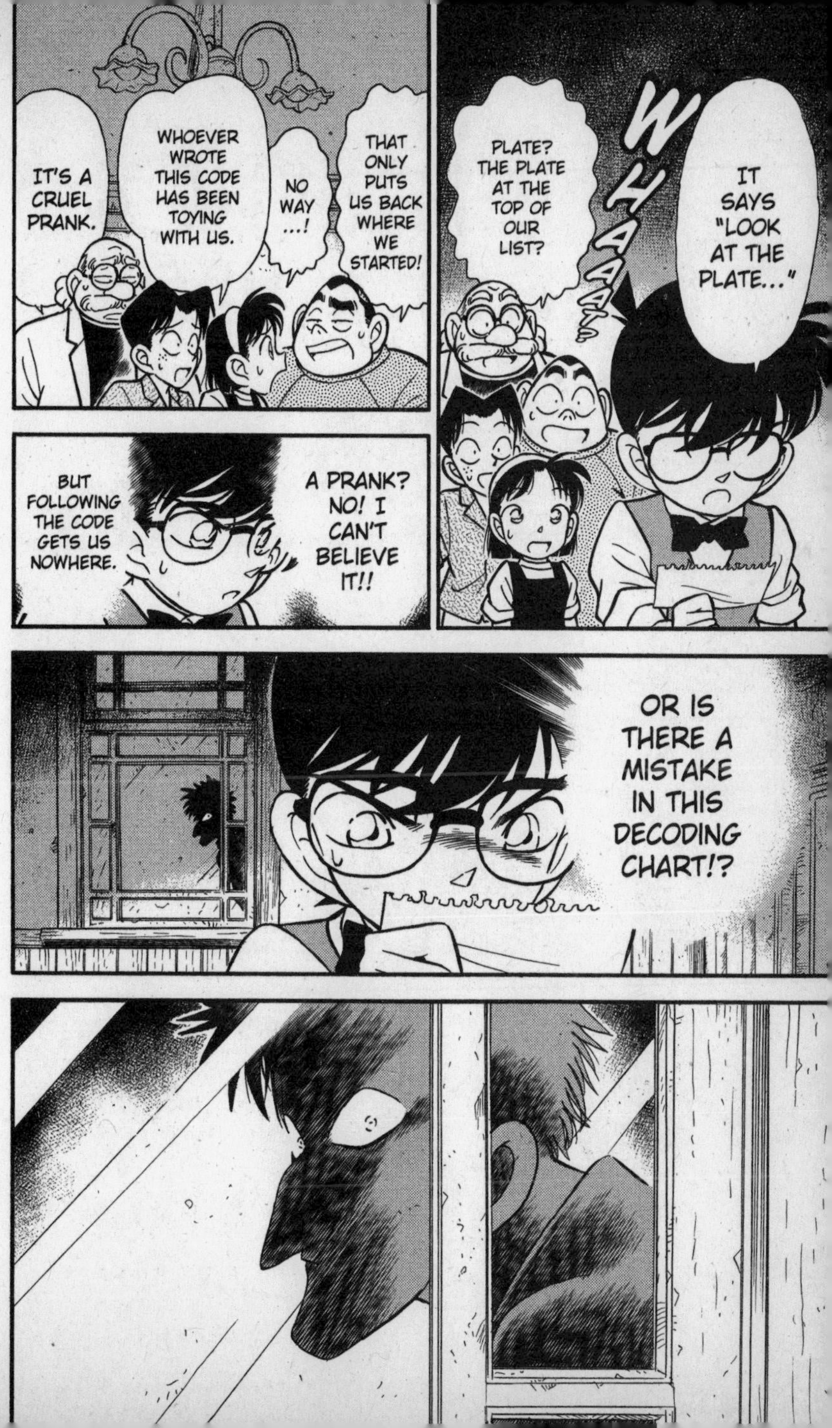

IT SAYS "LOOK AT THE PLATE..."
WHAAAA
PLATE? THE PLATE AT THE TOP OF OUR LIST?
THAT ONLY PUTS US BACK WHERE WE STARTED!
NO WAY ...!
WHOEVER WROTE THIS CODE HAS BEEN TOYING WITH US.
IT'S A CRUEL PRANK.
A PRANK? NO! I CAN'T BELIEVE IT!!
BUT FOLLOWING THE CODE GETS US NOWHERE.
OR IS THERE A MISTAKE IN THIS DECODING CHART!?

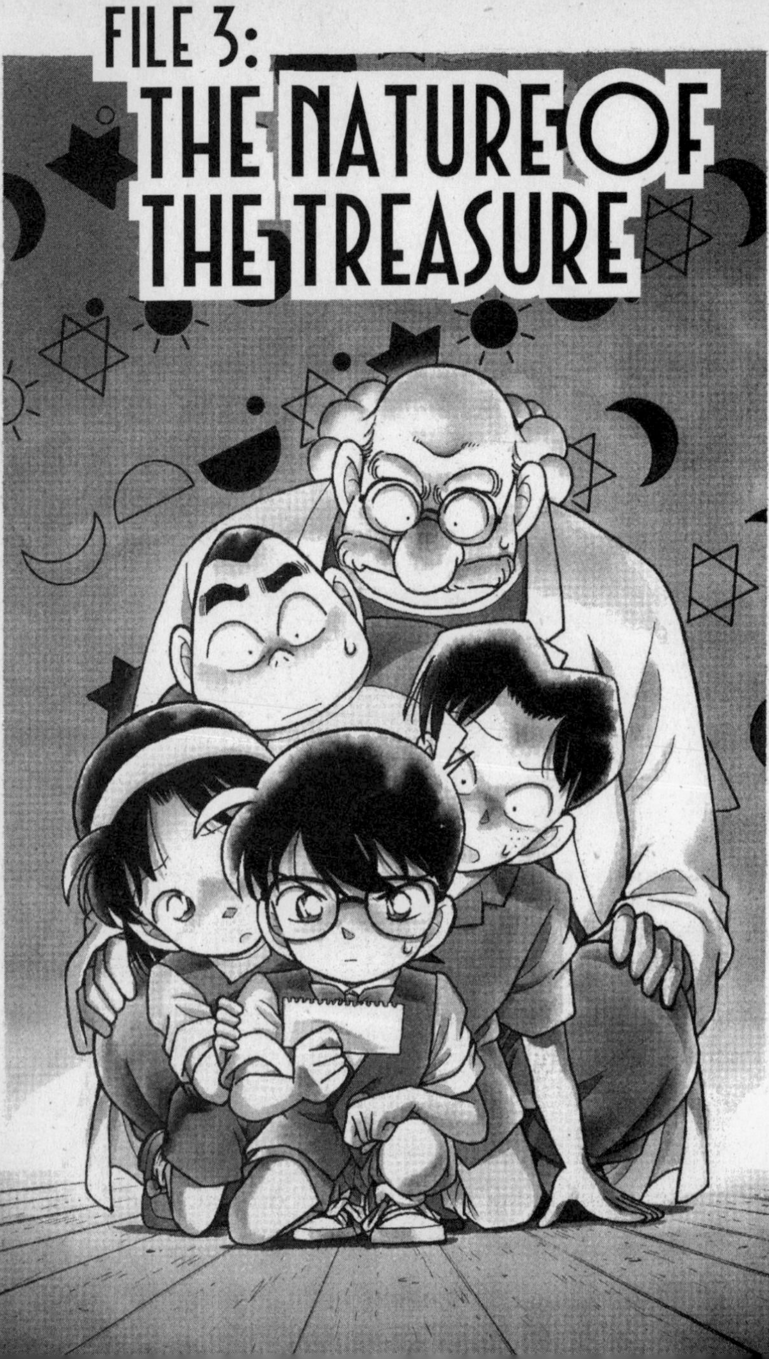
FILE 3:
THE NATURE OF THE TREASURE

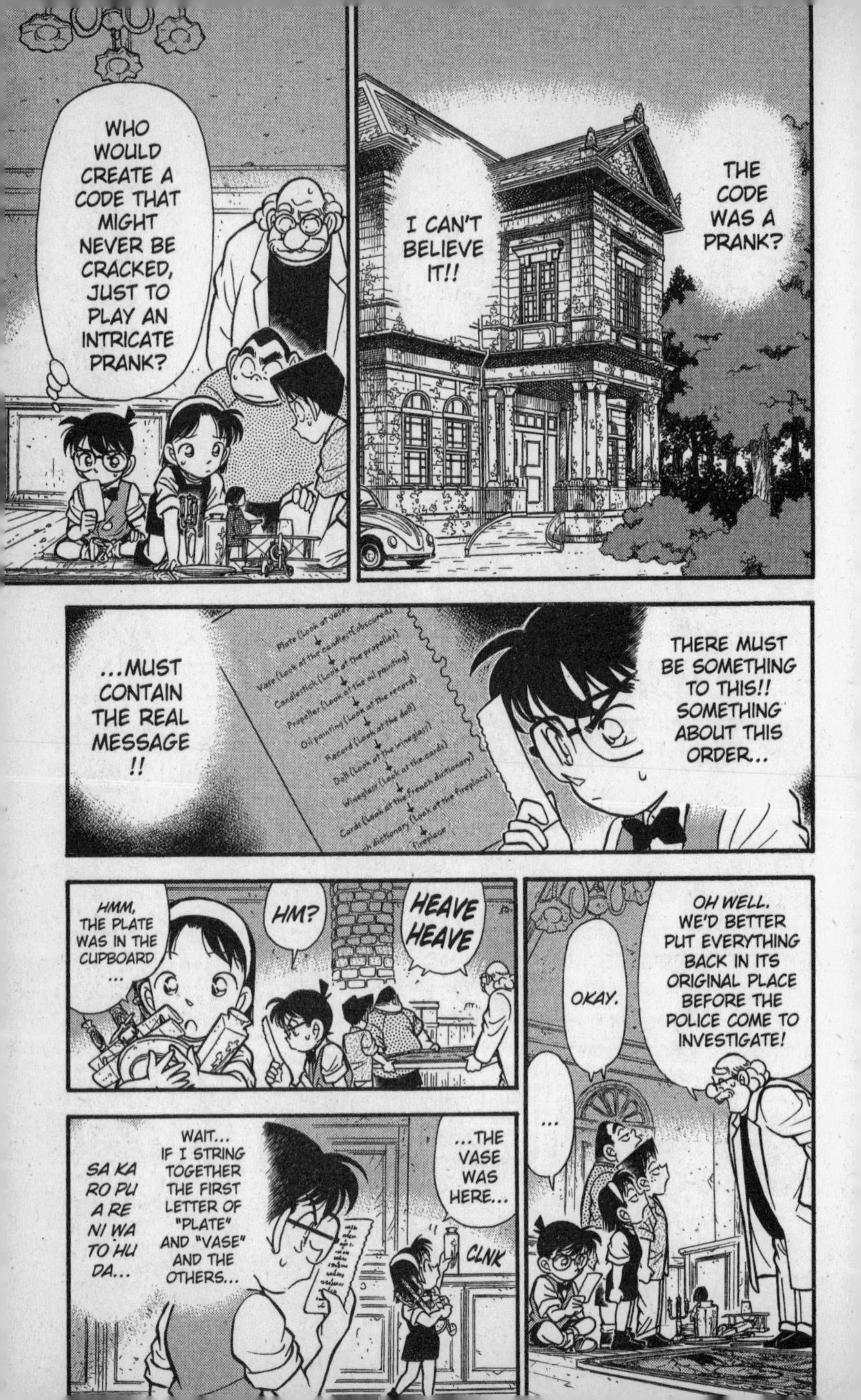
WHO WOULD CREATE A CODE THAT MIGHT NEVER BE CRACKED, JUST TO PLAY AN INTRICATE PRANK?
I CAN'T BELIEVE IT!!
THE CODE WAS A PRANK?
...MUST CONTAIN THE REAL MESSAGE !!
Plate (Look at vase)
Vase (Look at the candles) (obscured)
Candlestick (Look at the propeller)
Propeller (Look at the oil painting)
Oil painting (Look at the record)
Record (Look at the doll)
Doll (Look at the wineglass)
Wineglass (Look at the cards)
Cards (Look at the French dictionary)
h dictionary (Look at the fireplace)
Fireplace
THERE MUST BE SOMETHING TO THIS!! SOMETHING ABOUT THIS ORDER...
HMM, THE PLATE WAS IN THE CUPBOARD ...
HM?
HEAVE HEAVE
OH WELL. WE'D BETTER PUT EVERYTHING BACK IN ITS ORIGINAL PLACE BEFORE THE POLICE COME TO INVESTIGATE!
OKAY.
...
...THE VASE WAS HERE...
CLNK
WAIT... IF I STRING TOGETHER THE FIRST LETTER OF "PLATE" AND "VASE" AND THE OTHERS...
SA KA RO PU A RE NI WA TO HU DA...

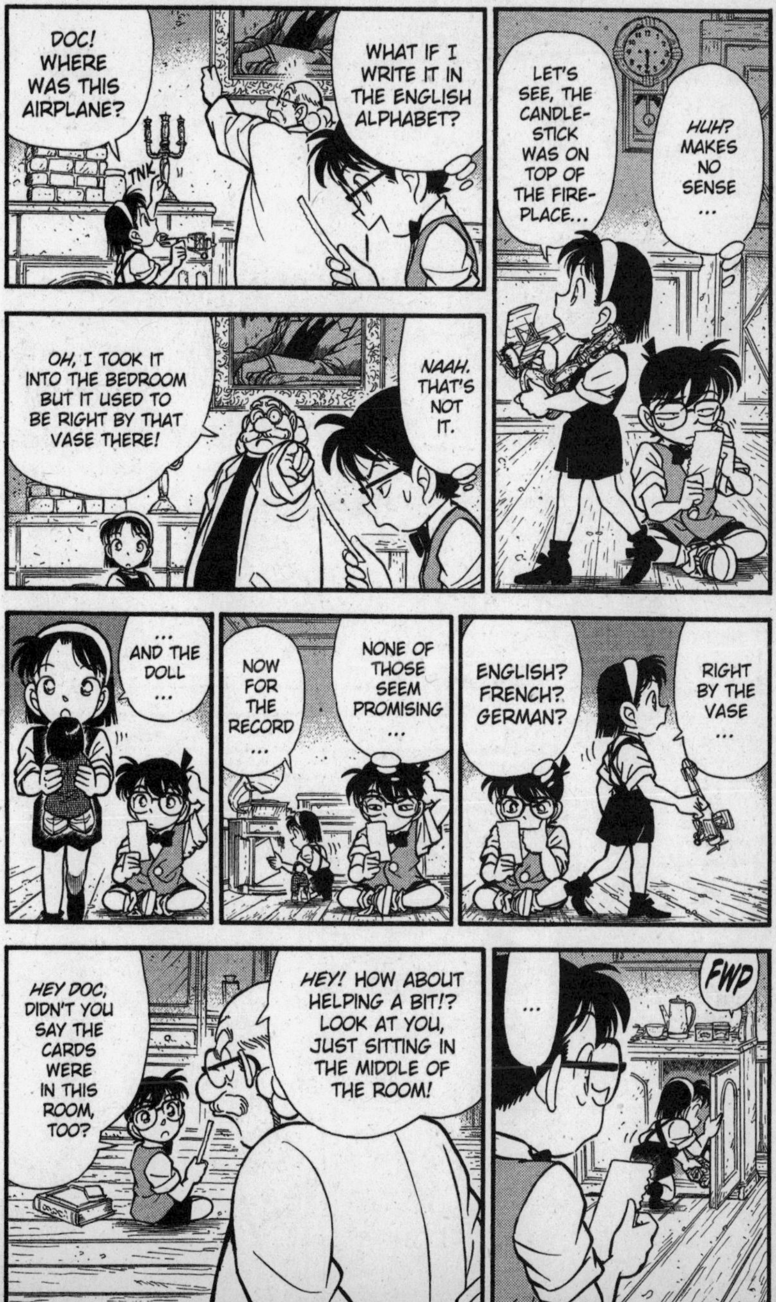
HUH? MAKES NO SENSE ...
LET'S SEE, THE CANDLE-STICK WAS ON TOP OF THE FIRE-PLACE...
WHAT IF I WRITE IT IN THE ENGLISH ALPHABET?
DOC! WHERE WAS THIS AIRPLANE?
TNK
NAAH. THAT'S NOT IT.
OH, I TOOK IT INTO THE BEDROOM BUT IT USED TO BE RIGHT BY THAT VASE THERE!
RIGHT BY THE VASE ...
ENGLISH? FRENCH? GERMAN?
NONE OF THOSE SEEM PROMISING ...
NOW FOR THE RECORD ...
... AND THE DOLL ...
FWP
...
HEY! HOW ABOUT HELPING A BIT!? LOOK AT YOU, JUST SITTING IN THE MIDDLE OF THE ROOM!
HEY DOC, DIDN'T YOU SAY THE CARDS WERE IN THIS ROOM, TOO?

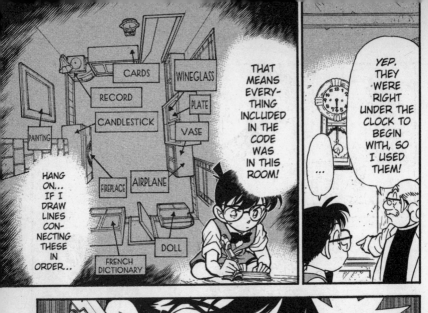

YEP. THEY WERE RIGHT UNDER THE CLOCK TO BEGIN WITH, SO I USED THEM!
...
THAT MEANS EVERY-THING INCLUDED IN THE CODE WAS IN THIS ROOM!
CARDS
WINEGLASS
RECORD
PLATE
CANDLESTICK
VASE
PAINTING
FIREPLACE
AIRPLANE
DOLL
FRENCH DICTIONARY
HANG ON... IF I DRAW LINES CON-NECTING THESE IN ORDER...
!?
THEY ALL CONVERGE AT THE CENTER OF THE ROOM!!
plate
vase
wineglass
airplane
cards
doll
painting
candlestick
fireplace
French dictionary
THE DIC-TIONARY...
SO THAT'S WHY AMY KEEPS PASSING RIGHT BY ME.
THIS IS THE CENTER OF THE ROOM, BUT THERE'S NOTHING UNUSUAL HERE...
BUT THAT'S STRANGE...
IF IT'S NOT IN THE FLOOR, MAYBE...

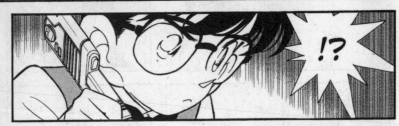

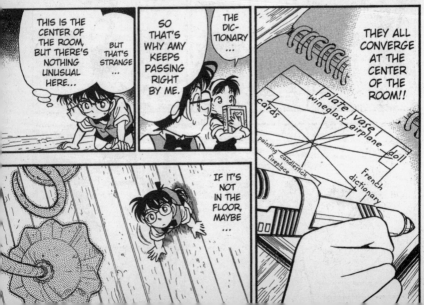

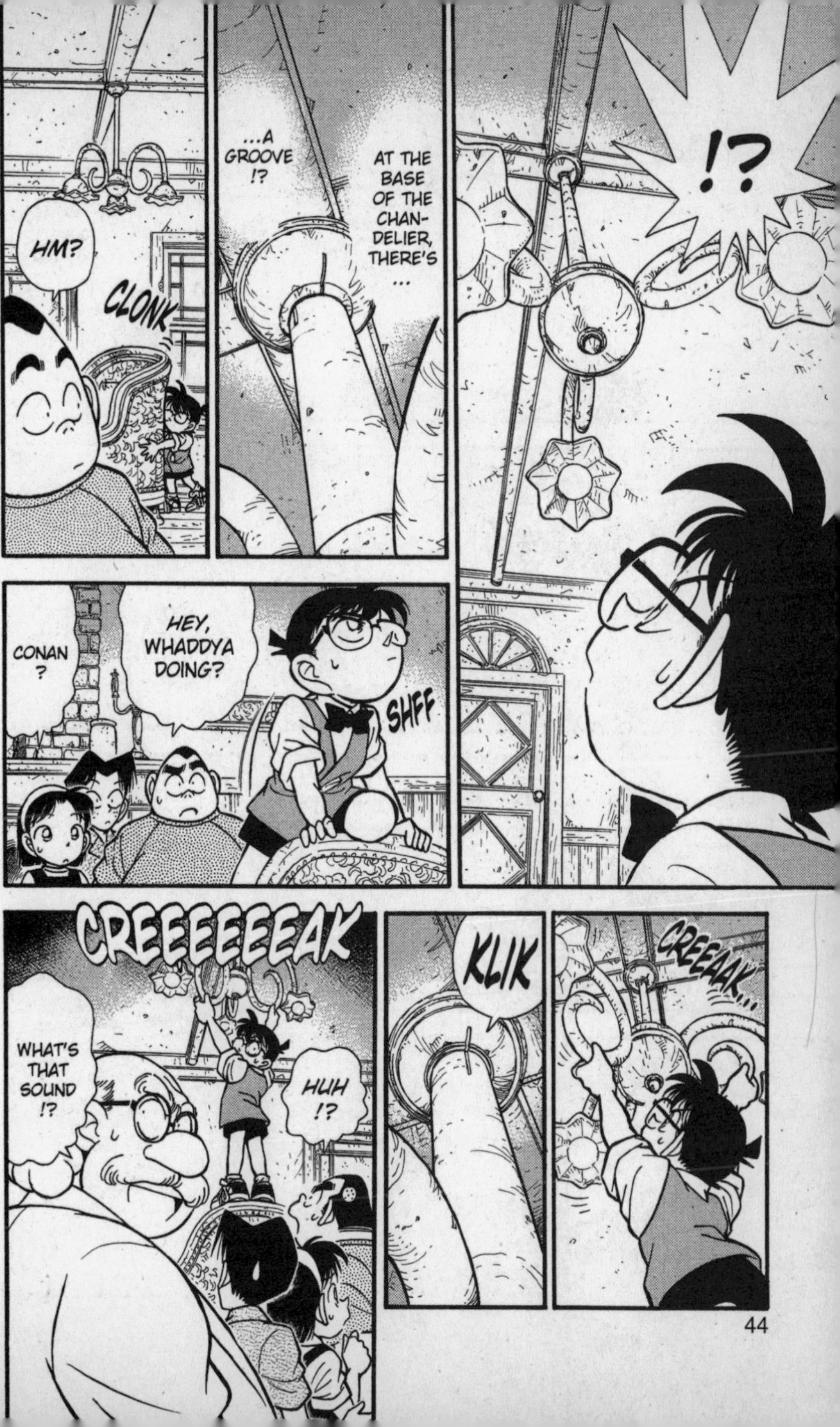
!?
AT THE BASE OF THE CHAN-DELIER, THERE'S ...
...A GROOVE !?
HM?
CLONK
SHFF
HEY, WHADDYA DOING?
CONAN ?
CREEAAK...
KLIK
CREEEEEEEAK
HUH !?
WHAT'S THAT SOUND !?

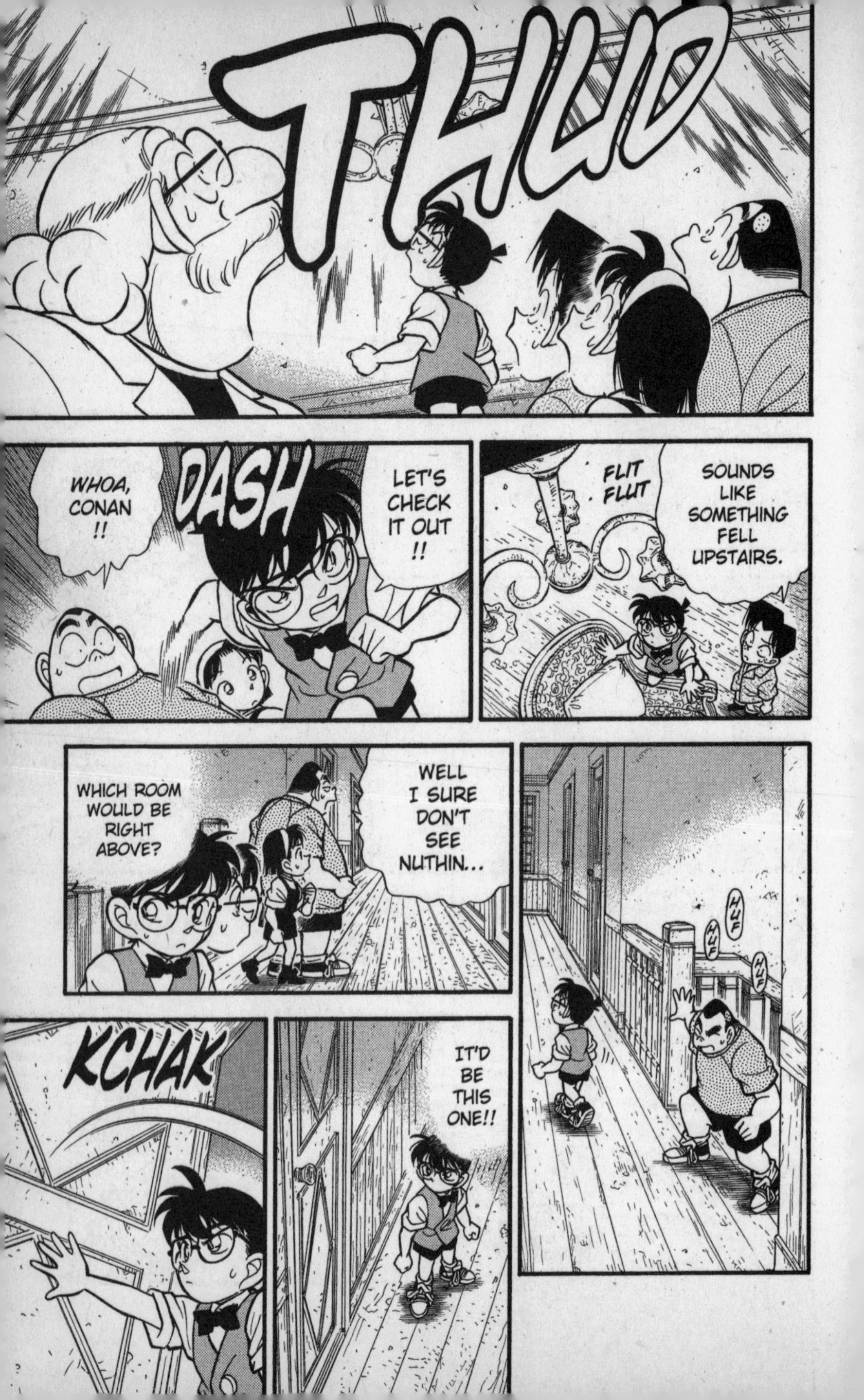
THUD
SOUNDS LIKE SOMETHING FELL UPSTAIRS.
FLIT FLUT
LET'S CHECK IT OUT!!
DASH
WHOA, CONAN!!
HUF
HUF
HUF
WELL I SURE DON'T SEE NUTHIN...
WHICH ROOM WOULD BE RIGHT ABOVE?
IT'D BE THIS ONE!!
KCHAK

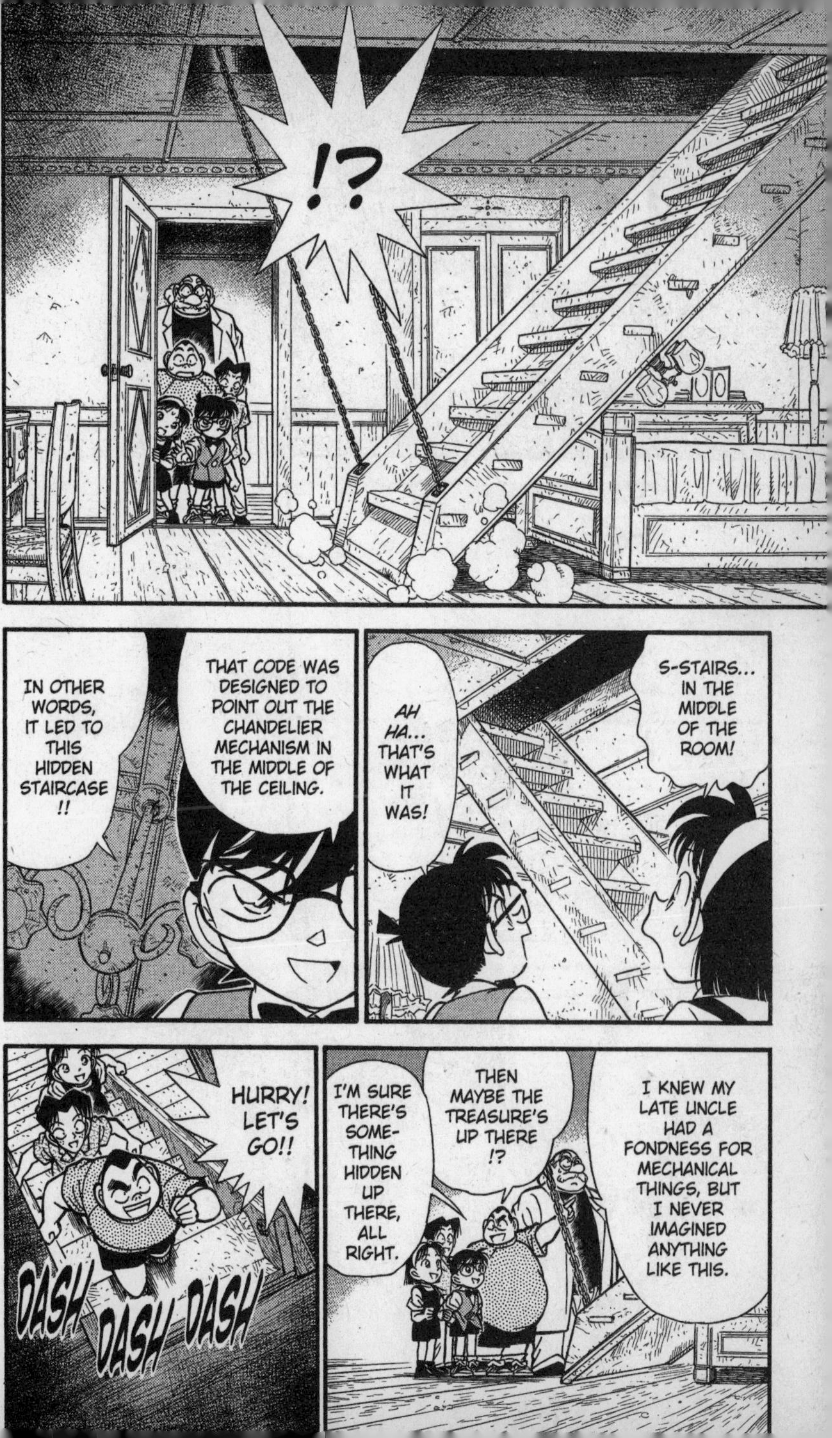
!?
S-STAIRS... IN THE MIDDLE OF THE ROOM!
AH HA... THAT'S WHAT IT WAS!
THAT CODE WAS DESIGNED TO POINT OUT THE CHANDELIER MECHANISM IN THE MIDDLE OF THE CEILING.
IN OTHER WORDS, IT LED TO THIS HIDDEN STAIRCASE !!
I KNEW MY LATE UNCLE HAD A FONDNESS FOR MECHANICAL THINGS, BUT I NEVER IMAGINED ANYTHING LIKE THIS.
THEN MAYBE THE TREASURE'S UP THERE !?
I'M SURE THERE'S SOME-THING HIDDEN UP THERE, ALL RIGHT.
HURRY! LET'S GO!!
DASH DASH DASH

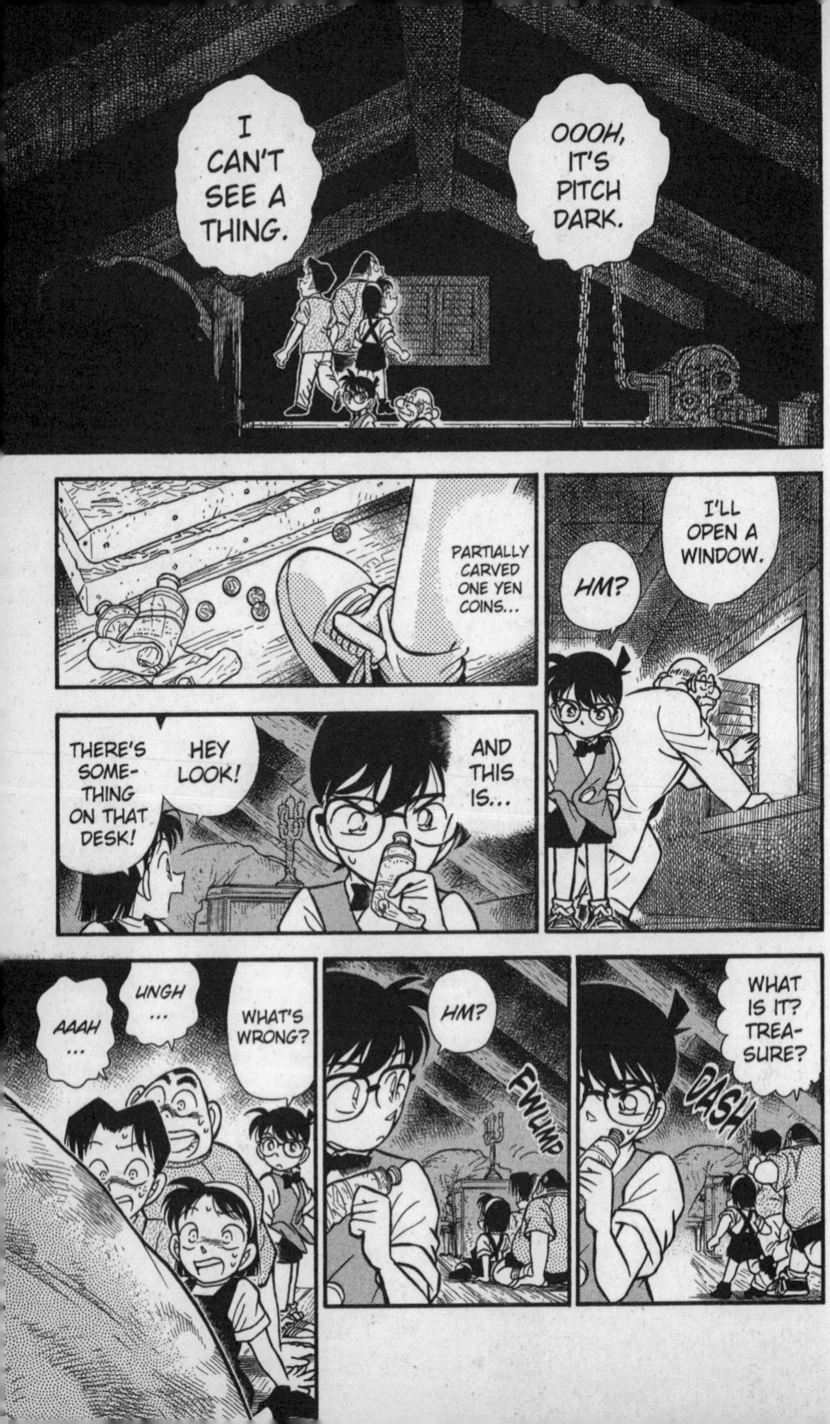

OOOH, IT'S PITCH DARK.
I CAN'T SEE A THING.
I'LL OPEN A WINDOW.
HM?
PARTIALLY CARVED ONE YEN COINS...
AND THIS IS...
HEY LOOK!
THERE'S SOMETHING ON THAT DESK!
WHAT IS IT? TREASURE?
DASH
HM?
FWUMP
WHAT'S WRONG?
UNGH ...
AAAH ...

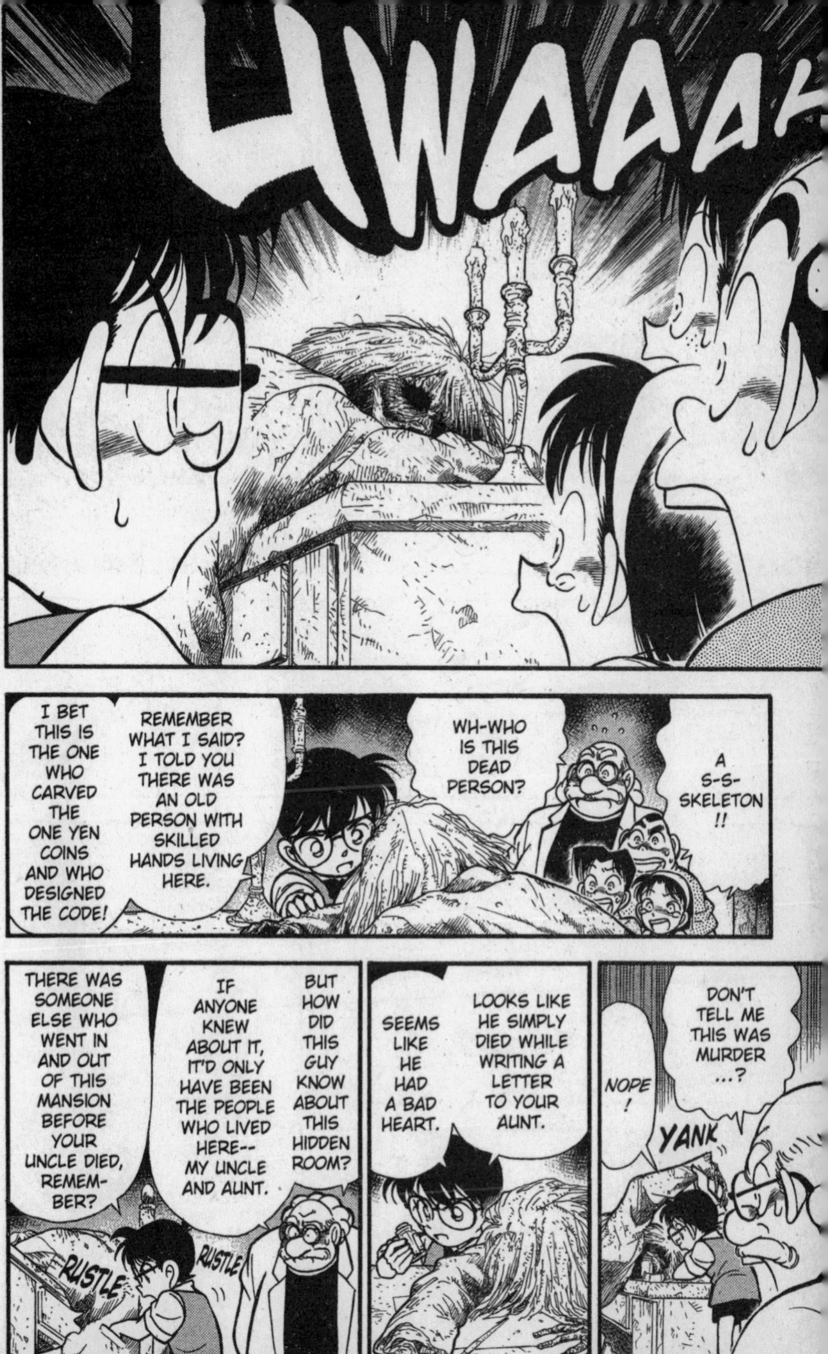
UWAAAK
A S-S-SKELETON!!
WH-WHO IS THIS DEAD PERSON?
REMEMBER WHAT I SAID? I TOLD YOU THERE WAS AN OLD PERSON WITH SKILLED HANDS LIVING HERE.
I BET THIS IS THE ONE WHO CARVED THE ONE YEN COINS AND WHO DESIGNED THE CODE!
DON'T TELL ME THIS WAS MURDER ...?
NOPE!
YANK
LOOKS LIKE HE SIMPLY DIED WHILE WRITING A LETTER TO YOUR AUNT.
SEEMS LIKE HE HAD A BAD HEART.
BUT HOW DID THIS GUY KNOW ABOUT THIS HIDDEN ROOM?
IF ANYONE KNEW ABOUT IT, IT'D ONLY HAVE BEEN THE PEOPLE WHO LIVED HERE-- MY UNCLE AND AUNT.
RUSTLE
RUSTLE
THERE WAS SOMEONE ELSE WHO WENT IN AND OUT OF THIS MANSION BEFORE YOUR UNCLE DIED, REMEMBER?

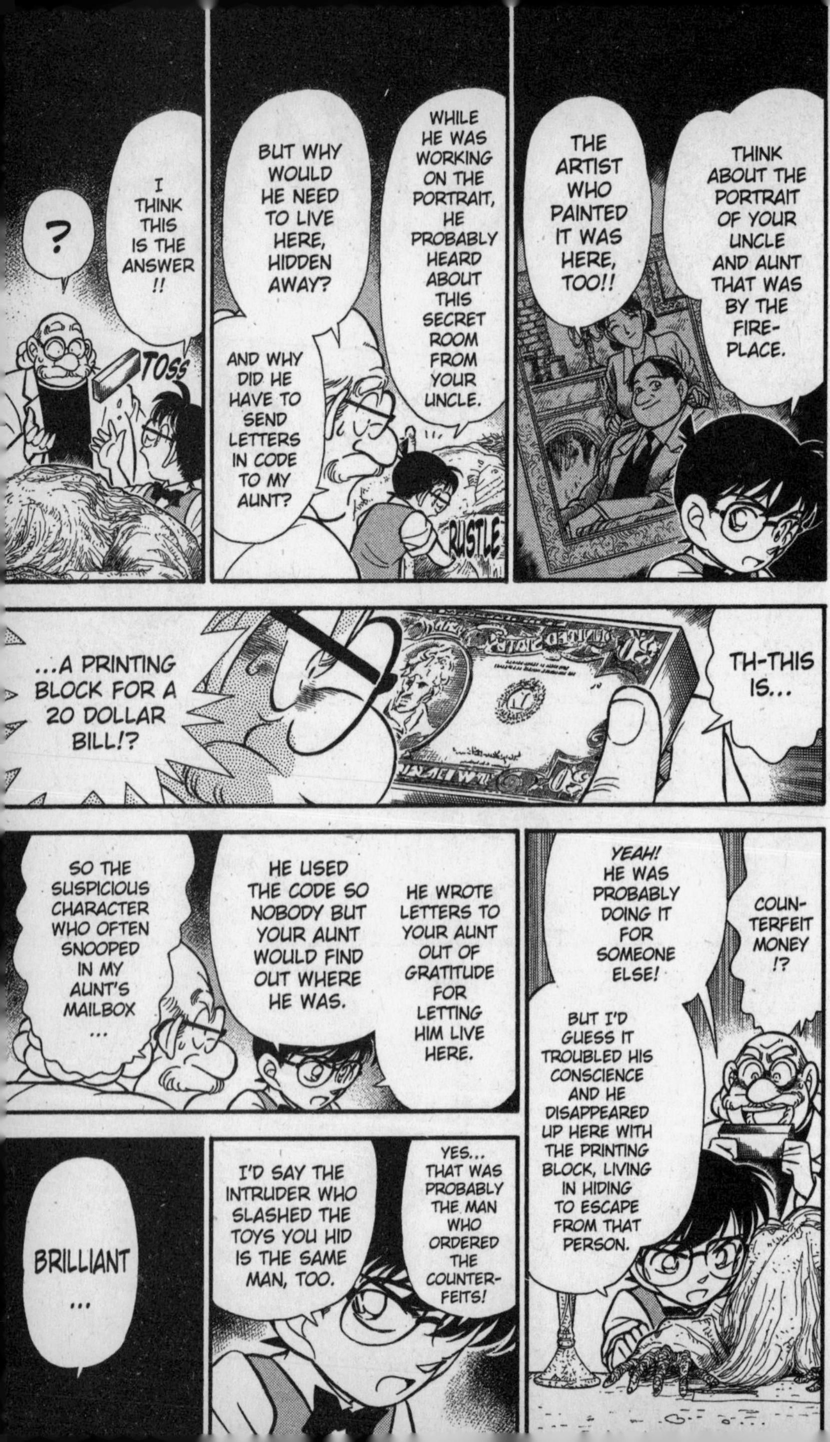
THINK ABOUT THE PORTRAIT OF YOUR UNCLE AND AUNT THAT WAS BY THE FIRE-PLACE.
THE ARTIST WHO PAINTED IT WAS HERE, TOO!!
WHILE HE WAS WORKING ON THE PORTRAIT, HE PROBABLY HEARD ABOUT THIS SECRET ROOM FROM YOUR UNCLE.
BUT WHY WOULD HE NEED TO LIVE HERE, HIDDEN AWAY?
AND WHY DID HE HAVE TO SEND LETTERS IN CODE TO MY AUNT?
RUSTLE
I THINK THIS IS THE ANSWER!!
?
TOSS
TH-THIS IS...
...A PRINTING BLOCK FOR A 20 DOLLAR BILL!?
COUNTERFEIT MONEY!?
YEAH! HE WAS PROBABLY DOING IT FOR SOMEONE ELSE!
BUT I'D GUESS IT TROUBLED HIS CONSCIENCE AND HE DISAPPEARED UP HERE WITH THE PRINTING BLOCK, LIVING IN HIDING TO ESCAPE FROM THAT PERSON.
HE WROTE LETTERS TO YOUR AUNT OUT OF GRATITUDE FOR LETTING HIM LIVE HERE.
HE USED THE CODE SO NOBODY BUT YOUR AUNT WOULD FIND OUT WHERE HE WAS.
SO THE SUSPICIOUS CHARACTER WHO OFTEN SNOOPED IN MY AUNT'S MAILBOX...
YES... THAT WAS PROBABLY THE MAN WHO ORDERED THE COUNTERFEITS!
I'D SAY THE INTRUDER WHO SLASHED THE TOYS YOU HID IS THE SAME MAN, TOO.
BRILLIANT...

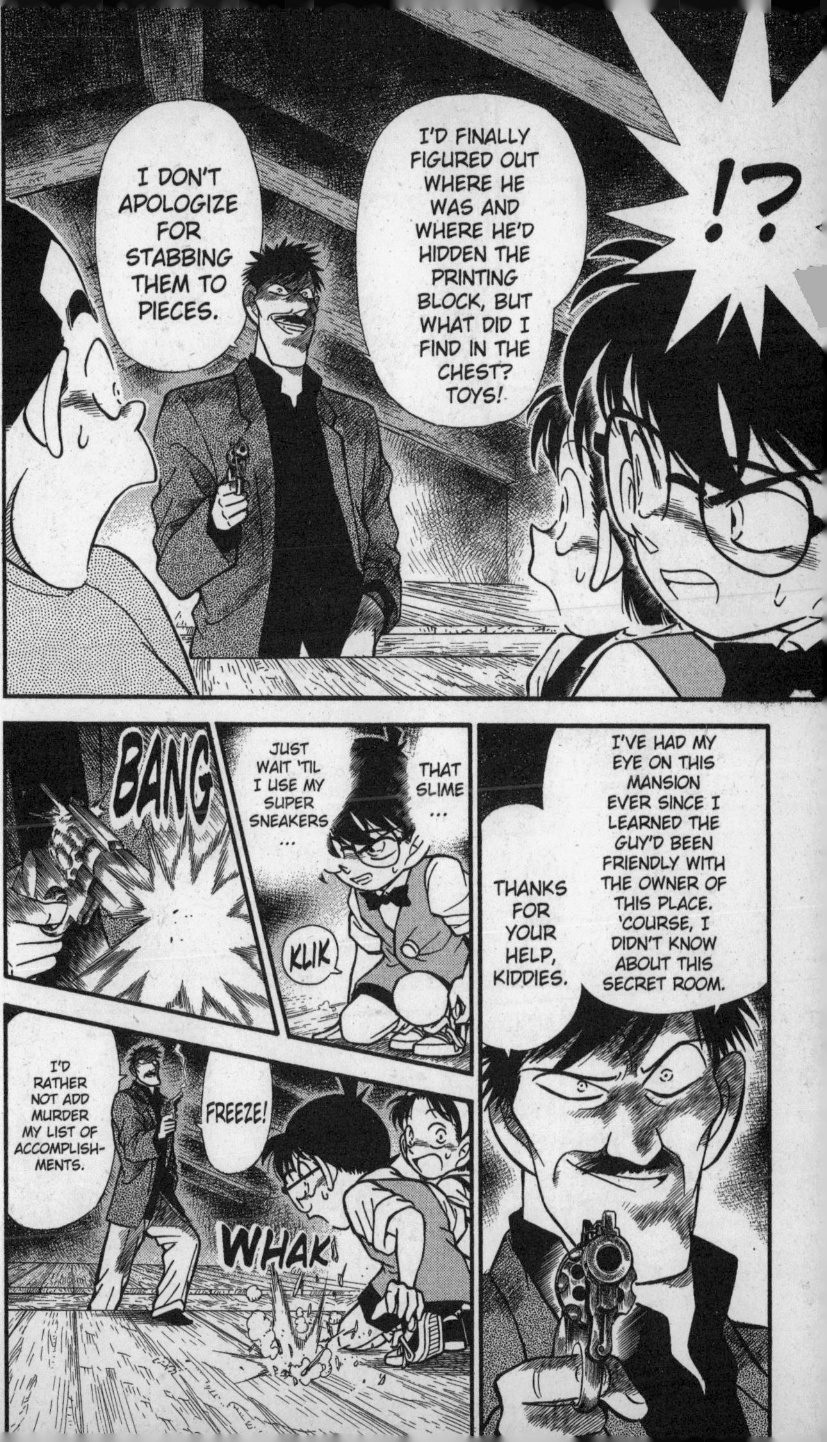
!?
I'D FINALLY FIGURED OUT WHERE HE WAS AND WHERE HE'D HIDDEN THE PRINTING BLOCK, BUT WHAT DID I FIND IN THE CHEST? TOYS!
I DON'T APOLOGIZE FOR STABBING THEM TO PIECES.
I'VE HAD MY EYE ON THIS MANSION EVER SINCE I LEARNED THE GUY'D BEEN FRIENDLY WITH THE OWNER OF THIS PLACE. 'COURSE, I DIDN'T KNOW ABOUT THIS SECRET ROOM.
THANKS FOR YOUR HELP, KIDDIES.
THAT SLIME ...
JUST WAIT 'TIL I USE MY SUPER SNEAKERS ...
KLIK
BANG
FREEZE!
I'D RATHER NOT ADD MURDER MY LIST OF ACCOMPLISHMENTS.
WHAK

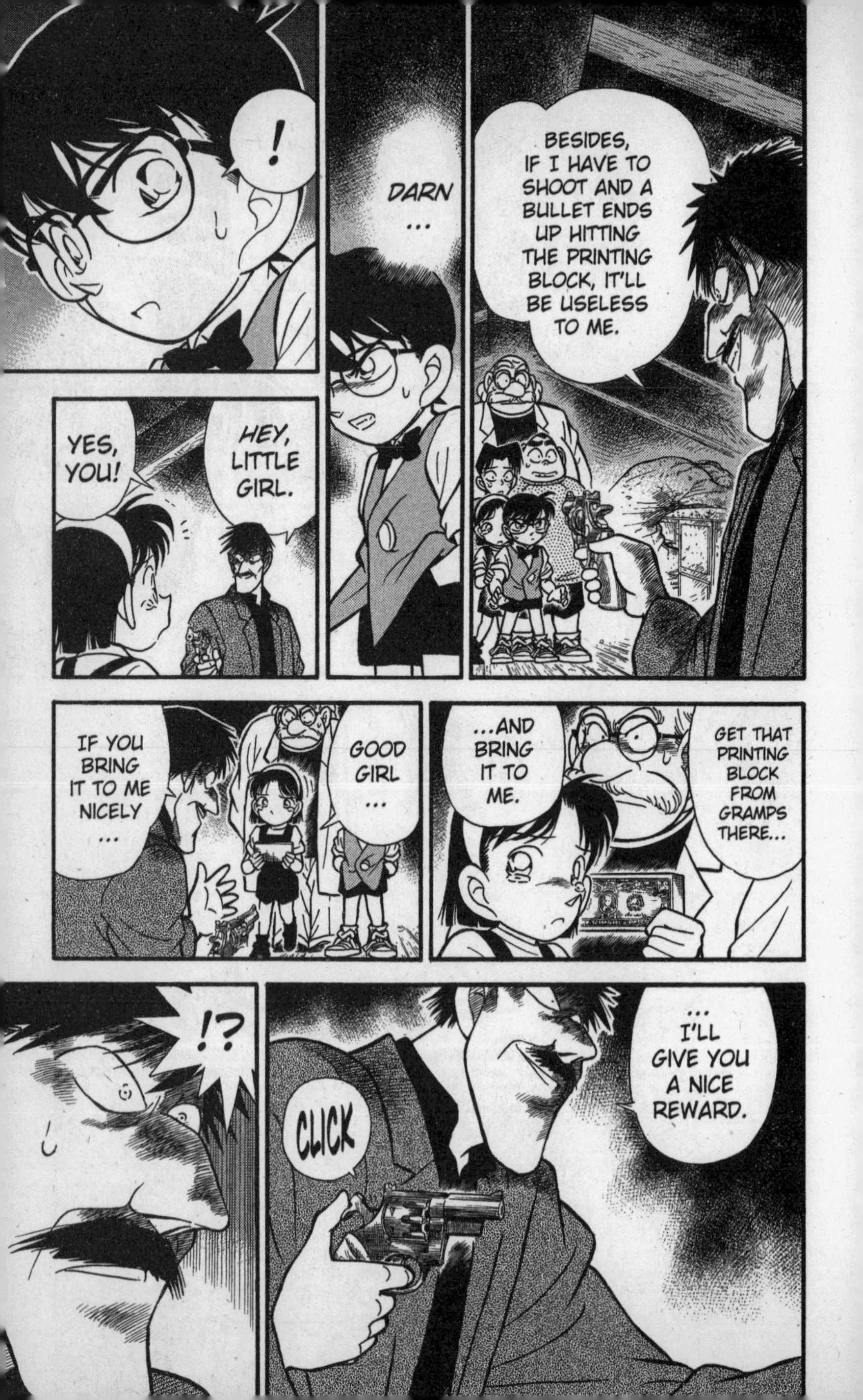
BESIDES, IF I HAVE TO SHOOT AND A BULLET ENDS UP HITTING THE PRINTING BLOCK, IT'LL BE USELESS TO ME.
DARN ...
!
HEY, LITTLE GIRL.
YES, YOU!
GET THAT PRINTING BLOCK FROM GRAMPS THERE...
...AND BRING IT TO ME.
GOOD GIRL ...
IF YOU BRING IT TO ME NICELY ...
... I'LL GIVE YOU A NICE REWARD.
CLICK
!?

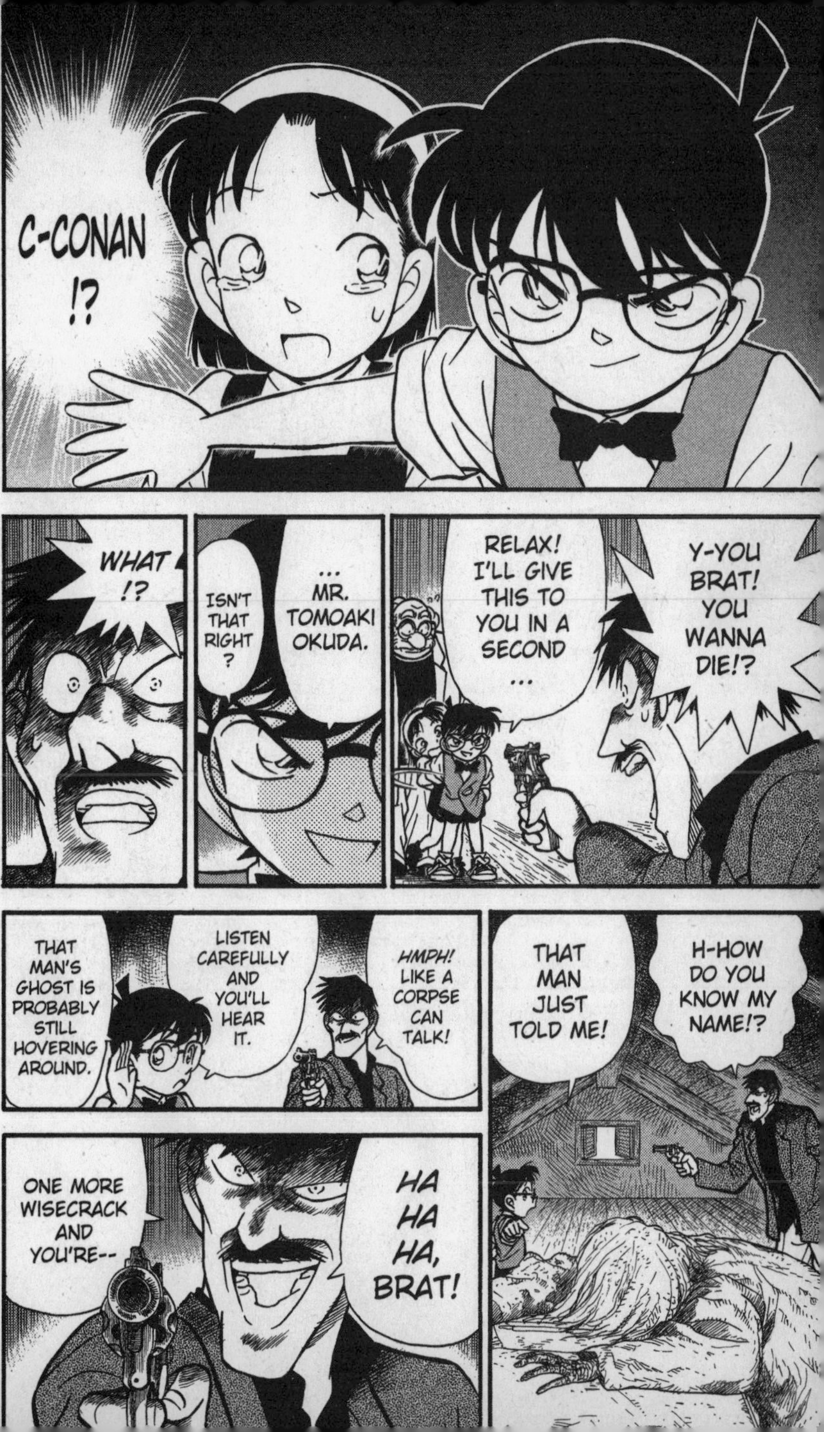
C-CONAN !?
Y-YOU BRAT! YOU WANNA DIE!?
RELAX! I'LL GIVE THIS TO YOU IN A SECOND ...
... MR. TOMOAKI OKUDA.
ISN'T THAT RIGHT ?
WHAT !?
H-HOW DO YOU KNOW MY NAME!?
THAT MAN JUST TOLD ME!
HMPH! LIKE A CORPSE CAN TALK!
LISTEN CAREFULLY AND YOU'LL HEAR IT.
THAT MAN'S GHOST IS PROBABLY STILL HOVERING AROUND.
HA HA HA, BRAT!
ONE MORE WISECRACK AND YOU'RE--

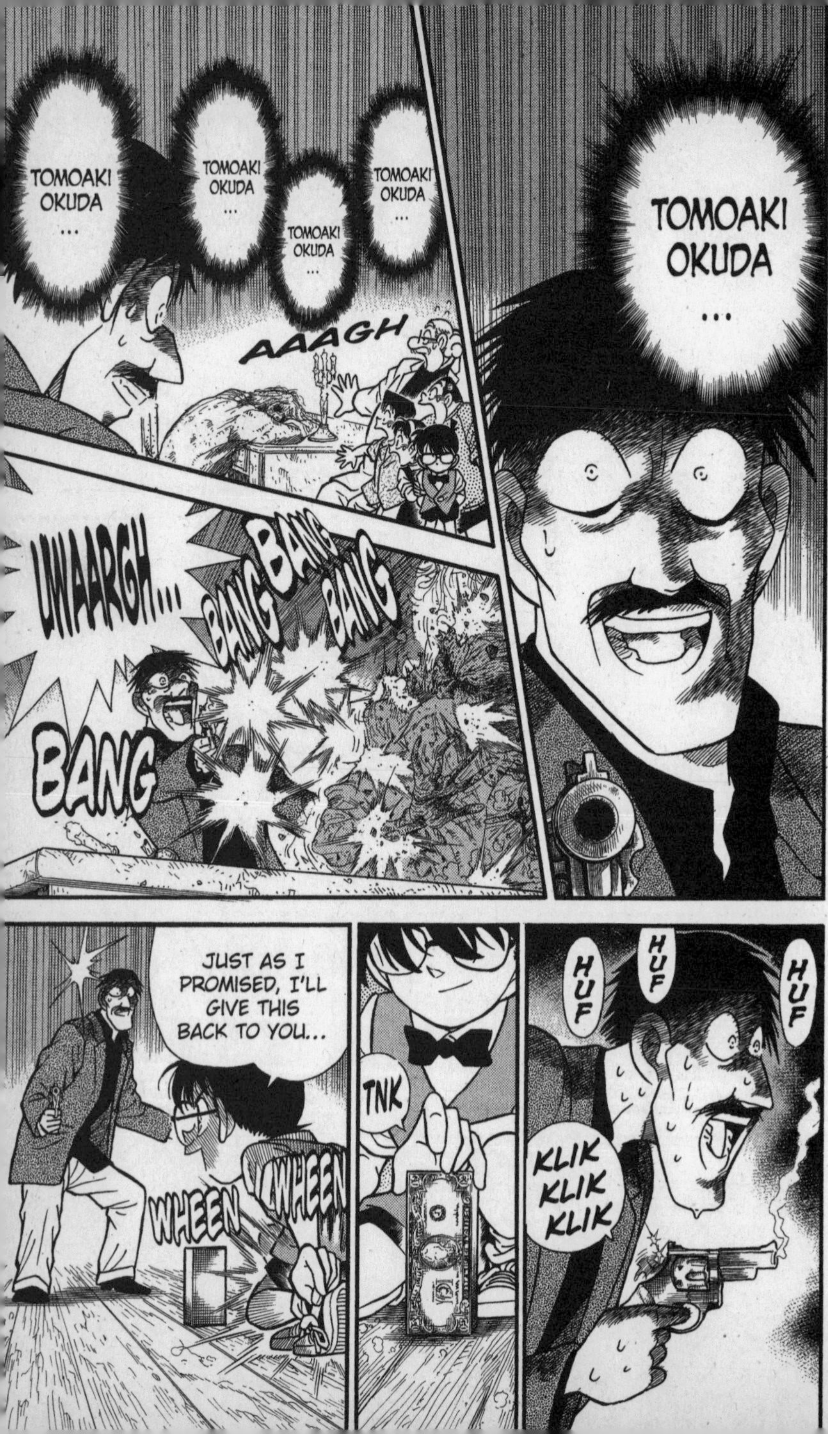
TOMOAKI OKUDA ...
TOMOAKI OKUDA ...
TOMOAKI OKUDA ...
TOMOAKI OKUDA ...
TOMOAKI OKUDA ...
AAAGH
UWAARGH...!
BANG BANG BANG
BANG
HUF HUF HUF
KLIK KLIK KLIK
TNK
JUST AS I PROMISED, I'LL GIVE THIS BACK TO YOU...
WHEEN WHEEN

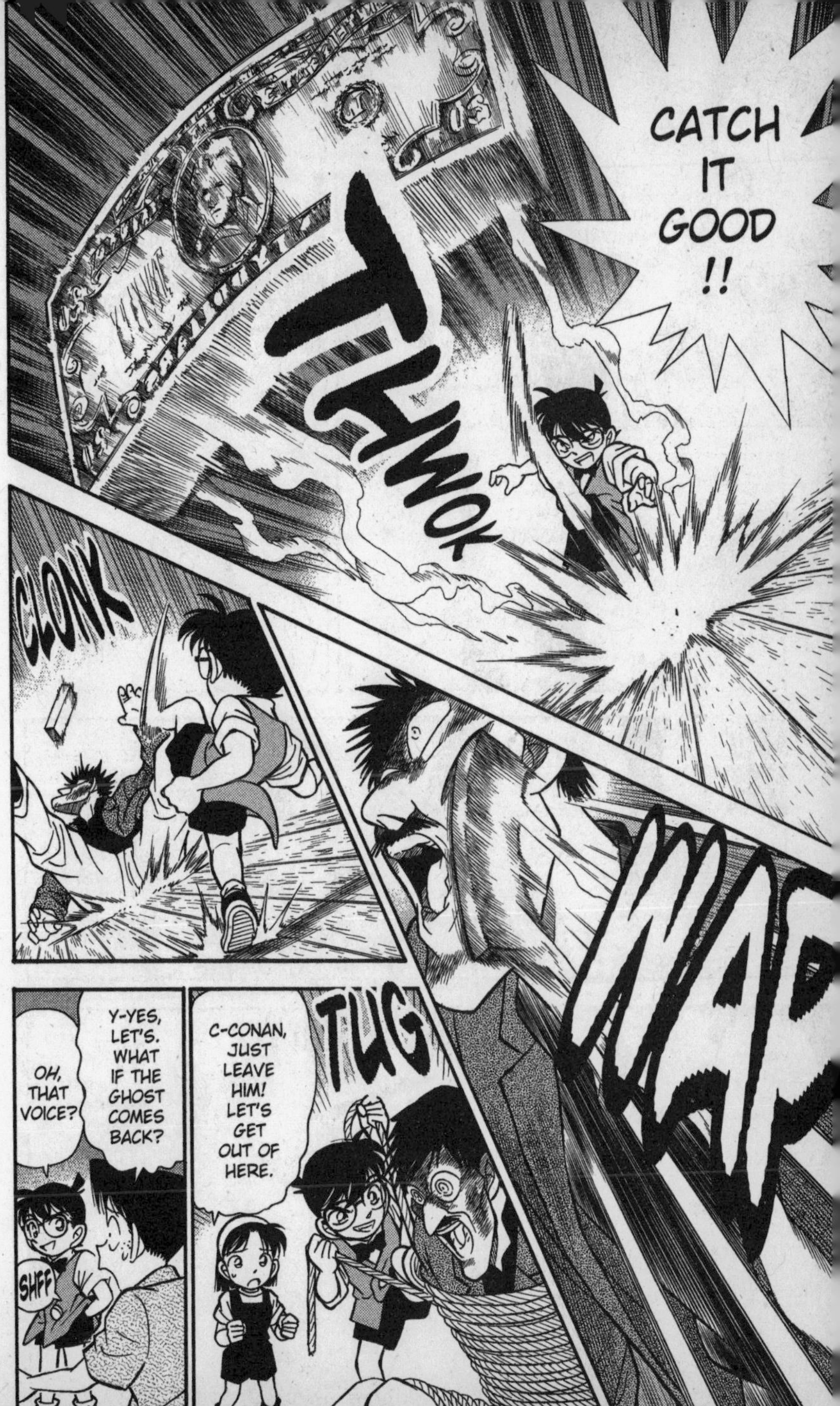
CATCH IT GOOD !!
THWOK
CLONK
WAP
TUG
C-CONAN, JUST LEAVE HIM! LET'S GET OUT OF HERE.
Y-YES, LET'S. WHAT IF THE GHOST COMES BACK?
OH, THAT VOICE?
SHFF

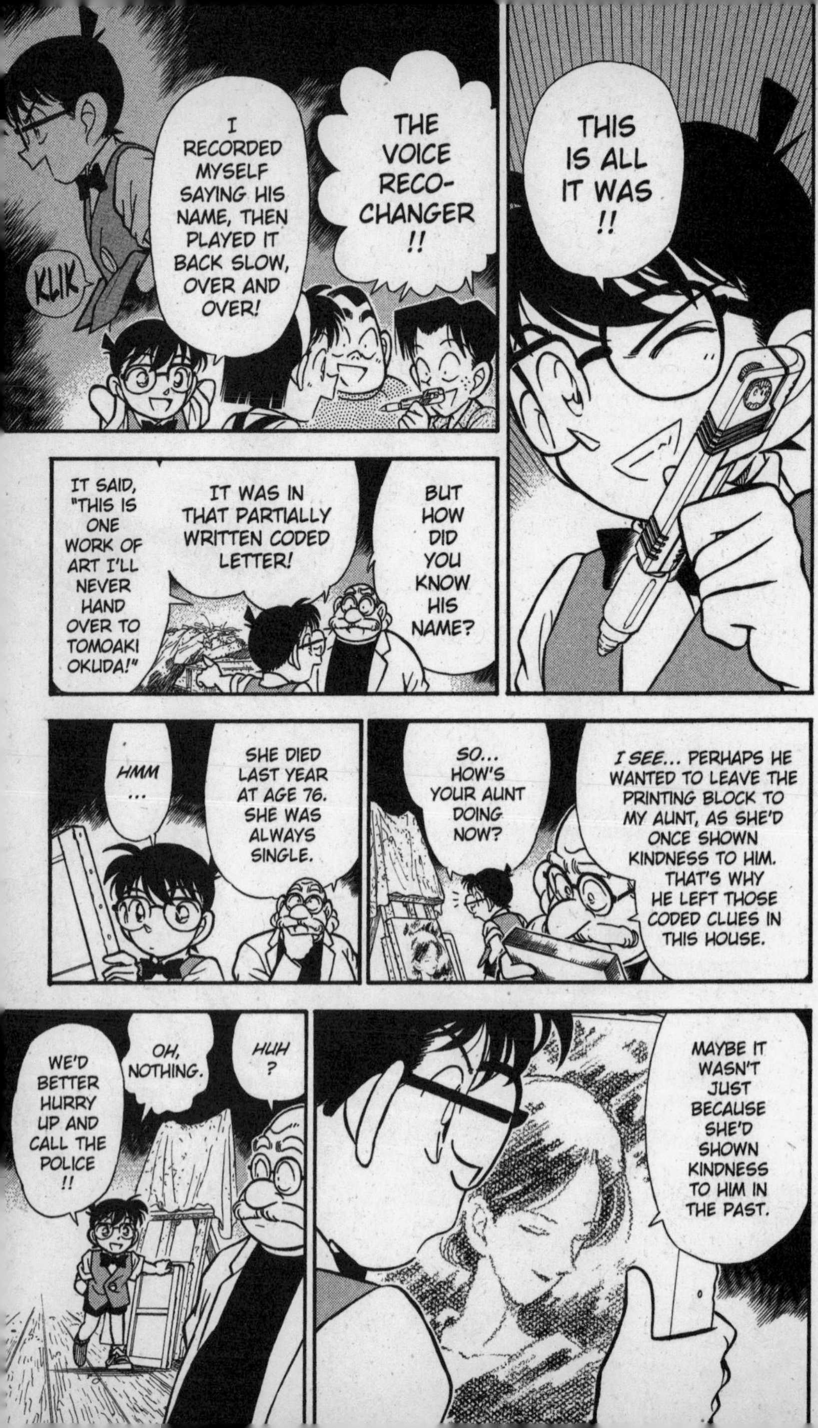
THIS IS ALL IT WAS !!
THE VOICE RECO-CHANGER !!
I RECORDED MYSELF SAYING HIS NAME, THEN PLAYED IT BACK SLOW, OVER AND OVER!
KLIK
BUT HOW DID YOU KNOW HIS NAME?
IT WAS IN THAT PARTIALLY WRITTEN CODED LETTER!
IT SAID, "THIS IS ONE WORK OF ART I'LL NEVER HAND OVER TO TOMOAKI OKUDA!"
I SEE... PERHAPS HE WANTED TO LEAVE THE PRINTING BLOCK TO MY AUNT, AS SHE'D ONCE SHOWN KINDNESS TO HIM. THAT'S WHY HE LEFT THOSE CODED CLUES IN THIS HOUSE.
SO... HOW'S YOUR AUNT DOING NOW?
SHE DIED LAST YEAR AT AGE 76. SHE WAS ALWAYS SINGLE.
HMM ...
MAYBE IT WASN'T JUST BECAUSE SHE'D SHOWN KINDNESS TO HIM IN THE PAST.
HUH ?
OH, NOTHING.
WE'D BETTER HURRY UP AND CALL THE POLICE !!

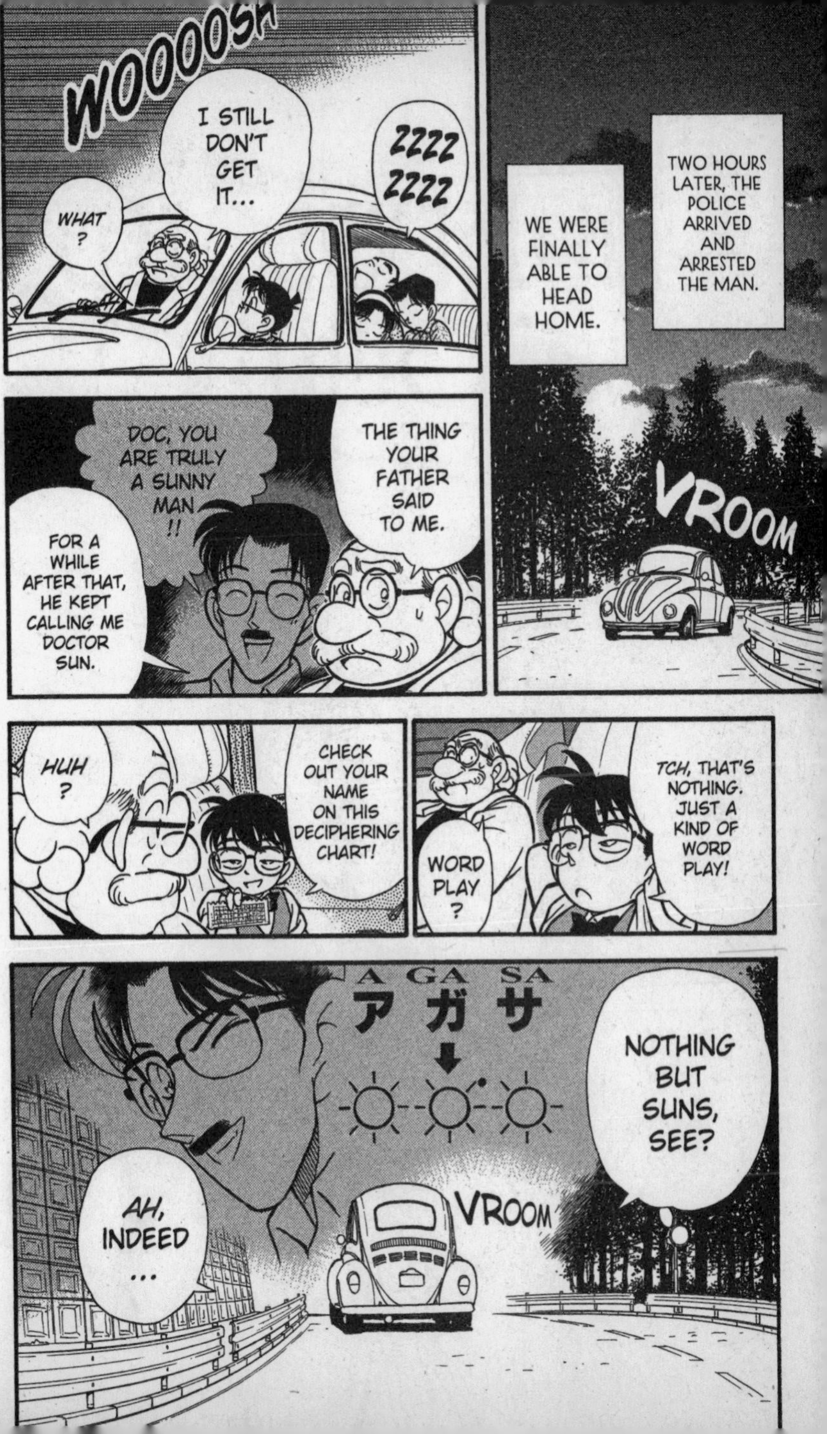
TWO HOURS LATER, THE POLICE ARRIVED AND ARRESTED THE MAN.
WE WERE FINALLY ABLE TO HEAD HOME.
VROOM
WOOOOSH
ZZZZ ZZZZ
I STILL DON'T GET IT...
WHAT?
THE THING YOUR FATHER SAID TO ME.
DOC, YOU ARE TRULY A SUNNY MAN!!
FOR A WHILE AFTER THAT, HE KEPT CALLING ME DOCTOR SUN.
TCH, THAT'S NOTHING. JUST A KIND OF WORD PLAY!
WORD PLAY?
CHECK OUT YOUR NAME ON THIS DECIPHERING CHART!
HUH?
A GA SA
アガサ
NOTHING BUT SUNS, SEE?
VROOM
AH, INDEED...

FILE 4: AN UNEXPECTED ENCOUNTER

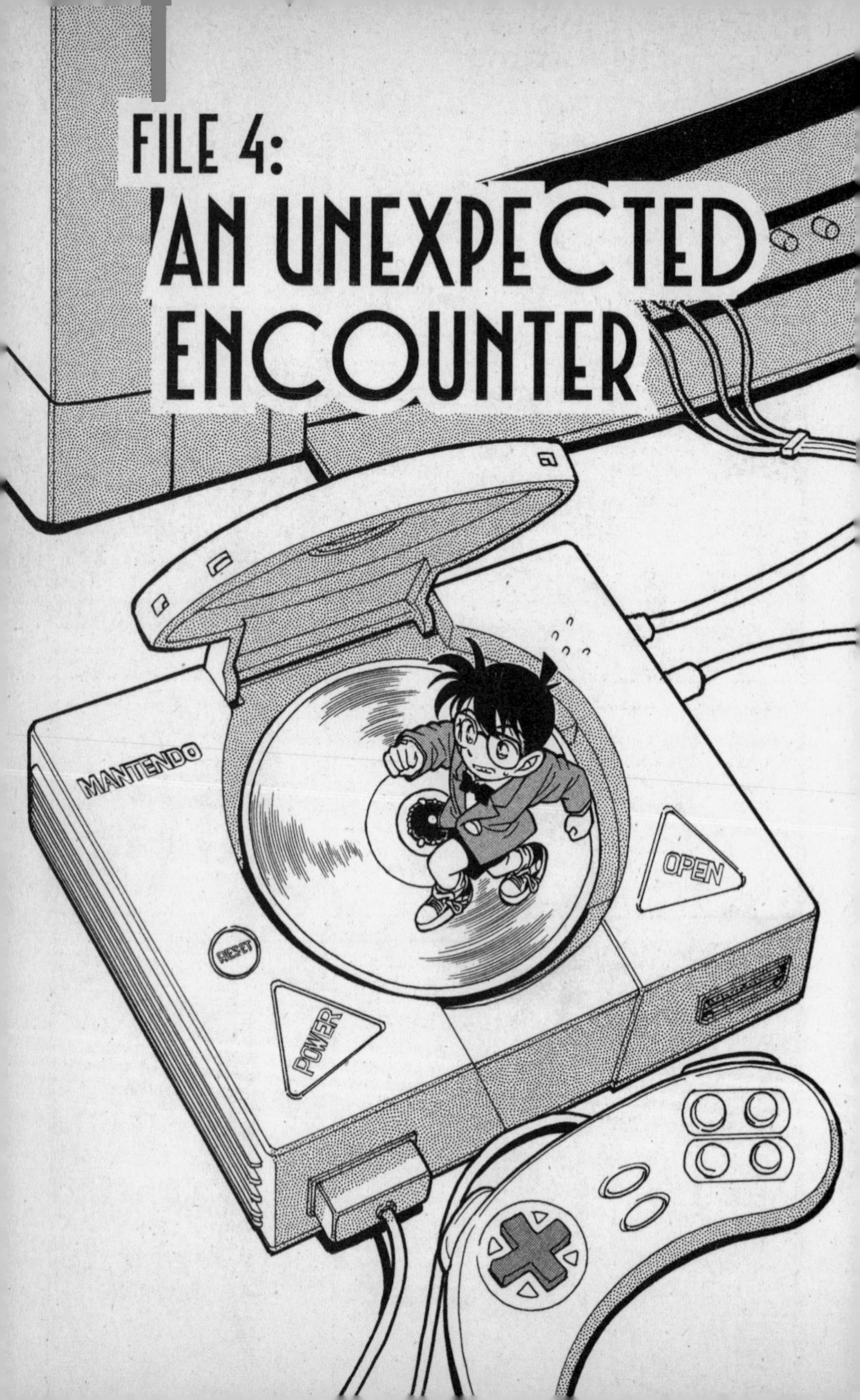
MANTENDO
RESET
POWER
OPEN

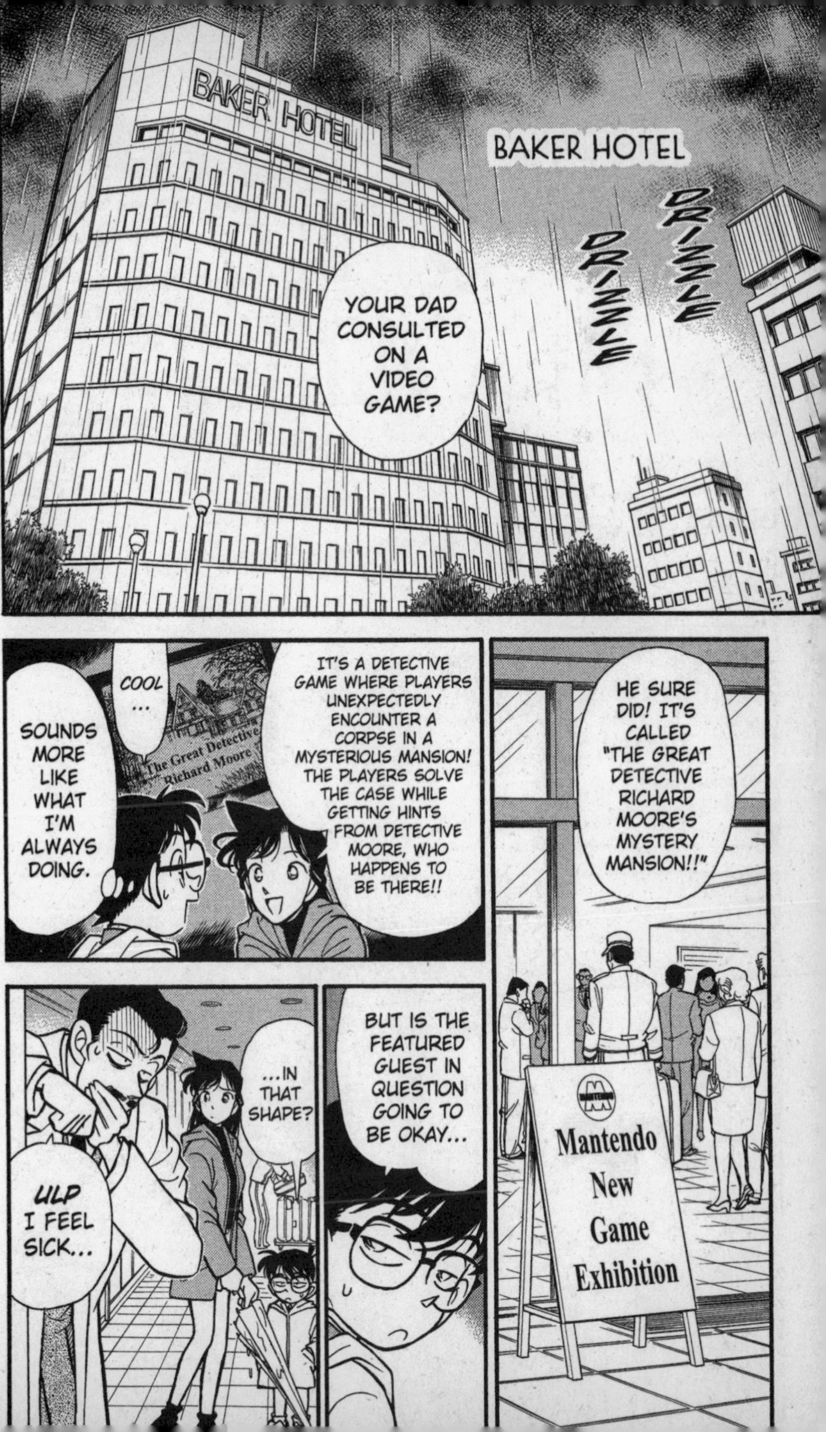
BAKER HOTEL
BAKER HOTEL
DRIZZLE DRIZZLE
YOUR DAD CONSULTED ON A VIDEO GAME?
HE SURE DID! IT'S CALLED "THE GREAT DETECTIVE RICHARD MOORE'S MYSTERY MANSION!!"
IT'S A DETECTIVE GAME WHERE PLAYERS UNEXPECTEDLY ENCOUNTER A CORPSE IN A MYSTERIOUS MANSION! THE PLAYERS SOLVE THE CASE WHILE GETTING HINTS FROM DETECTIVE MOORE, WHO HAPPENS TO BE THERE!!
The Great Detective Richard Moore
COOL...
SOUNDS MORE LIKE WHAT I'M ALWAYS DOING.
Mantendo New Game Exhibition
BUT IS THE FEATURED GUEST IN QUESTION GOING TO BE OKAY...
...IN THAT SHAPE?
ULP I FEEL SICK...

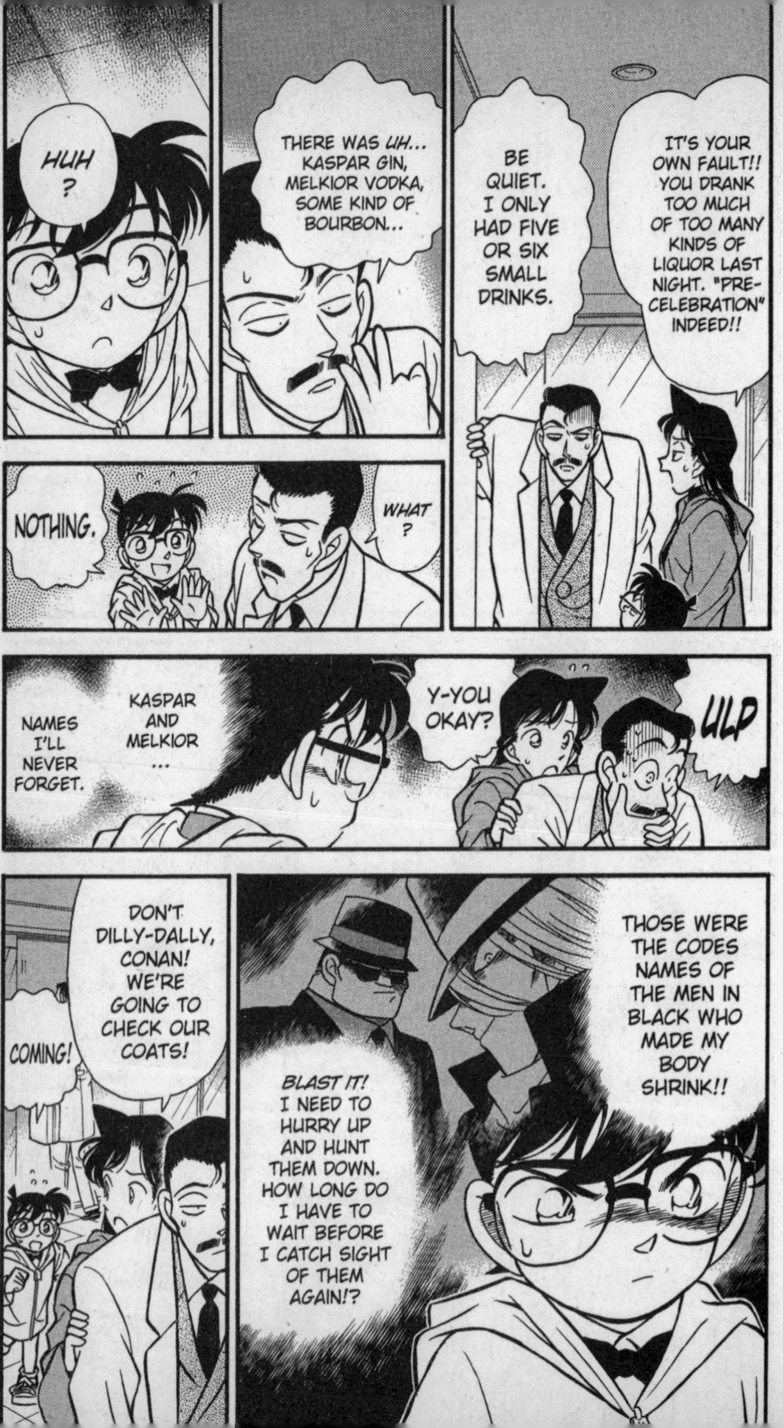
HUH ?
THERE WAS UH... KASPAR GIN, MELKIOR VODKA, SOME KIND OF BOURBON...
IT'S YOUR OWN FAULT!! YOU DRANK TOO MUCH OF TOO MANY KINDS OF LIQUOR LAST NIGHT. "PRE-CELEBRATION" INDEED!!
BE QUIET. I ONLY HAD FIVE OR SIX SMALL DRINKS.
NOTHING.
WHAT ?
NAMES I'LL NEVER FORGET.
KASPAR AND MELKIOR ...
Y-YOU OKAY?
ULP
DON'T DILLY-DALLY, CONAN! WE'RE GOING TO CHECK OUR COATS!
COMING!
THOSE WERE THE CODES NAMES OF THE MEN IN BLACK WHO MADE MY BODY SHRINK!!
BLAST IT! I NEED TO HURRY UP AND HUNT THEM DOWN. HOW LONG DO I HAVE TO WAIT BEFORE I CATCH SIGHT OF THEM AGAIN!?

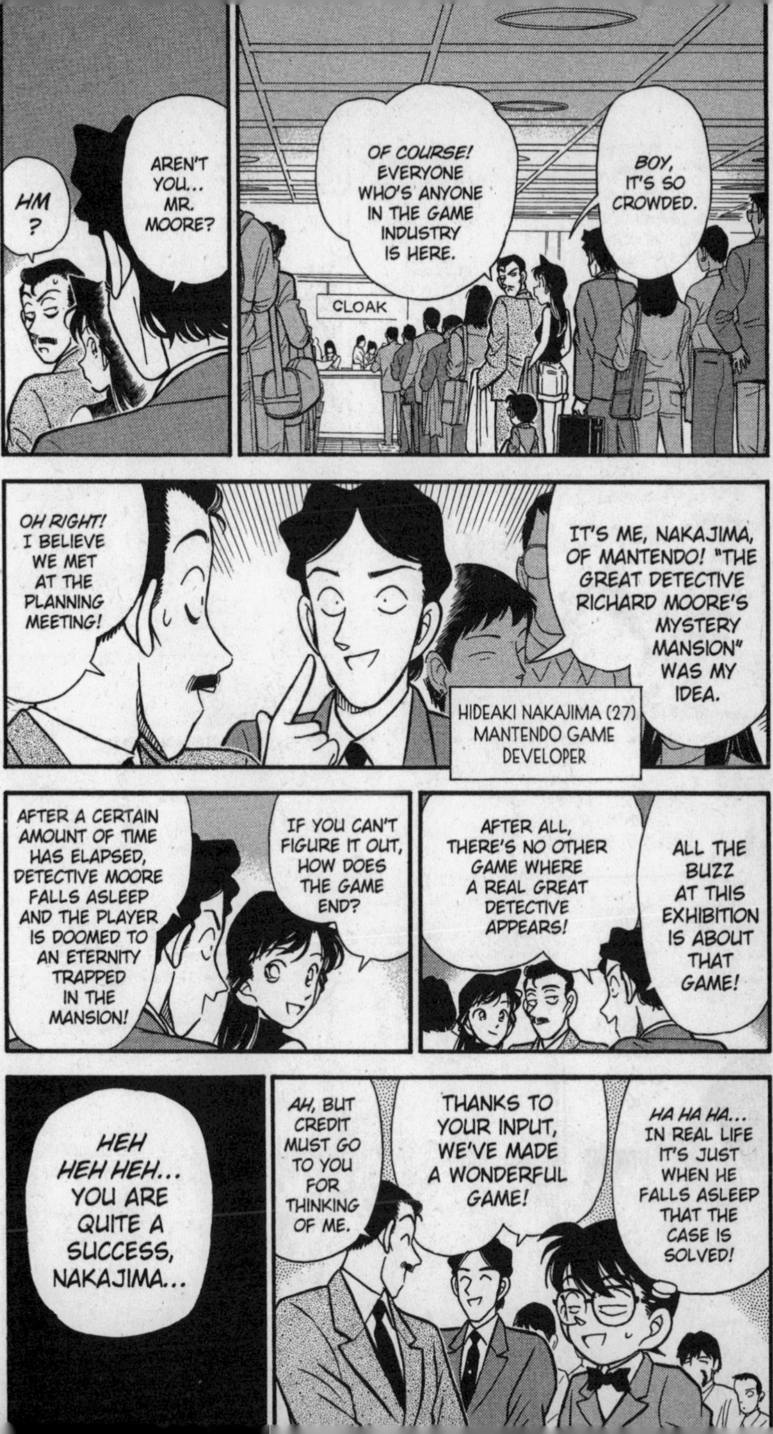
BOY, IT'S SO CROWDED.
OF COURSE! EVERYONE WHO'S ANYONE IN THE GAME INDUSTRY IS HERE.
CLOAK
AREN'T YOU... MR. MOORE?
HM ?
IT'S ME, NAKAJIMA, OF MANTENDO! "THE GREAT DETECTIVE RICHARD MOORE'S MYSTERY MANSION" WAS MY IDEA.
HIDEAKI NAKAJIMA (27) MANTENDO GAME DEVELOPER
OH RIGHT! I BELIEVE WE MET AT THE PLANNING MEETING!
ALL THE BUZZ AT THIS EXHIBITION IS ABOUT THAT GAME!
AFTER ALL, THERE'S NO OTHER GAME WHERE A REAL GREAT DETECTIVE APPEARS!
IF YOU CAN'T FIGURE IT OUT, HOW DOES THE GAME END?
AFTER A CERTAIN AMOUNT OF TIME HAS ELAPSED, DETECTIVE MOORE FALLS ASLEEP AND THE PLAYER IS DOOMED TO AN ETERNITY TRAPPED IN THE MANSION!
THANKS TO YOUR INPUT, WE'VE MADE A WONDERFUL GAME!
AH, BUT CREDIT MUST GO TO YOU FOR THINKING OF ME.
HA HA HA... IN REAL LIFE IT'S JUST WHEN HE FALLS ASLEEP THAT THE CASE IS SOLVED!
HEH HEH HEH... YOU ARE QUITE A SUCCESS, NAKAJIMA...

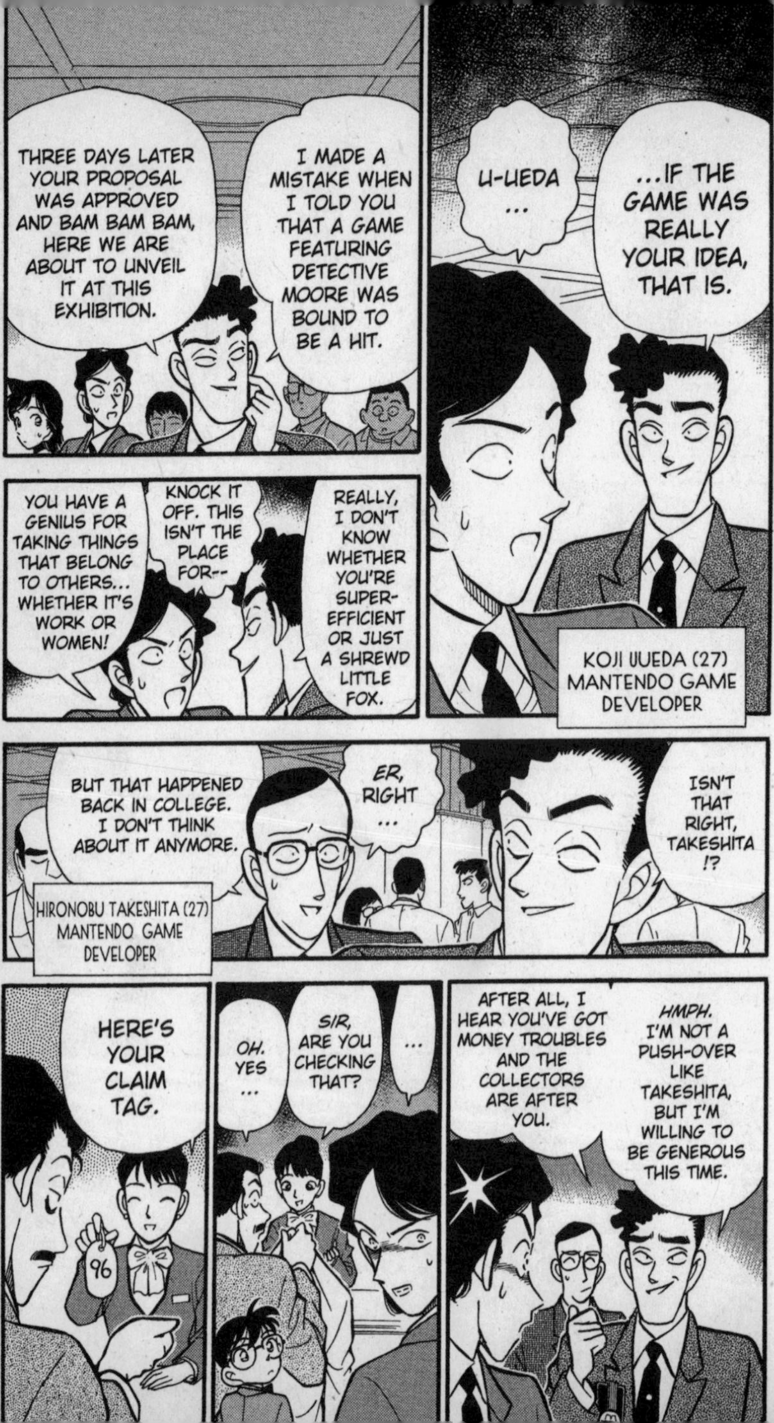
THREE DAYS LATER YOUR PROPOSAL WAS APPROVED AND BAM BAM BAM, HERE WE ARE ABOUT TO UNVEIL IT AT THIS EXHIBITION.
I MADE A MISTAKE WHEN I TOLD YOU THAT A GAME FEATURING DETECTIVE MOORE WAS BOUND TO BE A HIT.
...IF THE GAME WAS REALLY YOUR IDEA, THAT IS.
U-UEDA...
KOJI UUEDA (27) MANTENDO GAME DEVELOPER
REALLY, I DON'T KNOW WHETHER YOU'RE SUPER-EFFICIENT OR JUST A SHREWD LITTLE FOX.
KNOCK IT OFF. THIS ISN'T THE PLACE FOR--
YOU HAVE A GENIUS FOR TAKING THINGS THAT BELONG TO OTHERS... WHETHER IT'S WORK OR WOMEN!
ISN'T THAT RIGHT, TAKESHITA!?
ER, RIGHT...
BUT THAT HAPPENED BACK IN COLLEGE. I DON'T THINK ABOUT IT ANYMORE.
HIRONOBU TAKESHITA (27) MANTENDO GAME DEVELOPER
HMPH. I'M NOT A PUSH-OVER LIKE TAKESHITA, BUT I'M WILLING TO BE GENEROUS THIS TIME.
AFTER ALL, I HEAR YOU'VE GOT MONEY TROUBLES AND THE COLLECTORS ARE AFTER YOU.
...
SIR, ARE YOU CHECKING THAT?
OH. YES...
HERE'S YOUR CLAIM TAG.
96

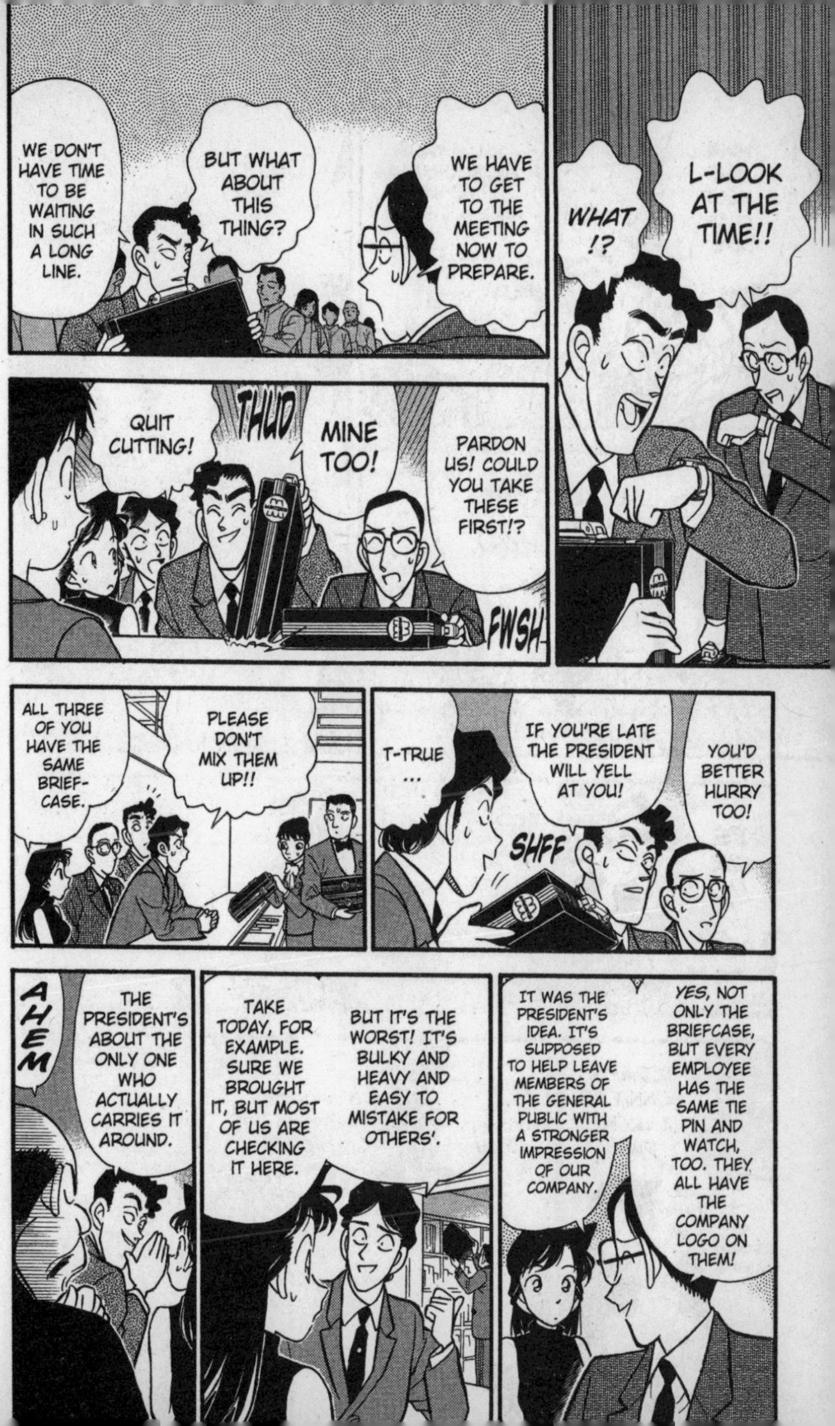
WE DON'T HAVE TIME TO BE WAITING IN SUCH A LONG LINE.
BUT WHAT ABOUT THIS THING?
WE HAVE TO GET TO THE MEETING NOW TO PREPARE.
WHAT !?
L-LOOK AT THE TIME!!
QUIT CUTTING!
THUD
MINE TOO!
PARDON US! COULD YOU TAKE THESE FIRST!?
FWSH
ALL THREE OF YOU HAVE THE SAME BRIEF-CASE.
PLEASE DON'T MIX THEM UP!!
T-TRUE ...
IF YOU'RE LATE THE PRESIDENT WILL YELL AT YOU!
YOU'D BETTER HURRY TOO!
SHFF
AHEM
THE PRESIDENT'S ABOUT THE ONLY ONE WHO ACTUALLY CARRIES IT AROUND.
TAKE TODAY, FOR EXAMPLE. SURE WE BROUGHT IT, BUT MOST OF US ARE CHECKING IT HERE.
BUT IT'S THE WORST! IT'S BULKY AND HEAVY AND EASY TO MISTAKE FOR OTHERS'.
IT WAS THE PRESIDENT'S IDEA. IT'S SUPPOSED TO HELP LEAVE MEMBERS OF THE GENERAL PUBLIC WITH A STRONGER IMPRESSION OF OUR COMPANY.
YES, NOT ONLY THE BRIEFCASE, BUT EVERY EMPLOYEE HAS THE SAME TIE PIN AND WATCH, TOO. THEY ALL HAVE THE COMPANY LOGO ON THEM!

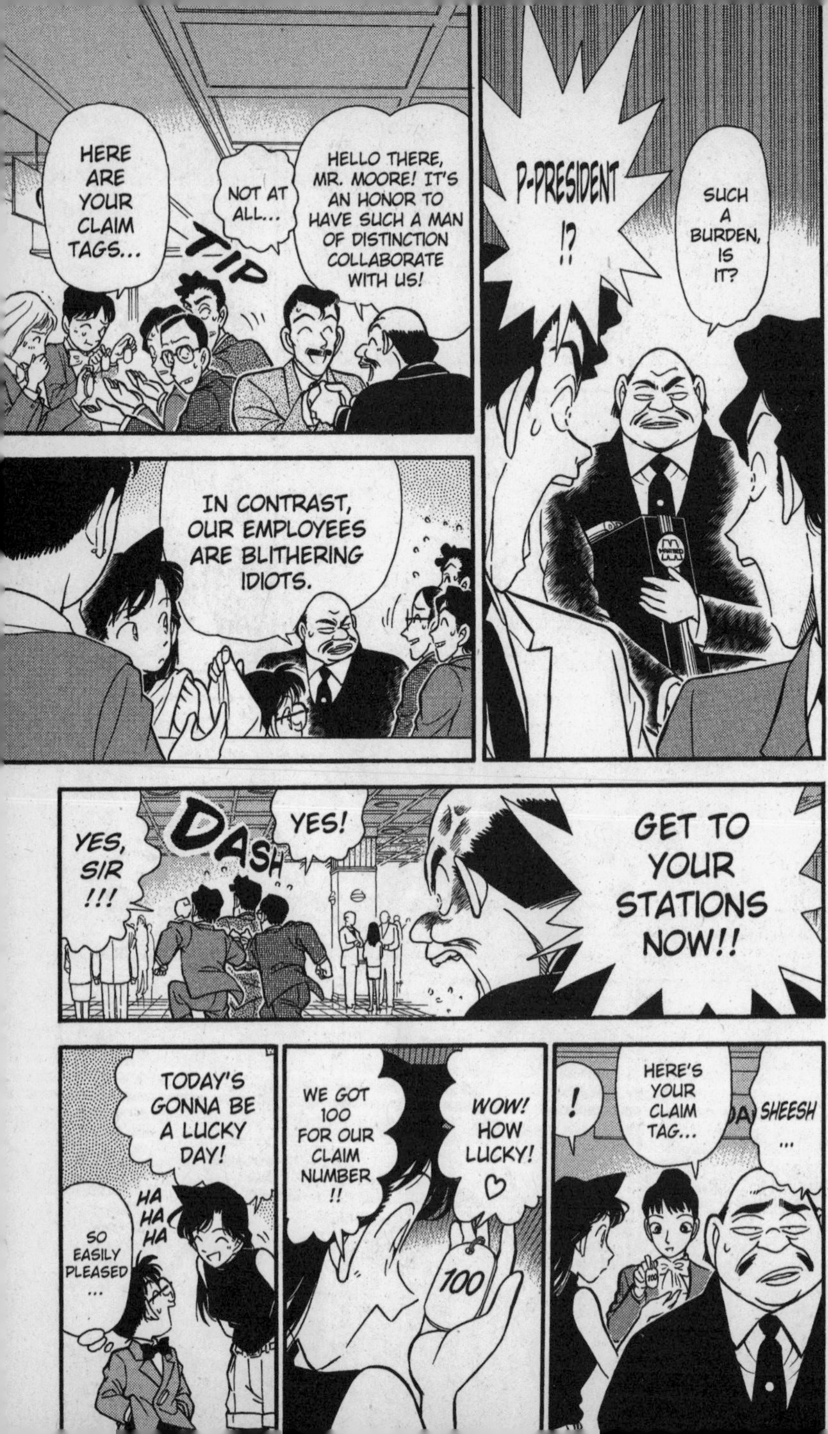
HERE ARE YOUR CLAIM TAGS...
NOT AT ALL...
TIP
HELLO THERE, MR. MOORE! IT'S AN HONOR TO HAVE SUCH A MAN OF DISTINCTION COLLABORATE WITH US!
P-PRESIDENT !?
SUCH A BURDEN, IS IT?
IN CONTRAST, OUR EMPLOYEES ARE BLITHERING IDIOTS.
YES, SIR !!!
DASH
YES!
GET TO YOUR STATIONS NOW!!
TODAY'S GONNA BE A LUCKY DAY!
HA HA HA
SO EASILY PLEASED ...
WE GOT 100 FOR OUR CLAIM NUMBER !!
WOW! HOW LUCKY! ♡
100
!
HERE'S YOUR CLAIM TAG...
SHEESH ...

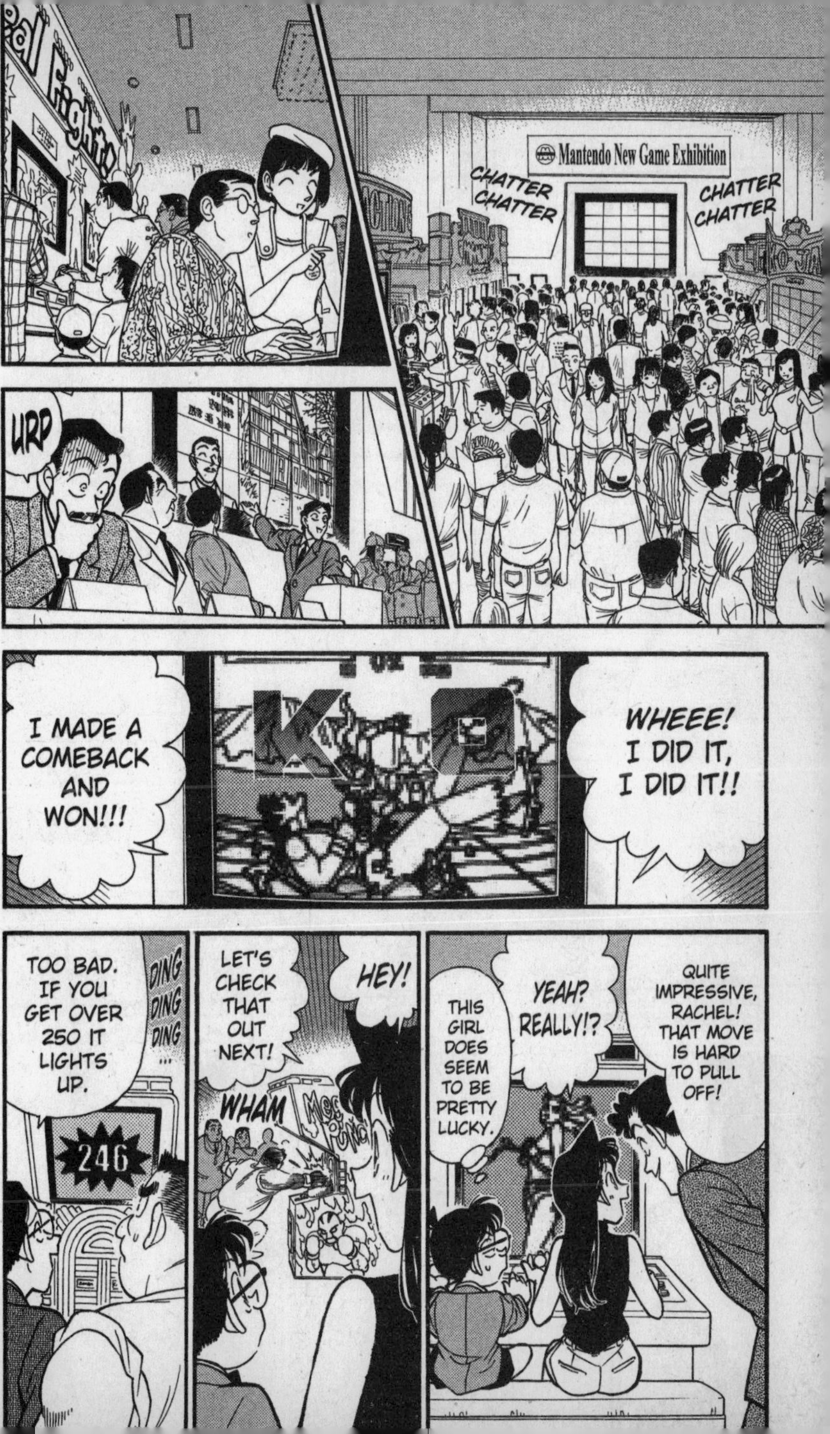
Mantendo New Game Exhibition
CHATTER CHATTER
CHATTER CHATTER
URP
I MADE A COMEBACK AND WON!!!
WHEEE! I DID IT, I DID IT!!
TOO BAD. IF YOU GET OVER 250 IT LIGHTS UP.
DING DING DING...
246
LET'S CHECK THAT OUT NEXT!
WHAM
HEY!
QUITE IMPRESSIVE, RACHEL! THAT MOVE IS HARD TO PULL OFF!
YEAH? REALLY!?
THIS GIRL DOES SEEM TO BE PRETTY LUCKY.

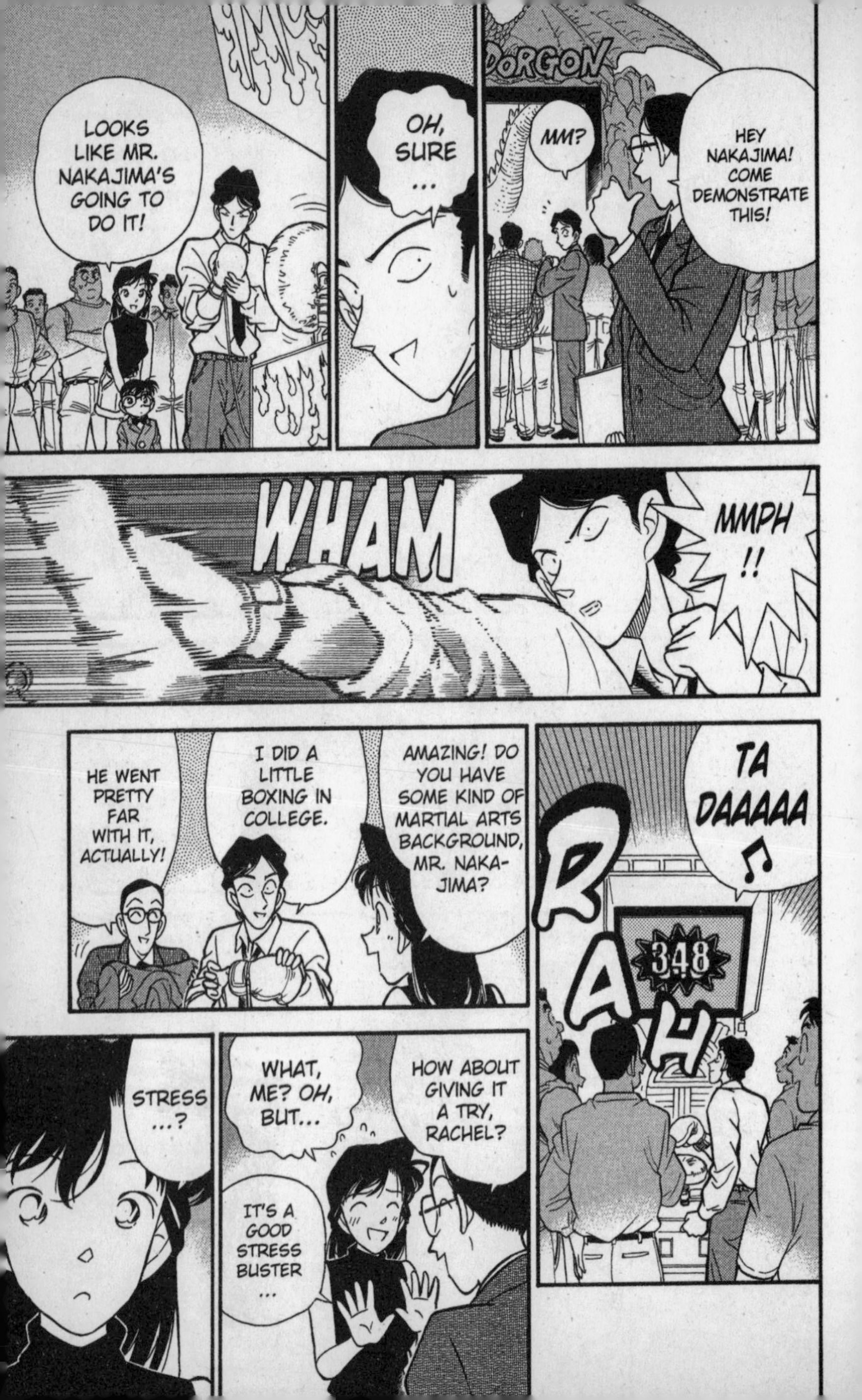
HEY NAKAJIMA! COME DEMONSTRATE THIS!
MM?
OH, SURE ...
LOOKS LIKE MR. NAKAJIMA'S GOING TO DO IT!
MMPH !!
WHAM
TA DAAAAA ♫
RAH
348
AMAZING! DO YOU HAVE SOME KIND OF MARTIAL ARTS BACKGROUND, MR. NAKA-JIMA?
I DID A LITTLE BOXING IN COLLEGE.
HE WENT PRETTY FAR WITH IT, ACTUALLY!
HOW ABOUT GIVING IT A TRY, RACHEL?
WHAT, ME? OH, BUT...
IT'S A GOOD STRESS BUSTER ...
STRESS ...?

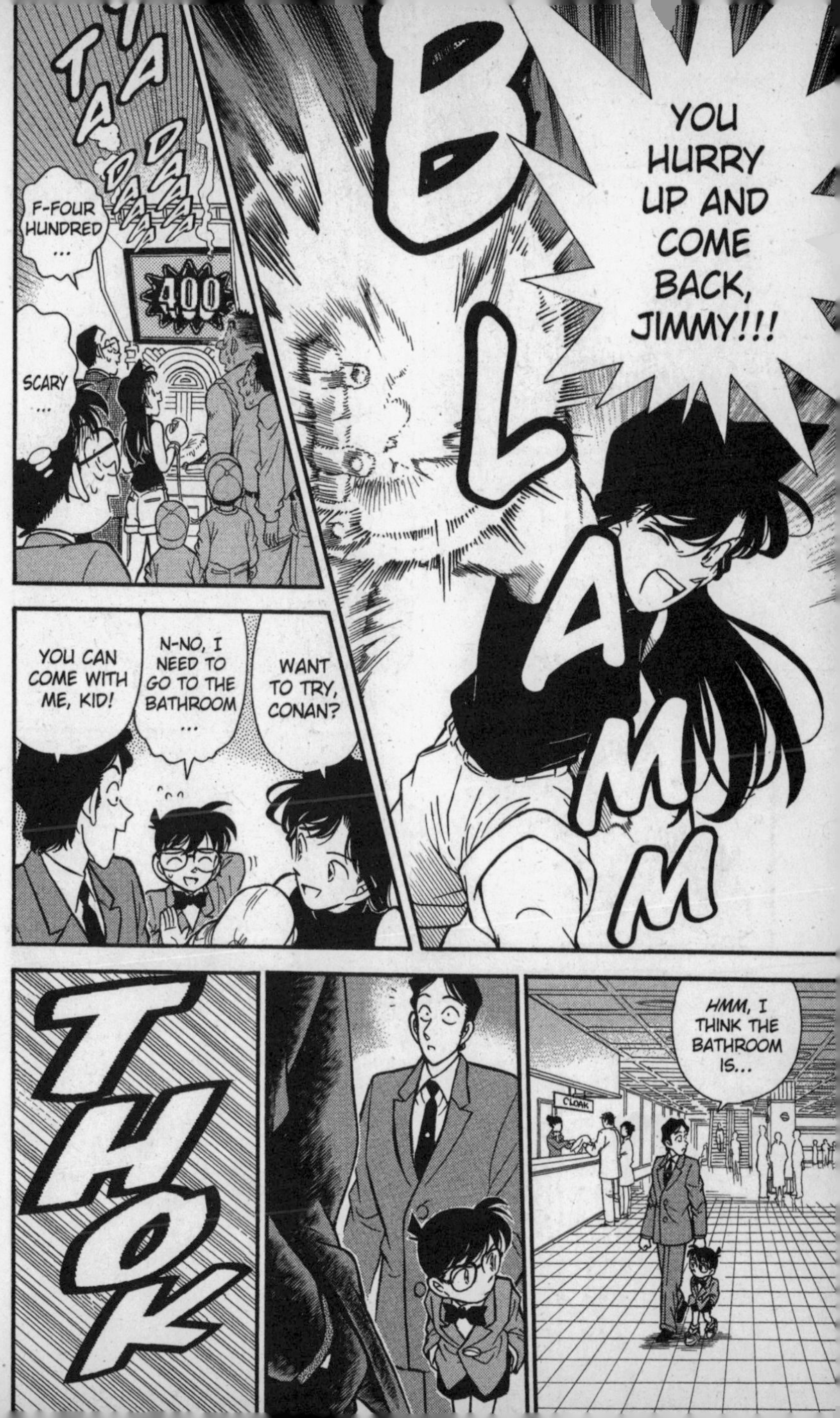
BLAMM
YOU HURRY UP AND COME BACK, JIMMY!!!
TA TA
F-FOUR HUNDRED ...
400
SCARY ...
WANT TO TRY, CONAN?
N-NO, I NEED TO GO TO THE BATHROOM ...
YOU CAN COME WITH ME, KID!
HMM, I THINK THE BATHROOM IS...
CLOAK
THOK

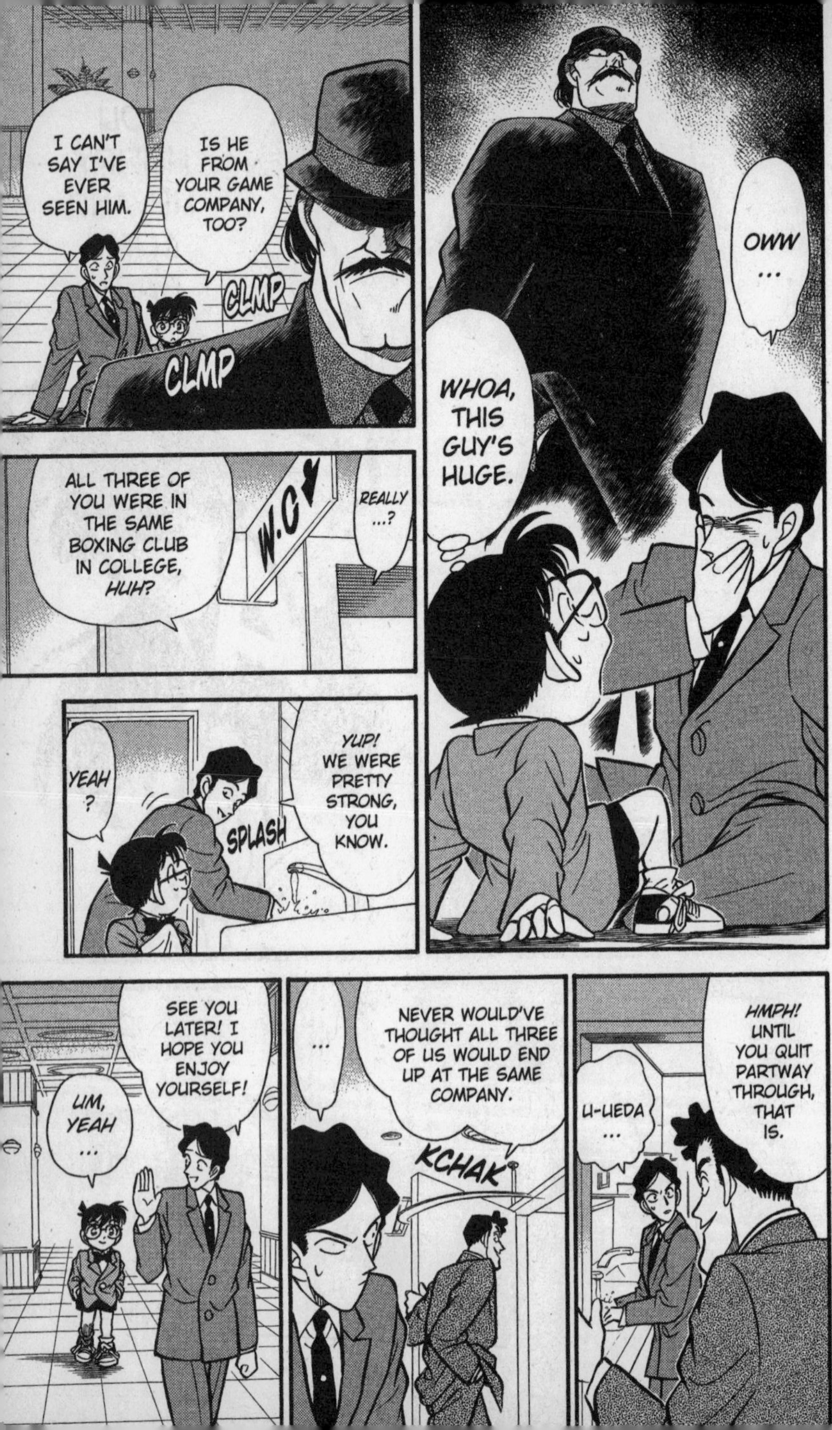
OWW ...
WHOA, THIS GUY'S HUGE.
IS HE FROM YOUR GAME COMPANY, TOO?
I CAN'T SAY I'VE EVER SEEN HIM.
CLMP
CLMP
W.C
ALL THREE OF YOU WERE IN THE SAME BOXING CLUB IN COLLEGE, HUH?
REALLY ...?
YUP! WE WERE PRETTY STRONG, YOU KNOW.
YEAH ?
SPLASH
HMPH! UNTIL YOU QUIT PARTWAY THROUGH, THAT IS.
U-UEDA ...
NEVER WOULD'VE THOUGHT ALL THREE OF US WOULD END UP AT THE SAME COMPANY.
...
KCHAK
SEE YOU LATER! I HOPE YOU ENJOY YOURSELF!
UM, YEAH ...

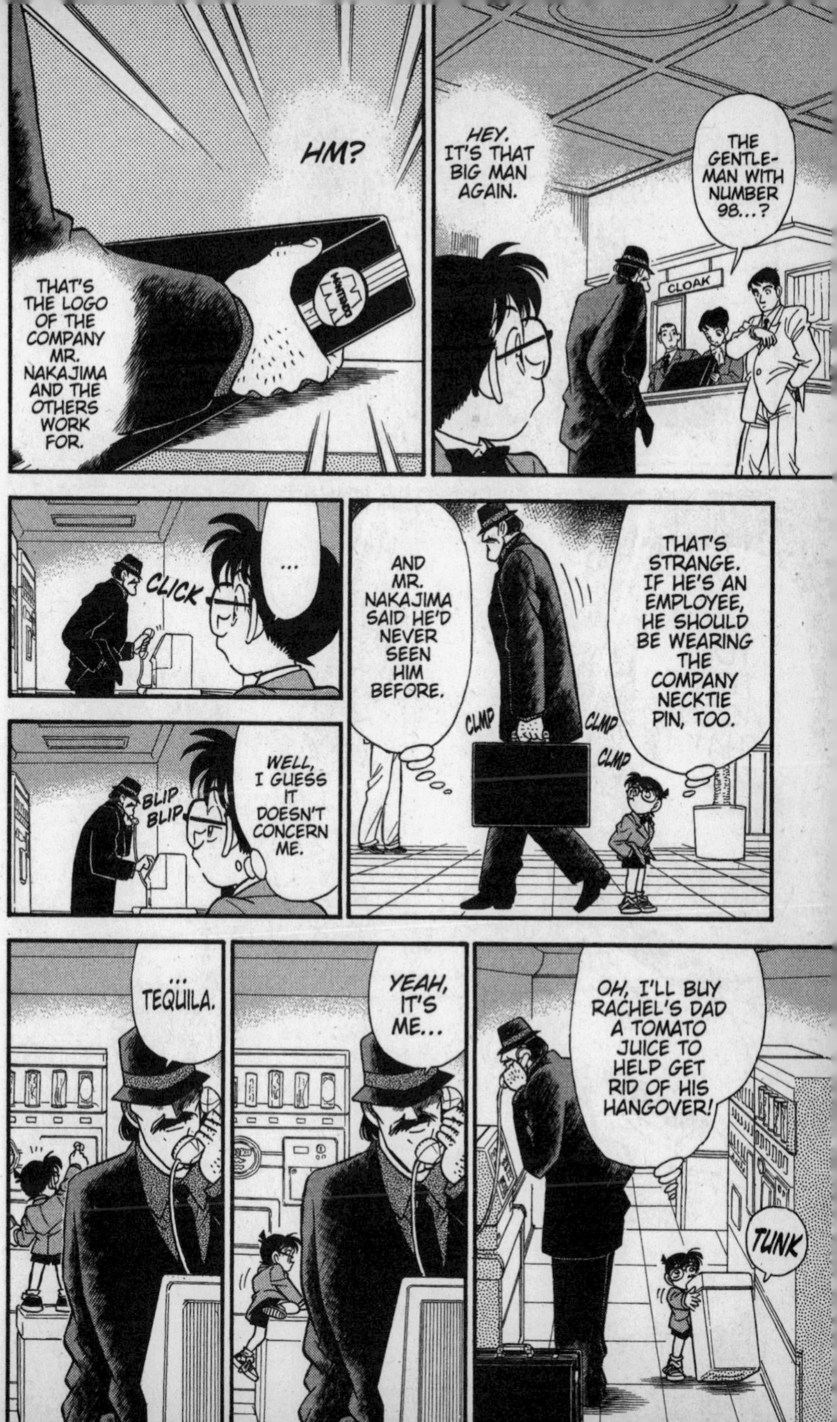
HM?
THAT'S THE LOGO OF THE COMPANY MR. NAKAJIMA AND THE OTHERS WORK FOR.
HEY. IT'S THAT BIG MAN AGAIN.
THE GENTLEMAN WITH NUMBER 98...?
CLOAK
CLICK
...
AND MR. NAKAJIMA SAID HE'D NEVER SEEN HIM BEFORE.
THAT'S STRANGE. IF HE'S AN EMPLOYEE, HE SHOULD BE WEARING THE COMPANY NECKTIE PIN, TOO.
CLMP
CLMP
CLMP
BLIP BLIP
WELL, I GUESS IT DOESN'T CONCERN ME.
... TEQUILA.
YEAH, IT'S ME...
OH, I'LL BUY RACHEL'S DAD A TOMATO JUICE TO HELP GET RID OF HIS HANGOVER!
TUNK

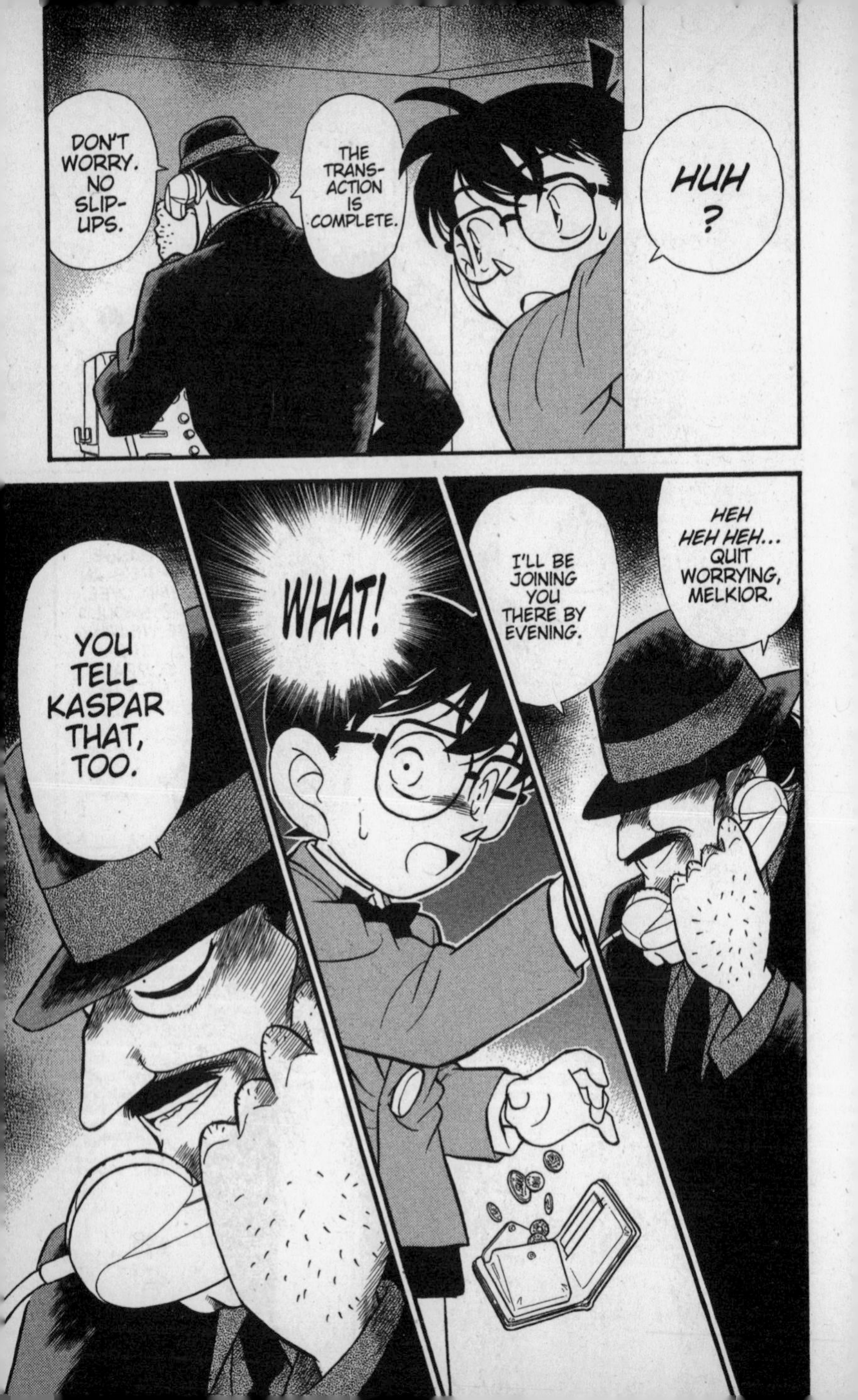
HUH ?
THE TRANS-ACTION IS COMPLETE.
DON'T WORRY. NO SLIP-UPS.
HEH HEH HEH... QUIT WORRYING, MELKIOR.
I'LL BE JOINING YOU THERE BY EVENING.
WHAT!
YOU TELL KASPAR THAT, TOO.

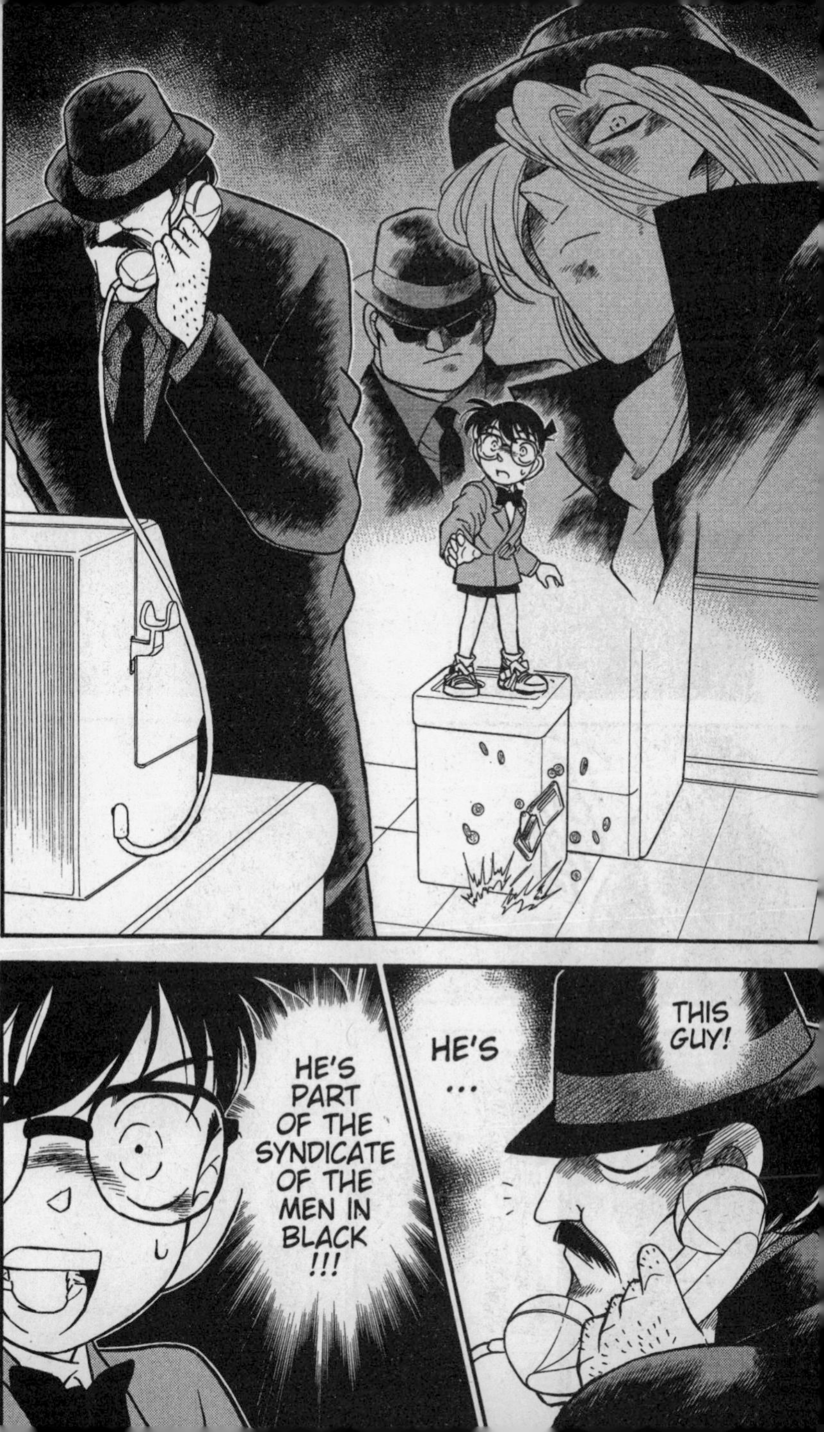
THIS GUY!
HE'S ...
HE'S PART OF THE SYNDICATE OF THE MEN IN BLACK !!!

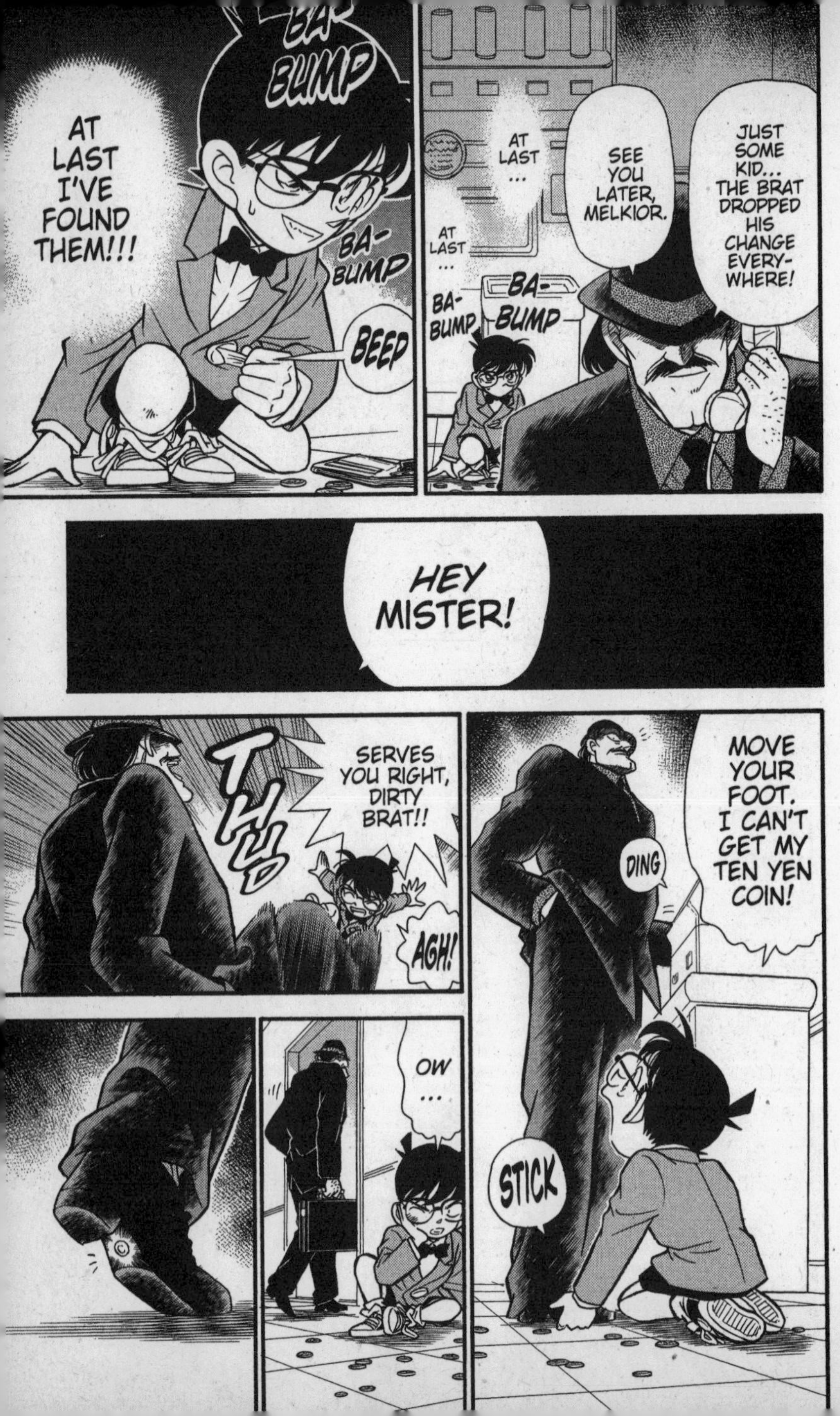
JUST SOME KID... THE BRAT DROPPED HIS CHANGE EVERY-WHERE!
SEE YOU LATER, MELKIOR.
AT LAST ...
AT LAST ...
BA-BUMP
BA-BUMP
BA-BUMP
AT LAST I'VE FOUND THEM!!!
BA-BUMP
BEEP
HEY MISTER!
MOVE YOUR FOOT. I CAN'T GET MY TEN YEN COIN!
DING
STICK
SERVES YOU RIGHT, DIRTY BRAT!!
THUD
AGH!
OW ...

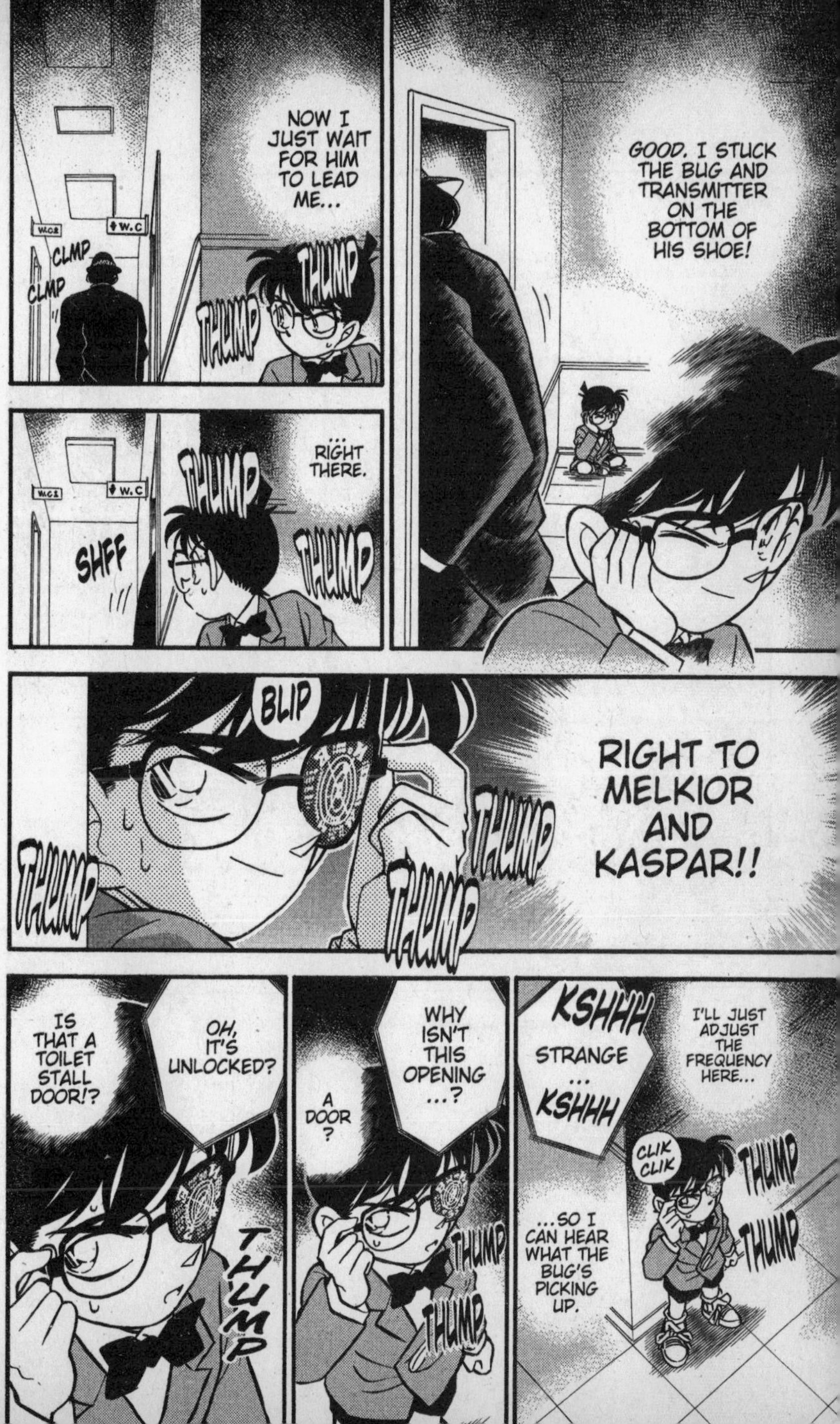
GOOD. I STUCK THE BUG AND TRANSMITTER ON THE BOTTOM OF HIS SHOE!
NOW I JUST WAIT FOR HIM TO LEAD ME...
W.C
CLMP
CLMP
THUMP
THUMP
...RIGHT THERE.
W.C
THUMP
THUMP
SHFF
BLIP
RIGHT TO MELKIOR AND KASPAR!!
THUMP
THUMP
THUMP
I'LL JUST ADJUST THE FREQUENCY HERE...
...SO I CAN HEAR WHAT THE BUG'S PICKING UP.
CLIK CLIK
THUMP
THUMP
KSHHH
STRANGE...
KSHHH
WHY ISN'T THIS OPENING...?
A DOOR?
THUMP
THUMP
OH, IT'S UNLOCKED?
IS THAT A TOILET STALL DOOR!?
THUMP

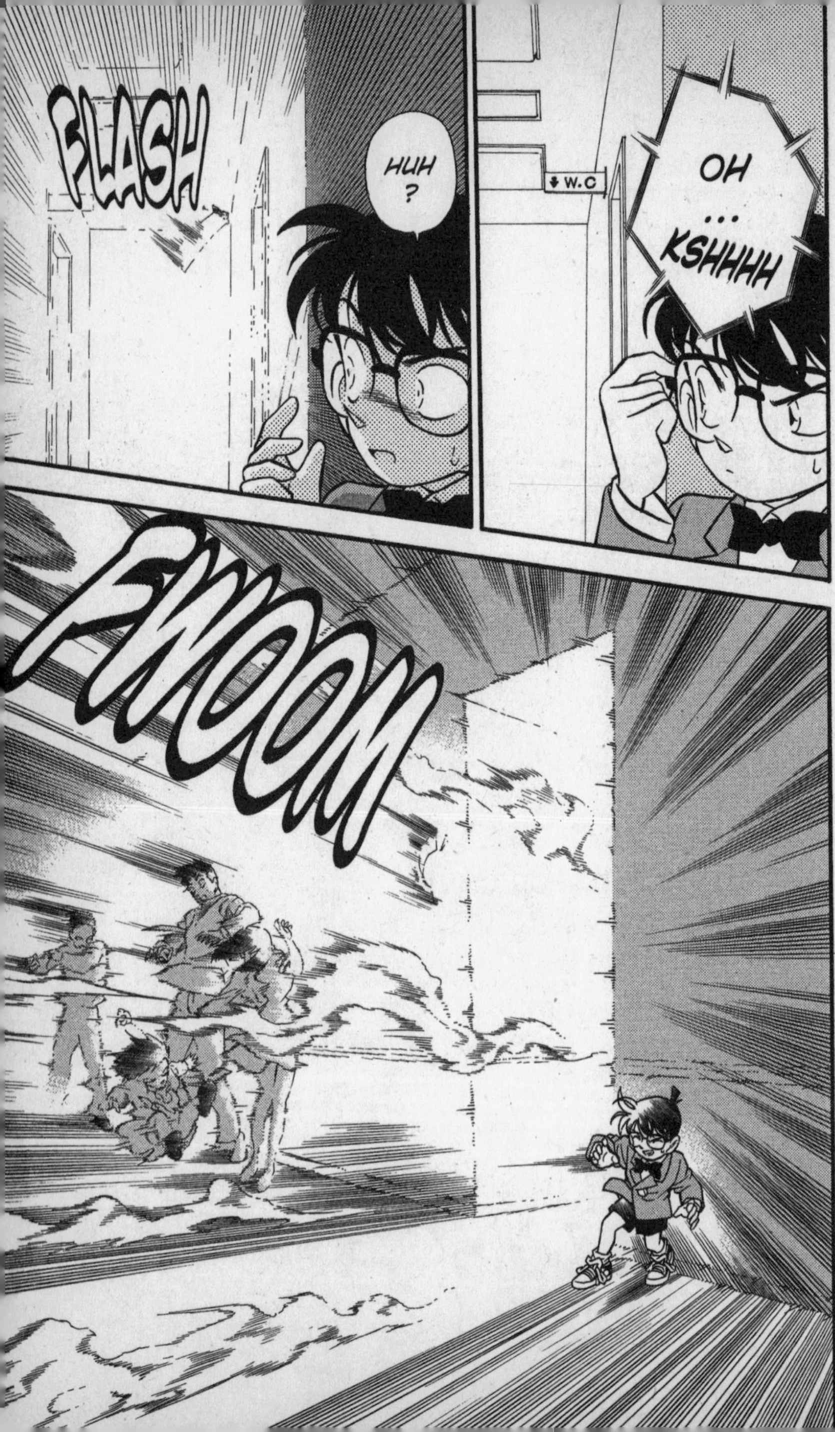
OH ... KSHHHH
W.C
HUH ?
FLASH
FWOOM

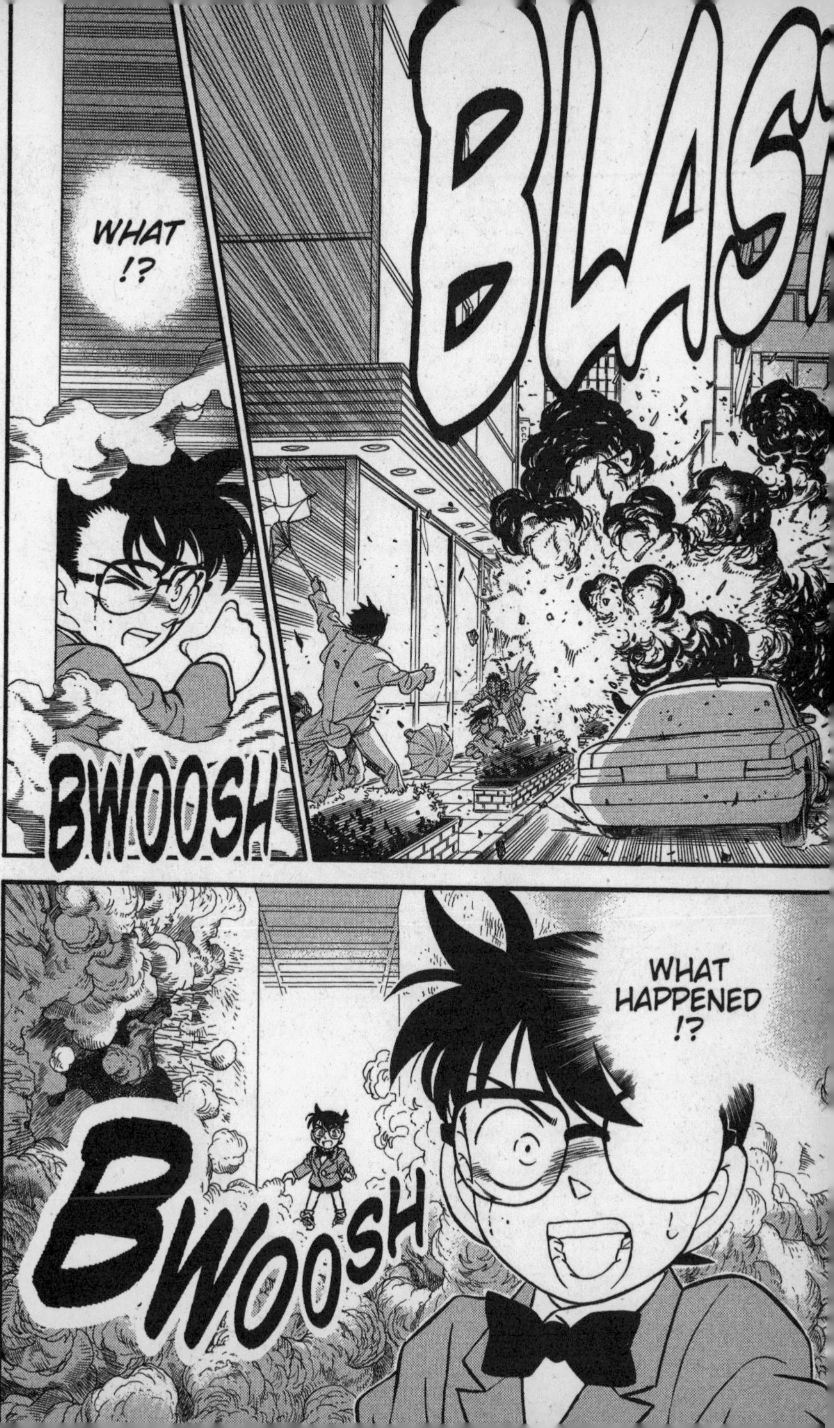
BLAS
WHAT !?
BWOOSH
WHAT HAPPENED !?
BWOOSH

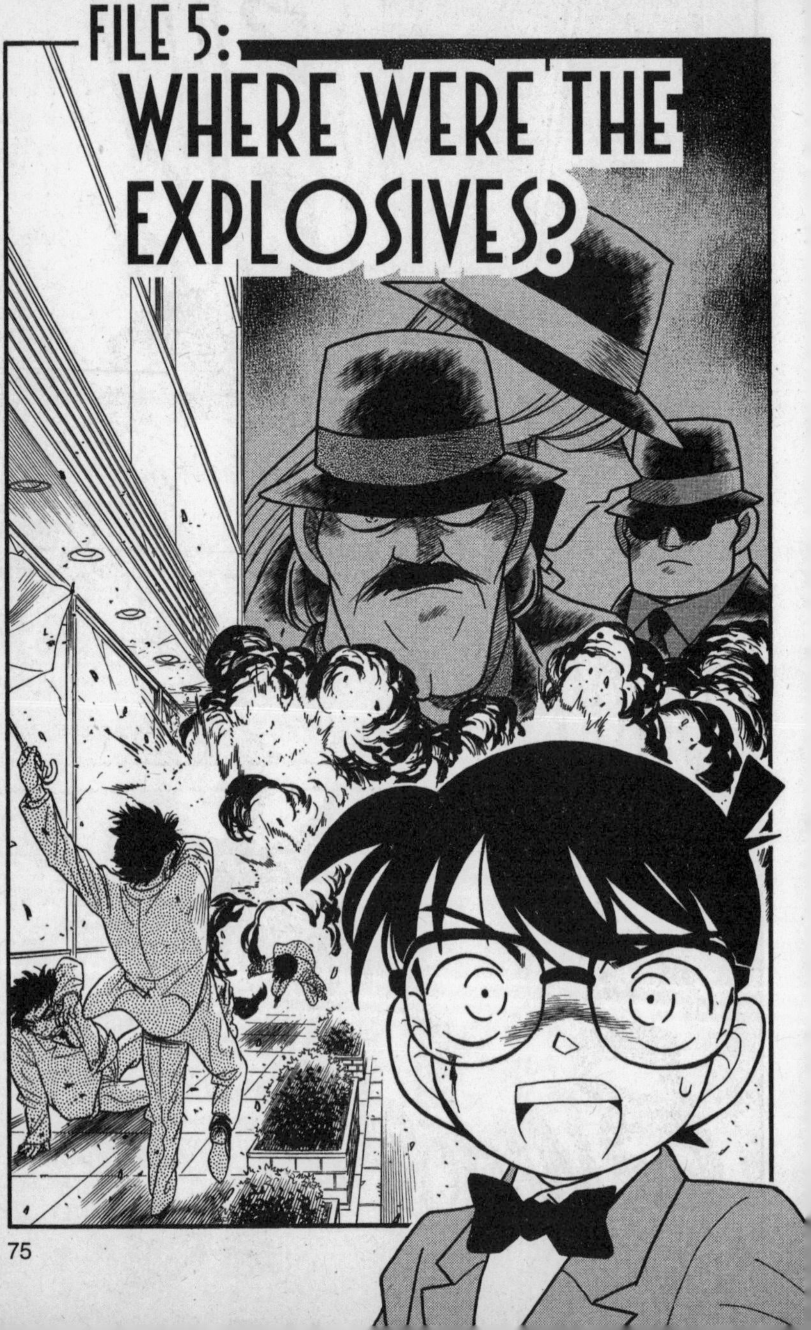
FILE 5:
WHERE WERE THE EXPLOSIVES?

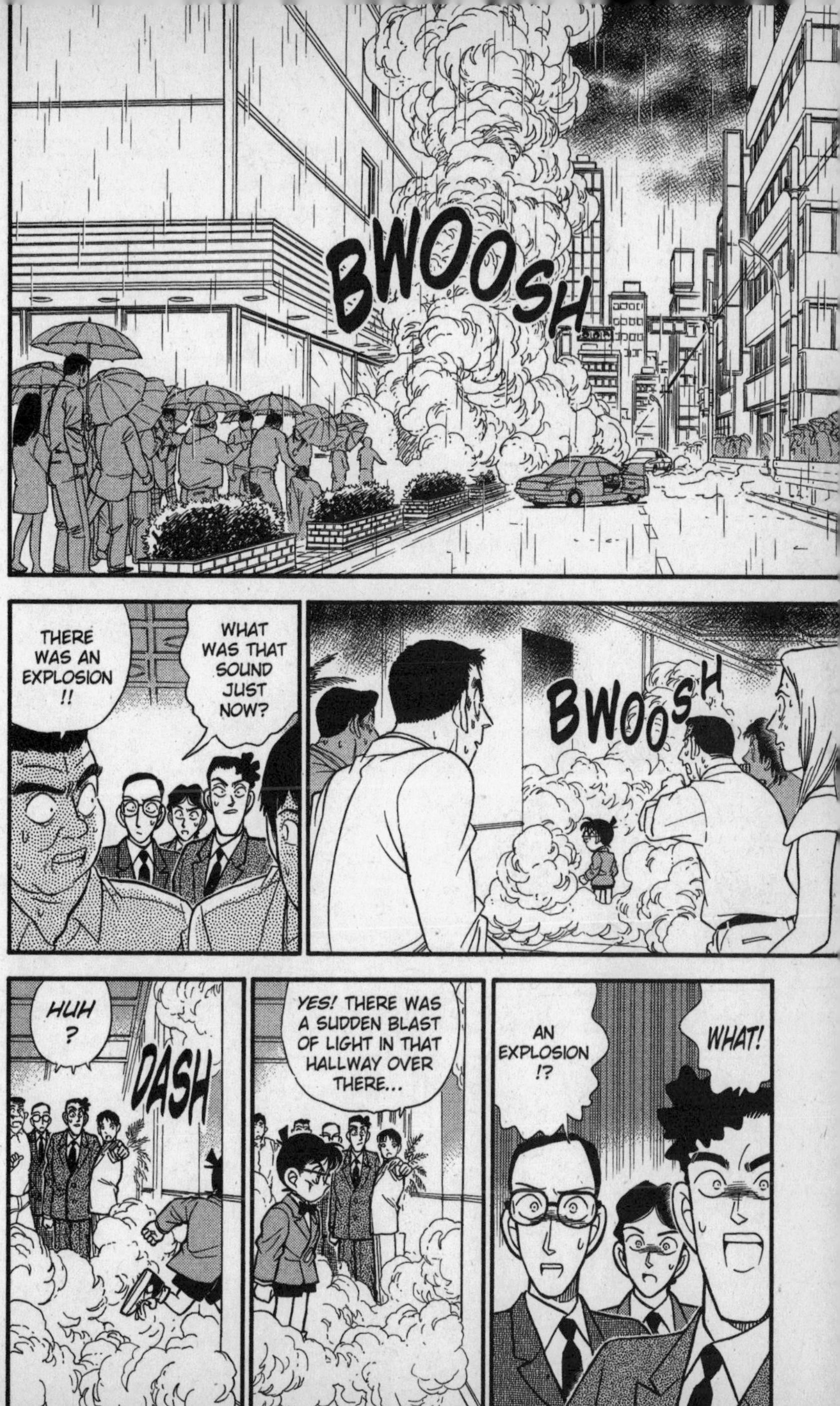
BWOOSH
BWOOSH
WHAT WAS THAT SOUND JUST NOW?
THERE WAS AN EXPLOSION !!
WHAT!
AN EXPLOSION !?
YES! THERE WAS A SUDDEN BLAST OF LIGHT IN THAT HALLWAY OVER THERE...
HUH ?
DASH

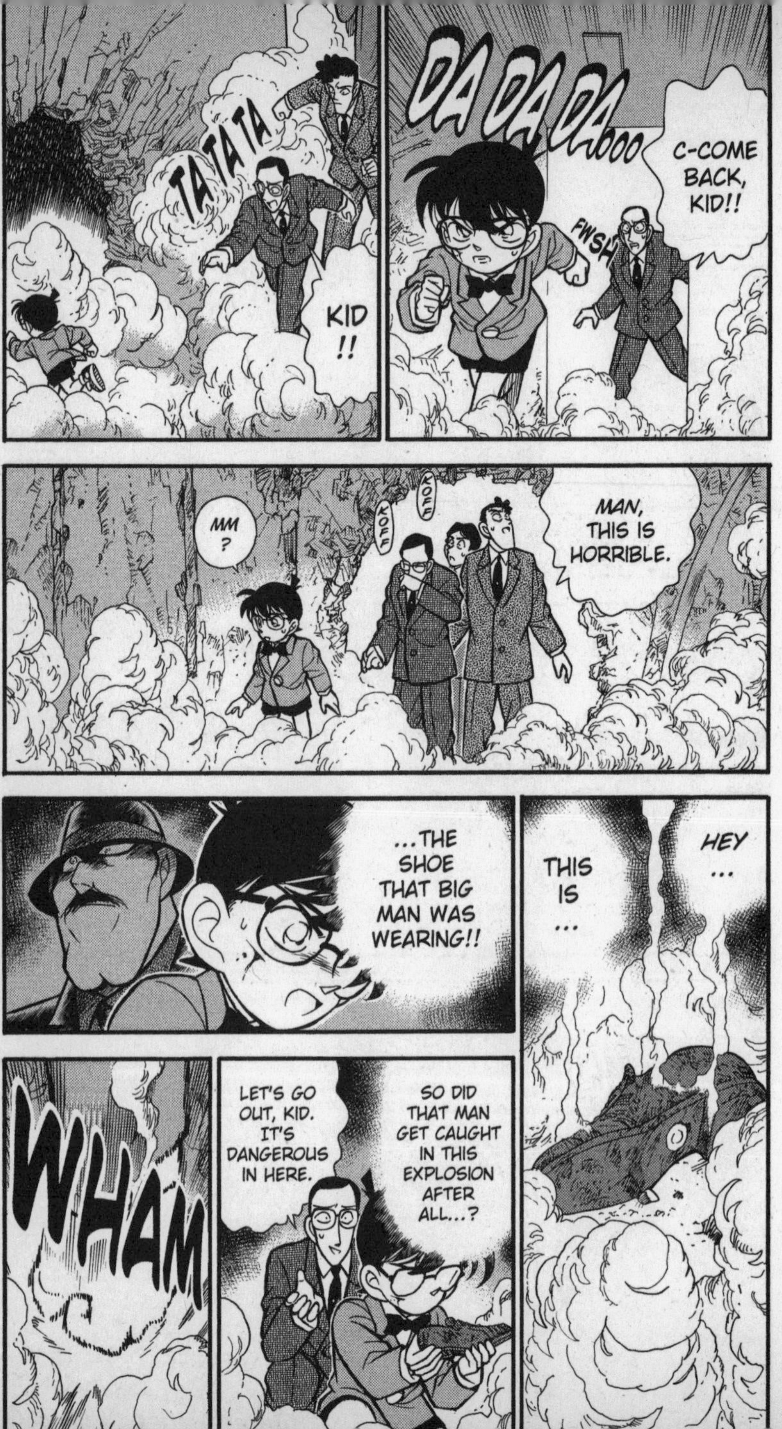
TA TA TA
KID !!
DA DA DA DOOO
FWSH
C-COME BACK, KID!!
MM ?
KOFF KOFF
MAN, THIS IS HORRIBLE.
HEY ...
THIS IS ...
...THE SHOE THAT BIG MAN WAS WEARING!!
WHAM
SO DID THAT MAN GET CAUGHT IN THIS EXPLOSION AFTER ALL...?
LET'S GO OUT, KID. IT'S DANGEROUS IN HERE.

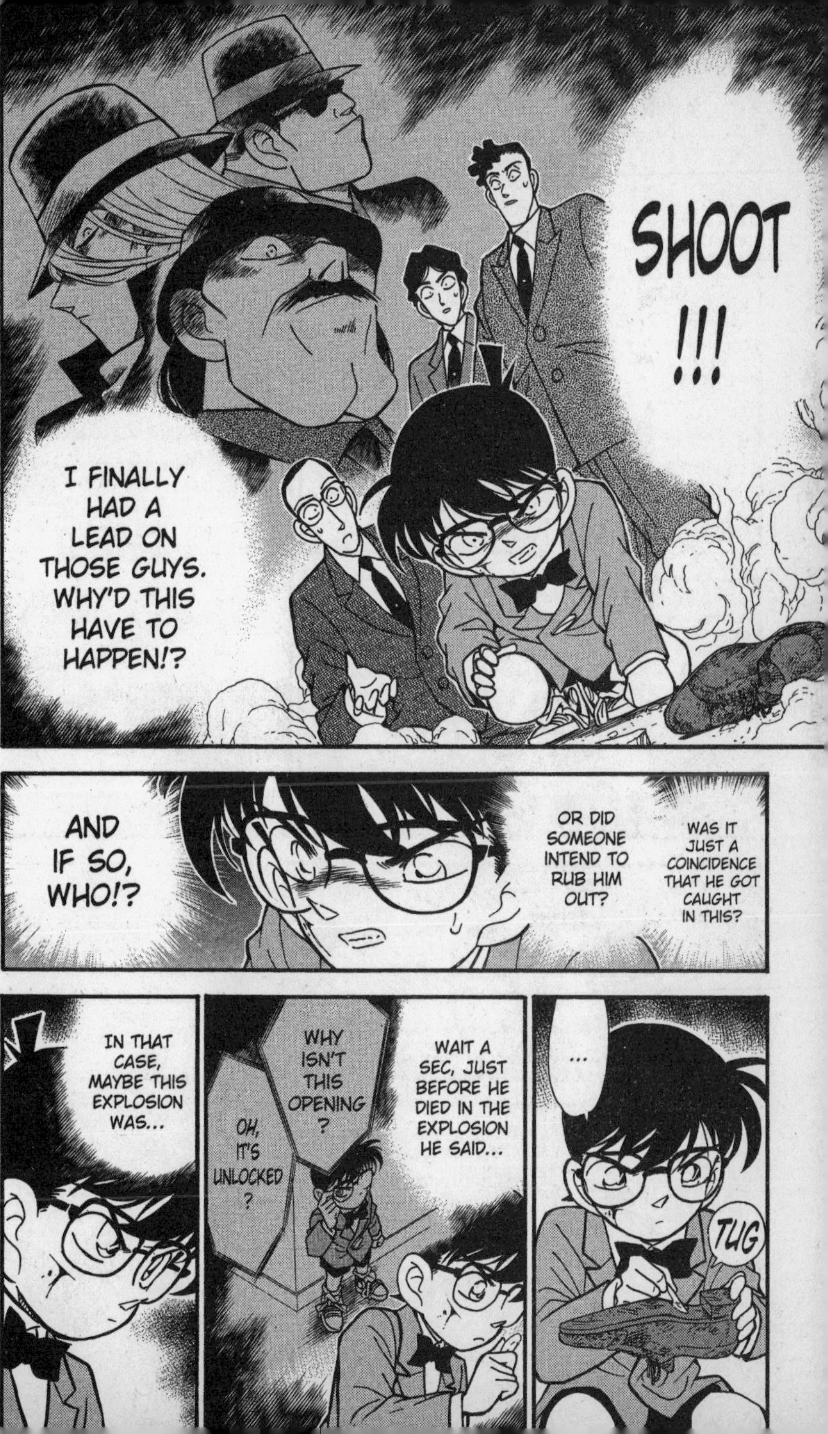
SHOOT !!!
I FINALLY HAD A LEAD ON THOSE GUYS. WHY'D THIS HAVE TO HAPPEN!?
WAS IT JUST A COINCIDENCE THAT HE GOT CAUGHT IN THIS?
OR DID SOMEONE INTEND TO RUB HIM OUT?
AND IF SO, WHO!?
...
TUG
WAIT A SEC, JUST BEFORE HE DIED IN THE EXPLOSION HE SAID...
WHY ISN'T THIS OPENING?
OH, IT'S UNLOCKED?
IN THAT CASE, MAYBE THIS EXPLOSION WAS...

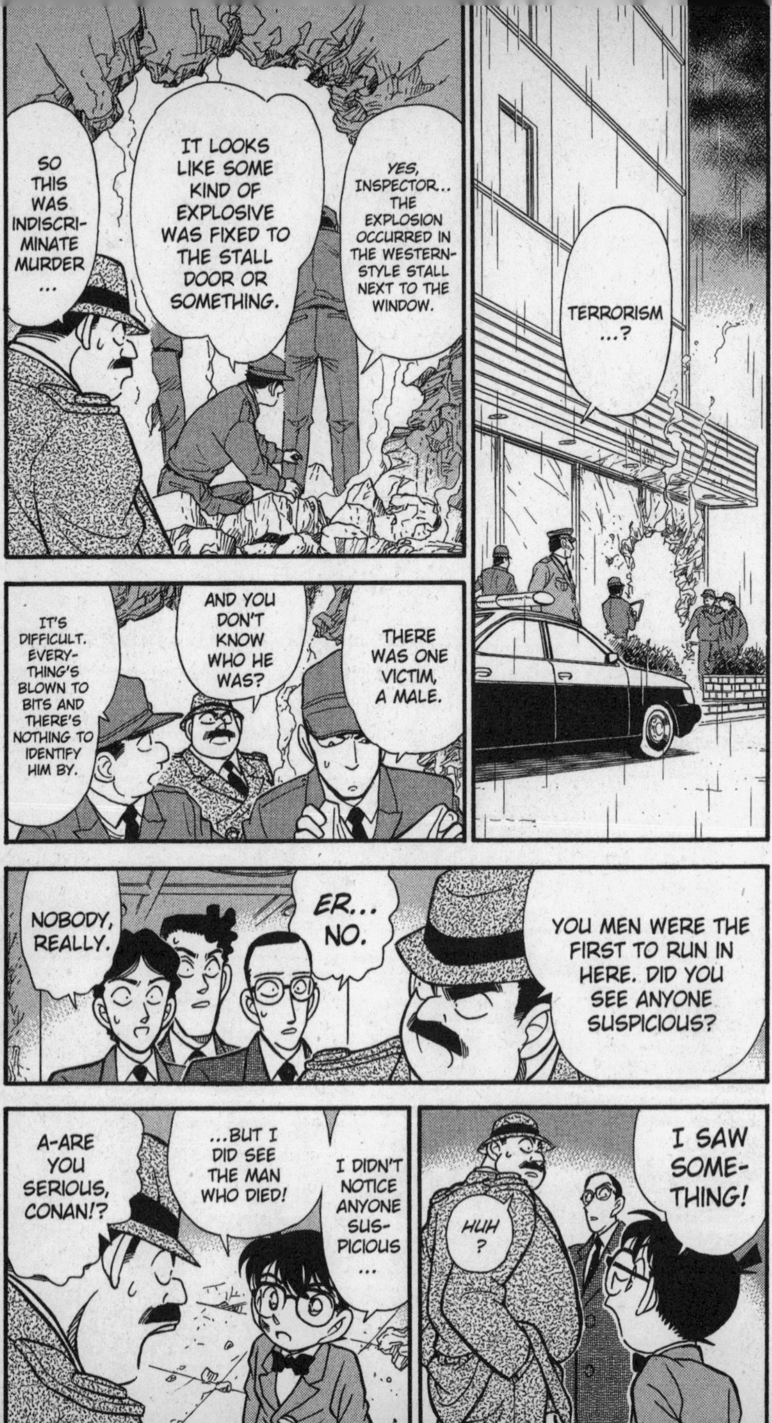
TERRORISM ...?
YES, INSPECTOR... THE EXPLOSION OCCURRED IN THE WESTERN-STYLE STALL NEXT TO THE WINDOW.
IT LOOKS LIKE SOME KIND OF EXPLOSIVE WAS FIXED TO THE STALL DOOR OR SOMETHING.
SO THIS WAS INDISCRIMINATE MURDER ...
THERE WAS ONE VICTIM, A MALE.
AND YOU DON'T KNOW WHO HE WAS?
IT'S DIFFICULT. EVERYTHING'S BLOWN TO BITS AND THERE'S NOTHING TO IDENTIFY HIM BY.
YOU MEN WERE THE FIRST TO RUN IN HERE. DID YOU SEE ANYONE SUSPICIOUS?
ER... NO.
NOBODY, REALLY.
I SAW SOMETHING!
HUH ?
I DIDN'T NOTICE ANYONE SUSPICIOUS ...
...BUT I DID SEE THE MAN WHO DIED!
A-ARE YOU SERIOUS, CONAN!?

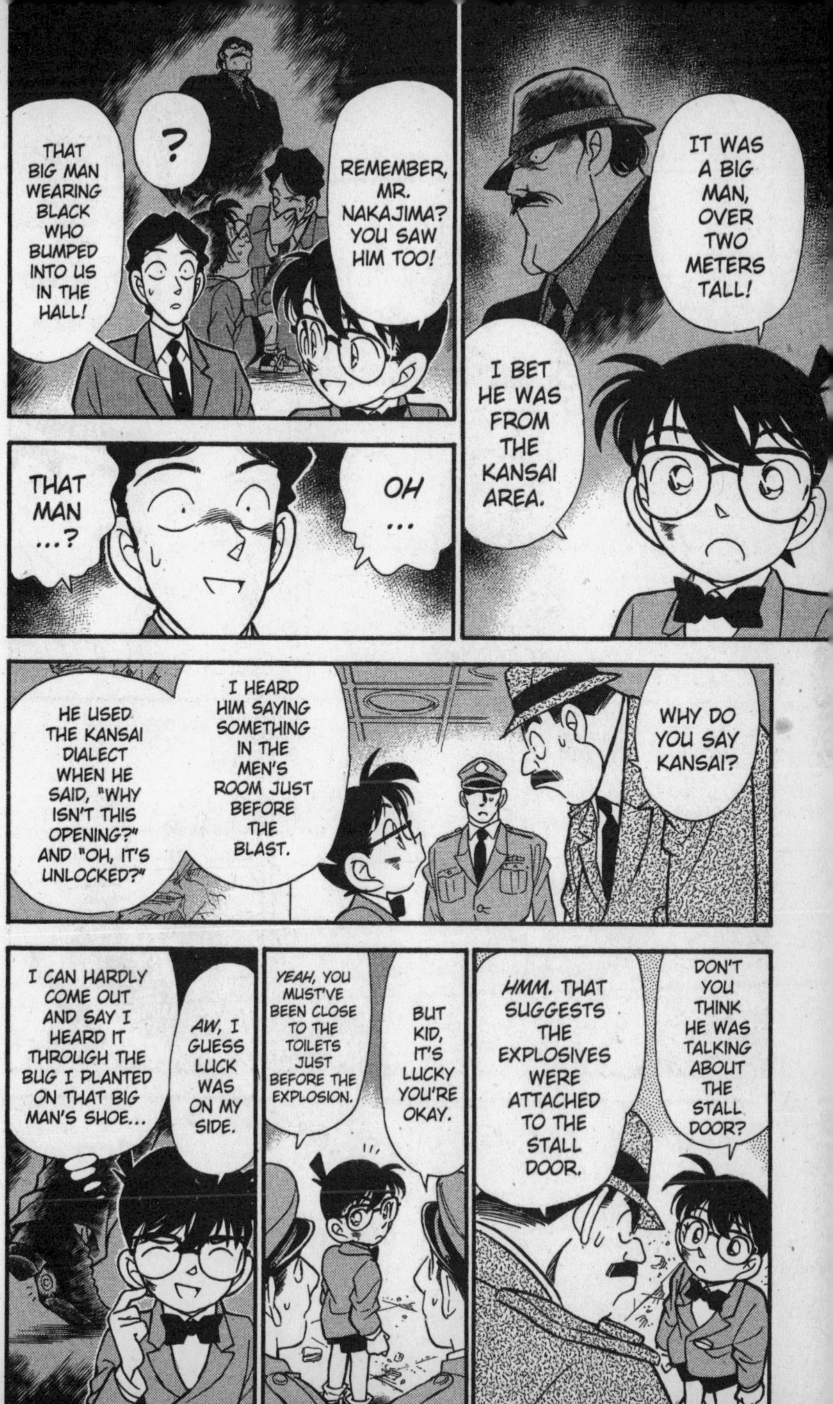
IT WAS A BIG MAN, OVER TWO METERS TALL!
I BET HE WAS FROM THE KANSAI AREA.
REMEMBER, MR. NAKAJIMA? YOU SAW HIM TOO!
?
THAT BIG MAN WEARING BLACK WHO BUMPED INTO US IN THE HALL!
OH ...
THAT MAN ...?
WHY DO YOU SAY KANSAI?
I HEARD HIM SAYING SOMETHING IN THE MEN'S ROOM JUST BEFORE THE BLAST.
HE USED THE KANSAI DIALECT WHEN HE SAID, "WHY ISN'T THIS OPENING?" AND "OH, IT'S UNLOCKED?"
DON'T YOU THINK HE WAS TALKING ABOUT THE STALL DOOR?
HMM. THAT SUGGESTS THE EXPLOSIVES WERE ATTACHED TO THE STALL DOOR.
BUT KID, IT'S LUCKY YOU'RE OKAY.
YEAH, YOU MUST'VE BEEN CLOSE TO THE TOILETS JUST BEFORE THE EXPLOSION.
AW, I GUESS LUCK WAS ON MY SIDE.
I CAN HARDLY COME OUT AND SAY I HEARD IT THROUGH THE BUG I PLANTED ON THAT BIG MAN'S SHOE...

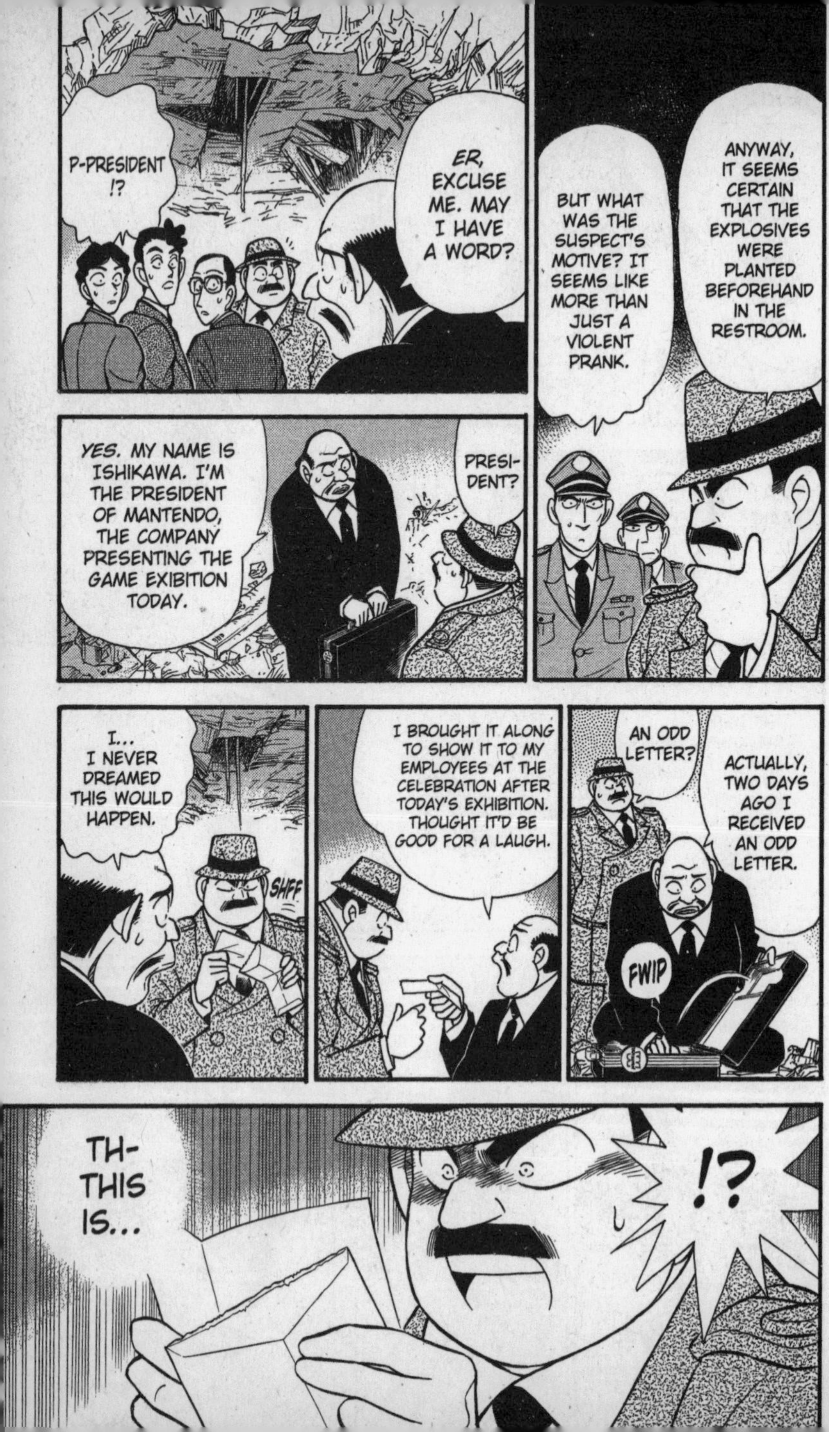
ANYWAY, IT SEEMS CERTAIN THAT THE EXPLOSIVES WERE PLANTED BEFOREHAND IN THE RESTROOM.
BUT WHAT WAS THE SUSPECT'S MOTIVE? IT SEEMS LIKE MORE THAN JUST A VIOLENT PRANK.
ER, EXCUSE ME. MAY I HAVE A WORD?
P-PRESIDENT !?
PRESI-DENT?
YES. MY NAME IS ISHIKAWA. I'M THE PRESIDENT OF MANTENDO, THE COMPANY PRESENTING THE GAME EXIBITION TODAY.
ACTUALLY, TWO DAYS AGO I RECEIVED AN ODD LETTER.
AN ODD LETTER?
FWIP
I BROUGHT IT ALONG TO SHOW IT TO MY EMPLOYEES AT THE CELEBRATION AFTER TODAY'S EXHIBITION. THOUGHT IT'D BE GOOD FOR A LAUGH.
I... I NEVER DREAMED THIS WOULD HAPPEN.
SHFF
TH-THIS IS...
!?

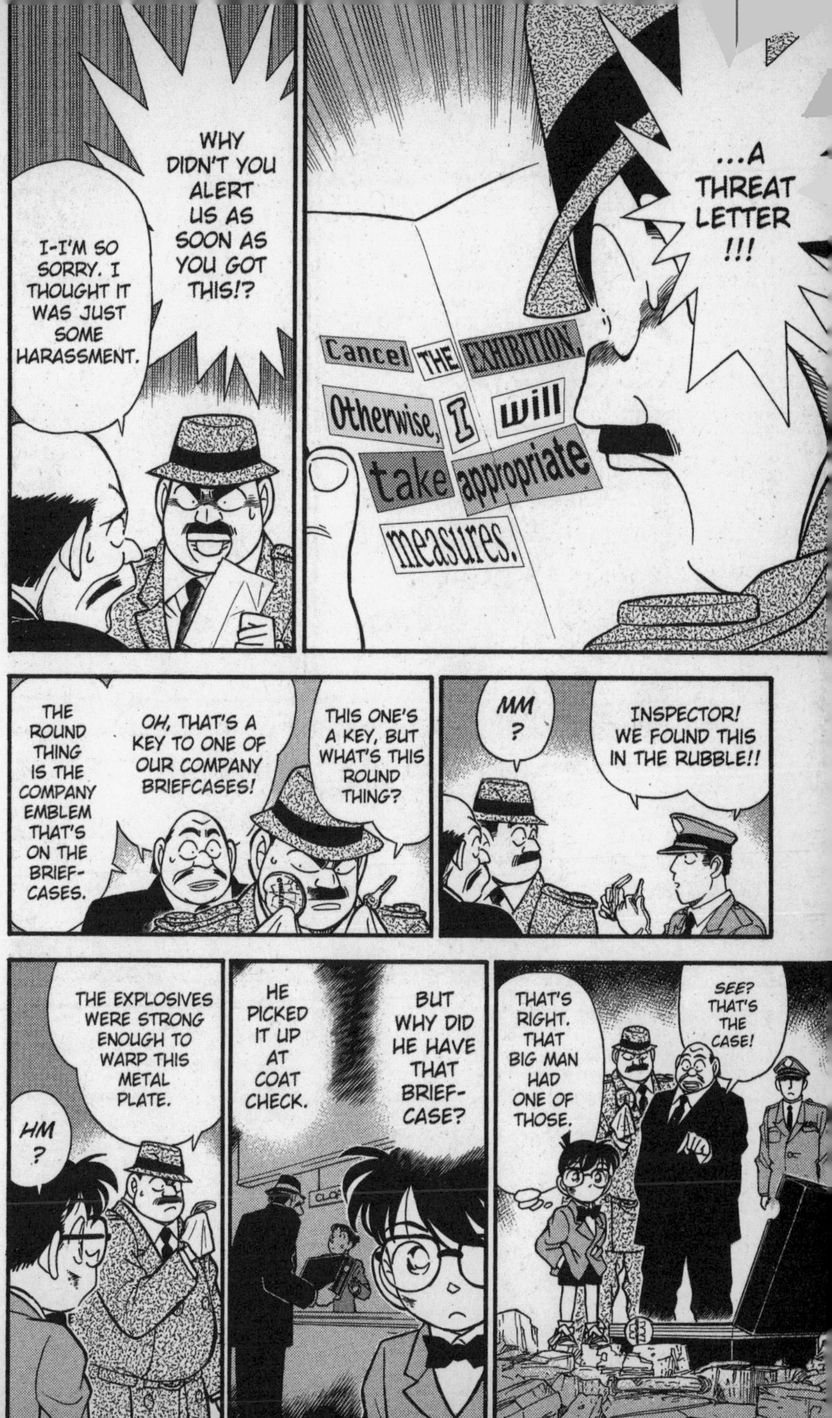
...A THREAT LETTER!!!
Cancel THE EXHIBITION. Otherwise, I will take appropriate measures.
WHY DIDN'T YOU ALERT US AS SOON AS YOU GOT THIS!?
I-I'M SO SORRY. I THOUGHT IT WAS JUST SOME HARASSMENT.
INSPECTOR! WE FOUND THIS IN THE RUBBLE!!
MM?
THIS ONE'S A KEY, BUT WHAT'S THIS ROUND THING?
OH, THAT'S A KEY TO ONE OF OUR COMPANY BRIEFCASES!
THE ROUND THING IS THE COMPANY EMBLEM THAT'S ON THE BRIEF-CASES.
SEE? THAT'S THE CASE!
THAT'S RIGHT. THAT BIG MAN HAD ONE OF THOSE.
BUT WHY DID HE HAVE THAT BRIEF-CASE?
HE PICKED IT UP AT COAT CHECK.
THE EXPLOSIVES WERE STRONG ENOUGH TO WARP THIS METAL PLATE.
HM?

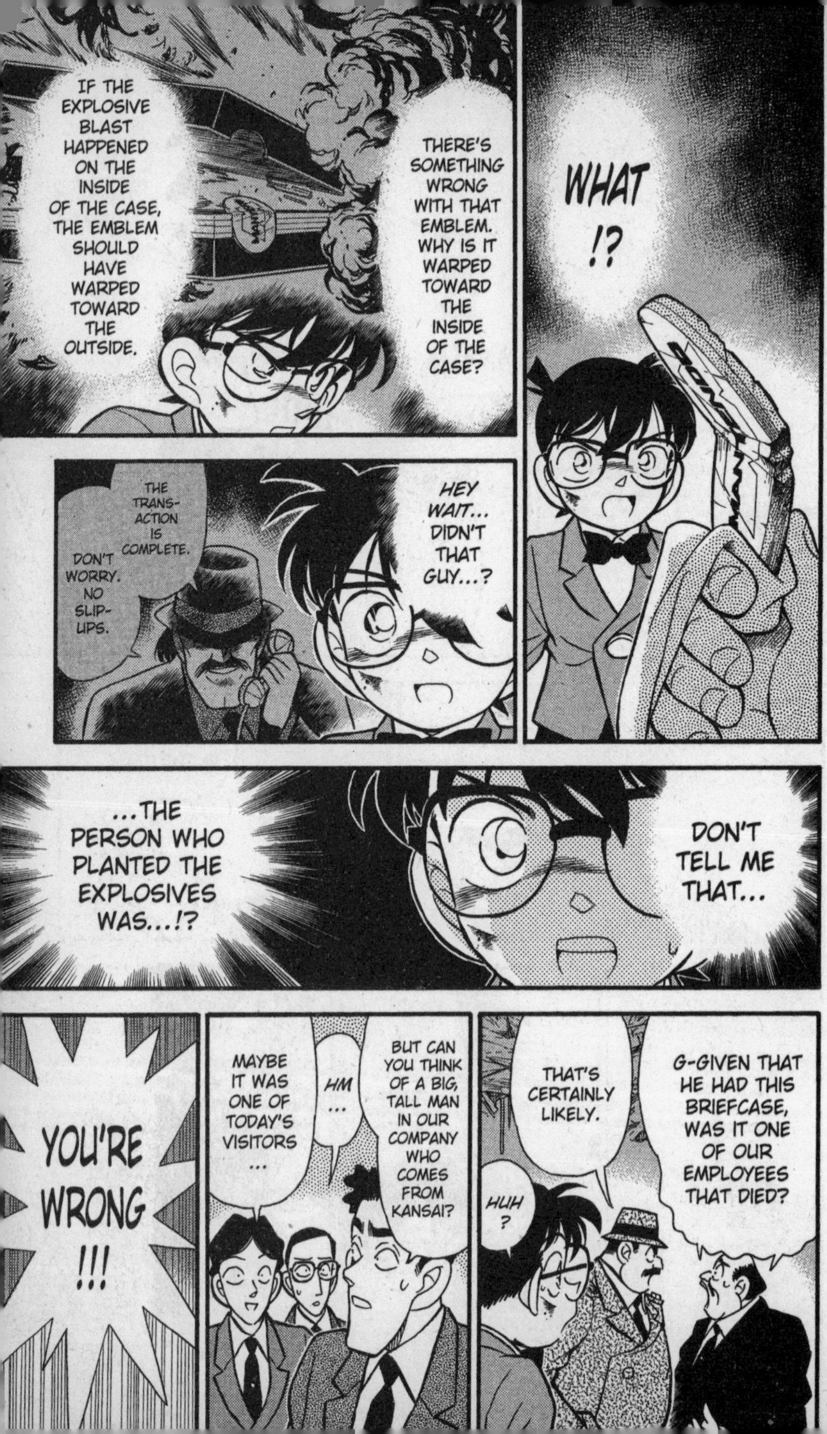
WHAT !?
THERE'S SOMETHING WRONG WITH THAT EMBLEM. WHY IS IT WARPED TOWARD THE INSIDE OF THE CASE?
IF THE EXPLOSIVE BLAST HAPPENED ON THE INSIDE OF THE CASE, THE EMBLEM SHOULD HAVE WARPED TOWARD THE OUTSIDE.
HEY WAIT... DIDN'T THAT GUY...?
THE TRANS-ACTION IS COMPLETE.
DON'T WORRY. NO SLIP-UPS.
DON'T TELL ME THAT...
...THE PERSON WHO PLANTED THE EXPLOSIVES WAS...!?
G-GIVEN THAT HE HAD THIS BRIEFCASE, WAS IT ONE OF OUR EMPLOYEES THAT DIED?
THAT'S CERTAINLY LIKELY.
HUH ?
BUT CAN YOU THINK OF A BIG, TALL MAN IN OUR COMPANY WHO COMES FROM KANSAI?
HM ...
MAYBE IT WAS ONE OF TODAY'S VISITORS ...
YOU'RE WRONG !!!

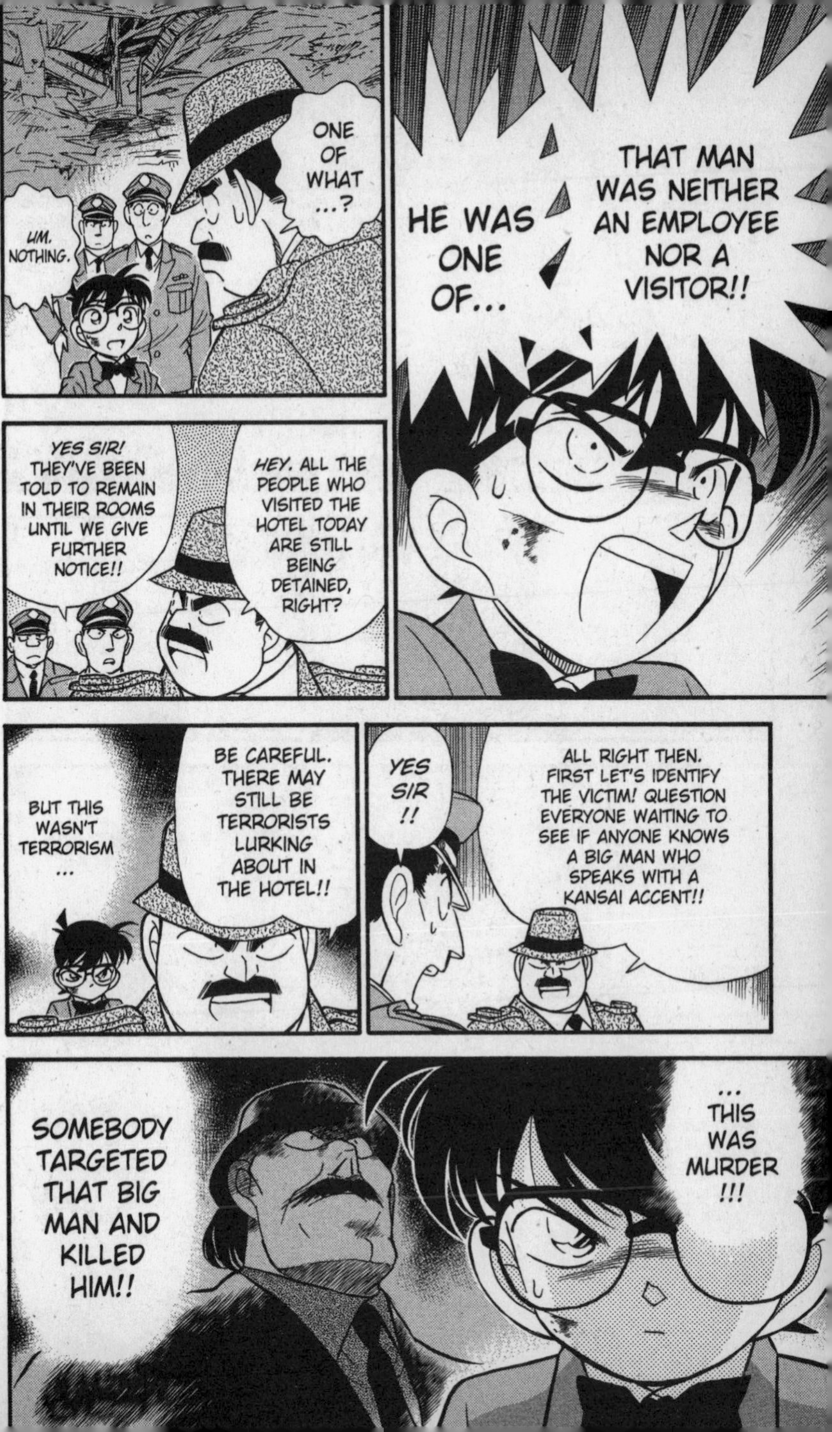
THAT MAN WAS NEITHER AN EMPLOYEE NOR A VISITOR!!
HE WAS ONE OF...
ONE OF WHAT ...?
UM. NOTHING.
HEY. ALL THE PEOPLE WHO VISITED THE HOTEL TODAY ARE STILL BEING DETAINED, RIGHT?
YES SIR! THEY'VE BEEN TOLD TO REMAIN IN THEIR ROOMS UNTIL WE GIVE FURTHER NOTICE!!
ALL RIGHT THEN. FIRST LET'S IDENTIFY THE VICTIM! QUESTION EVERYONE WAITING TO SEE IF ANYONE KNOWS A BIG MAN WHO SPEAKS WITH A KANSAI ACCENT!!
YES SIR !!
BE CAREFUL. THERE MAY STILL BE TERRORISTS LURKING ABOUT IN THE HOTEL!!
BUT THIS WASN'T TERRORISM ...
... THIS WAS MURDER !!!
SOMEBODY TARGETED THAT BIG MAN AND KILLED HIM!!

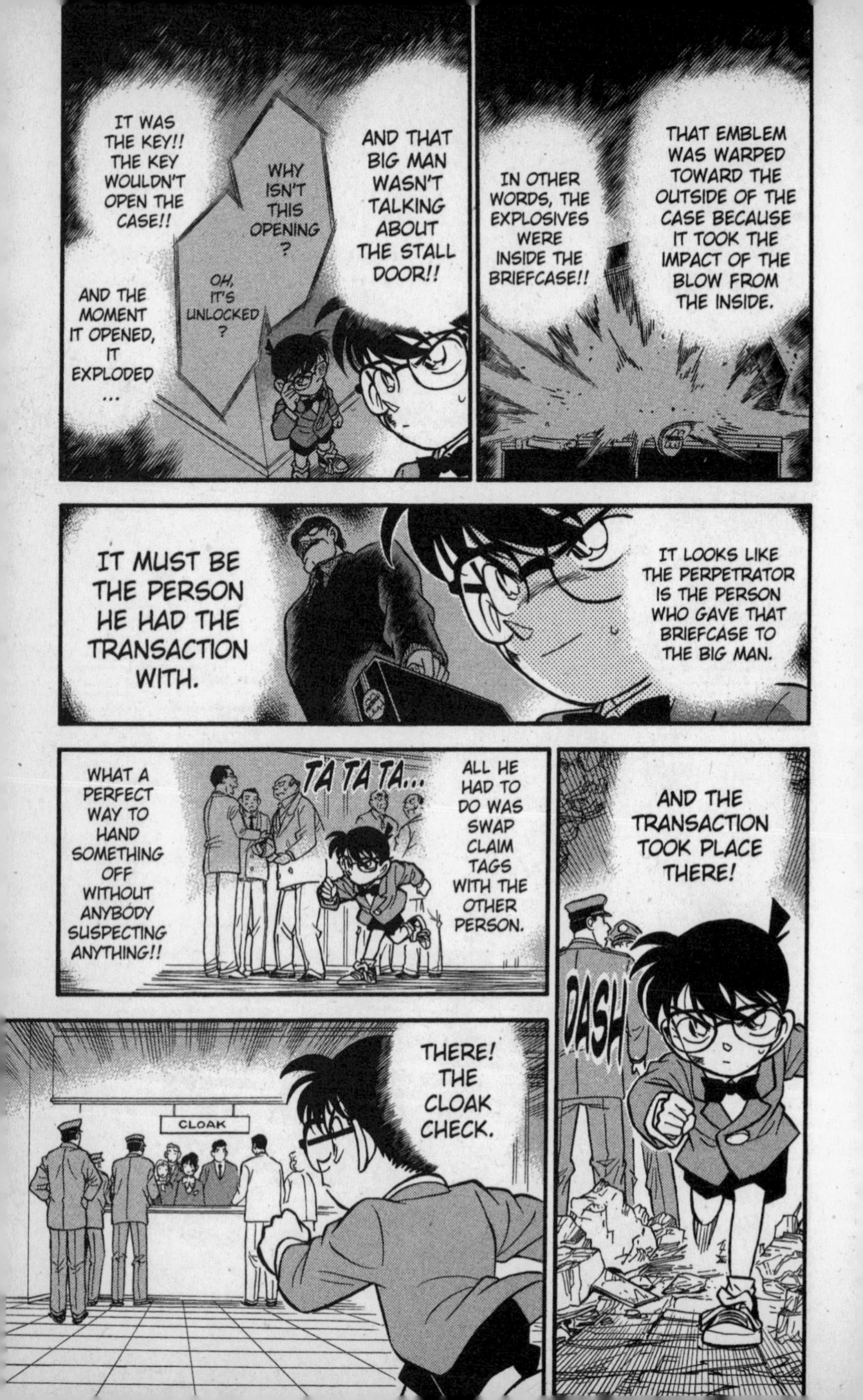
THAT EMBLEM WAS WARPED TOWARD THE OUTSIDE OF THE CASE BECAUSE IT TOOK THE IMPACT OF THE BLOW FROM THE INSIDE.
IN OTHER WORDS, THE EXPLOSIVES WERE INSIDE THE BRIEFCASE!!
AND THAT BIG MAN WASN'T TALKING ABOUT THE STALL DOOR!!
WHY ISN'T THIS OPENING?
IT WAS THE KEY!! THE KEY WOULDN'T OPEN THE CASE!!
OH, IT'S UNLOCKED?
AND THE MOMENT IT OPENED, IT EXPLODED...
IT LOOKS LIKE THE PERPETRATOR IS THE PERSON WHO GAVE THAT BRIEFCASE TO THE BIG MAN.
IT MUST BE THE PERSON HE HAD THE TRANSACTION WITH.
AND THE TRANSACTION TOOK PLACE THERE!
DASH
TA TA TA...
ALL HE HAD TO DO WAS SWAP CLAIM TAGS WITH THE OTHER PERSON.
WHAT A PERFECT WAY TO HAND SOMETHING OFF WITHOUT ANYBODY SUSPECTING ANYTHING!!
THERE! THE CLOAK CHECK.
CLOAK

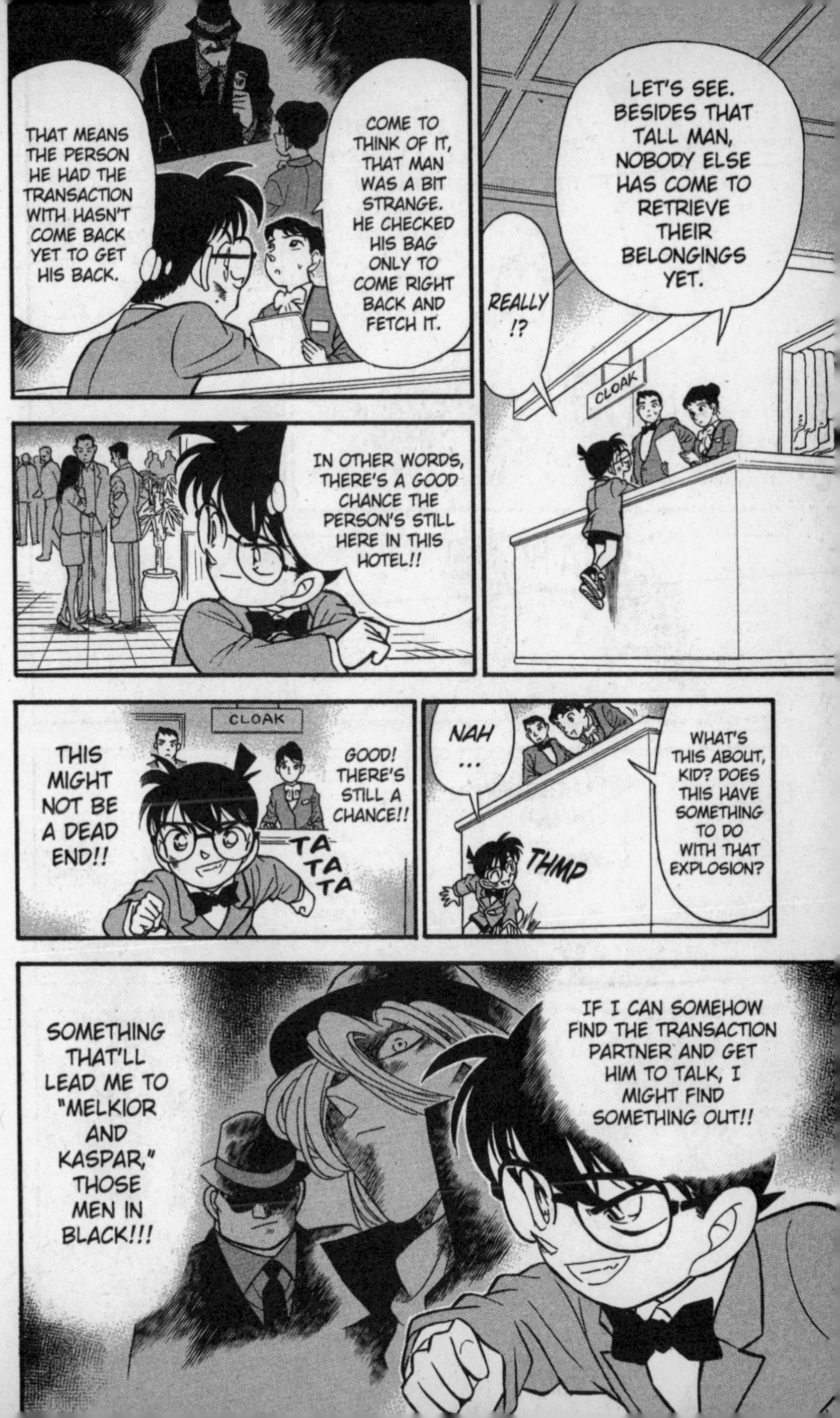
LET'S SEE. BESIDES THAT TALL MAN, NOBODY ELSE HAS COME TO RETRIEVE THEIR BELONGINGS YET.
REALLY !?
CLOAK
COME TO THINK OF IT, THAT MAN WAS A BIT STRANGE. HE CHECKED HIS BAG ONLY TO COME RIGHT BACK AND FETCH IT.
THAT MEANS THE PERSON HE HAD THE TRANSACTION WITH HASN'T COME BACK YET TO GET HIS BACK.
IN OTHER WORDS, THERE'S A GOOD CHANCE THE PERSON'S STILL HERE IN THIS HOTEL!!
WHAT'S THIS ABOUT, KID? DOES THIS HAVE SOMETHING TO DO WITH THAT EXPLOSION?
NAH ...
THMP
CLOAK
GOOD! THERE'S STILL A CHANCE!!
THIS MIGHT NOT BE A DEAD END!!
TA TA TA
IF I CAN SOMEHOW FIND THE TRANSACTION PARTNER AND GET HIM TO TALK, I MIGHT FIND SOMETHING OUT!!
SOMETHING THAT'LL LEAD ME TO "MELKIOR AND KASPAR," THOSE MEN IN BLACK!!!

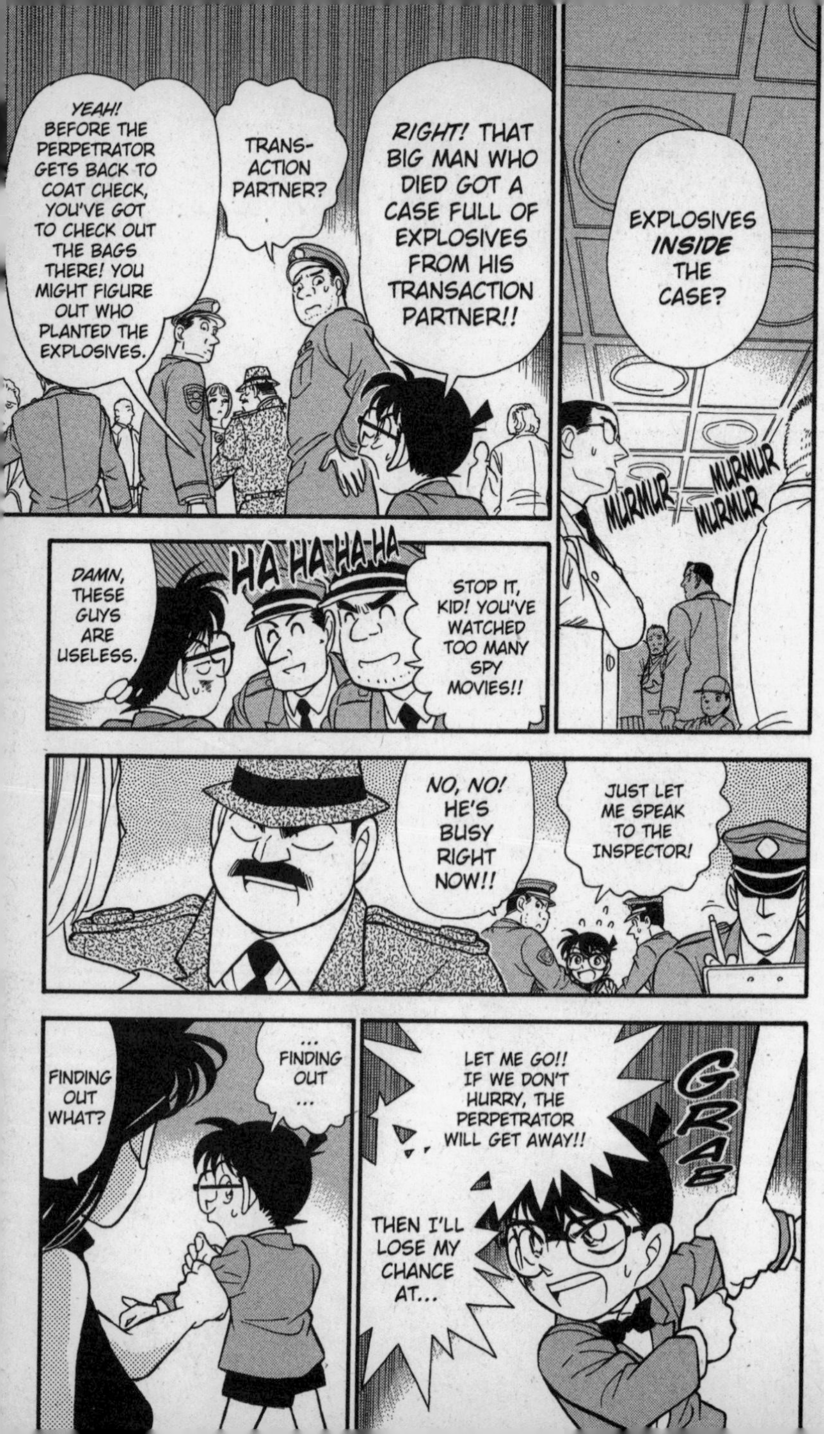
YEAH! BEFORE THE PERPETRATOR GETS BACK TO COAT CHECK, YOU'VE GOT TO CHECK OUT THE BAGS THERE! YOU MIGHT FIGURE OUT WHO PLANTED THE EXPLOSIVES.
TRANS-ACTION PARTNER?
RIGHT! THAT BIG MAN WHO DIED GOT A CASE FULL OF EXPLOSIVES FROM HIS TRANSACTION PARTNER!!
EXPLOSIVES INSIDE THE CASE?
MURMUR
MURMUR MURMUR
HA HA HA HA
STOP IT, KID! YOU'VE WATCHED TOO MANY SPY MOVIES!!
DAMN, THESE GUYS ARE USELESS.
JUST LET ME SPEAK TO THE INSPECTOR!
NO, NO! HE'S BUSY RIGHT NOW!!
FINDING OUT WHAT?
... FINDING OUT ...
LET ME GO!! IF WE DON'T HURRY, THE PERPETRATOR WILL GET AWAY!!
GRAB
THEN I'LL LOSE MY CHANCE AT...

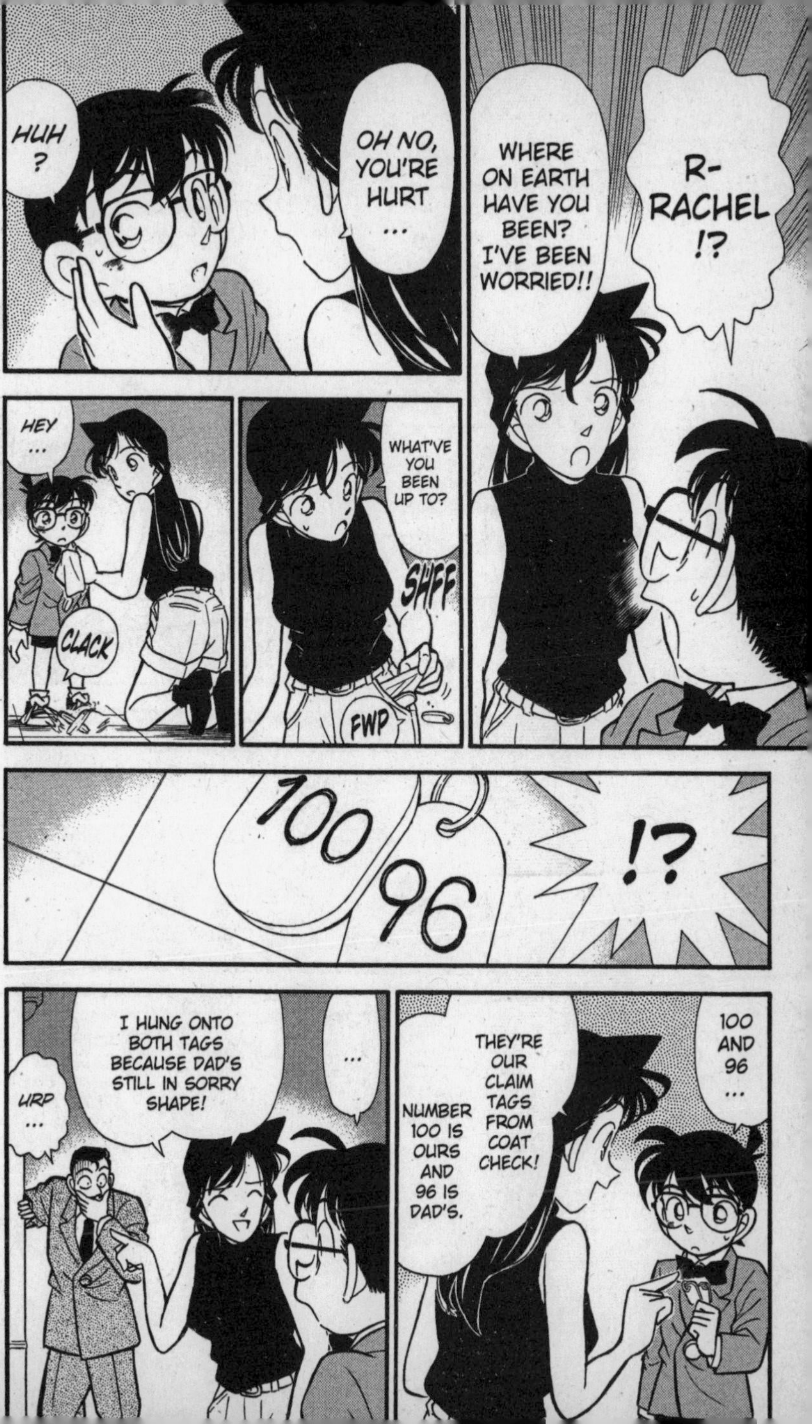
R-RACHEL!?
WHERE ON EARTH HAVE YOU BEEN? I'VE BEEN WORRIED!!
OH NO, YOU'RE HURT...
HUH?
WHAT'VE YOU BEEN UP TO?
SHFF
FWP
HEY...
CLACK
100
96
!?
100 AND 96...
THEY'RE OUR CLAIM TAGS FROM COAT CHECK!
NUMBER 100 IS OURS AND 96 IS DAD'S.
...
I HUNG ONTO BOTH TAGS BECAUSE DAD'S STILL IN SORRY SHAPE!
URP...

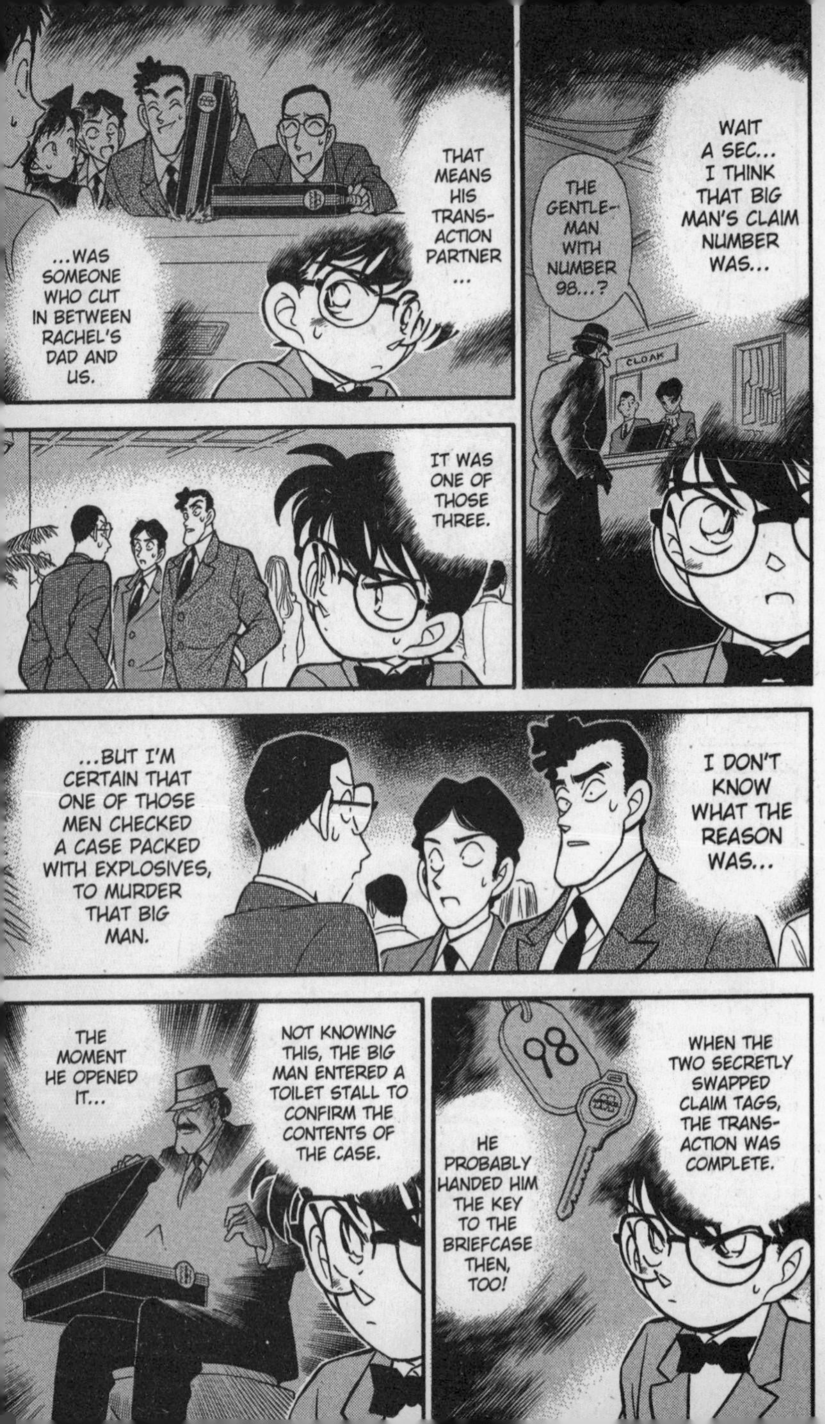
WAIT A SEC... I THINK THAT BIG MAN'S CLAIM NUMBER WAS...
THE GENTLEMAN WITH NUMBER 98...?
CLOAK
THAT MEANS HIS TRANSACTION PARTNER...
...WAS SOMEONE WHO CUT IN BETWEEN RACHEL'S DAD AND US.
IT WAS ONE OF THOSE THREE.
I DON'T KNOW WHAT THE REASON WAS...
...BUT I'M CERTAIN THAT ONE OF THOSE MEN CHECKED A CASE PACKED WITH EXPLOSIVES, TO MURDER THAT BIG MAN.
WHEN THE TWO SECRETLY SWAPPED CLAIM TAGS, THE TRANSACTION WAS COMPLETE.
98
HE PROBABLY HANDED HIM THE KEY TO THE BRIEFCASE THEN, TOO!
NOT KNOWING THIS, THE BIG MAN ENTERED A TOILET STALL TO CONFIRM THE CONTENTS OF THE CASE.
THE MOMENT HE OPENED IT...

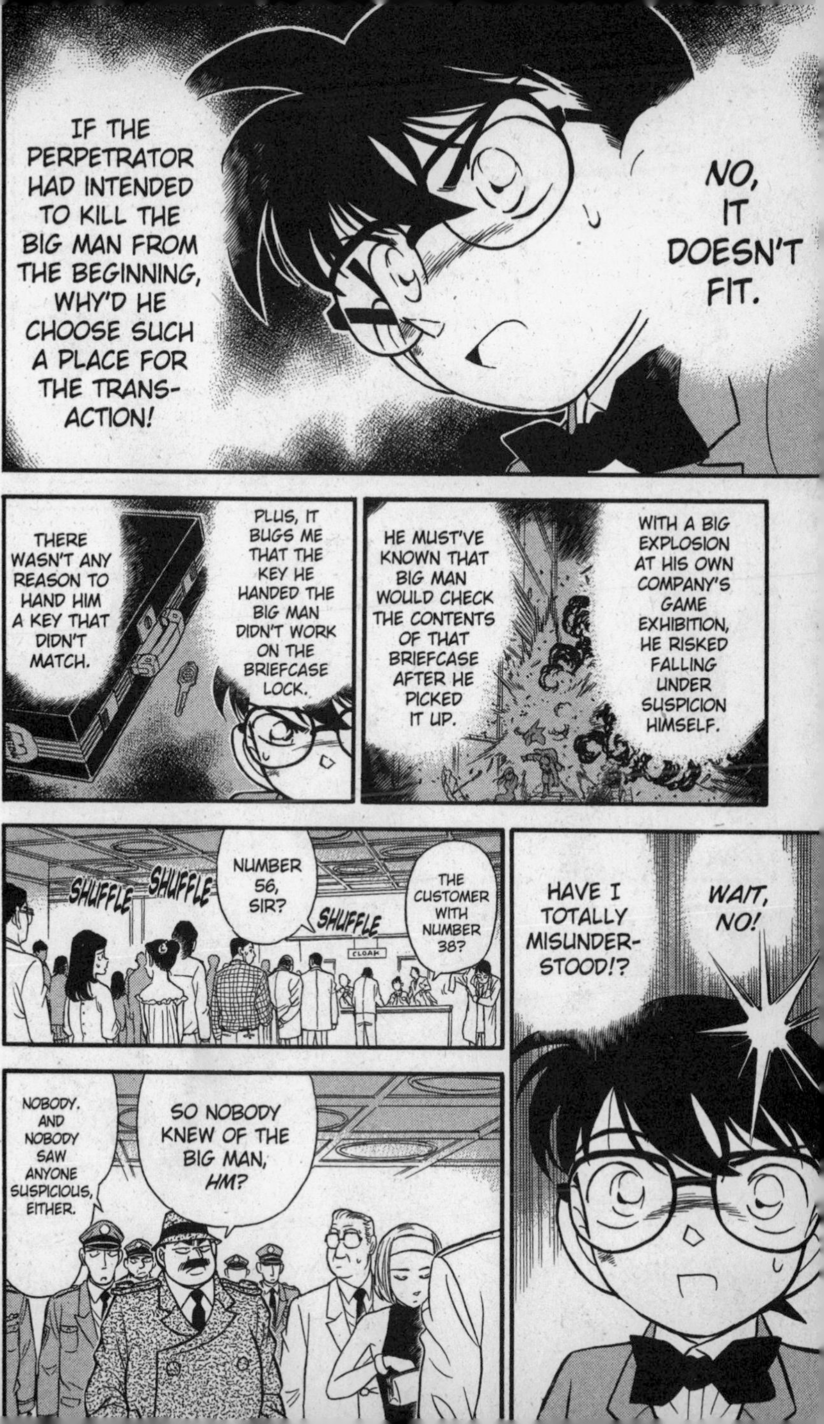
IF THE PERPETRATOR HAD INTENDED TO KILL THE BIG MAN FROM THE BEGINNING, WHY'D HE CHOOSE SUCH A PLACE FOR THE TRANS-ACTION!
NO, IT DOESN'T FIT.
THERE WASN'T ANY REASON TO HAND HIM A KEY THAT DIDN'T MATCH.
PLUS, IT BUGS ME THAT THE KEY HE HANDED THE BIG MAN DIDN'T WORK ON THE BRIEFCASE LOCK.
HE MUST'VE KNOWN THAT BIG MAN WOULD CHECK THE CONTENTS OF THAT BRIEFCASE AFTER HE PICKED IT UP.
WITH A BIG EXPLOSION AT HIS OWN COMPANY'S GAME EXHIBITION, HE RISKED FALLING UNDER SUSPICION HIMSELF.
SHUFFLE SHUFFLE
NUMBER 56, SIR?
SHUFFLE
CLOAK
THE CUSTOMER WITH NUMBER 38?
HAVE I TOTALLY MISUNDER-STOOD!?
WAIT, NO!
SO NOBODY KNEW OF THE BIG MAN, HM?
NOBODY. AND NOBODY SAW ANYONE SUSPICIOUS, EITHER.

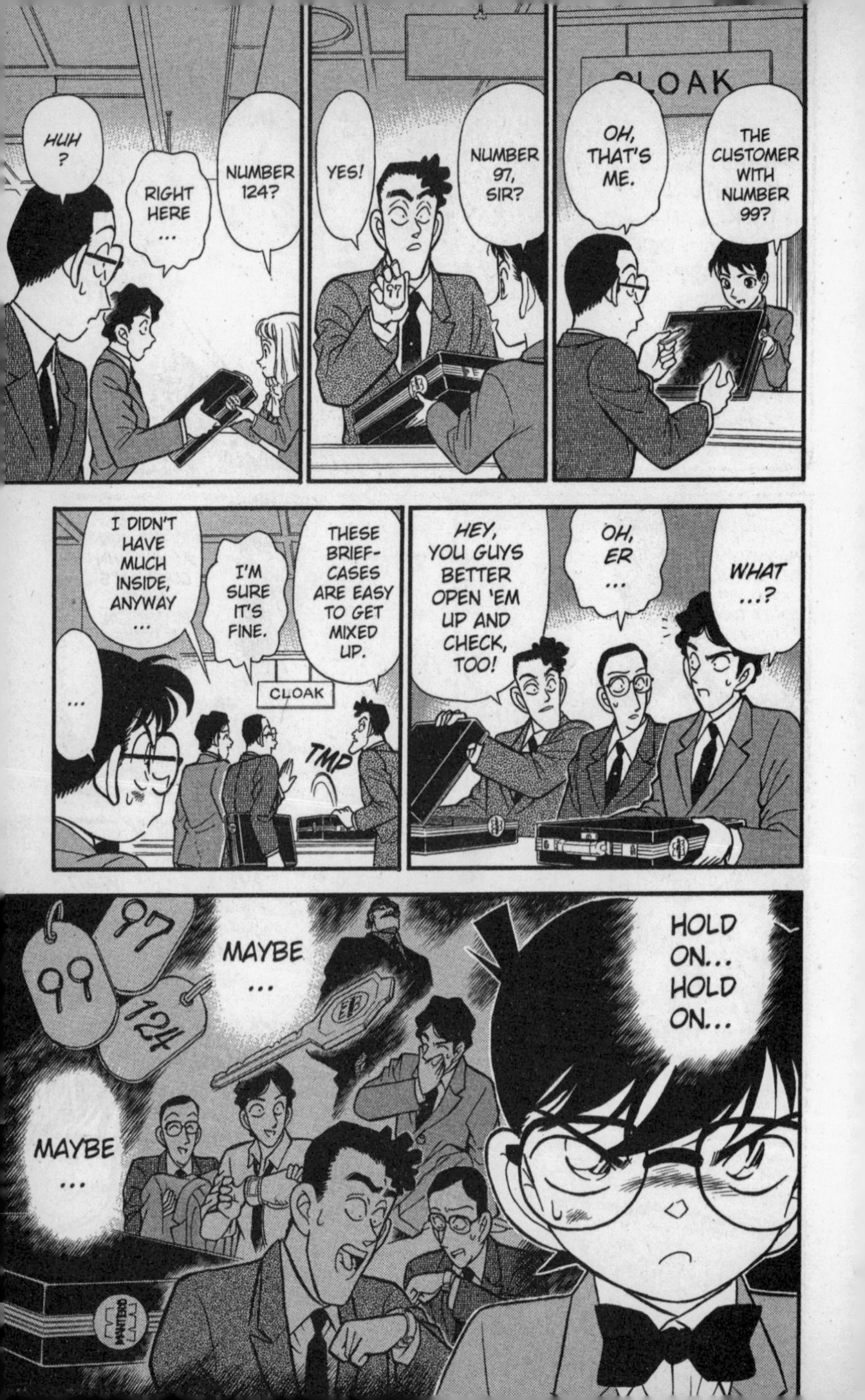
CLOAK
THE CUSTOMER WITH NUMBER 99?
OH, THAT'S ME.
NUMBER 97, SIR?
YES!
NUMBER 124?
RIGHT HERE ...
HUH ?
WHAT ...?
OH, ER ...
HEY, YOU GUYS BETTER OPEN 'EM UP AND CHECK, TOO!
THESE BRIEF-CASES ARE EASY TO GET MIXED UP.
I'M SURE IT'S FINE.
I DIDN'T HAVE MUCH INSIDE, ANYWAY ...
...
CLOAK
TMP
HOLD ON... HOLD ON...
97
99
124
MAYBE ...
MAYBE ...

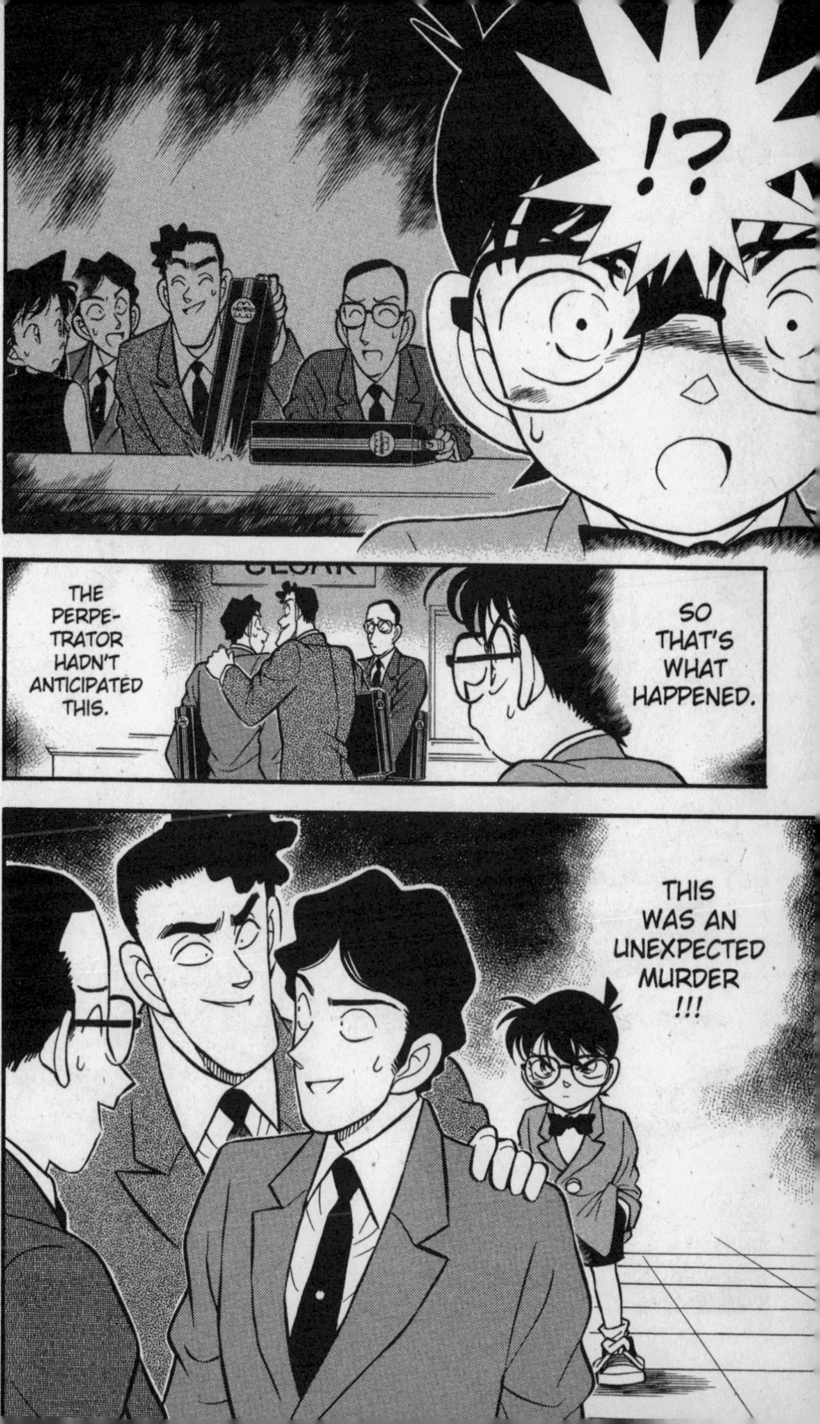
!?
SO THAT'S WHAT HAPPENED.
THE PERPE-TRATOR HADN'T ANTICIPATED THIS.
THIS WAS AN UNEXPECTED MURDER !!!

FILE 6:
CONAN'S MISCALCULATION

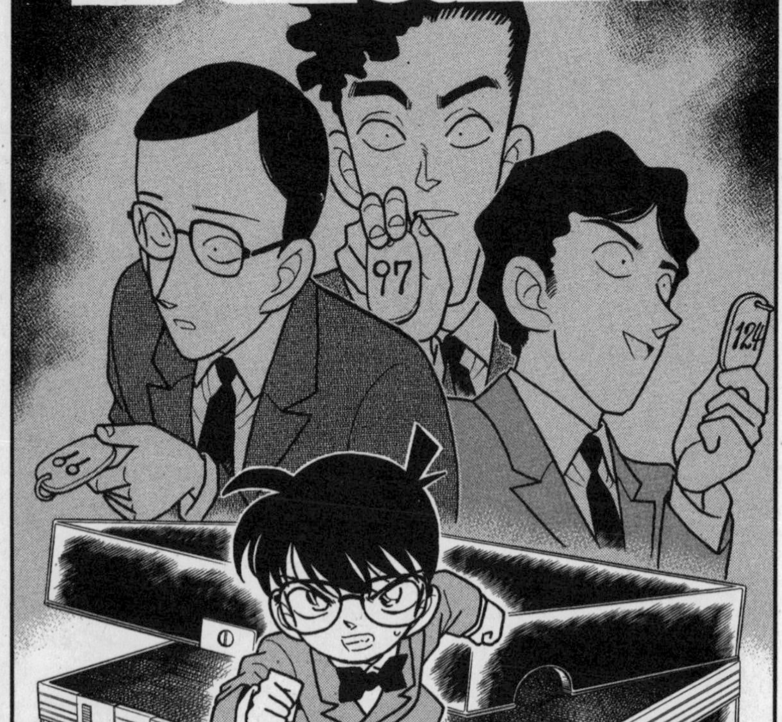
97
124

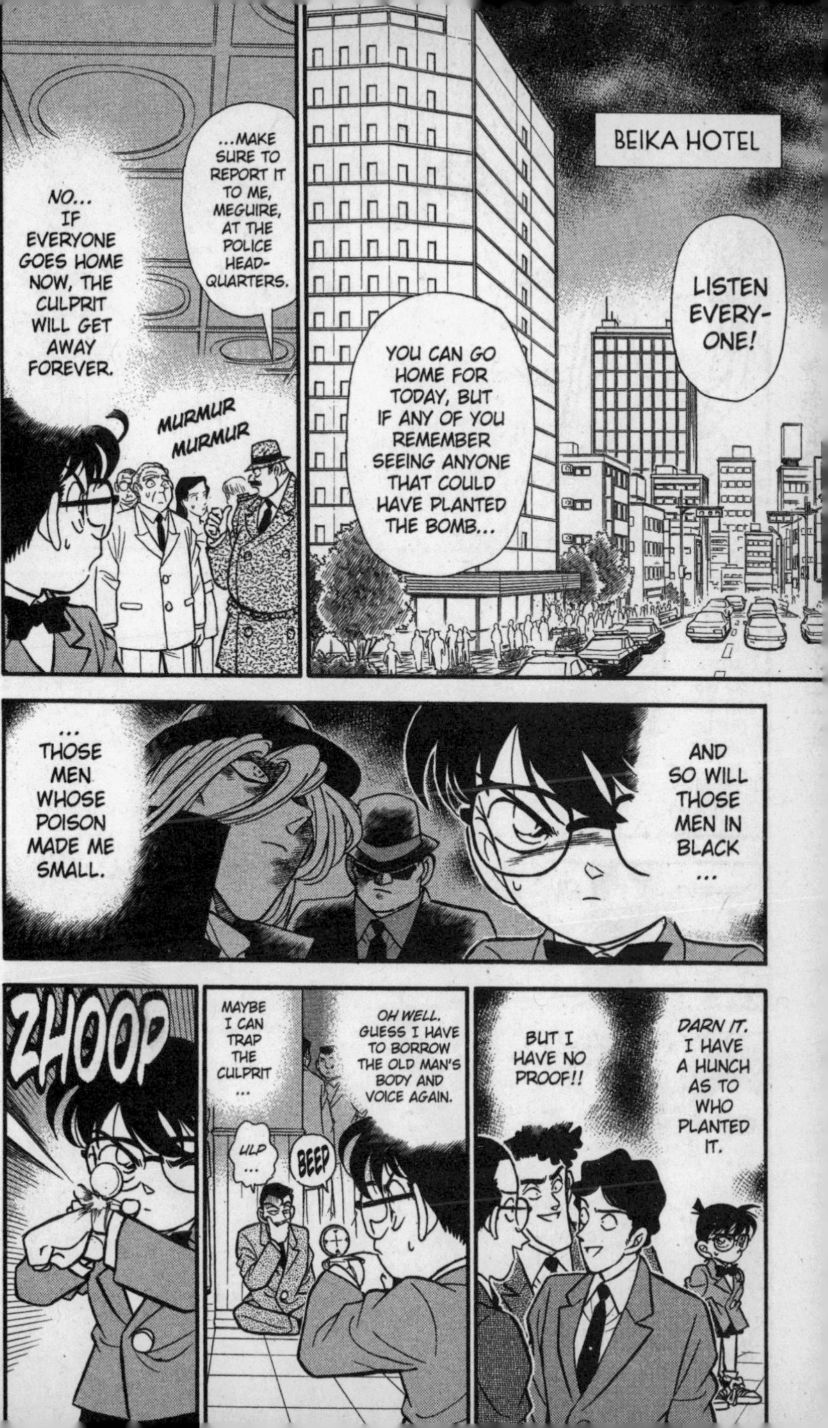
BEIKA HOTEL
LISTEN EVERYONE!
YOU CAN GO HOME FOR TODAY, BUT IF ANY OF YOU REMEMBER SEEING ANYONE THAT COULD HAVE PLANTED THE BOMB...
...MAKE SURE TO REPORT IT TO ME, MEGUIRE, AT THE POLICE HEADQUARTERS.
MURMUR MURMUR
NO... IF EVERYONE GOES HOME NOW, THE CULPRIT WILL GET AWAY FOREVER.
AND SO WILL THOSE MEN IN BLACK ...
... THOSE MEN WHOSE POISON MADE ME SMALL.
DARN IT. I HAVE A HUNCH AS TO WHO PLANTED IT.
BUT I HAVE NO PROOF!!
OH WELL. GUESS I HAVE TO BORROW THE OLD MAN'S BODY AND VOICE AGAIN.
MAYBE I CAN TRAP THE CULPRIT ...
BEEP
ULP ...
ZHOOP

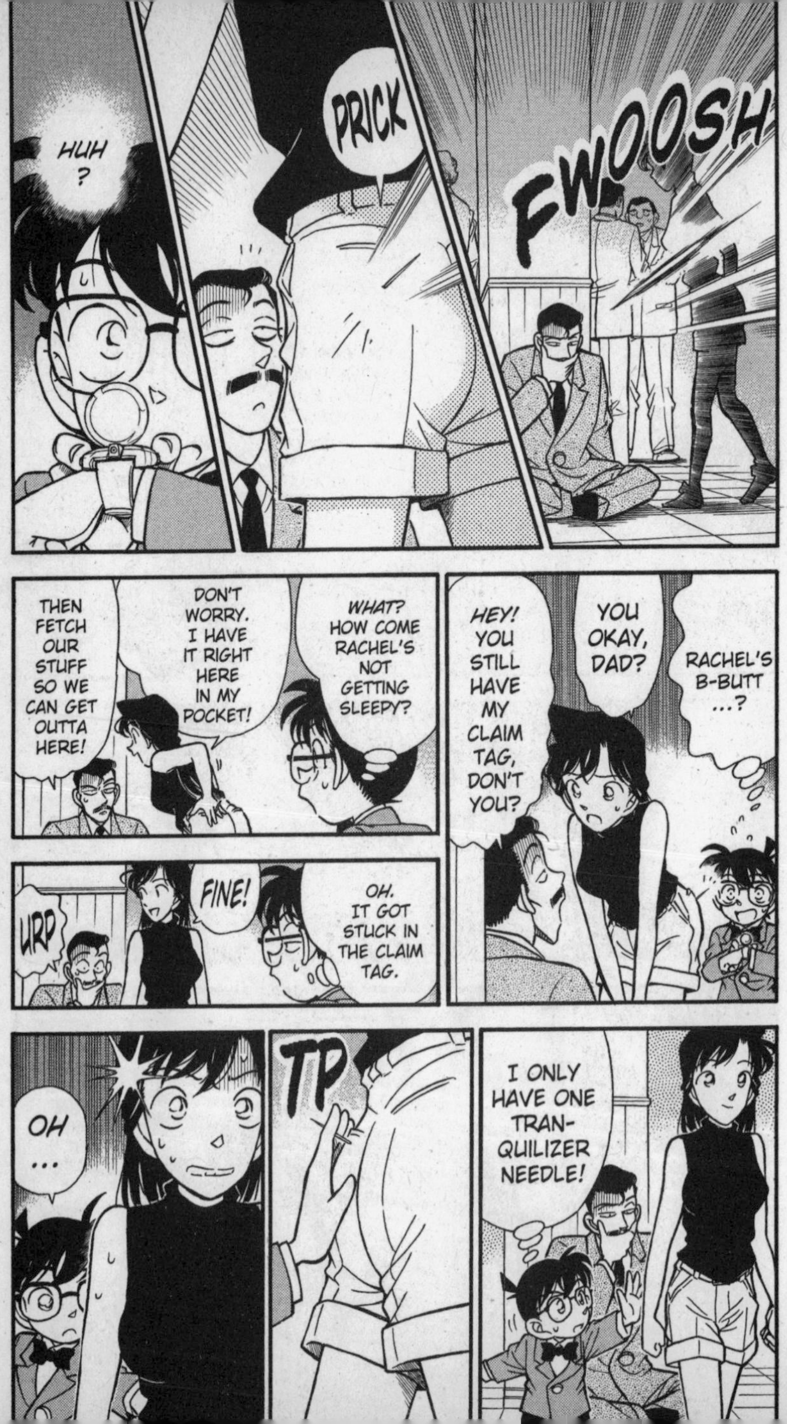
HUH ?
PRICK
FWOOSH
THEN FETCH OUR STUFF SO WE CAN GET OUTTA HERE!
DON'T WORRY. I HAVE IT RIGHT HERE IN MY POCKET!
WHAT? HOW COME RACHEL'S NOT GETTING SLEEPY?
HEY! YOU STILL HAVE MY CLAIM TAG, DON'T YOU?
YOU OKAY, DAD?
RACHEL'S B-BUTT ...?
URP
FINE!
OH. IT GOT STUCK IN THE CLAIM TAG.
OH ...
TP
I ONLY HAVE ONE TRAN-QUILIZER NEEDLE!

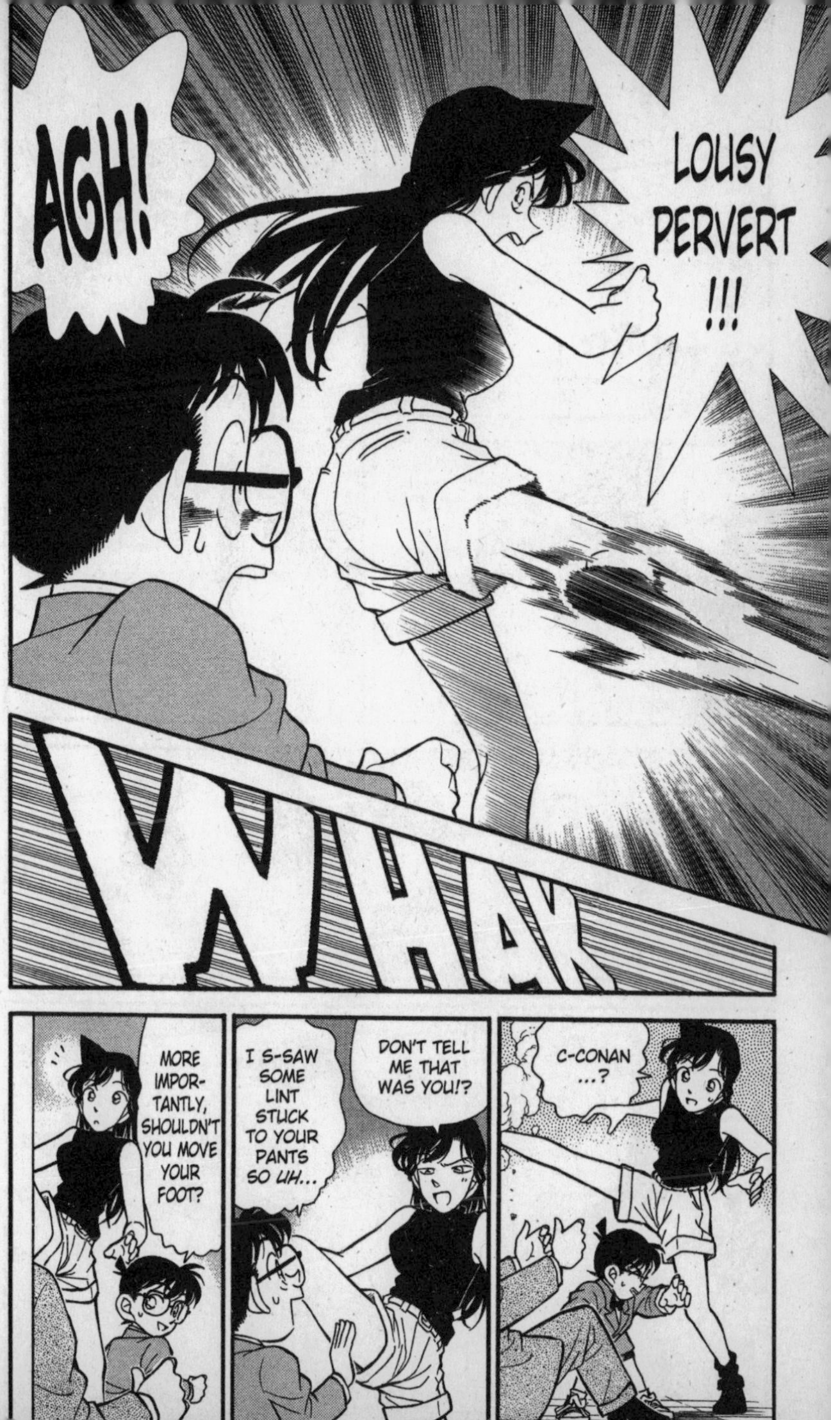
LOUSY PERVERT !!!
AGH!
WHAK
C-CONAN ...?
DON'T TELL ME THAT WAS YOU!?
I S-SAW SOME LINT STUCK TO YOUR PANTS SO UH...
MORE IMPOR-TANTLY, SHOULDN'T YOU MOVE YOUR FOOT?

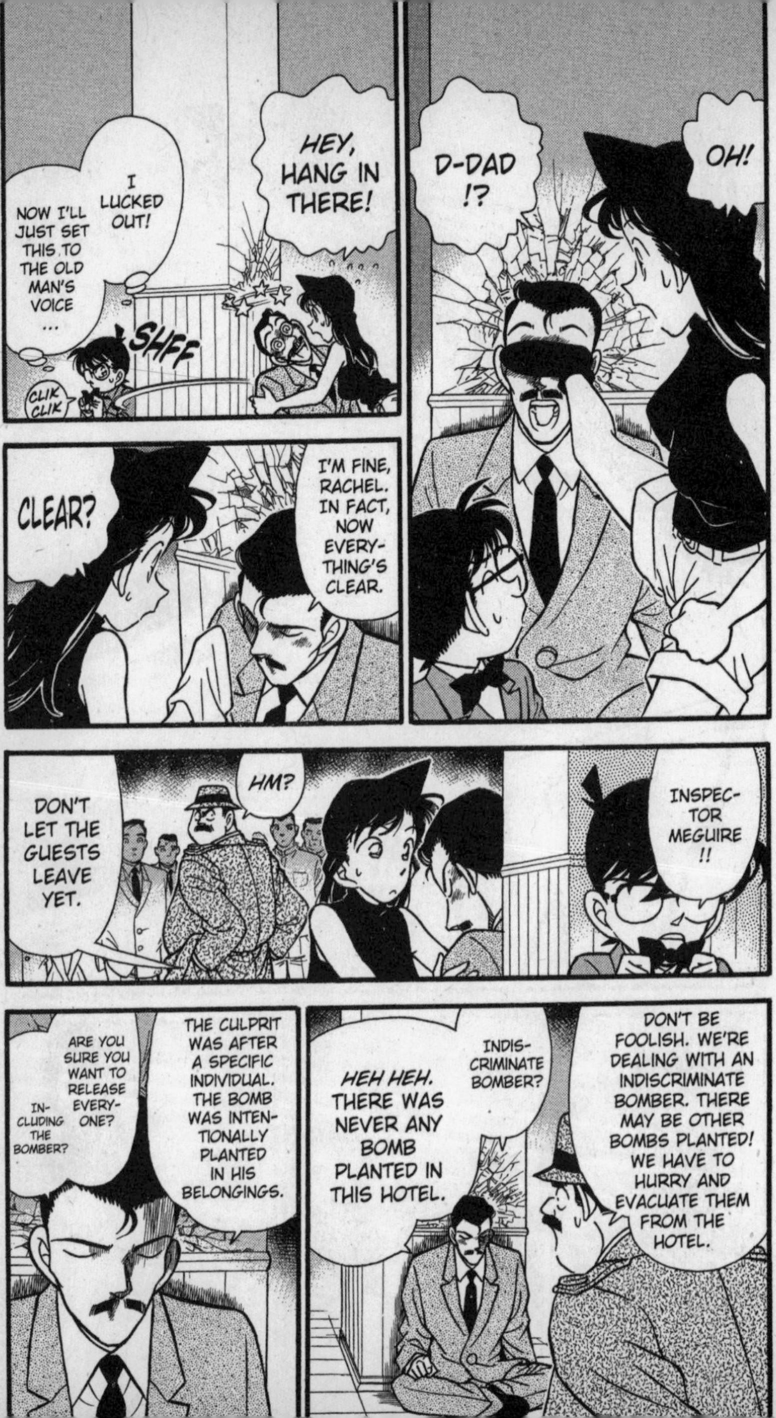
HEY, HANG IN THERE!
I LUCKED OUT!
NOW I'LL JUST SET THIS TO THE OLD MAN'S VOICE ...
SHFF
CLIK CLIK
OH!
D-DAD !?
I'M FINE, RACHEL. IN FACT, NOW EVERYTHING'S CLEAR.
CLEAR?
INSPECTOR MEGUIRE !!
DON'T LET THE GUESTS LEAVE YET.
HM?
DON'T BE FOOLISH. WE'RE DEALING WITH AN INDISCRIMINATE BOMBER. THERE MAY BE OTHER BOMBS PLANTED! WE HAVE TO HURRY AND EVACUATE THEM FROM THE HOTEL.
INDISCRIMINATE BOMBER?
HEH HEH. THERE WAS NEVER ANY BOMB PLANTED IN THIS HOTEL.
THE CULPRIT WAS AFTER A SPECIFIC INDIVIDUAL. THE BOMB WAS INTENTIONALLY PLANTED IN HIS BELONGINGS.
ARE YOU SURE YOU WANT TO RELEASE EVERYONE?
INCLUDING THE BOMBER?

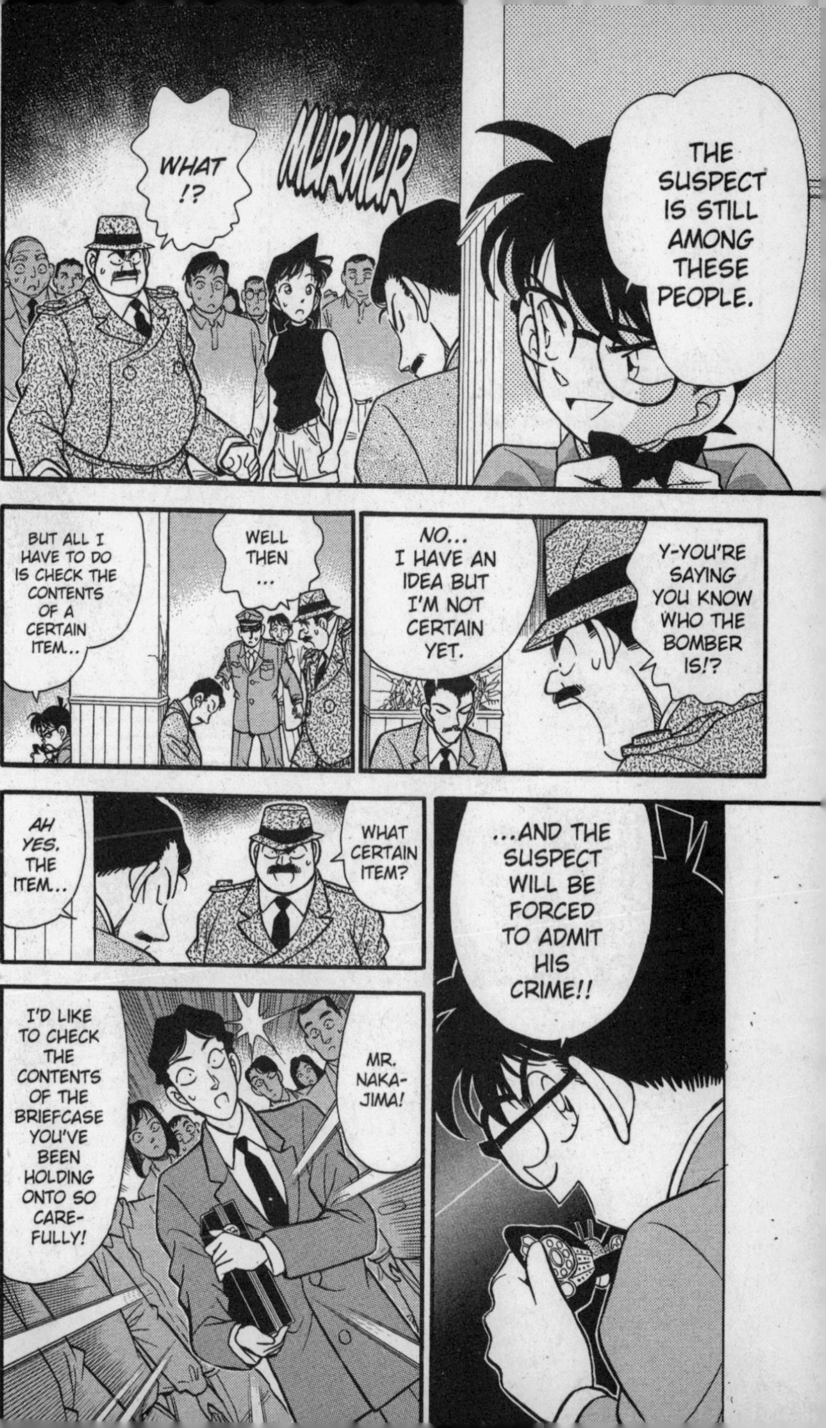
THE SUSPECT IS STILL AMONG THESE PEOPLE.
WHAT !?
MURMUR
Y-YOU'RE SAYING YOU KNOW WHO THE BOMBER IS!?
NO... I HAVE AN IDEA BUT I'M NOT CERTAIN YET.
WELL THEN ...
BUT ALL I HAVE TO DO IS CHECK THE CONTENTS OF A CERTAIN ITEM...
...AND THE SUSPECT WILL BE FORCED TO ADMIT HIS CRIME!!
WHAT CERTAIN ITEM?
AH YES. THE ITEM...
MR. NAKAJIMA!
I'D LIKE TO CHECK THE CONTENTS OF THE BRIEFCASE YOU'VE BEEN HOLDING ONTO SO CAREFULLY!

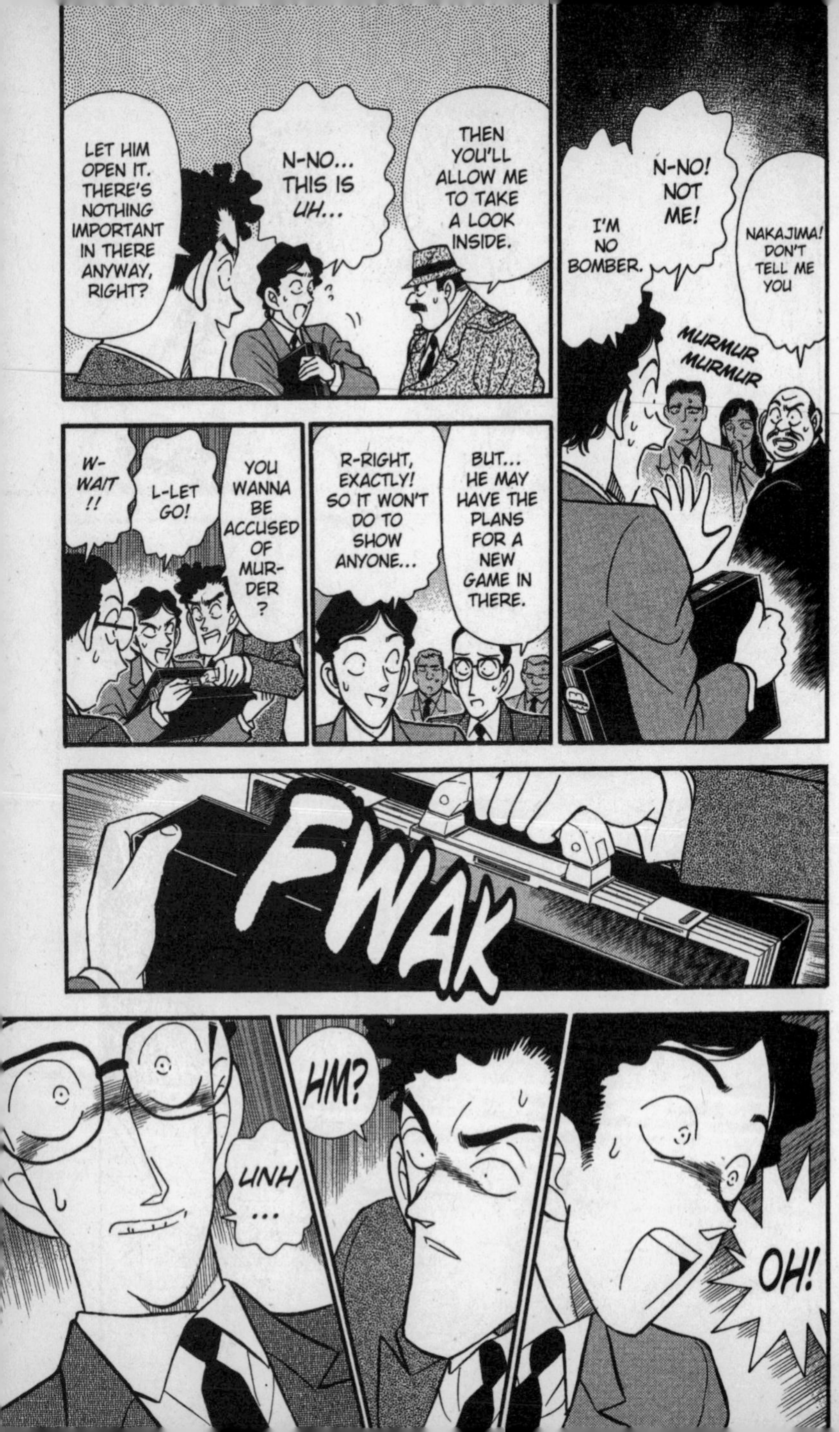

NAKAJIMA! DON'T TELL ME YOU
MURMUR MURMUR
N-NO! NOT ME!
I'M NO BOMBER.
THEN YOU'LL ALLOW ME TO TAKE A LOOK INSIDE.
N-NO... THIS IS UH...
LET HIM OPEN IT. THERE'S NOTHING IMPORTANT IN THERE ANYWAY, RIGHT?
BUT... HE MAY HAVE THE PLANS FOR A NEW GAME IN THERE.
R-RIGHT, EXACTLY! SO IT WON'T DO TO SHOW ANYONE...
YOU WANNA BE ACCUSED OF MUR-DER?
L-LET GO!
W-WAIT !!
FWAK
OH!
HM?
UNH ...

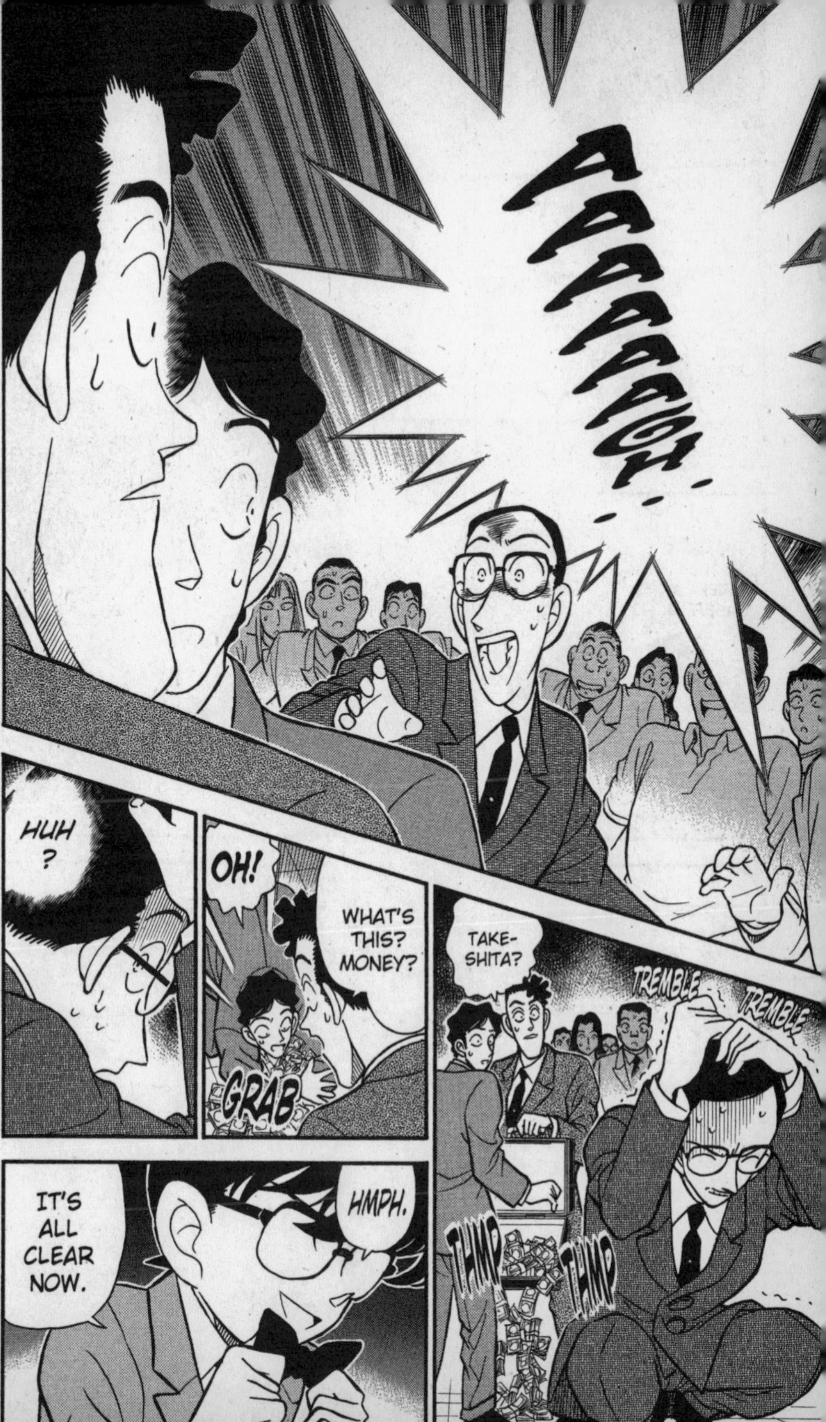

AAAAAAGH...!
TAKE-SHITA?
TREMBLE
TREMBLE
THMP
THMP
OH!
WHAT'S THIS? MONEY?
GRAB
HUH?
HMPH.
IT'S ALL CLEAR NOW.

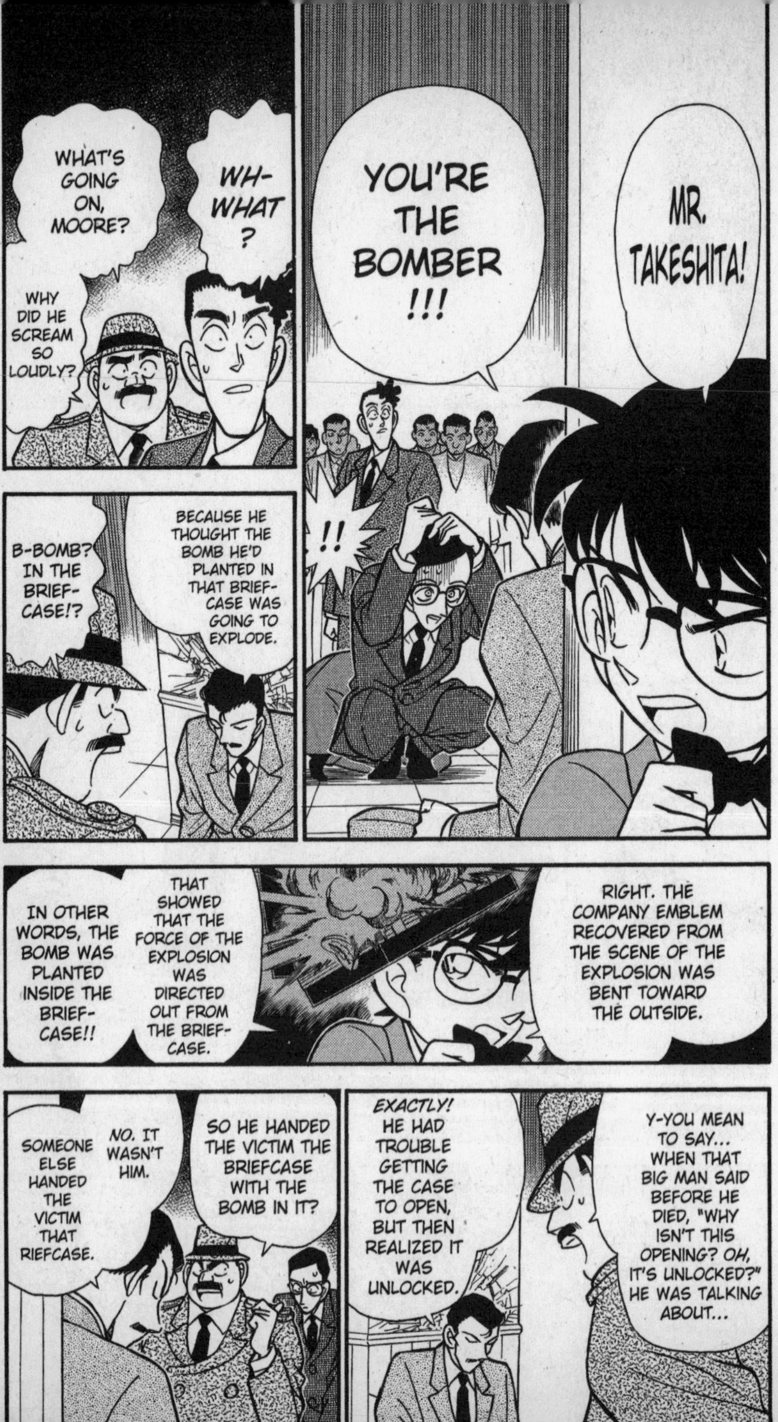
WH-WHAT?
WHAT'S GOING ON, MOORE?
WHY DID HE SCREAM SO LOUDLY?
MR. TAKESHITA!
YOU'RE THE BOMBER!!!
!!
B-BOMB? IN THE BRIEF-CASE!?
BECAUSE HE THOUGHT THE BOMB HE'D PLANTED IN THAT BRIEF-CASE WAS GOING TO EXPLODE.
RIGHT. THE COMPANY EMBLEM RECOVERED FROM THE SCENE OF THE EXPLOSION WAS BENT TOWARD THE OUTSIDE.
THAT SHOWED THAT THE FORCE OF THE EXPLOSION WAS DIRECTED OUT FROM THE BRIEF-CASE.
IN OTHER WORDS, THE BOMB WAS PLANTED INSIDE THE BRIEF-CASE!!
SO HE HANDED THE VICTIM THE BRIEFCASE WITH THE BOMB IN IT?
NO. IT WASN'T HIM.
SOMEONE ELSE HANDED THE VICTIM THAT RIEFCASE.
Y-YOU MEAN TO SAY... WHEN THAT BIG MAN SAID BEFORE HE DIED, "WHY ISN'T THIS OPENING? OH, IT'S UNLOCKED?" HE WAS TALKING ABOUT...
EXACTLY! HE HAD TROUBLE GETTING THE CASE TO OPEN, BUT THEN REALIZED IT WAS UNLOCKED.

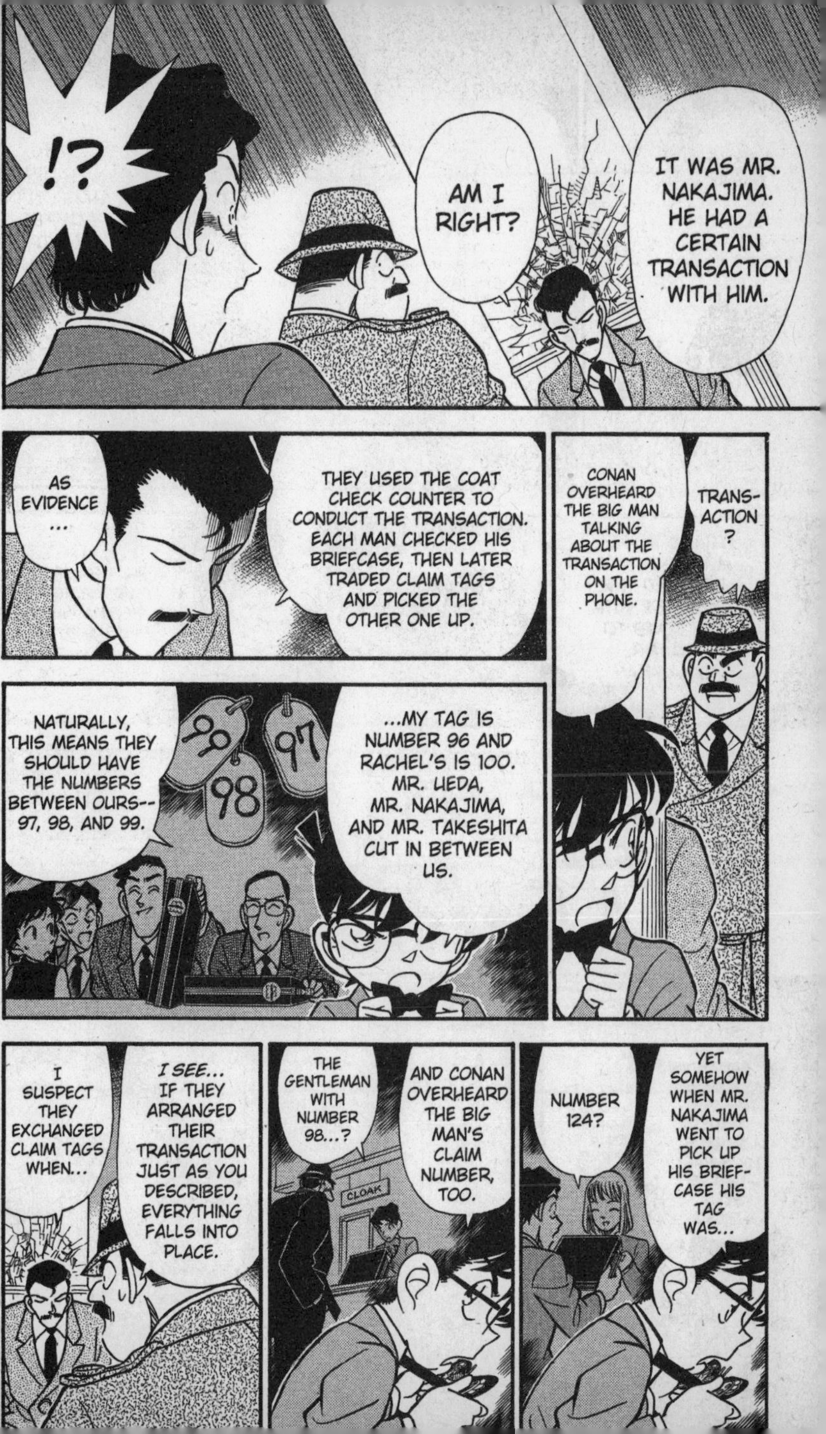
!?
IT WAS MR. NAKAJIMA. HE HAD A CERTAIN TRANSACTION WITH HIM.
AM I RIGHT?
TRANS-ACTION?
CONAN OVERHEARD THE BIG MAN TALKING ABOUT THE TRANSACTION ON THE PHONE.
AS EVIDENCE...
THEY USED THE COAT CHECK COUNTER TO CONDUCT THE TRANSACTION. EACH MAN CHECKED HIS BRIEFCASE, THEN LATER TRADED CLAIM TAGS AND PICKED THE OTHER ONE UP.
...MY TAG IS NUMBER 96 AND RACHEL'S IS 100. MR. UEDA, MR. NAKAJIMA, AND MR. TAKESHITA CUT IN BETWEEN US.
99
97
98
NATURALLY, THIS MEANS THEY SHOULD HAVE THE NUMBERS BETWEEN OURS-- 97, 98, AND 99.
YET SOMEHOW WHEN MR. NAKAJIMA WENT TO PICK UP HIS BRIEF-CASE HIS TAG WAS...
NUMBER 124?
AND CONAN OVERHEARD THE BIG MAN'S CLAIM NUMBER, TOO.
THE GENTLEMAN WITH NUMBER 98...?
CLOAK
I SEE... IF THEY ARRANGED THEIR TRANSACTION JUST AS YOU DESCRIBED, EVERYTHING FALLS INTO PLACE.
I SUSPECT THEY EXCHANGED CLAIM TAGS WHEN...

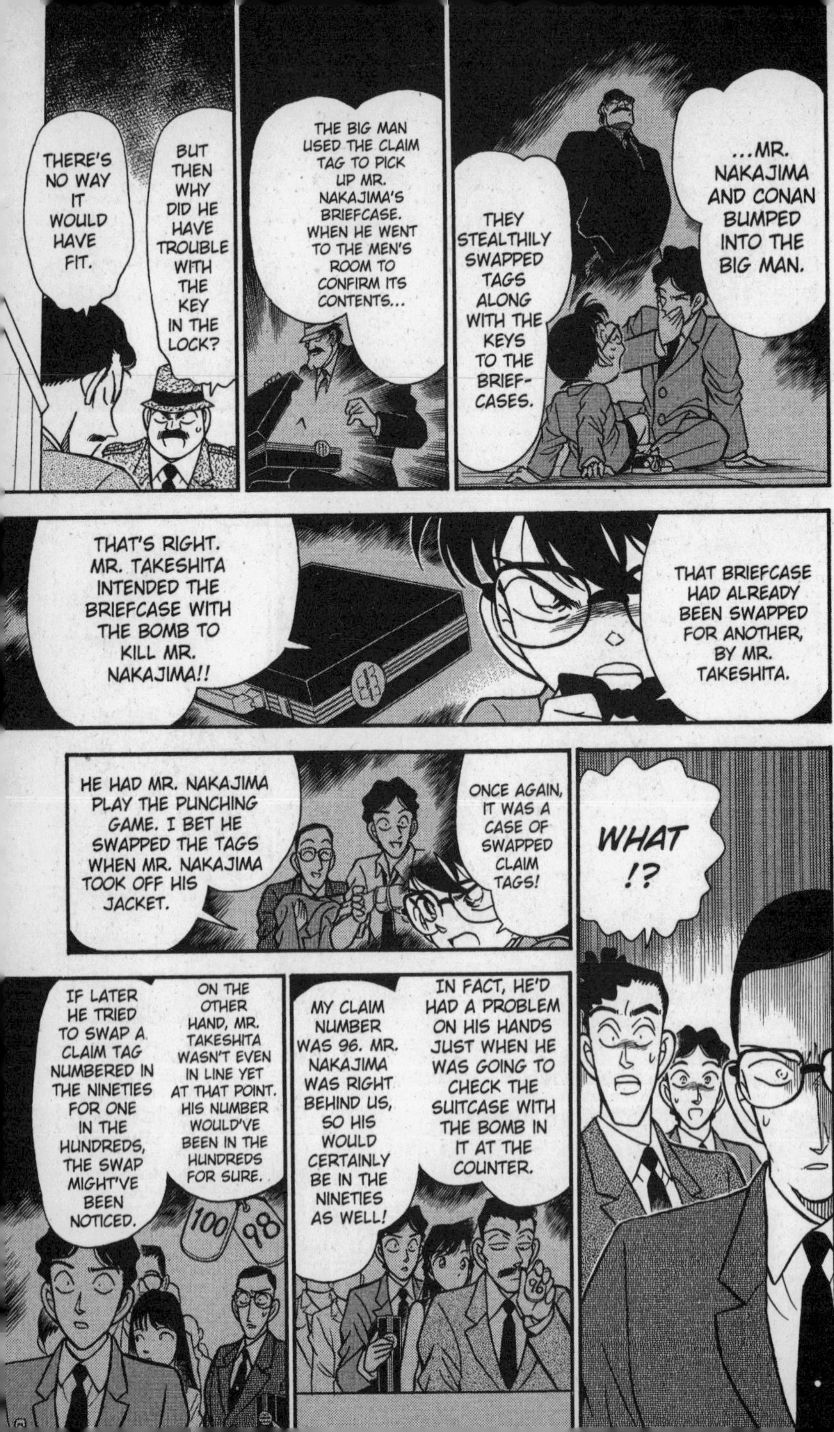
...MR. NAKAJIMA AND CONAN BUMPED INTO THE BIG MAN.
THEY STEALTHILY SWAPPED TAGS ALONG WITH THE KEYS TO THE BRIEF-CASES.
THE BIG MAN USED THE CLAIM TAG TO PICK UP MR. NAKAJIMA'S BRIEFCASE. WHEN HE WENT TO THE MEN'S ROOM TO CONFIRM ITS CONTENTS...
BUT THEN WHY DID HE HAVE TROUBLE WITH THE KEY IN THE LOCK?
THERE'S NO WAY IT WOULD HAVE FIT.
THAT BRIEFCASE HAD ALREADY BEEN SWAPPED FOR ANOTHER, BY MR. TAKESHITA.
THAT'S RIGHT. MR. TAKESHITA INTENDED THE BRIEFCASE WITH THE BOMB TO KILL MR. NAKAJIMA!!
WHAT !?
ONCE AGAIN, IT WAS A CASE OF SWAPPED CLAIM TAGS!
HE HAD MR. NAKAJIMA PLAY THE PUNCHING GAME. I BET HE SWAPPED THE TAGS WHEN MR. NAKAJIMA TOOK OFF HIS JACKET.
IN FACT, HE'D HAD A PROBLEM ON HIS HANDS JUST WHEN HE WAS GOING TO CHECK THE SUITCASE WITH THE BOMB IN IT AT THE COUNTER.
MY CLAIM NUMBER WAS 96. MR. NAKAJIMA WAS RIGHT BEHIND US, SO HIS WOULD CERTAINLY BE IN THE NINETIES AS WELL!
96
ON THE OTHER HAND, MR. TAKESHITA WASN'T EVEN IN LINE YET AT THAT POINT. HIS NUMBER WOULD'VE BEEN IN THE HUNDREDS FOR SURE.
IF LATER HE TRIED TO SWAP A CLAIM TAG NUMBERED IN THE NINETIES FOR ONE IN THE HUNDREDS, THE SWAP MIGHT'VE BEEN NOTICED.
100
98

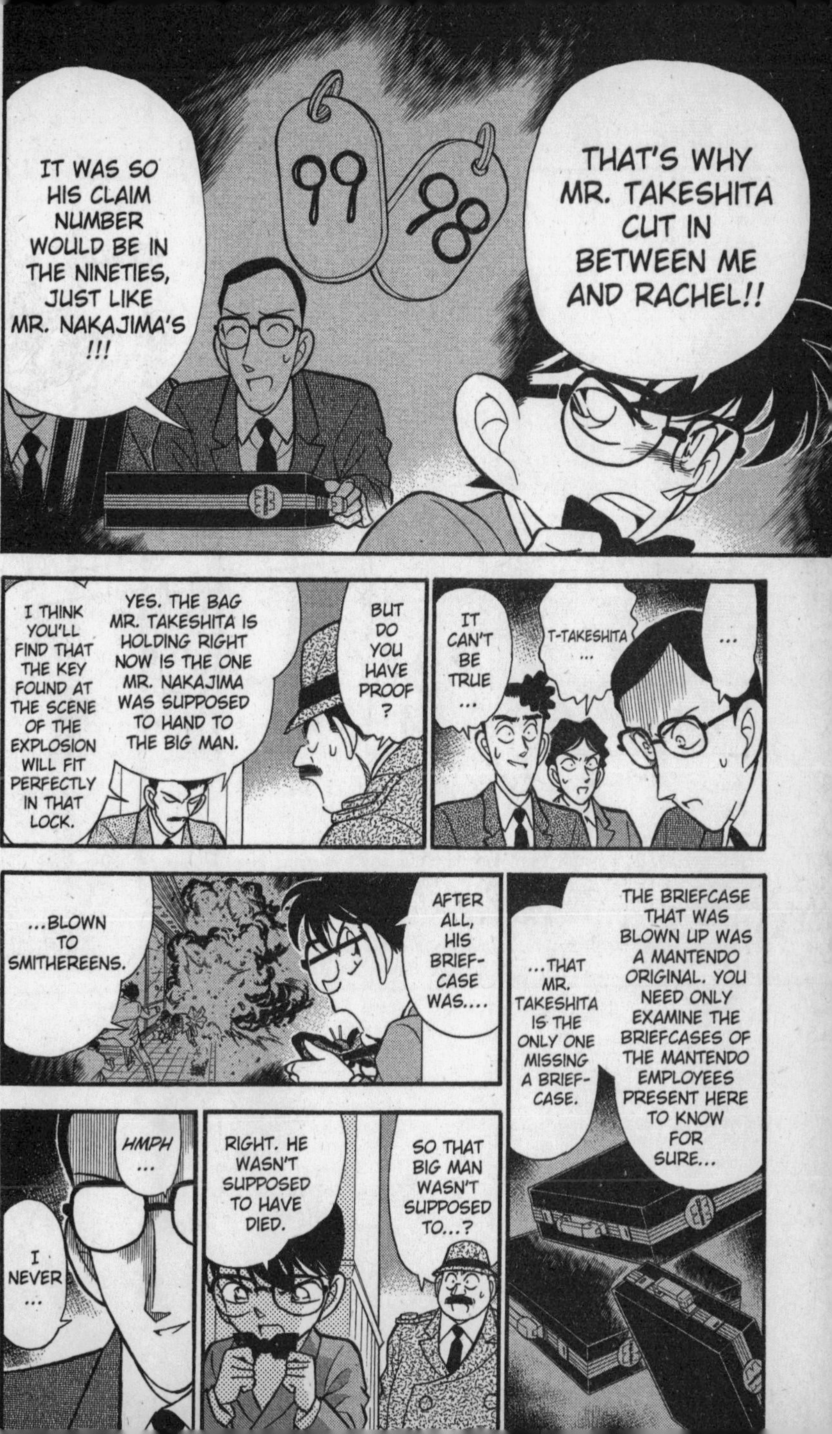

THAT'S WHY MR. TAKESHITA CUT IN BETWEEN ME AND RACHEL!!
IT WAS SO HIS CLAIM NUMBER WOULD BE IN THE NINETIES, JUST LIKE MR. NAKAJIMA'S !!!
99
98
...
T-TAKESHITA ...
IT CAN'T BE TRUE ...
BUT DO YOU HAVE PROOF ?
YES. THE BAG MR. TAKESHITA IS HOLDING RIGHT NOW IS THE ONE MR. NAKAJIMA WAS SUPPOSED TO HAND TO THE BIG MAN.
I THINK YOU'LL FIND THAT THE KEY FOUND AT THE SCENE OF THE EXPLOSION WILL FIT PERFECTLY IN THAT LOCK.
THE BRIEFCASE THAT WAS BLOWN UP WAS A MANTENDO ORIGINAL. YOU NEED ONLY EXAMINE THE BRIEFCASES OF THE MANTENDO EMPLOYEES PRESENT HERE TO KNOW FOR SURE...
...THAT MR. TAKESHITA IS THE ONLY ONE MISSING A BRIEF-CASE.
AFTER ALL, HIS BRIEF-CASE WAS....
...BLOWN TO SMITHEREENS.
SO THAT BIG MAN WASN'T SUPPOSED TO...?
RIGHT. HE WASN'T SUPPOSED TO HAVE DIED.
HMPH ...
I NEVER ...

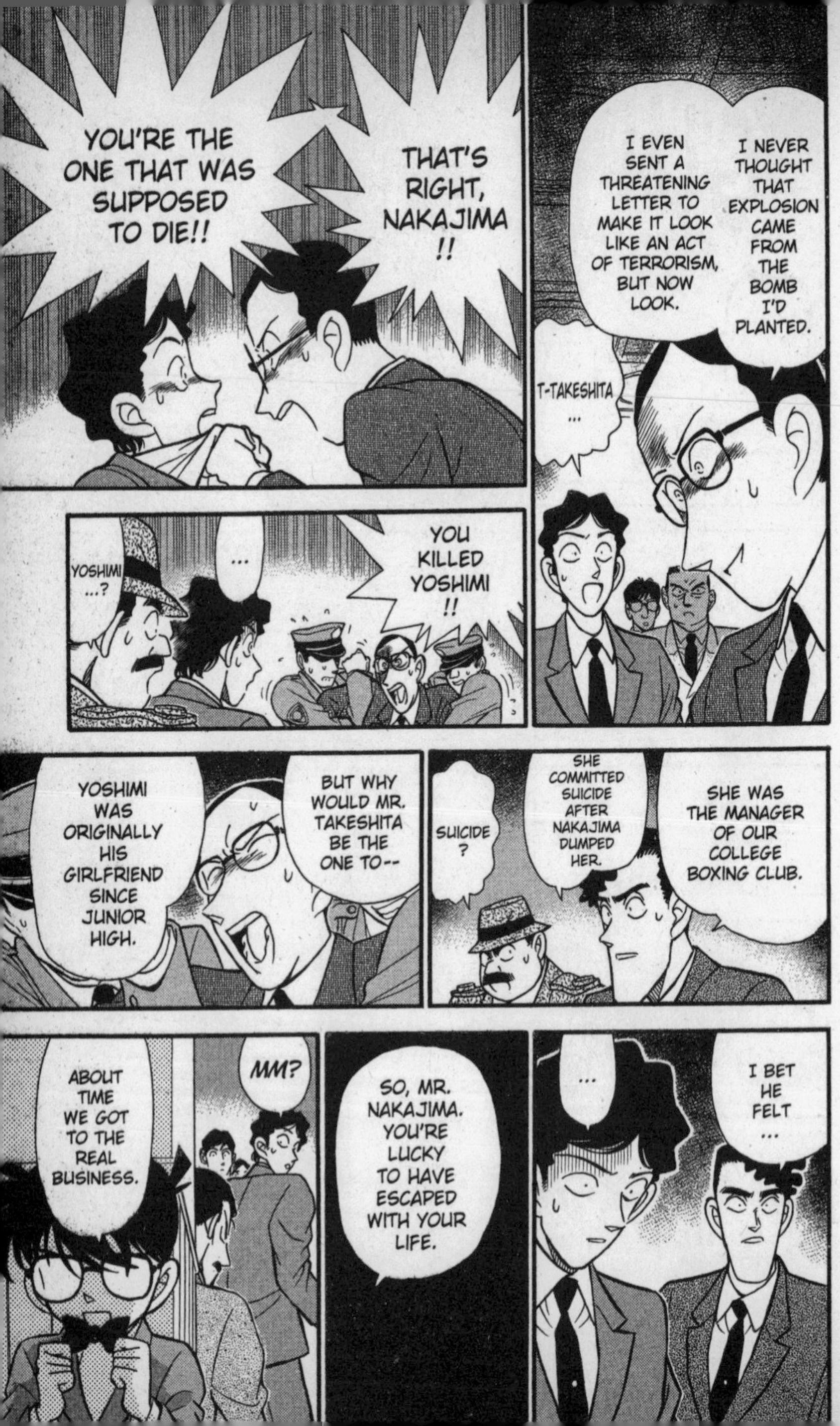
THAT'S RIGHT, NAKAJIMA!!
YOU'RE THE ONE THAT WAS SUPPOSED TO DIE!!
I NEVER THOUGHT THAT EXPLOSION CAME FROM THE BOMB I'D PLANTED.
I EVEN SENT A THREATENING LETTER TO MAKE IT LOOK LIKE AN ACT OF TERRORISM, BUT NOW LOOK.
T-TAKESHITA...
YOU KILLED YOSHIMI!!
...
YOSHIMI...?
BUT WHY WOULD MR. TAKESHITA BE THE ONE TO--
YOSHIMI WAS ORIGINALLY HIS GIRLFRIEND SINCE JUNIOR HIGH.
SHE WAS THE MANAGER OF OUR COLLEGE BOXING CLUB.
SHE COMMITTED SUICIDE AFTER NAKAJIMA DUMPED HER.
SUICIDE?
MM?
ABOUT TIME WE GOT TO THE REAL BUSINESS.
SO, MR. NAKAJIMA. YOU'RE LUCKY TO HAVE ESCAPED WITH YOUR LIFE.
I BET HE FELT...
...

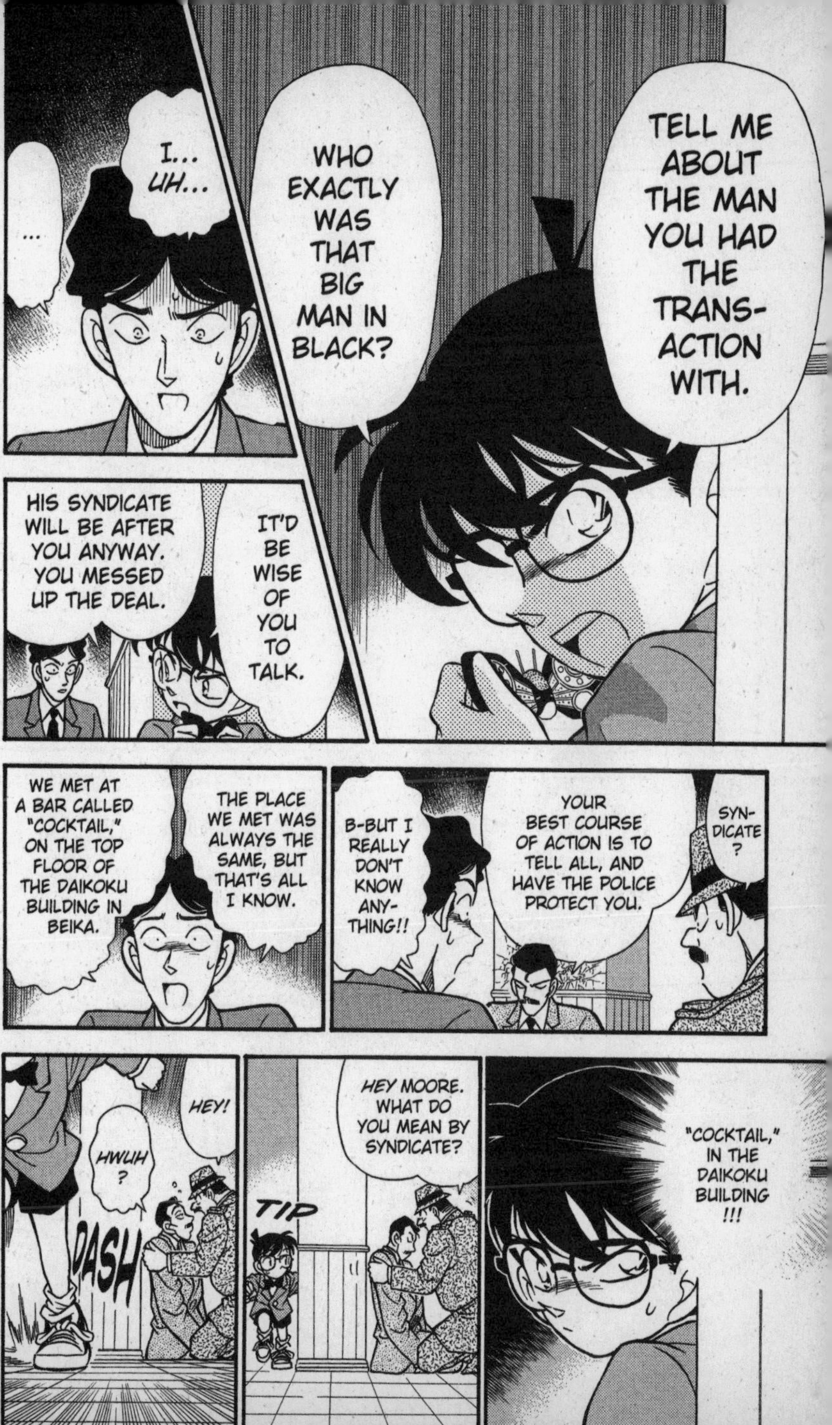
TELL ME ABOUT THE MAN YOU HAD THE TRANS-ACTION WITH.
WHO EXACTLY WAS THAT BIG MAN IN BLACK?
I... UH...
...
IT'D BE WISE OF YOU TO TALK.
HIS SYNDICATE WILL BE AFTER YOU ANYWAY. YOU MESSED UP THE DEAL.
SYN-DICATE ?
YOUR BEST COURSE OF ACTION IS TO TELL ALL, AND HAVE THE POLICE PROTECT YOU.
B-BUT I REALLY DON'T KNOW ANY-THING!!
THE PLACE WE MET WAS ALWAYS THE SAME, BUT THAT'S ALL I KNOW.
WE MET AT A BAR CALLED "COCKTAIL," ON THE TOP FLOOR OF THE DAIKOKU BUILDING IN BEIKA.
"COCKTAIL," IN THE DAIKOKU BUILDING !!!
HEY MOORE. WHAT DO YOU MEAN BY SYNDICATE?
TIP
HEY!
HWUH ?
DASH

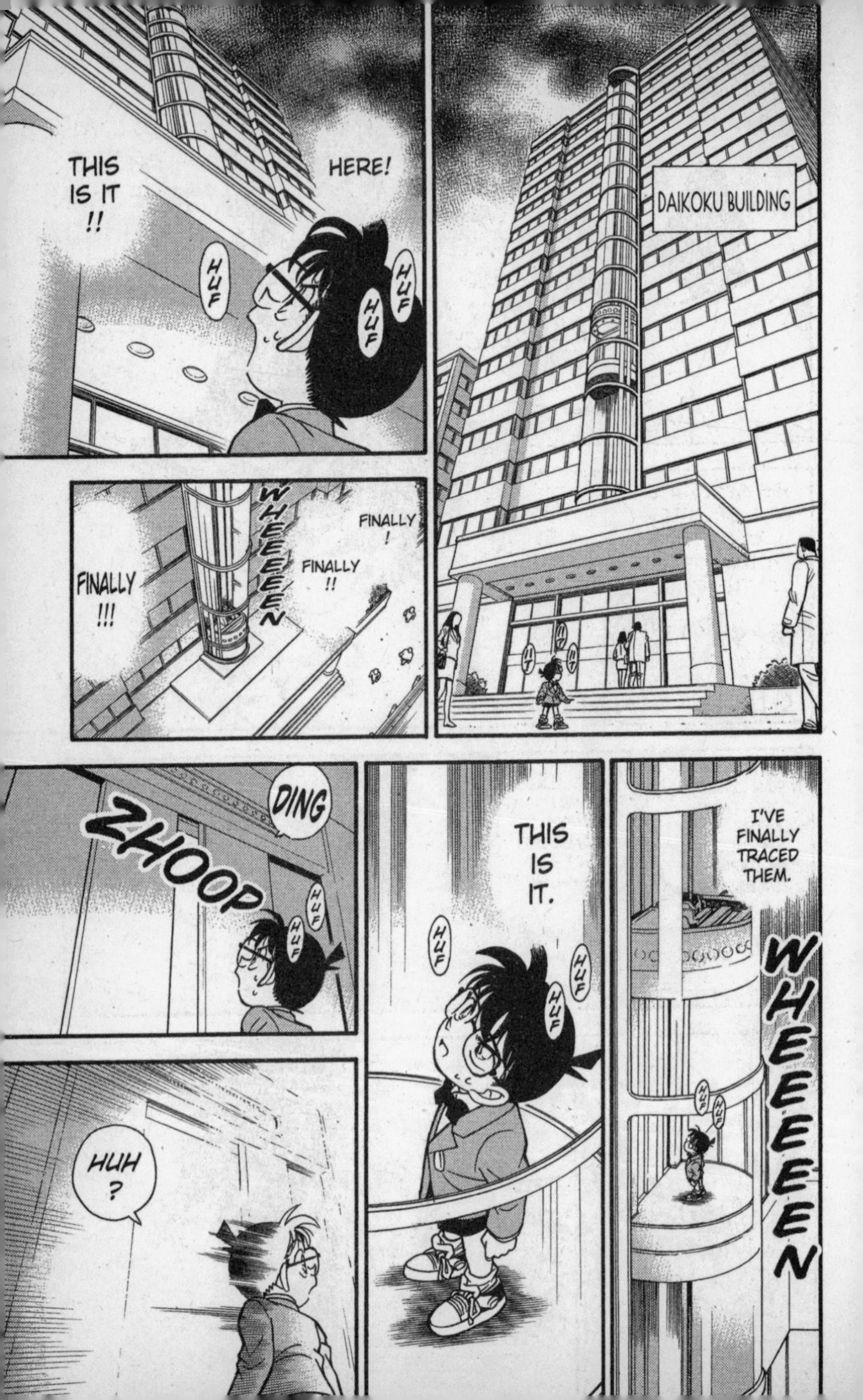
THIS IS IT !!
HERE!
HUF
HUF
HUF
FINALLY !
FINALLY !!
FINALLY !!!
WHEEEEEEN
DAIKOKU BUILDING
DING
ZHOOP
HUF
HUF
HUH ?
THIS IS IT.
HUF
HUF
HUF
I'VE FINALLY TRACED THEM.
HUF
HUF
WHEEEEEEN

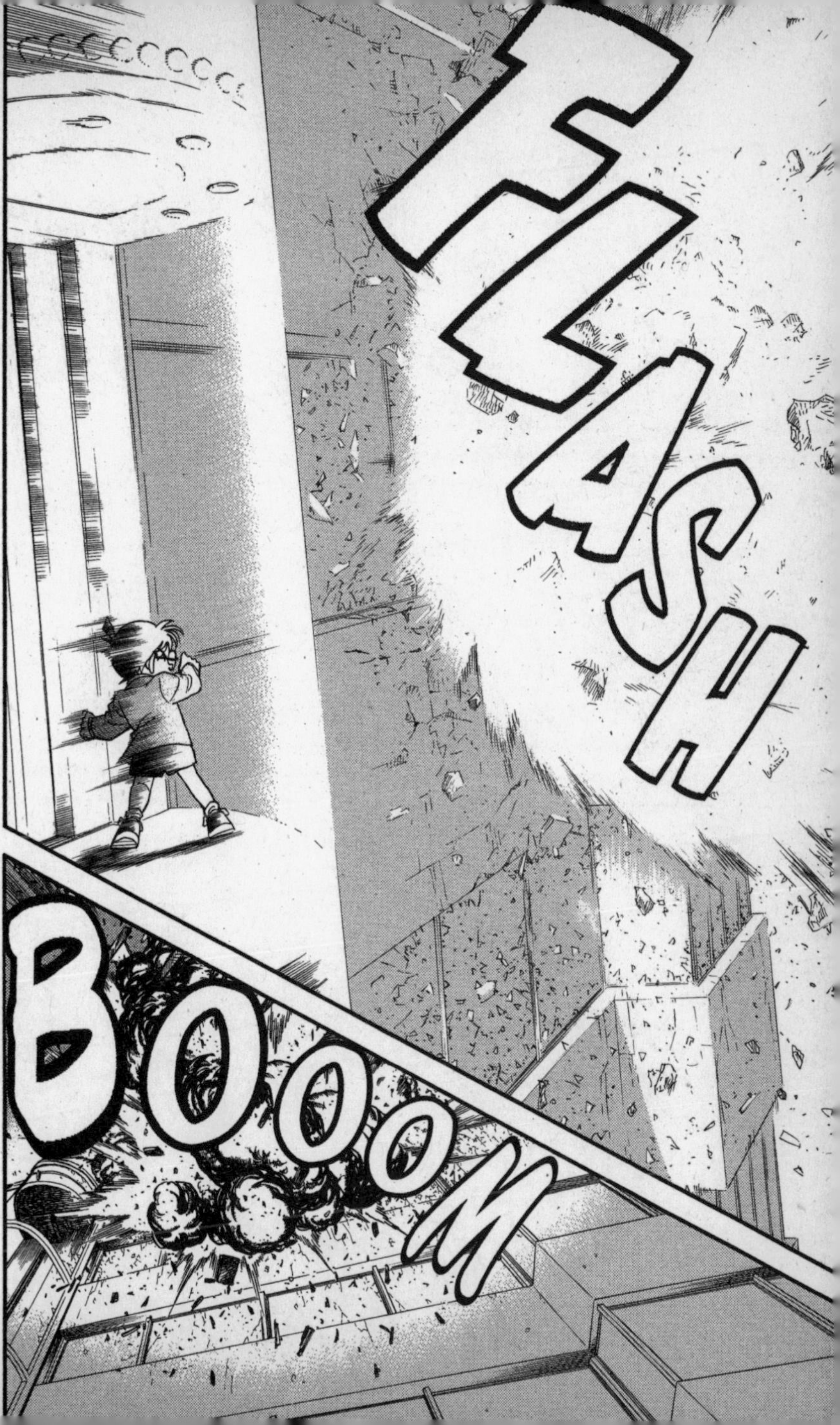
FLASH
BOOOOM

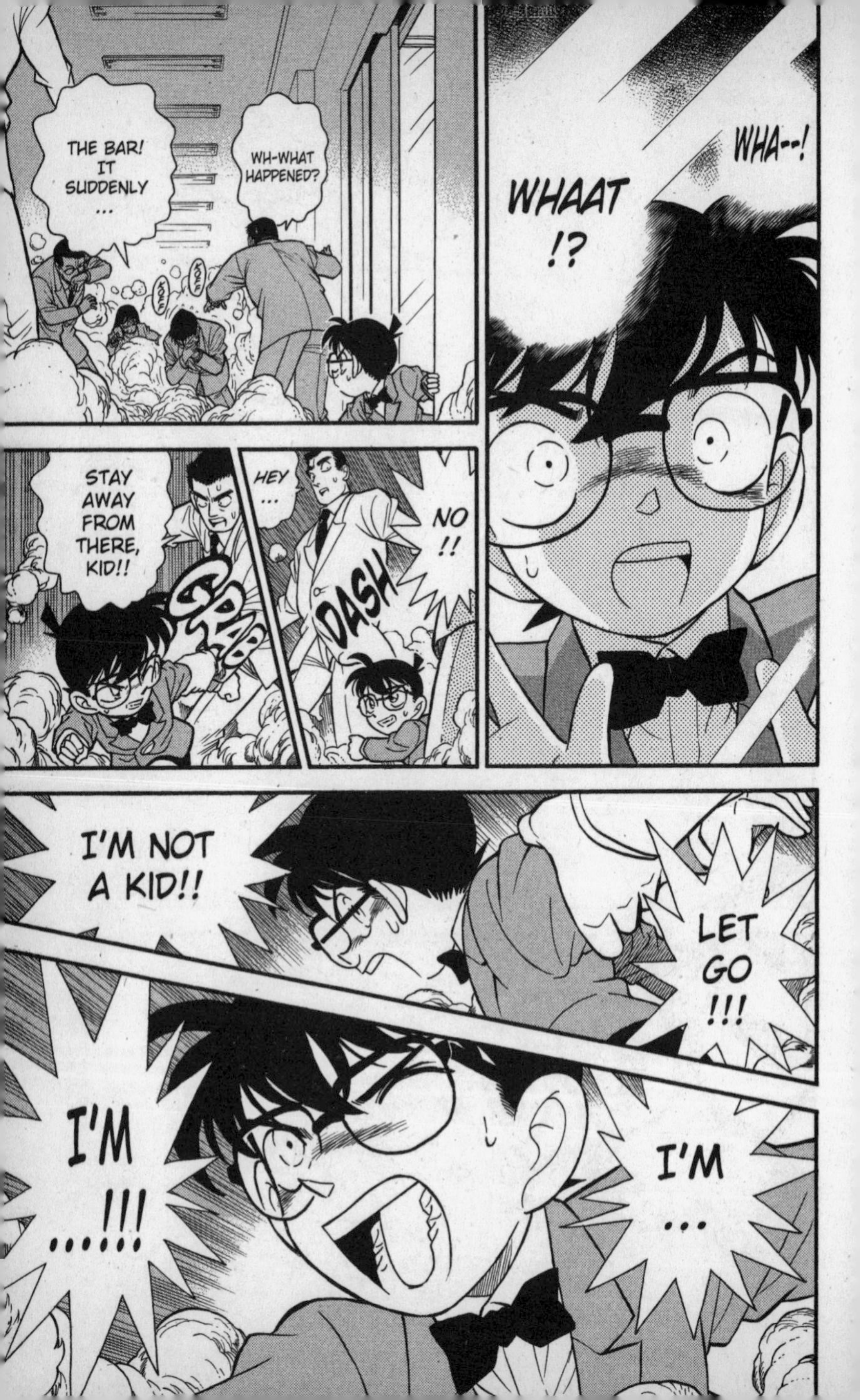

THE BAR! IT SUDDENLY ...
WH-WHAT HAPPENED?
STAY AWAY FROM THERE, KID!!
GRAB
HEY ...
DASH
NO !!
WHA--!
WHAAT !?
I'M NOT A KID!!
LET GO !!!
I'M ...
I'M ...!!!

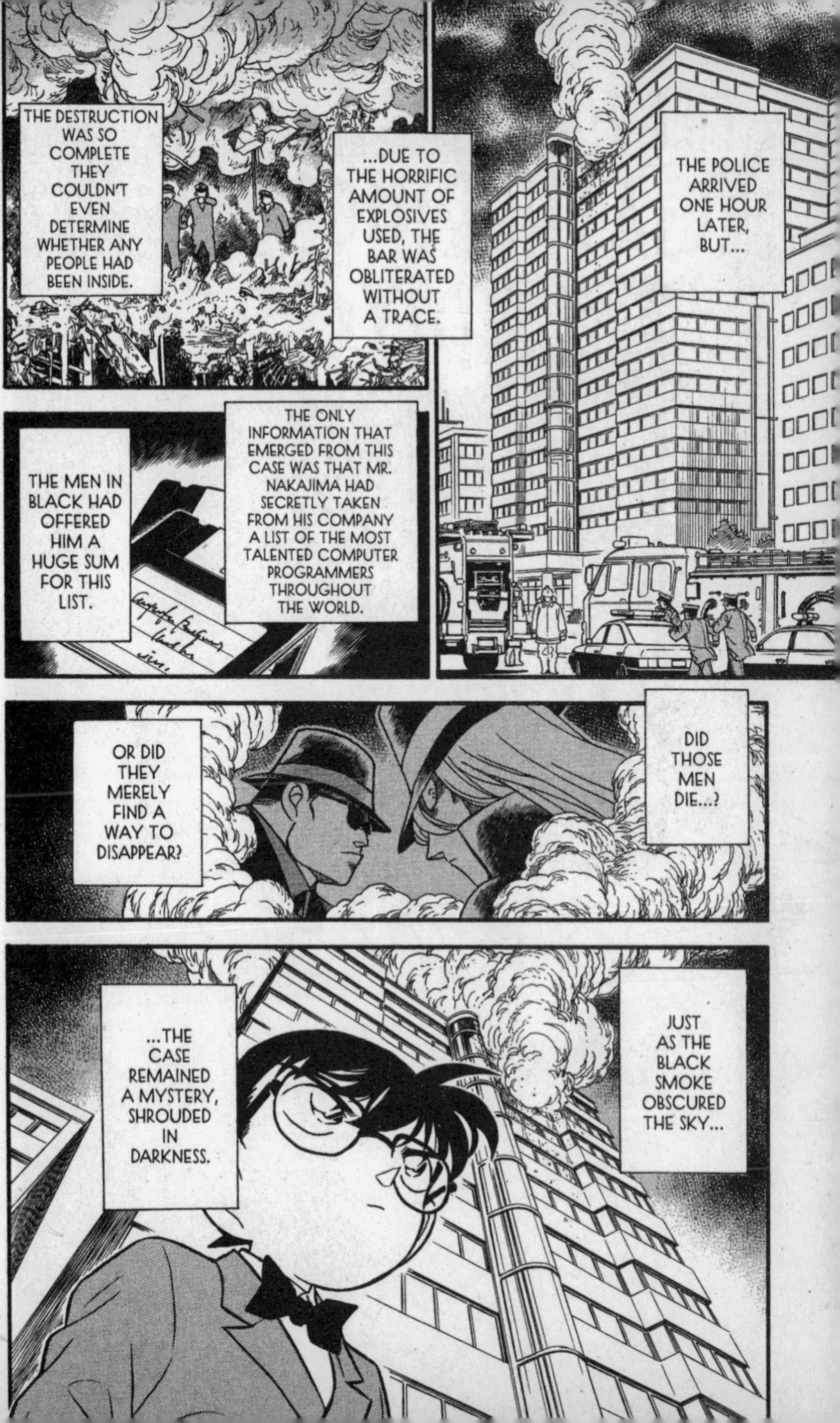
THE POLICE ARRIVED ONE HOUR LATER, BUT...
...DUE TO THE HORRIFIC AMOUNT OF EXPLOSIVES USED, THE BAR WAS OBLITERATED WITHOUT A TRACE.
THE DESTRUCTION WAS SO COMPLETE THEY COULDN'T EVEN DETERMINE WHETHER ANY PEOPLE HAD BEEN INSIDE.
THE ONLY INFORMATION THAT EMERGED FROM THIS CASE WAS THAT MR. NAKAJIMA HAD SECRETLY TAKEN FROM HIS COMPANY A LIST OF THE MOST TALENTED COMPUTER PROGRAMMERS THROUGHOUT THE WORLD.
THE MEN IN BLACK HAD OFFERED HIM A HUGE SUM FOR THIS LIST.
DID THOSE MEN DIE...?
OR DID THEY MERELY FIND A WAY TO DISAPPEAR?
JUST AS THE BLACK SMOKE OBSCURED THE SKY...
...THE CASE REMAINED A MYSTERY, SHROUDED IN DARKNESS.

FILE 7: GATHERING AT MYCROFT

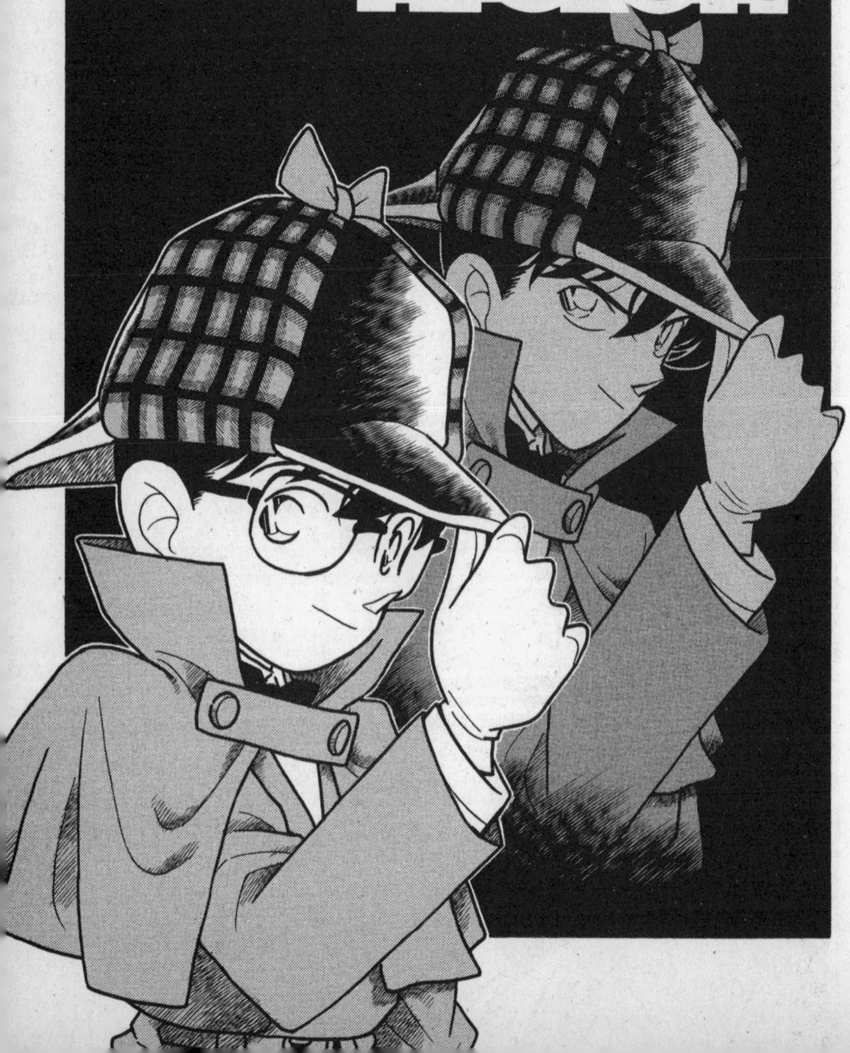

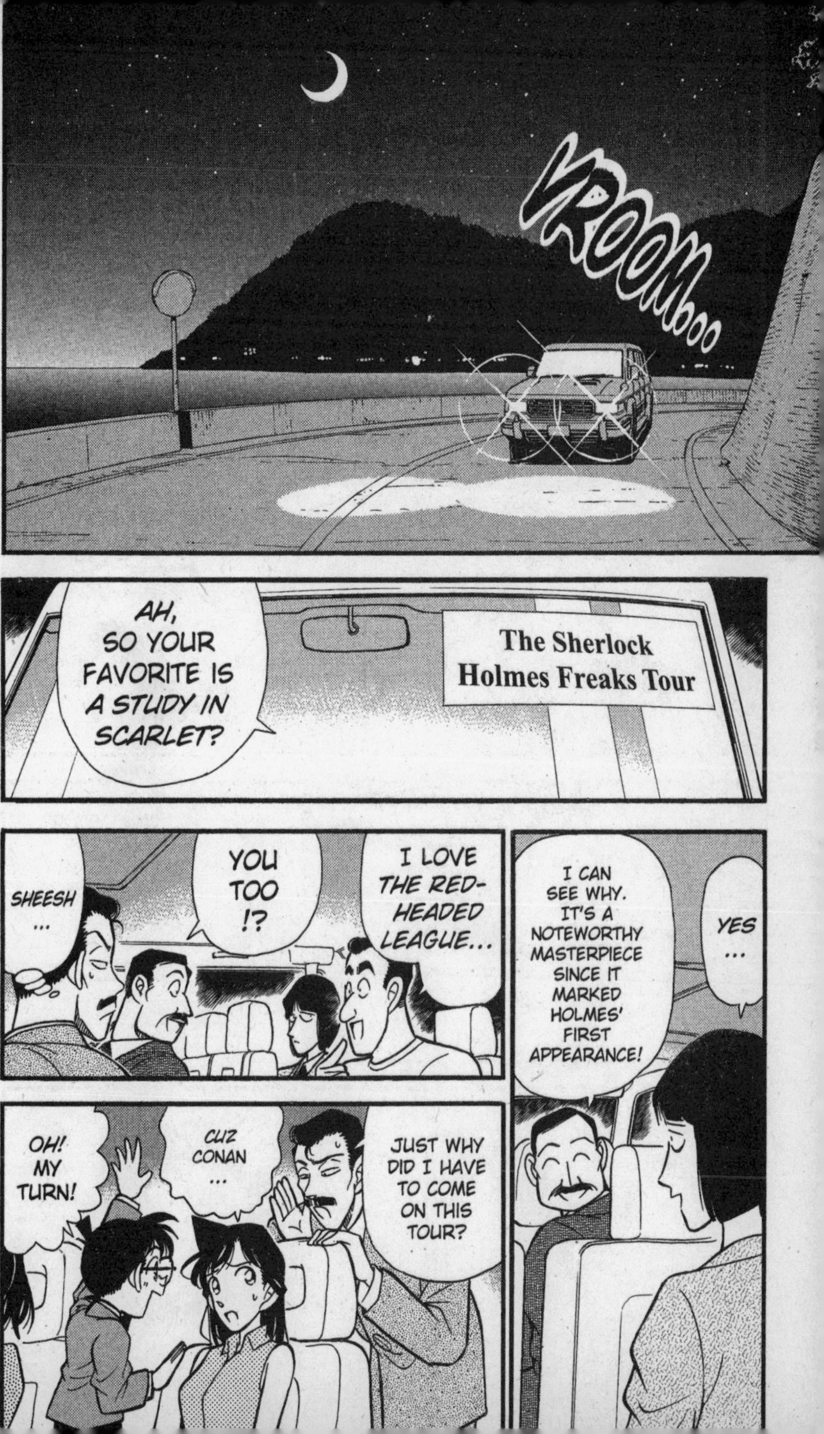
VROOMooo
The Sherlock Holmes Freaks Tour
AH, SO YOUR FAVORITE IS A STUDY IN SCARLET?
YES ...
I CAN SEE WHY. IT'S A NOTEWORTHY MASTERPIECE SINCE IT MARKED HOLMES' FIRST APPEARANCE!
I LOVE THE RED-HEADED LEAGUE...
YOU TOO !?
SHEESH ...
JUST WHY DID I HAVE TO COME ON THIS TOUR?
CUZ CONAN ...
OH! MY TURN!

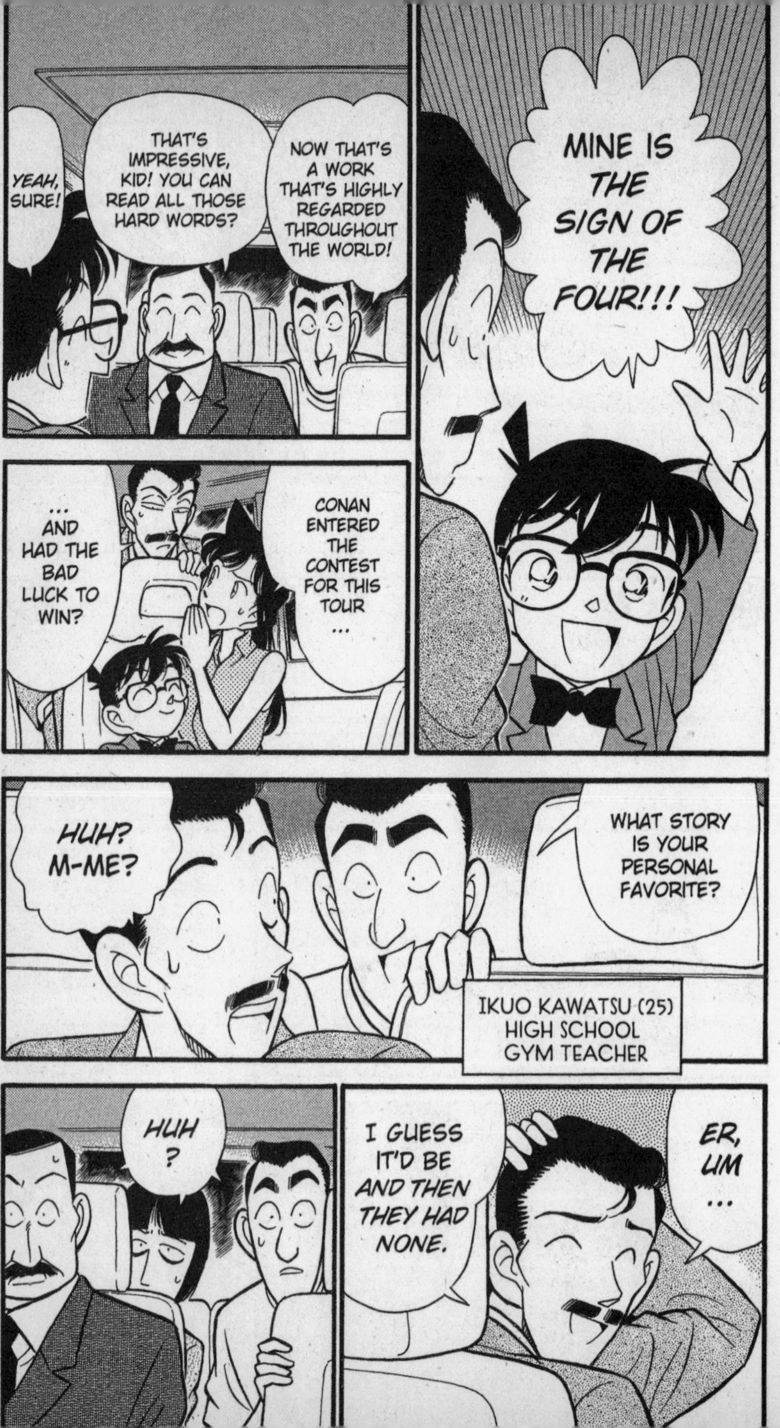
MINE IS THE SIGN OF THE FOUR!!!
NOW THAT'S A WORK THAT'S HIGHLY REGARDED THROUGHOUT THE WORLD!
THAT'S IMPRESSIVE, KID! YOU CAN READ ALL THOSE HARD WORDS?
YEAH, SURE!
CONAN ENTERED THE CONTEST FOR THIS TOUR ...
... AND HAD THE BAD LUCK TO WIN?
WHAT STORY IS YOUR PERSONAL FAVORITE?
IKUO KAWATSU (25) HIGH SCHOOL GYM TEACHER
HUH? M-ME?
ER, UM ...
I GUESS IT'D BE AND THEN THEY HAD NONE.
HUH ?

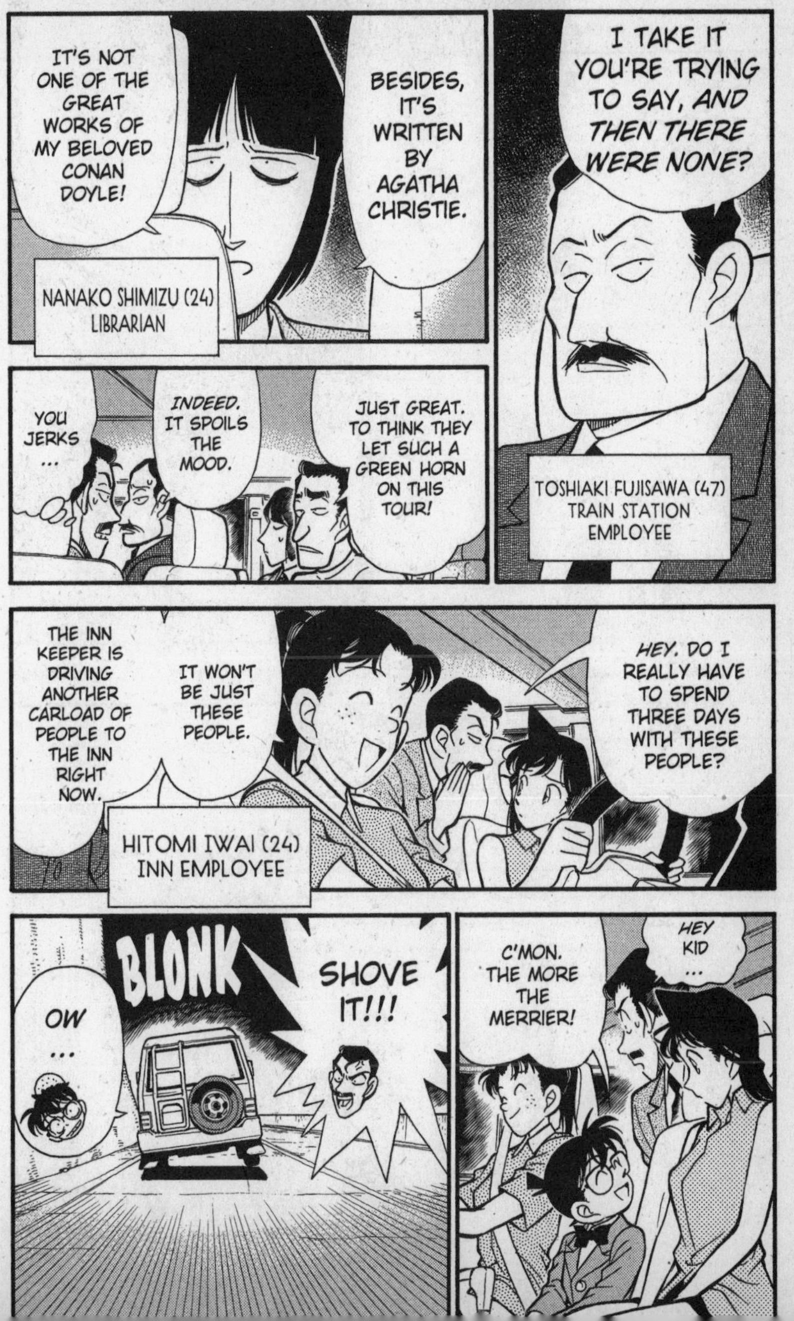
IT'S NOT ONE OF THE GREAT WORKS OF MY BELOVED CONAN DOYLE!
BESIDES, IT'S WRITTEN BY AGATHA CHRISTIE.
NANAKO SHIMIZU (24) LIBRARIAN
I TAKE IT YOU'RE TRYING TO SAY, *AND THEN THERE WERE NONE?*
TOSHIAKI FUJISAWA (47) TRAIN STATION EMPLOYEE
YOU JERKS ...
INDEED. IT SPOILS THE MOOD.
JUST GREAT. TO THINK THEY LET SUCH A GREEN HORN ON THIS TOUR!
THE INN KEEPER IS DRIVING ANOTHER CARLOAD OF PEOPLE TO THE INN RIGHT NOW.
IT WON'T BE JUST THESE PEOPLE.
HITOMI IWAI (24) INN EMPLOYEE
HEY. DO I REALLY HAVE TO SPEND THREE DAYS WITH THESE PEOPLE?
BLONK
OW ...
SHOVE IT!!!
C'MON. THE MORE THE MERRIER!
HEY KID ...

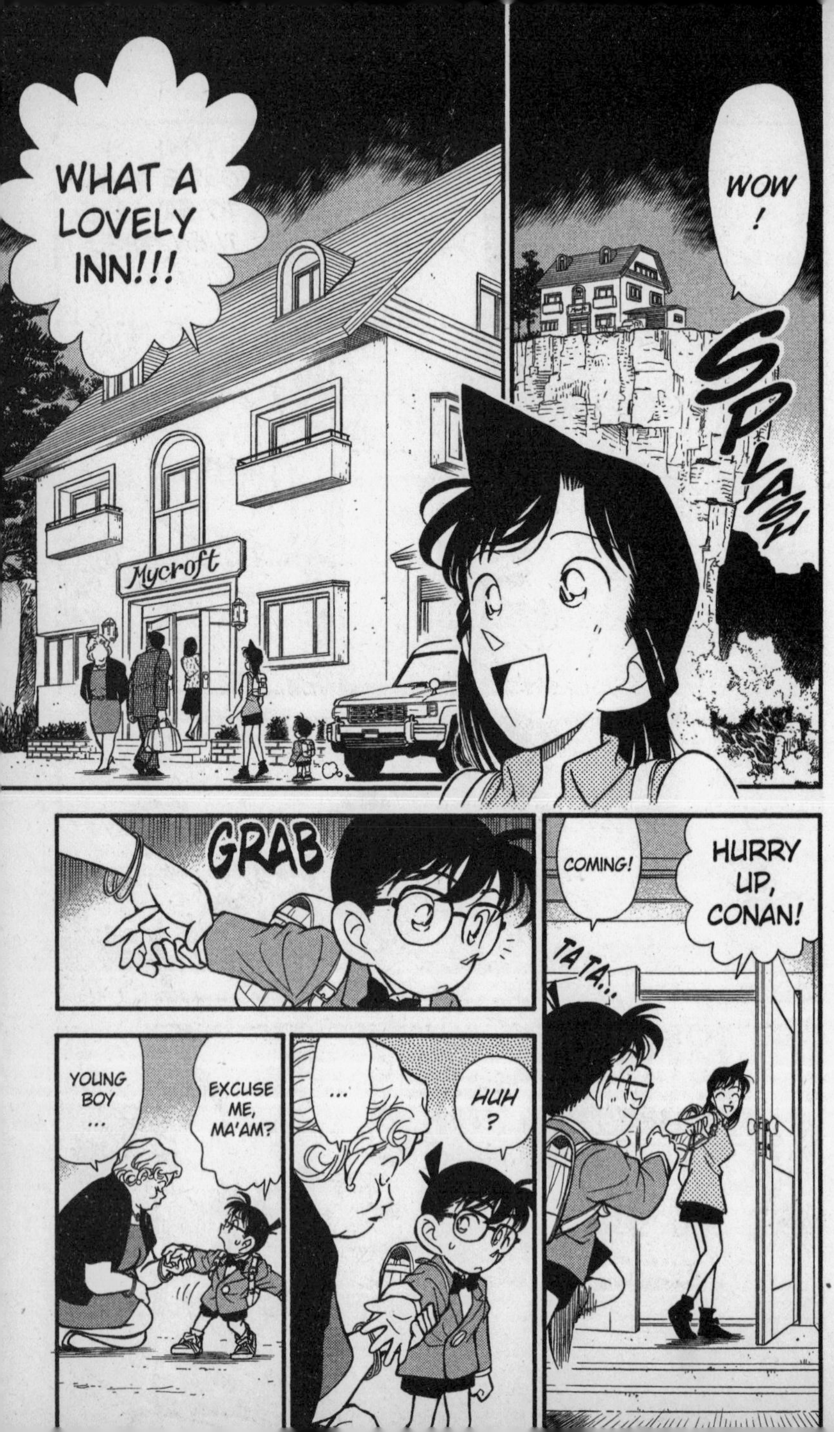
WOW!
SPLASH
WHAT A LOVELY INN!!!
Mycroft
HURRY UP, CONAN!
COMING!
TATA...
GRAB
HUH?
...
EXCUSE ME, MA'AM?
YOUNG BOY ...

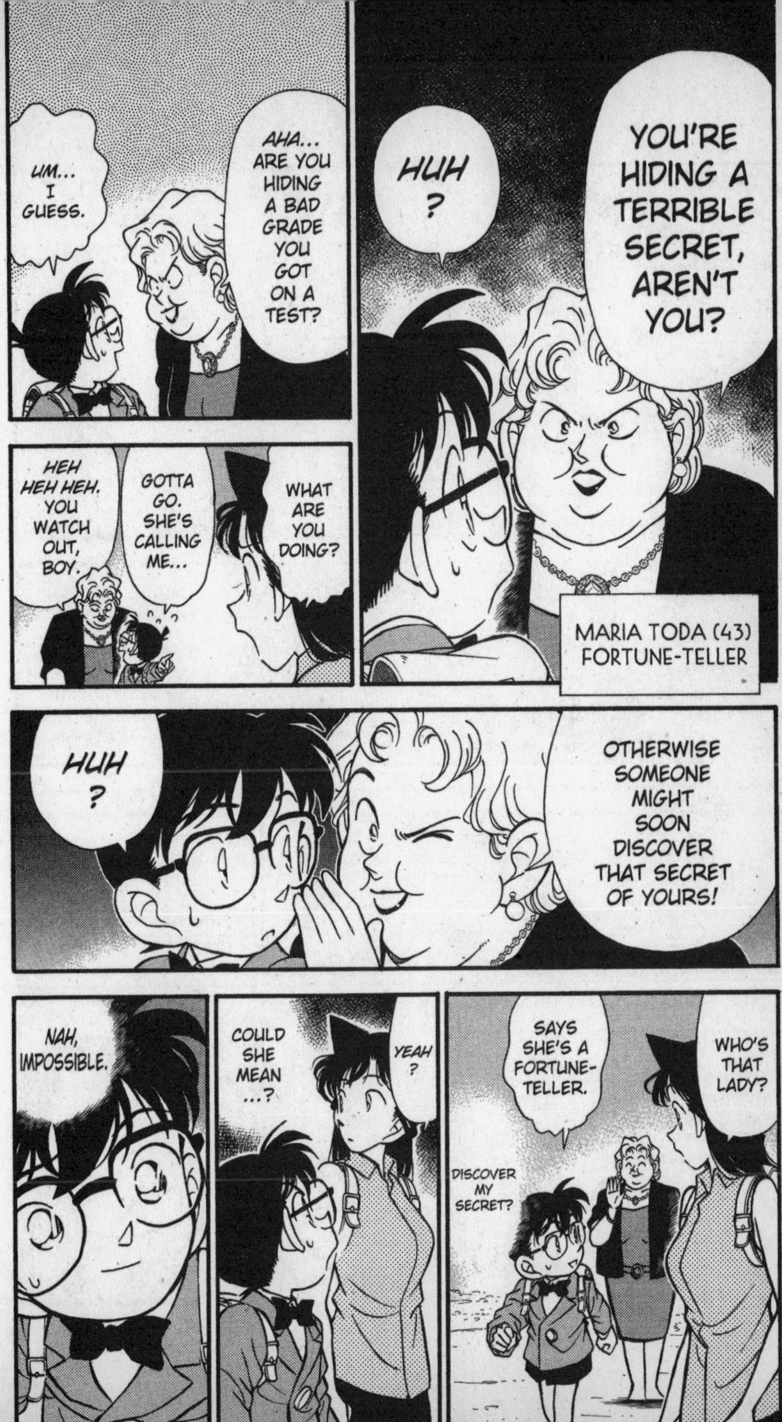
YOU'RE HIDING A TERRIBLE SECRET, AREN'T YOU?
HUH?
MARIA TODA (43) FORTUNE-TELLER
AHA... ARE YOU HIDING A BAD GRADE YOU GOT ON A TEST?
UM... I GUESS.
WHAT ARE YOU DOING?
GOTTA GO. SHE'S CALLING ME...
HEH HEH HEH. YOU WATCH OUT, BOY.
OTHERWISE SOMEONE MIGHT SOON DISCOVER THAT SECRET OF YOURS!
HUH?
WHO'S THAT LADY?
SAYS SHE'S A FORTUNE-TELLER.
DISCOVER MY SECRET?
YEAH?
COULD SHE MEAN ...?
NAH, IMPOSSIBLE.

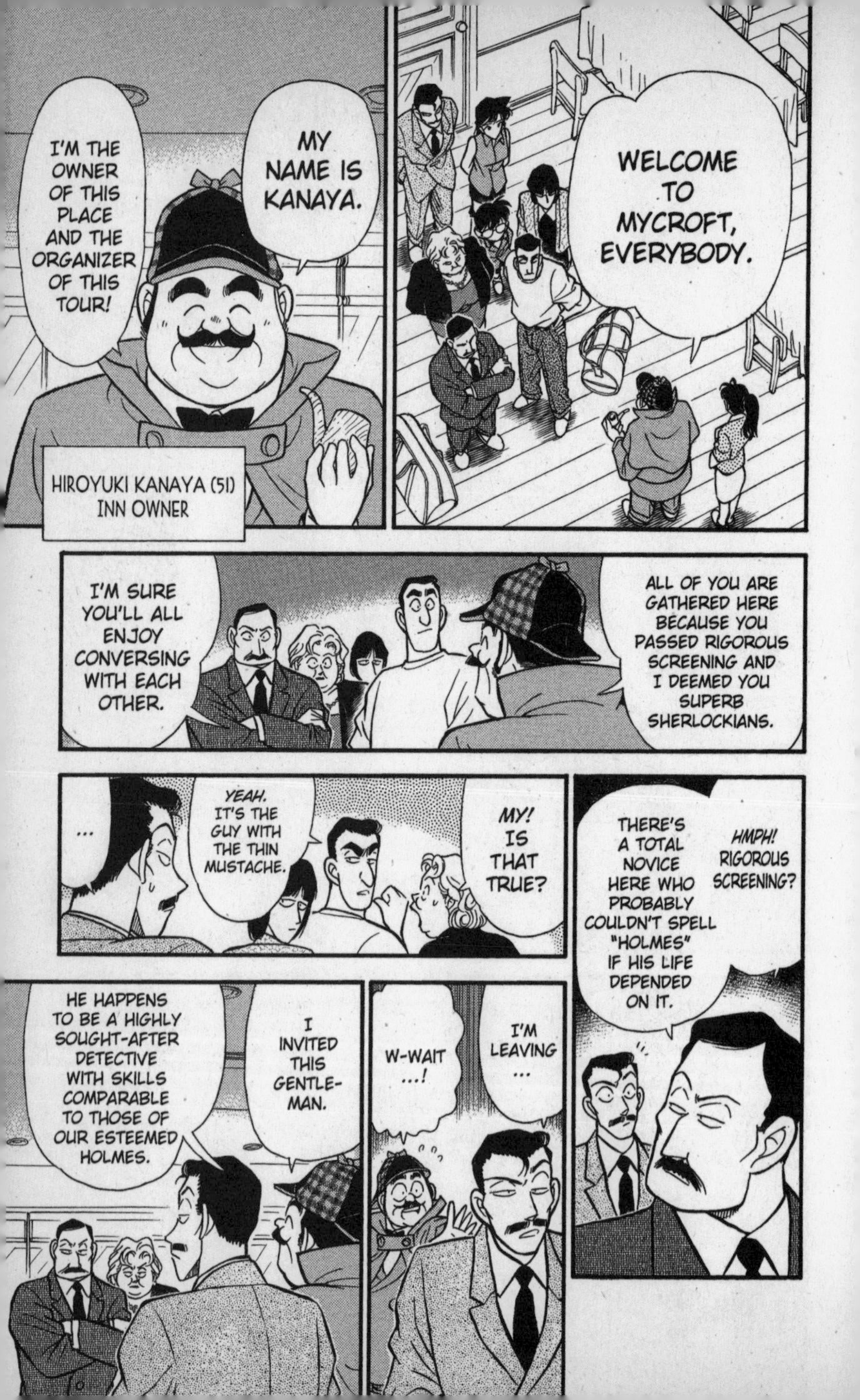

WELCOME TO MYCROFT, EVERYBODY.
MY NAME IS KANAYA.
I'M THE OWNER OF THIS PLACE AND THE ORGANIZER OF THIS TOUR!
HIROYUKI KANAYA (51) INN OWNER
ALL OF YOU ARE GATHERED HERE BECAUSE YOU PASSED RIGOROUS SCREENING AND I DEEMED YOU SUPERB SHERLOCKIANS.
I'M SURE YOU'LL ALL ENJOY CONVERSING WITH EACH OTHER.
HMPH! RIGOROUS SCREENING?
THERE'S A TOTAL NOVICE HERE WHO PROBABLY COULDN'T SPELL "HOLMES" IF HIS LIFE DEPENDED ON IT.
MY! IS THAT TRUE?
YEAH. IT'S THE GUY WITH THE THIN MUSTACHE.
...
I'M LEAVING...
W-WAIT...!
I INVITED THIS GENTLE-MAN.
HE HAPPENS TO BE A HIGHLY SOUGHT-AFTER DETECTIVE WITH SKILLS COMPARABLE TO THOSE OF OUR ESTEEMED HOLMES.

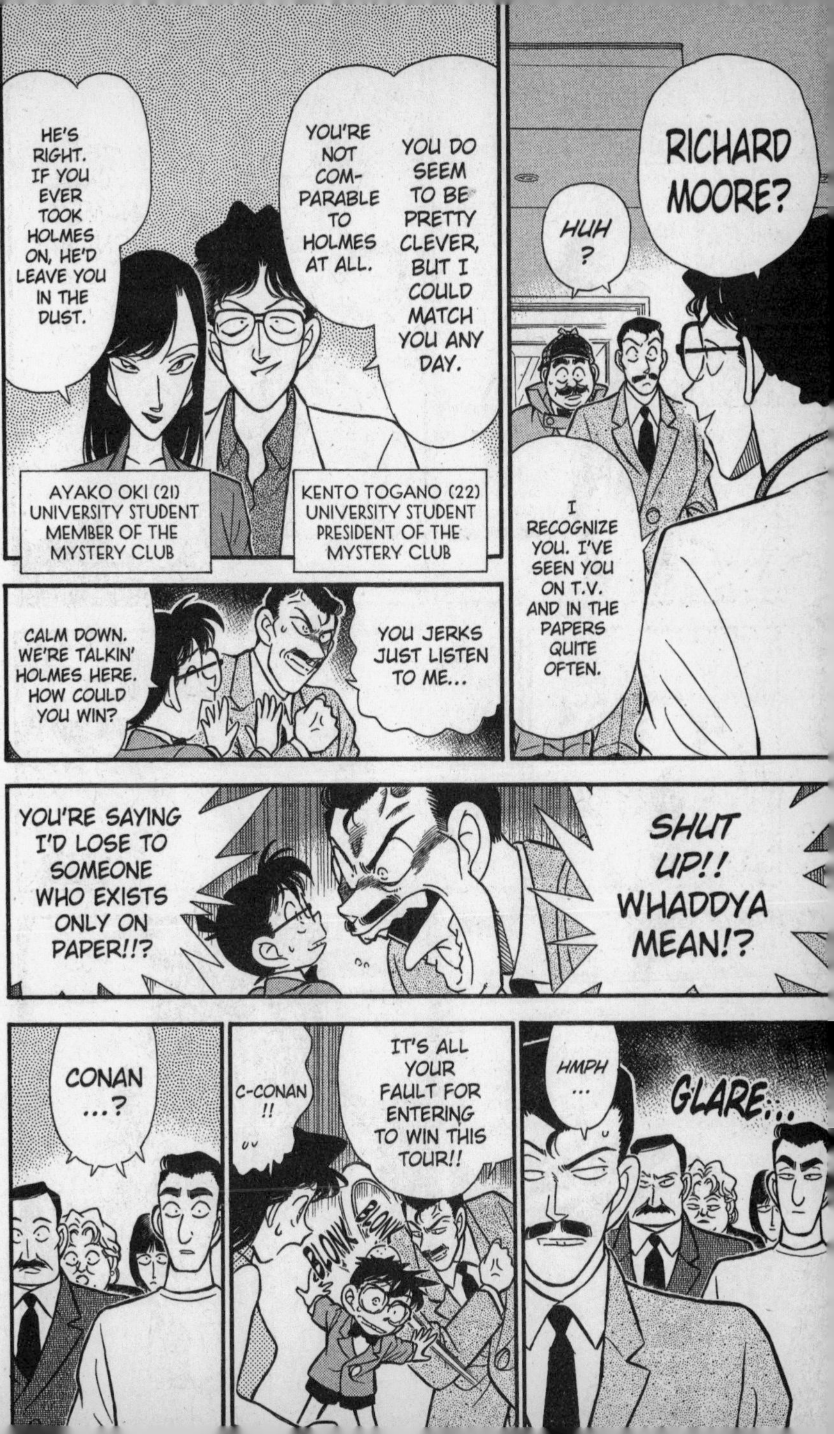
RICHARD MOORE?
HUH?
I RECOGNIZE YOU. I'VE SEEN YOU ON T.V. AND IN THE PAPERS QUITE OFTEN.
YOU DO SEEM TO BE PRETTY CLEVER, BUT I COULD MATCH YOU ANY DAY.
YOU'RE NOT COM-PARABLE TO HOLMES AT ALL.
HE'S RIGHT. IF YOU EVER TOOK HOLMES ON, HE'D LEAVE YOU IN THE DUST.
KENTO TOGANO (22) UNIVERSITY STUDENT PRESIDENT OF THE MYSTERY CLUB
AYAKO OKI (21) UNIVERSITY STUDENT MEMBER OF THE MYSTERY CLUB
YOU JERKS JUST LISTEN TO ME...
CALM DOWN. WE'RE TALKIN' HOLMES HERE. HOW COULD YOU WIN?
SHUT UP!! WHADDYA MEAN!?
YOU'RE SAYING I'D LOSE TO SOMEONE WHO EXISTS ONLY ON PAPER!!?
HMPH...
GLARE...
IT'S ALL YOUR FAULT FOR ENTERING TO WIN THIS TOUR!!
BLONK
BLONK
C-CONAN!!
CONAN...?

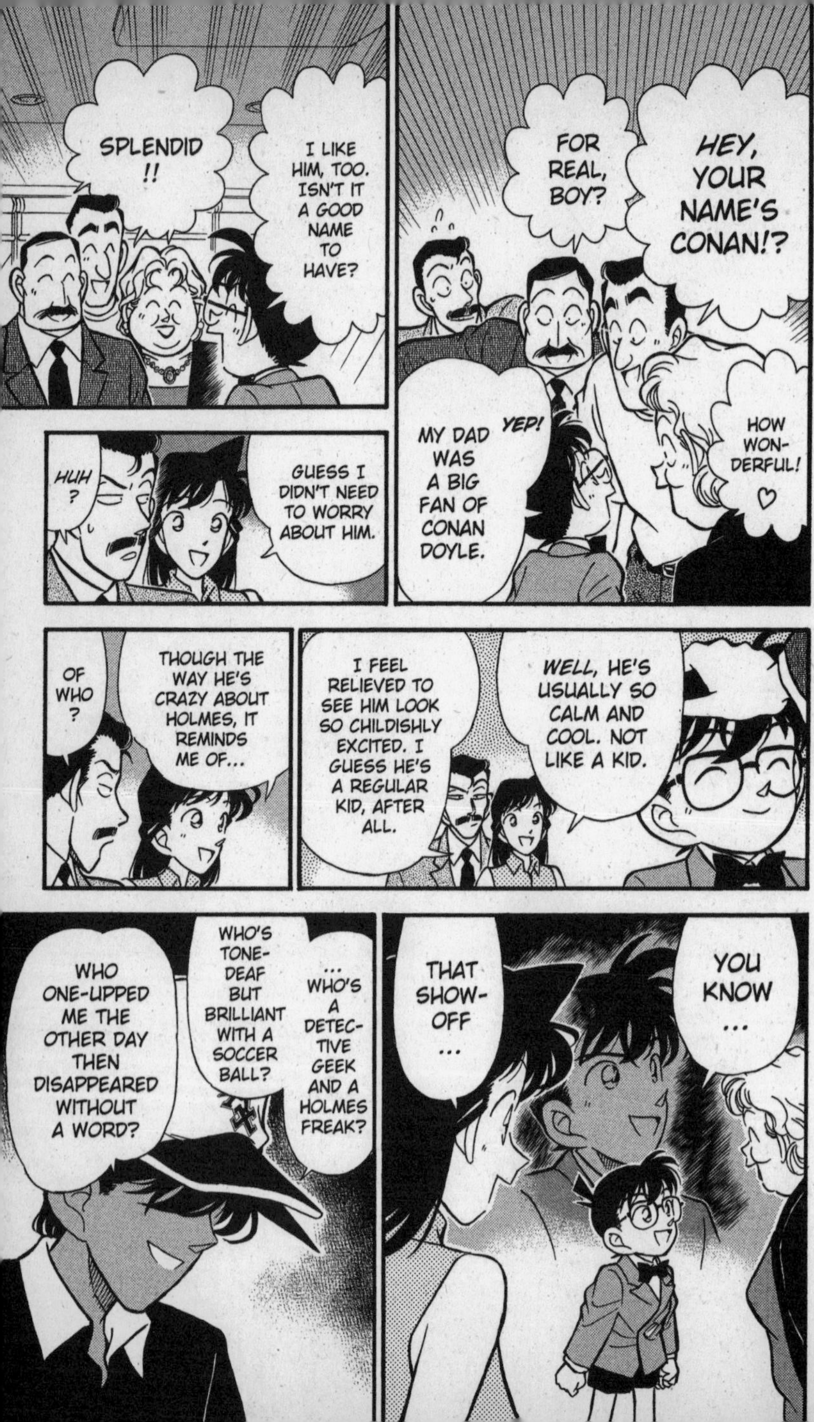
HEY, YOUR NAME'S CONAN!?
FOR REAL, BOY?
YEP!
MY DAD WAS A BIG FAN OF CONAN DOYLE.
HOW WON-DERFUL! ♥
I LIKE HIM, TOO. ISN'T IT A GOOD NAME TO HAVE?
SPLENDID!!
GUESS I DIDN'T NEED TO WORRY ABOUT HIM.
HUH?
WELL, HE'S USUALLY SO CALM AND COOL. NOT LIKE A KID.
I FEEL RELIEVED TO SEE HIM LOOK SO CHILDISHLY EXCITED. I GUESS HE'S A REGULAR KID, AFTER ALL.
THOUGH THE WAY HE'S CRAZY ABOUT HOLMES, IT REMINDS ME OF...
OF WHO?
YOU KNOW...
THAT SHOW-OFF...
...WHO'S A DETEC-TIVE GEEK AND A HOLMES FREAK?
WHO'S TONE-DEAF BUT BRILLIANT WITH A SOCCER BALL?
WHO ONE-UPPED ME THE OTHER DAY THEN DISAPPEARED WITHOUT A WORD?

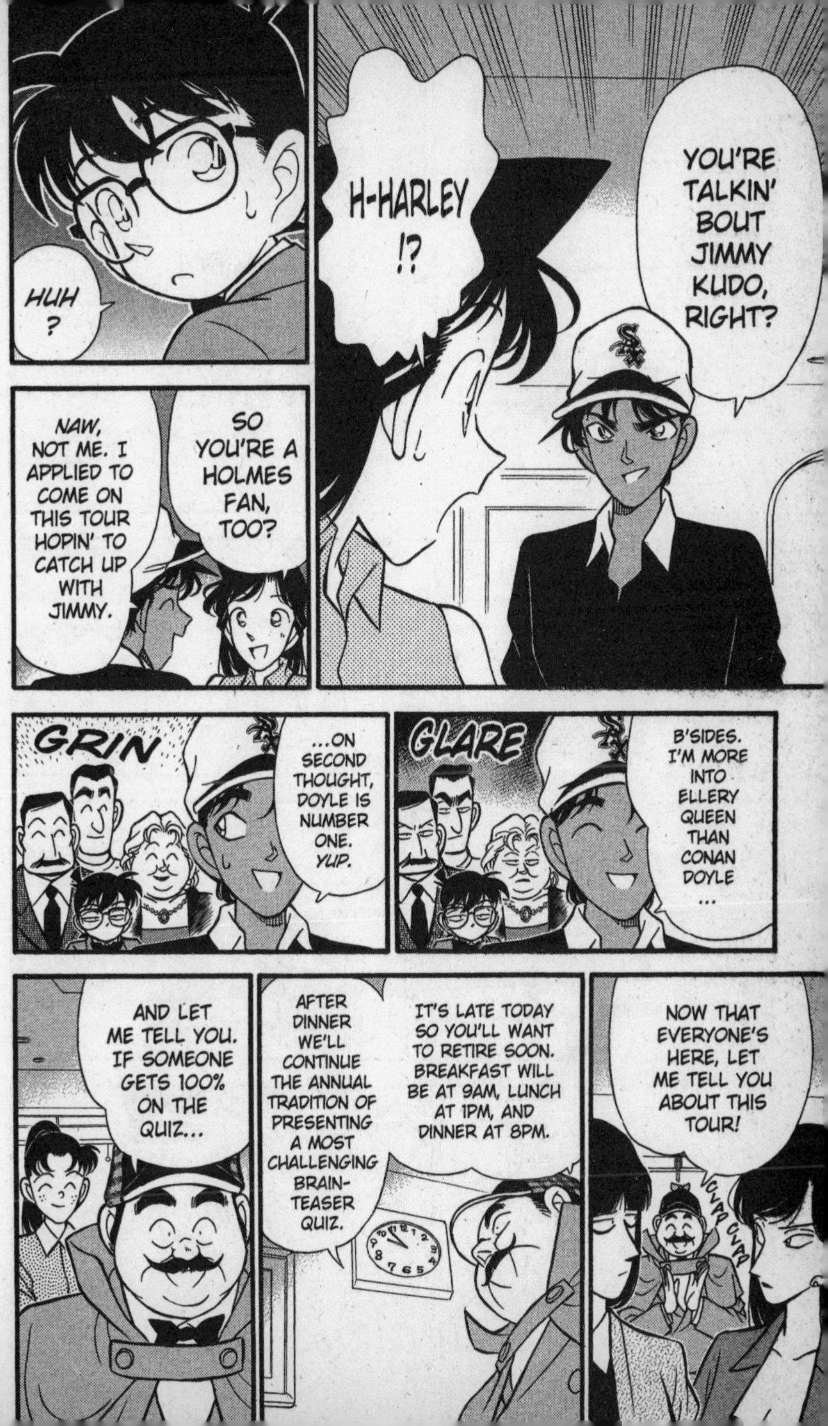
YOU'RE TALKIN' BOUT JIMMY KUDO, RIGHT?
H-HARLEY !?
HUH ?
SO YOU'RE A HOLMES FAN, TOO?
NAW, NOT ME. I APPLIED TO COME ON THIS TOUR HOPIN' TO CATCH UP WITH JIMMY.
GLARE
B'SIDES. I'M MORE INTO ELLERY QUEEN THAN CONAN DOYLE ...
GRIN
...ON SECOND THOUGHT, DOYLE IS NUMBER ONE. YUP.
NOW THAT EVERYONE'S HERE, LET ME TELL YOU ABOUT THIS TOUR!
IT'S LATE TODAY SO YOU'LL WANT TO RETIRE SOON. BREAKFAST WILL BE AT 9AM, LUNCH AT 1PM, AND DINNER AT 8PM.
AFTER DINNER WE'LL CONTINUE THE ANNUAL TRADITION OF PRESENTING A MOST CHALLENGING BRAIN-TEASER QUIZ.
AND LET ME TELL YOU. IF SOMEONE GETS 100% ON THE QUIZ...

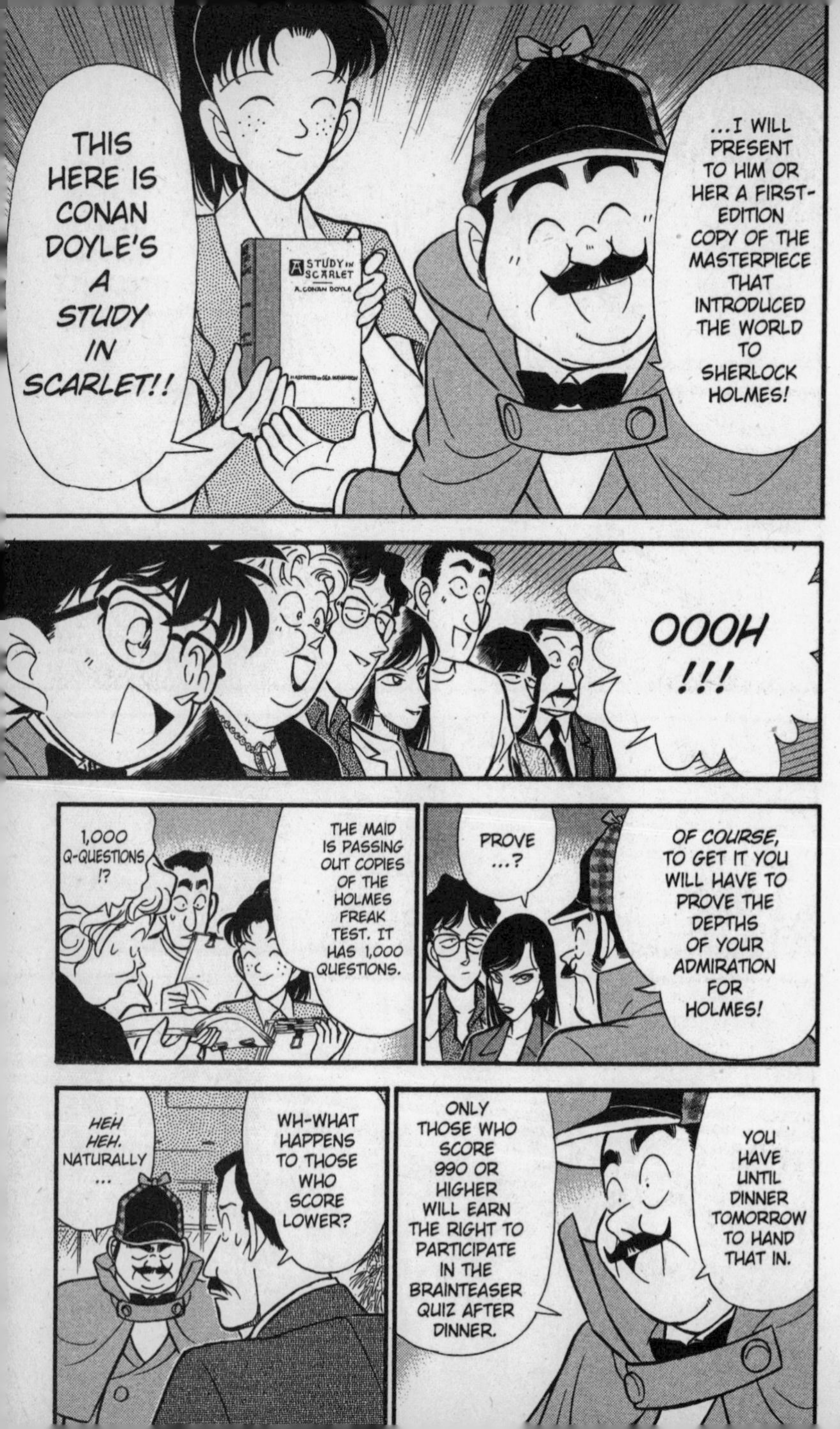
...I WILL PRESENT TO HIM OR HER A FIRST-EDITION COPY OF THE MASTERPIECE THAT INTRODUCED THE WORLD TO SHERLOCK HOLMES!
THIS HERE IS CONAN DOYLE'S A STUDY IN SCARLET!!
A STUDY IN SCARLET A. CONAN DOYLE
OOOH !!!
OF COURSE, TO GET IT YOU WILL HAVE TO PROVE THE DEPTHS OF YOUR ADMIRATION FOR HOLMES!
PROVE ...?
THE MAID IS PASSING OUT COPIES OF THE HOLMES FREAK TEST. IT HAS 1,000 QUESTIONS.
1,000 Q-QUESTIONS !?
YOU HAVE UNTIL DINNER TOMORROW TO HAND THAT IN.
ONLY THOSE WHO SCORE 990 OR HIGHER WILL EARN THE RIGHT TO PARTICIPATE IN THE BRAINTEASER QUIZ AFTER DINNER.
WH-WHAT HAPPENS TO THOSE WHO SCORE LOWER?
HEH HEH. NATURALLY ...

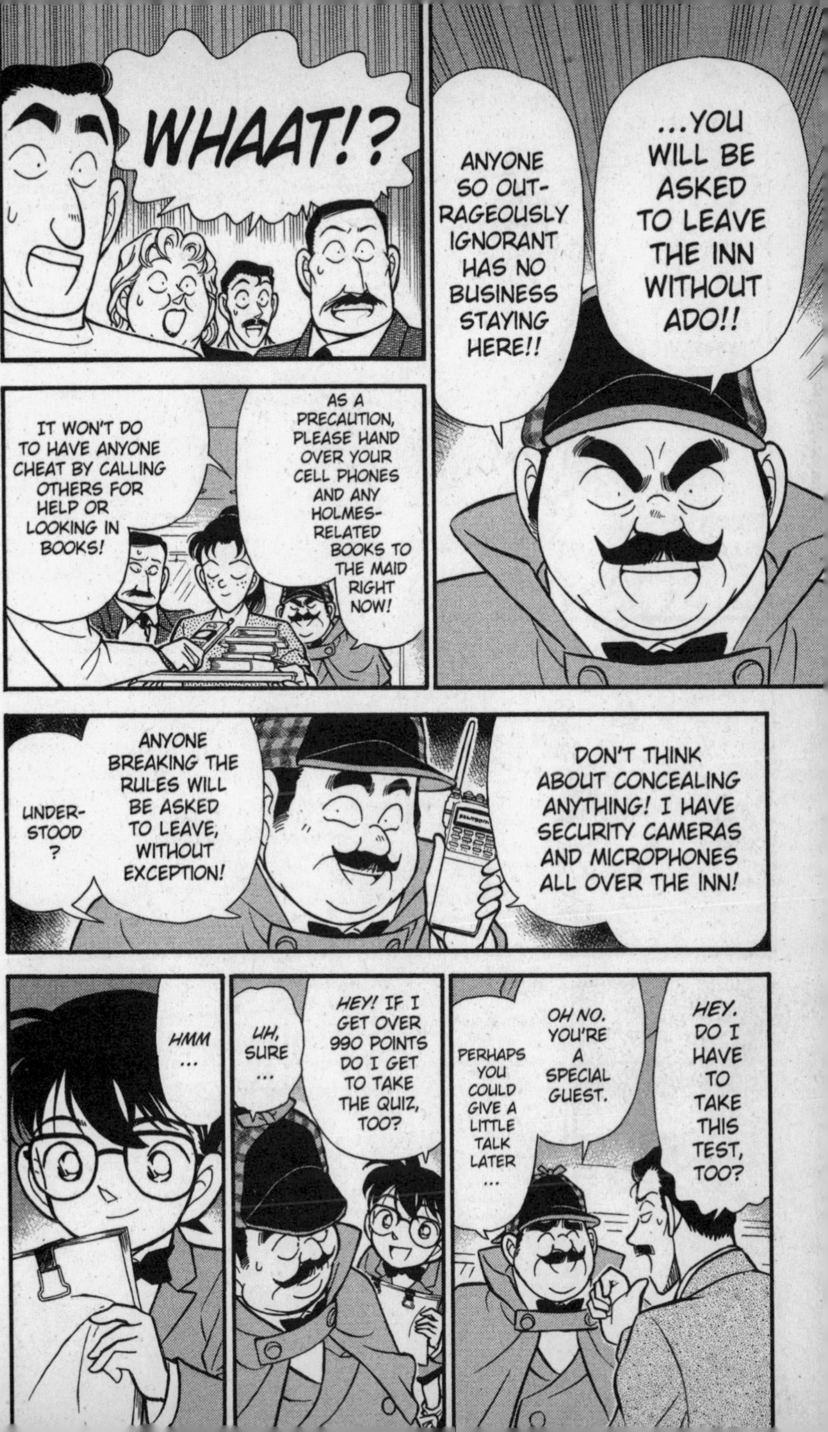
...YOU WILL BE ASKED TO LEAVE THE INN WITHOUT ADO!!
ANYONE SO OUT-RAGEOUSLY IGNORANT HAS NO BUSINESS STAYING HERE!!
WHAAT!?
AS A PRECAUTION, PLEASE HAND OVER YOUR CELL PHONES AND ANY HOLMES-RELATED BOOKS TO THE MAID RIGHT NOW!
IT WON'T DO TO HAVE ANYONE CHEAT BY CALLING OTHERS FOR HELP OR LOOKING IN BOOKS!
DON'T THINK ABOUT CONCEALING ANYTHING! I HAVE SECURITY CAMERAS AND MICROPHONES ALL OVER THE INN!
ANYONE BREAKING THE RULES WILL BE ASKED TO LEAVE, WITHOUT EXCEPTION!
UNDER-STOOD?
HEY. DO I HAVE TO TAKE THIS TEST, TOO?
OH NO. YOU'RE A SPECIAL GUEST.
PERHAPS YOU COULD GIVE A LITTLE TALK LATER...
HEY! IF I GET OVER 990 POINTS DO I GET TO TAKE THE QUIZ, TOO?
UH, SURE...
HMM...

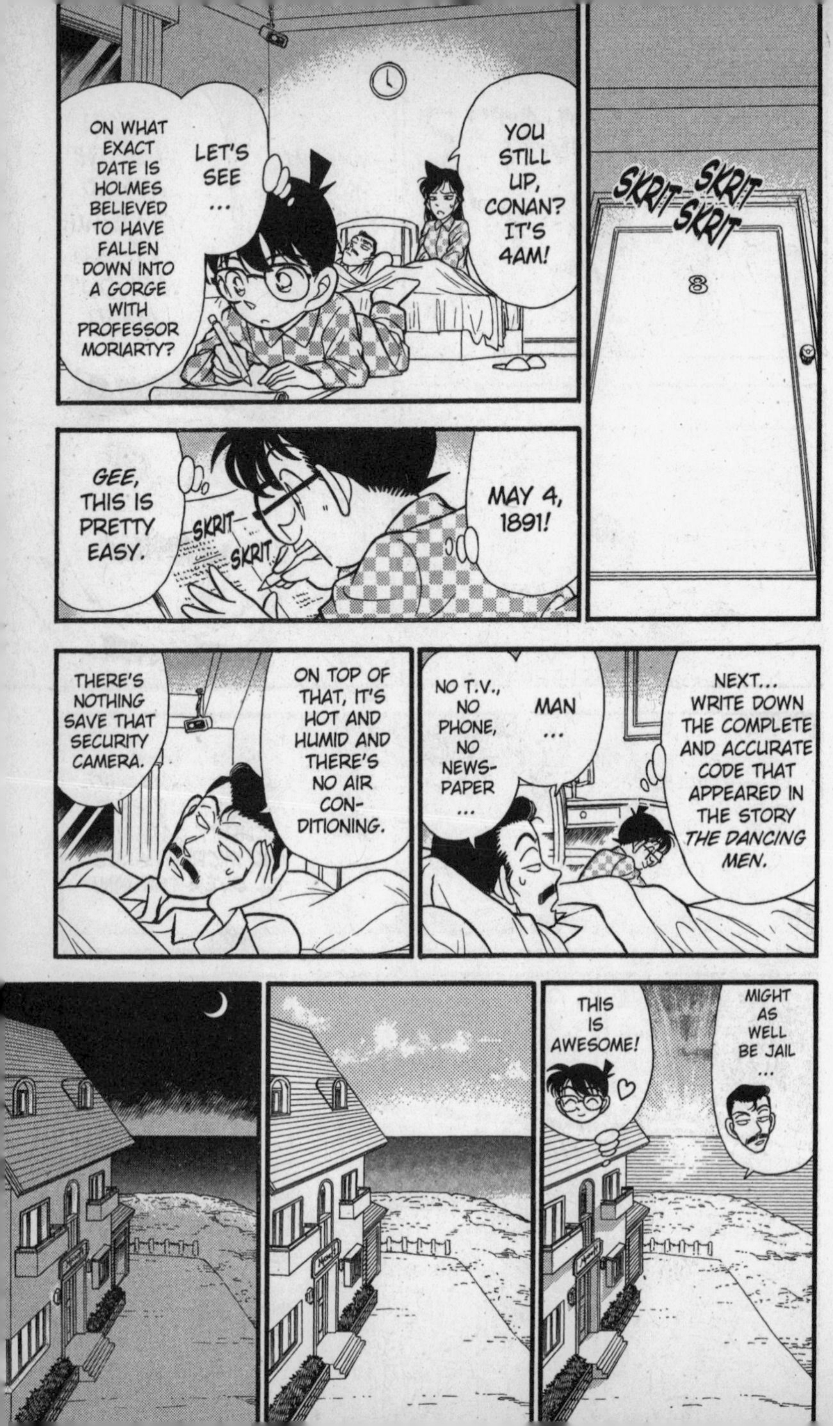
SKRIT SKRIT
SKRIT
YOU STILL UP, CONAN? IT'S 4AM!
LET'S SEE ...
ON WHAT EXACT DATE IS HOLMES BELIEVED TO HAVE FALLEN DOWN INTO A GORGE WITH PROFESSOR MORIARTY?
MAY 4, 1891!
SKRIT
SKRIT
GEE, THIS IS PRETTY EASY.
NEXT... WRITE DOWN THE COMPLETE AND ACCURATE CODE THAT APPEARED IN THE STORY *THE DANCING MEN*.
MAN ...
NO T.V., NO PHONE, NO NEWS-PAPER ...
ON TOP OF THAT, IT'S HOT AND HUMID AND THERE'S NO AIR CON-DITIONING.
THERE'S NOTHING SAVE THAT SECURITY CAMERA.
MIGHT AS WELL BE JAIL ...
THIS IS AWESOME!

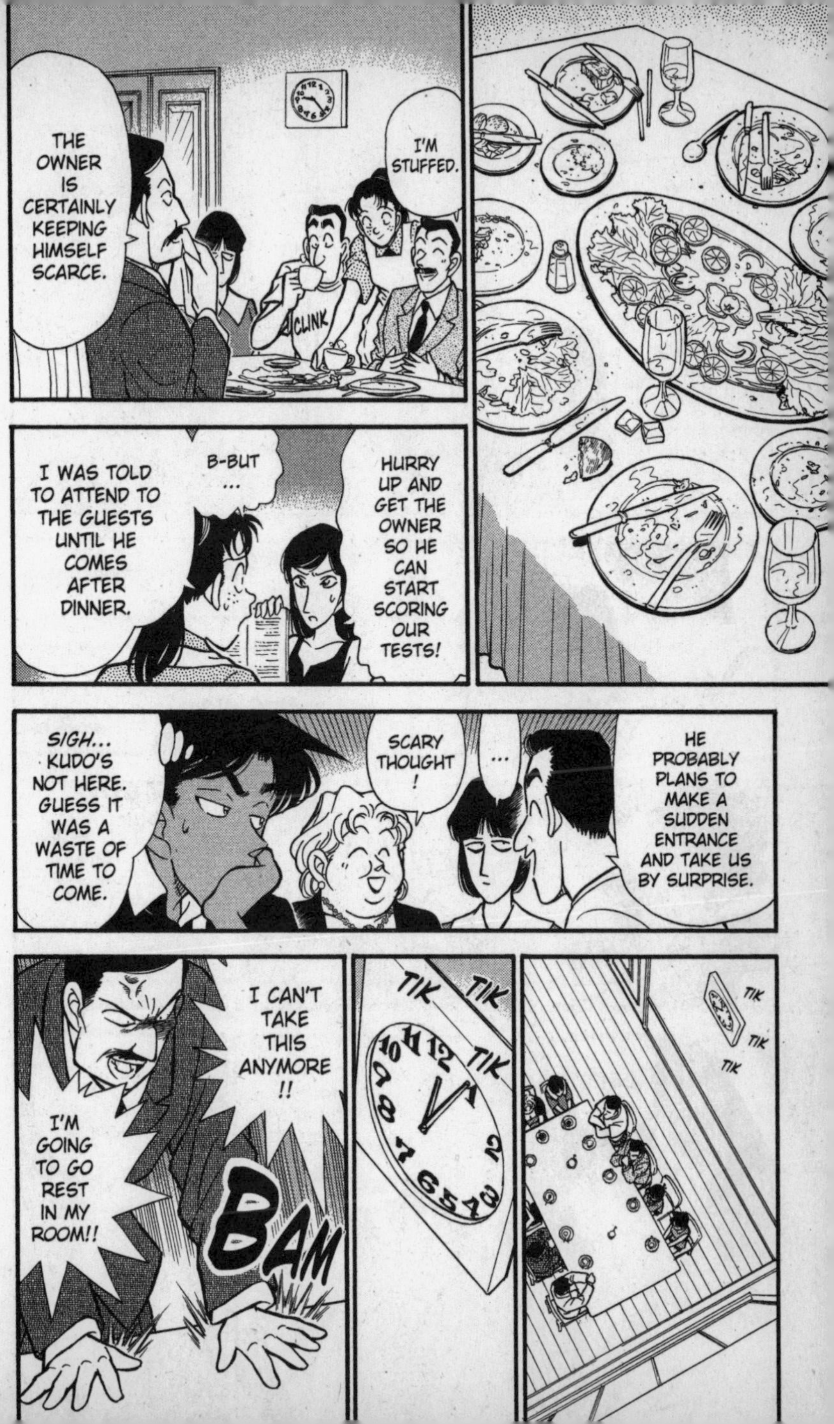
THE OWNER IS CERTAINLY KEEPING HIMSELF SCARCE.
CLINK
I'M STUFFED.
I WAS TOLD TO ATTEND TO THE GUESTS UNTIL HE COMES AFTER DINNER.
B-BUT ...
HURRY UP AND GET THE OWNER SO HE CAN START SCORING OUR TESTS!
SIGH... KUDO'S NOT HERE. GUESS IT WAS A WASTE OF TIME TO COME.
SCARY THOUGHT !
...
HE PROBABLY PLANS TO MAKE A SUDDEN ENTRANCE AND TAKE US BY SURPRISE.
I'M GOING TO GO REST IN MY ROOM!!
I CAN'T TAKE THIS ANYMORE !!
BAM
TIK TIK TIK
TIK TIK TIK

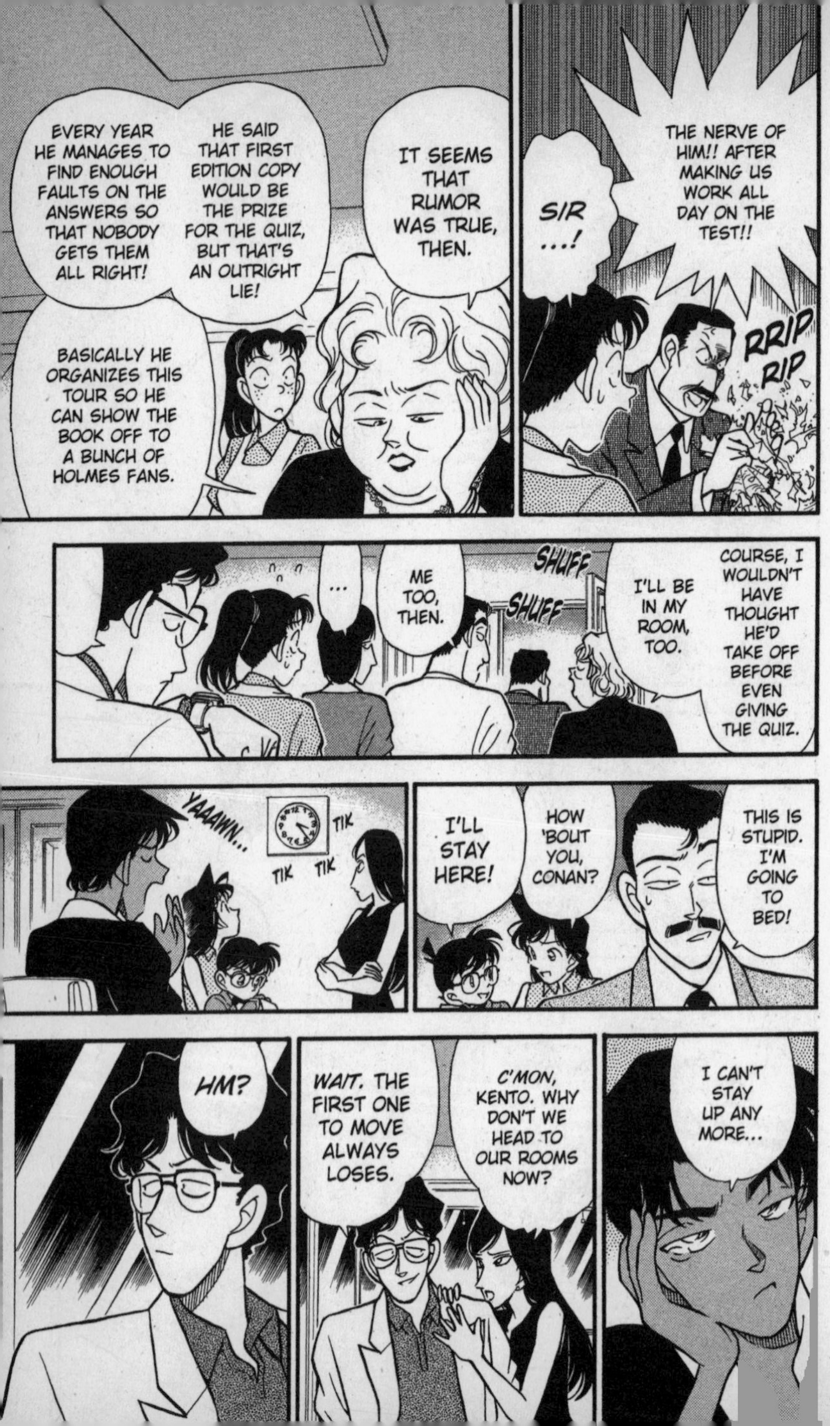
THE NERVE OF HIM!! AFTER MAKING US WORK ALL DAY ON THE TEST!!
SIR ...!
RRIP RIP
IT SEEMS THAT RUMOR WAS TRUE, THEN.
HE SAID THAT FIRST EDITION COPY WOULD BE THE PRIZE FOR THE QUIZ, BUT THAT'S AN OUTRIGHT LIE!
EVERY YEAR HE MANAGES TO FIND ENOUGH FAULTS ON THE ANSWERS SO THAT NOBODY GETS THEM ALL RIGHT!
BASICALLY HE ORGANIZES THIS TOUR SO HE CAN SHOW THE BOOK OFF TO A BUNCH OF HOLMES FANS.
COURSE, I WOULDN'T HAVE THOUGHT HE'D TAKE OFF BEFORE EVEN GIVING THE QUIZ.
I'LL BE IN MY ROOM, TOO.
SHUFF
SHUFF
ME TOO, THEN.
...
THIS IS STUPID. I'M GOING TO BED!
HOW 'BOUT YOU, CONAN?
I'LL STAY HERE!
TIK
TIK
TIK
YAAAWN...
I CAN'T STAY UP ANY MORE...
C'MON, KENTO. WHY DON'T WE HEAD TO OUR ROOMS NOW?
WAIT. THE FIRST ONE TO MOVE ALWAYS LOSES.
HM?

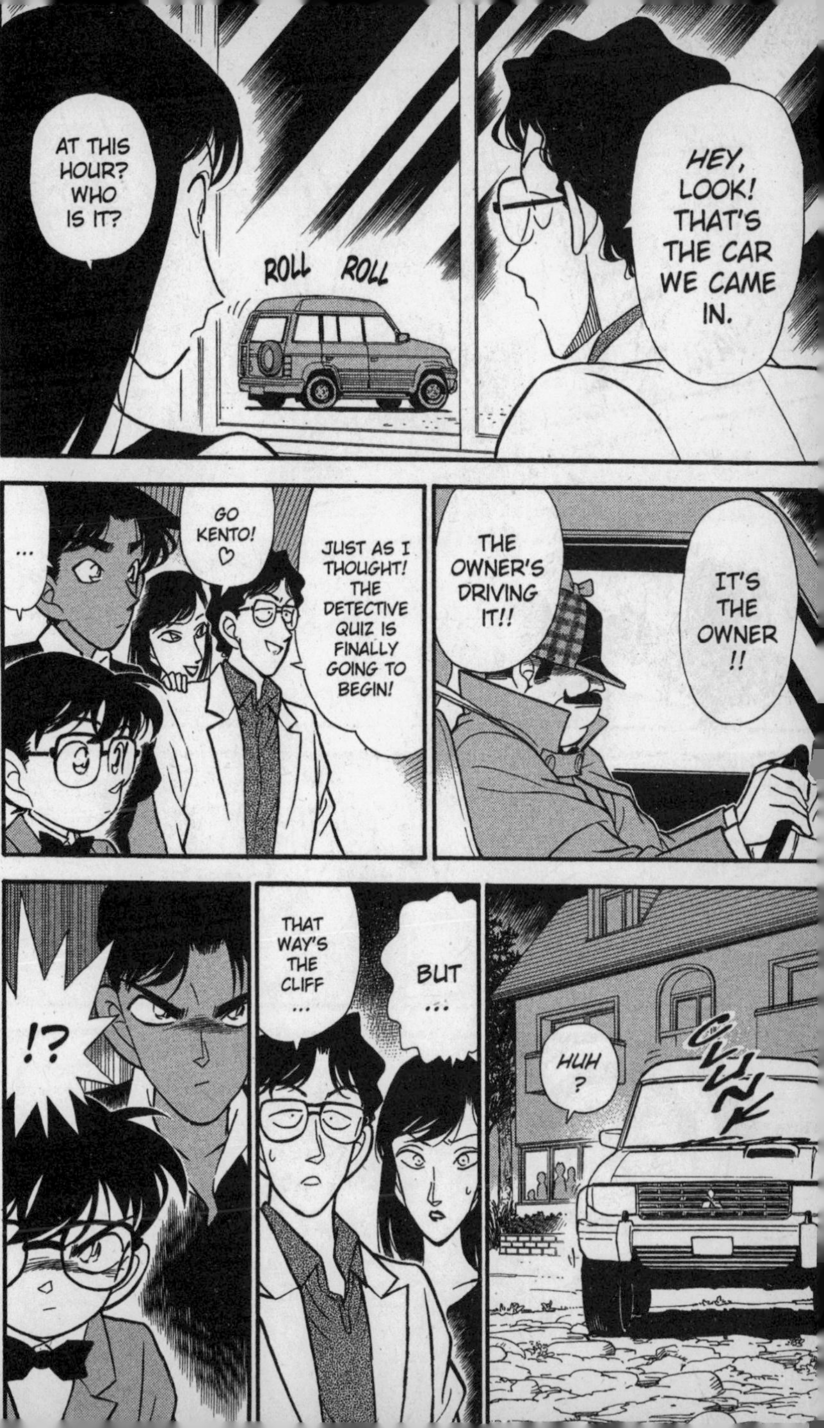
HEY, LOOK! THAT'S THE CAR WE CAME IN.
AT THIS HOUR? WHO IS IT?
ROLL ROLL
IT'S THE OWNER !!
THE OWNER'S DRIVING IT!!
JUST AS I THOUGHT! THE DETECTIVE QUIZ IS FINALLY GOING TO BEGIN!
GO KENTO! ♡
...
HUH ?
BUT ...
THAT WAY'S THE CLIFF ...
!?

WHOA, IT'S SPEEDING UP!!

CLANK CVRNK

FWSH

DA-DA-DA...

YA GOTTA STOP NOW OR YOU'LL FALL OFF!!

BAM BAM

HEY MISTER! WHATCHA DOIN'!?

IT'S NOT THE SOUND OF AN ENGINE!!

AND WHAT'S THAT SOUND?

WHRRRM

THERE'S A BLANKET OVER THE DASH-BOARD...?

MISTER!!!

TILT

VRM VRM

HEY! HEY MISTER!!

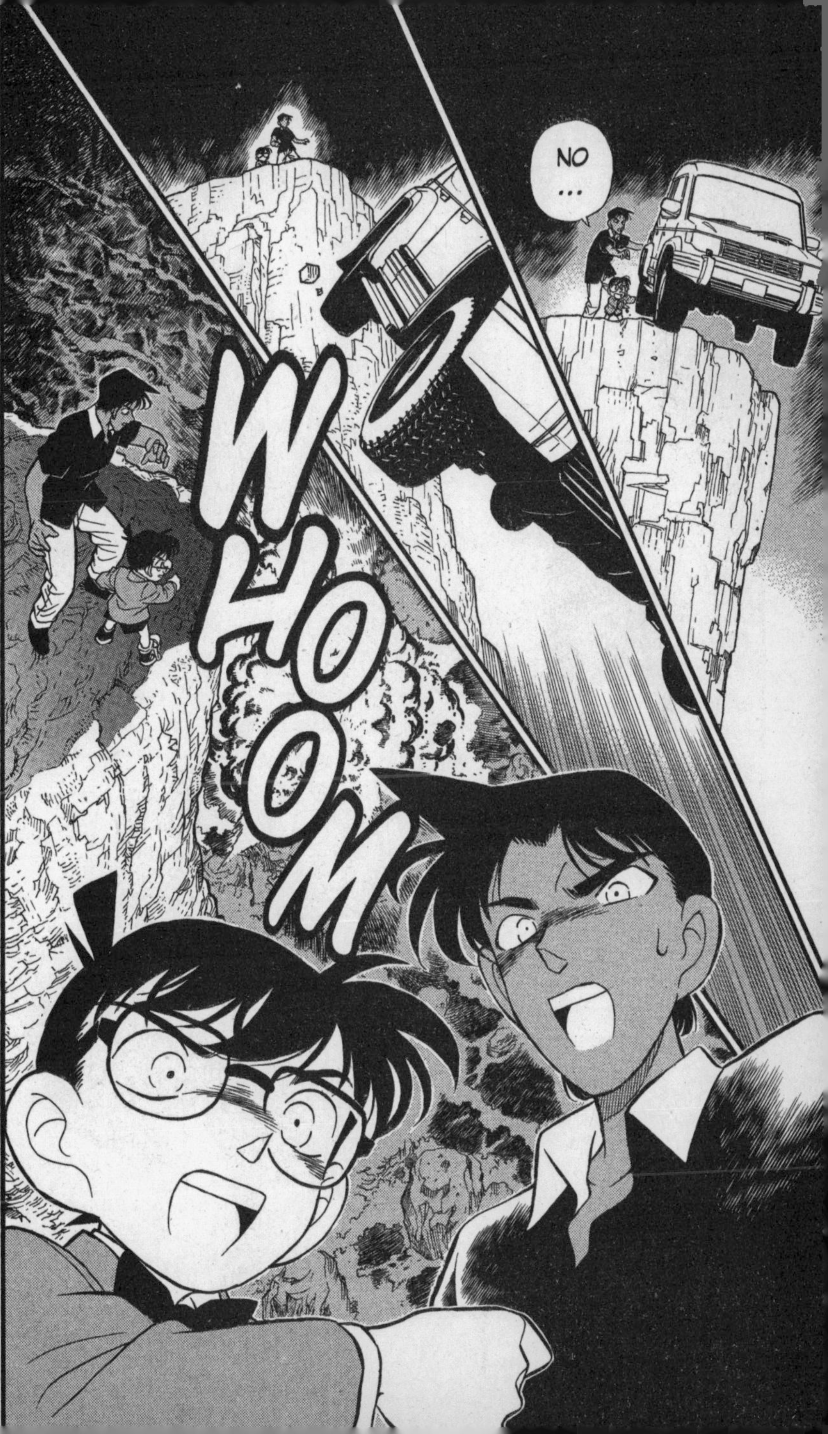
NO ...
WHOOM

FILE 8: THE WOMAN WHO KNEW TOO MUCH

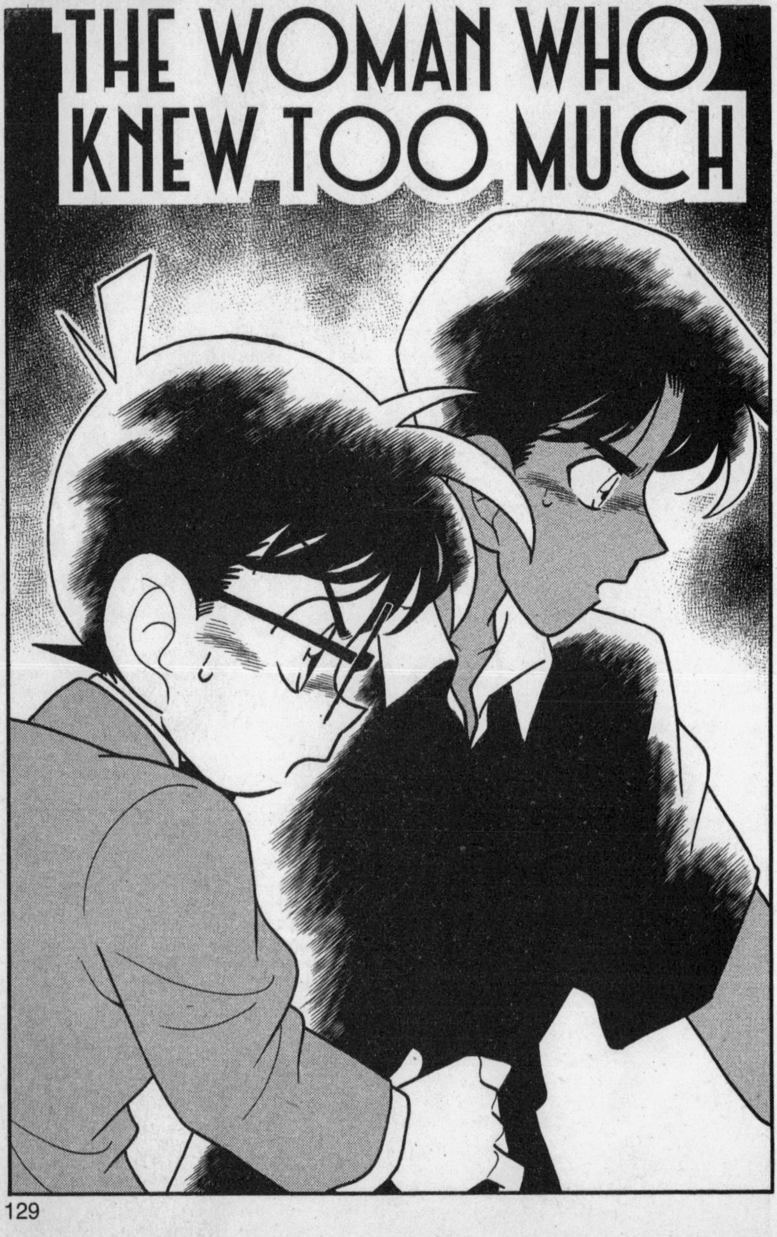

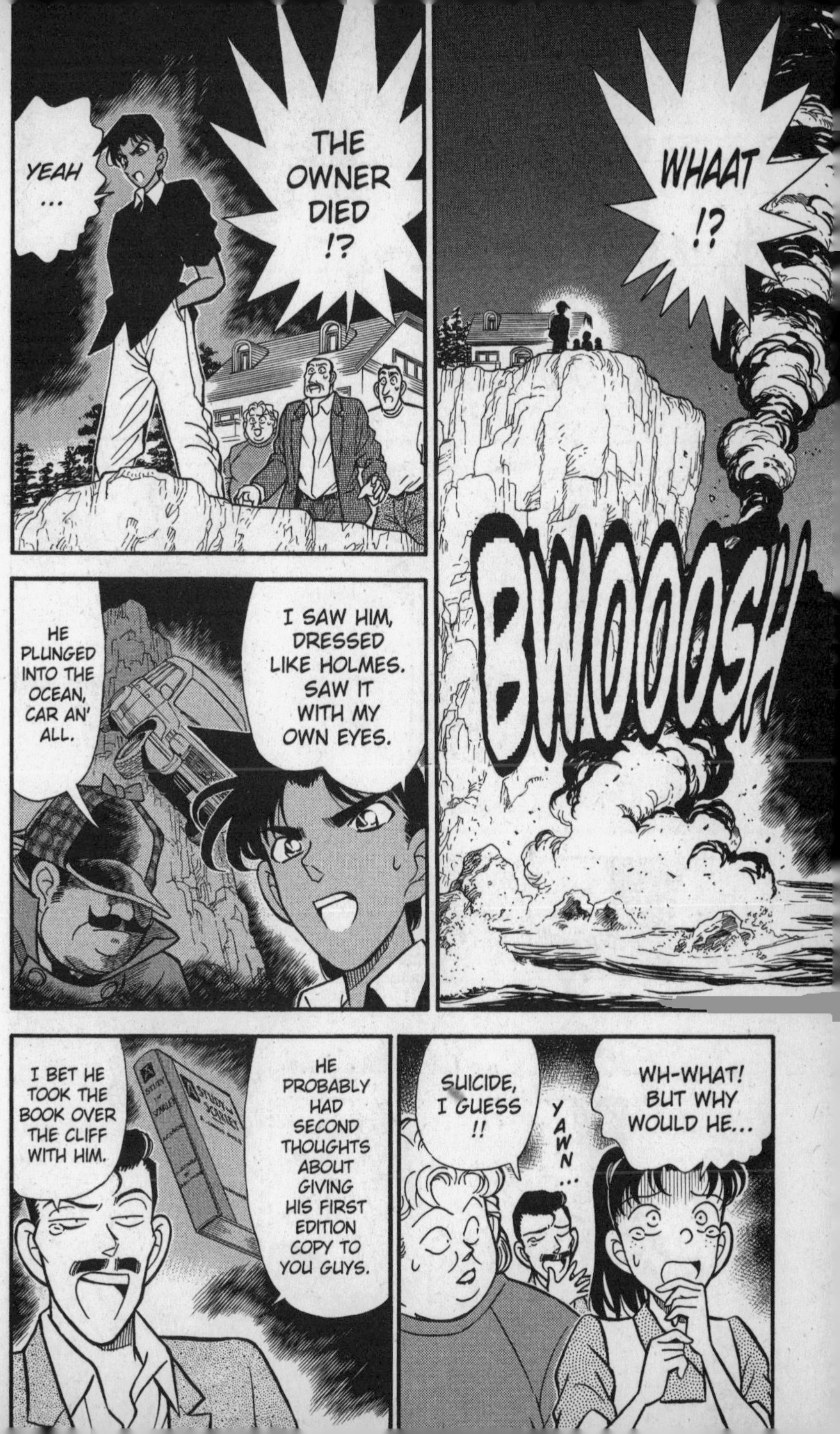

WHAAT !?
BWOOOSH
THE OWNER DIED !?
YEAH ...
I SAW HIM, DRESSED LIKE HOLMES. SAW IT WITH MY OWN EYES.
HE PLUNGED INTO THE OCEAN, CAR AN' ALL.
WH-WHAT! BUT WHY WOULD HE...
YAWN...
SUICIDE, I GUESS !!
HE PROBABLY HAD SECOND THOUGHTS ABOUT GIVING HIS FIRST EDITION COPY TO YOU GUYS.
I BET HE TOOK THE BOOK OVER THE CLIFF WITH HIM.

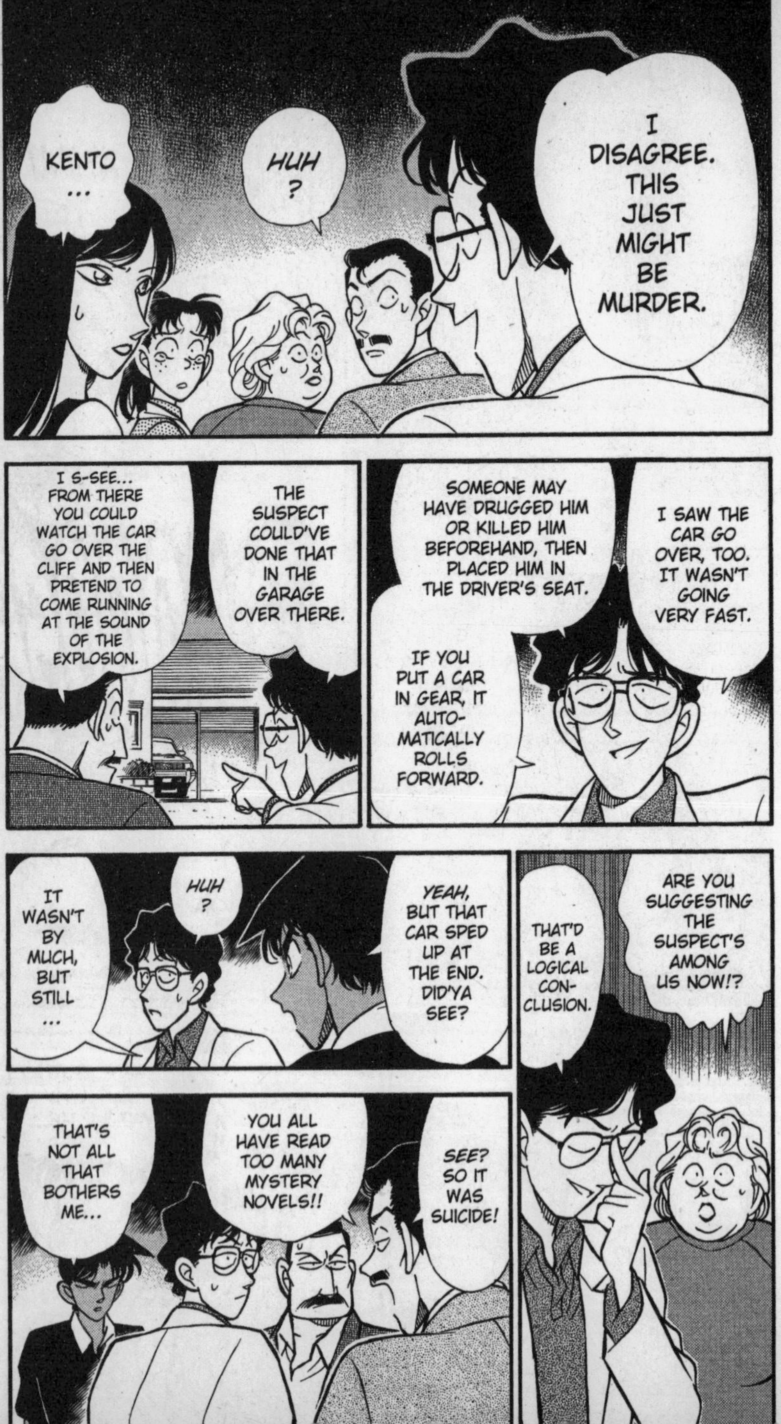
I DISAGREE. THIS JUST MIGHT BE MURDER.
HUH?
KENTO...
I SAW THE CAR GO OVER, TOO. IT WASN'T GOING VERY FAST.
SOMEONE MAY HAVE DRUGGED HIM OR KILLED HIM BEFOREHAND, THEN PLACED HIM IN THE DRIVER'S SEAT.
IF YOU PUT A CAR IN GEAR, IT AUTO-MATICALLY ROLLS FORWARD.
THE SUSPECT COULD'VE DONE THAT IN THE GARAGE OVER THERE.
I S-SEE... FROM THERE YOU COULD WATCH THE CAR GO OVER THE CLIFF AND THEN PRETEND TO COME RUNNING AT THE SOUND OF THE EXPLOSION.
ARE YOU SUGGESTING THE SUSPECT'S AMONG US NOW!?
THAT'D BE A LOGICAL CON-CLUSION.
YEAH, BUT THAT CAR SPED UP AT THE END. DID'YA SEE?
HUH?
IT WASN'T BY MUCH, BUT STILL...
SEE? SO IT WAS SUICIDE!
YOU ALL HAVE READ TOO MANY MYSTERY NOVELS!!
THAT'S NOT ALL THAT BOTHERS ME...

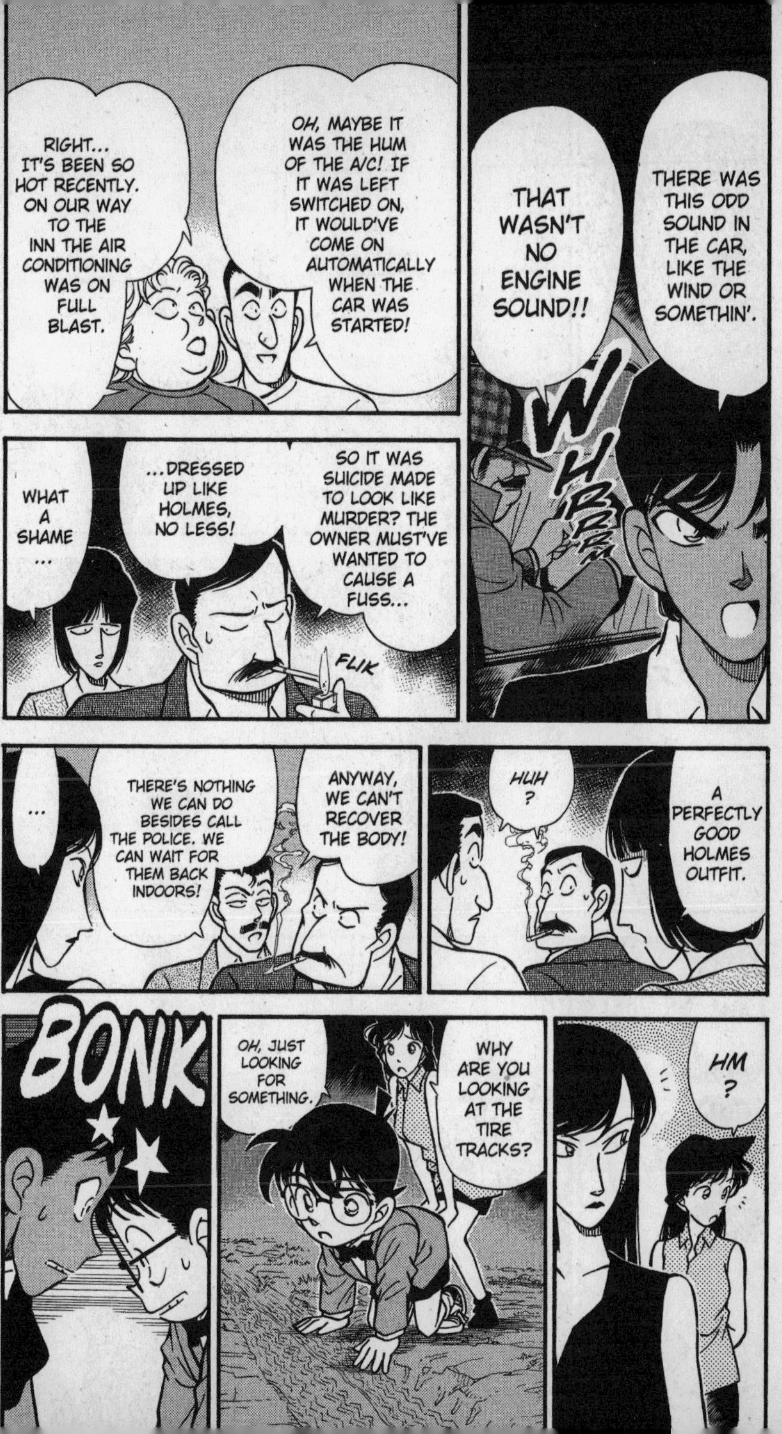
THERE WAS THIS ODD SOUND IN THE CAR, LIKE THE WIND OR SOMETHIN'.
THAT WASN'T NO ENGINE SOUND!!
WHRRR
OH, MAYBE IT WAS THE HUM OF THE A/C! IF IT WAS LEFT SWITCHED ON, IT WOULD'VE COME ON AUTOMATICALLY WHEN THE CAR WAS STARTED!
RIGHT... IT'S BEEN SO HOT RECENTLY. ON OUR WAY TO THE INN THE AIR CONDITIONING WAS ON FULL BLAST.
SO IT WAS SUICIDE MADE TO LOOK LIKE MURDER? THE OWNER MUST'VE WANTED TO CAUSE A FUSS...
...DRESSED UP LIKE HOLMES, NO LESS!
WHAT A SHAME...
FLIK
A PERFECTLY GOOD HOLMES OUTFIT.
HUH?
ANYWAY, WE CAN'T RECOVER THE BODY!
THERE'S NOTHING WE CAN DO BESIDES CALL THE POLICE. WE CAN WAIT FOR THEM BACK INDOORS!
...
HM?
WHY ARE YOU LOOKING AT THE TIRE TRACKS?
OH, JUST LOOKING FOR SOMETHING.
BONK

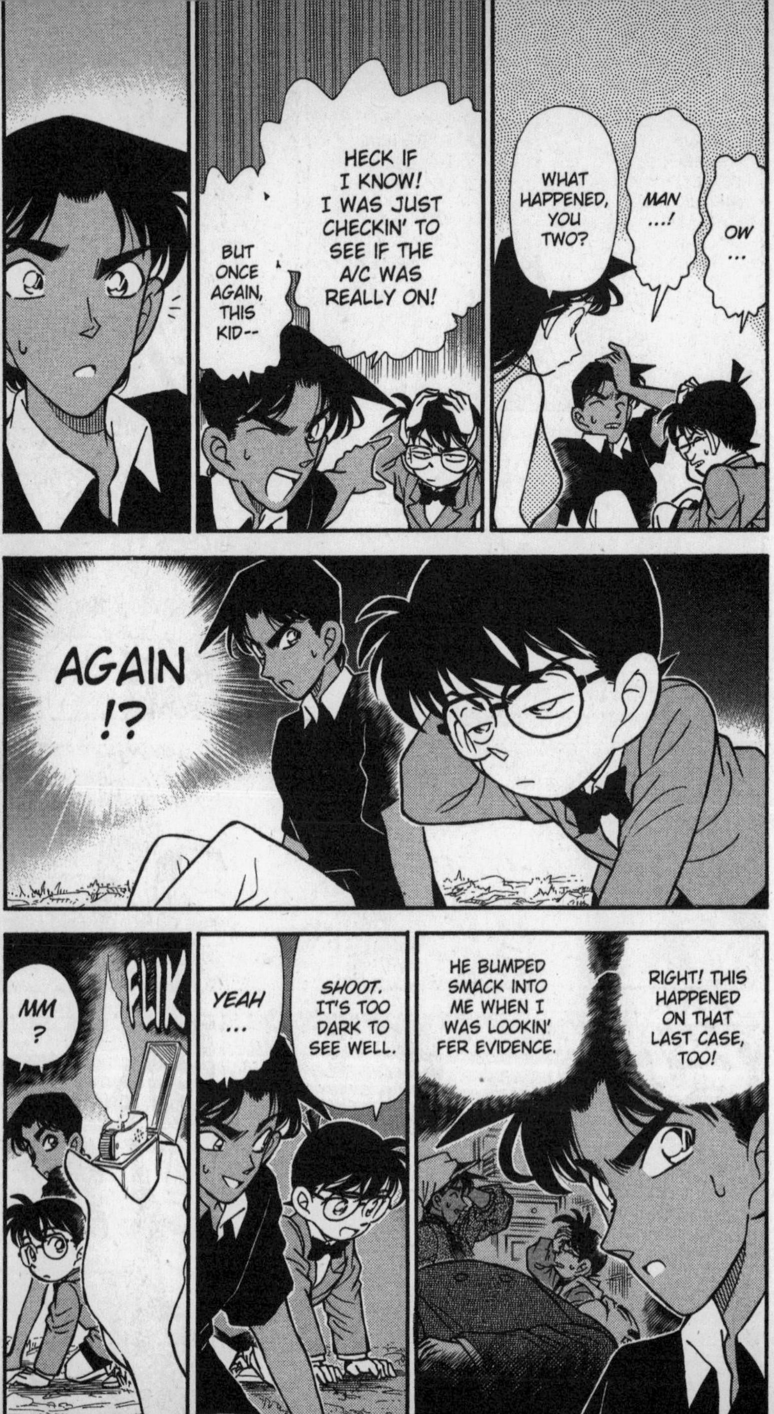
OW ...
MAN ...!
WHAT HAPPENED, YOU TWO?
HECK IF I KNOW! I WAS JUST CHECKIN' TO SEE IF THE A/C WAS REALLY ON!
BUT ONCE AGAIN, THIS KID--
AGAIN !?
RIGHT! THIS HAPPENED ON THAT LAST CASE, TOO!
HE BUMPED SMACK INTO ME WHEN I WAS LOOKIN' FER EVIDENCE.
SHOOT. IT'S TOO DARK TO SEE WELL.
YEAH ...
FLIK
MM ?

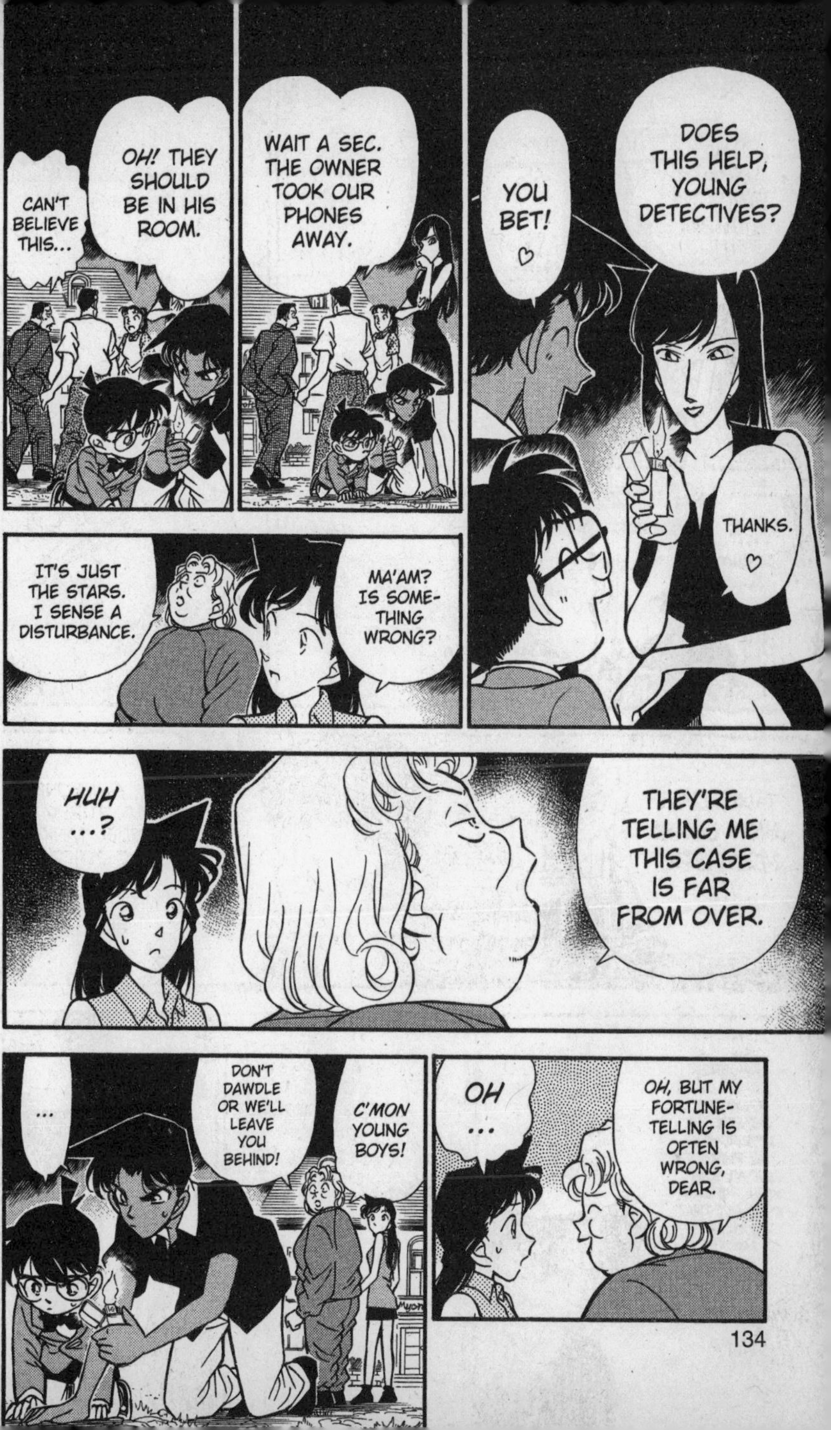

CAN'T BELIEVE THIS...
OH! THEY SHOULD BE IN HIS ROOM.
WAIT A SEC. THE OWNER TOOK OUR PHONES AWAY.
YOU BET! ♡
DOES THIS HELP, YOUNG DETECTIVES?
THANKS. ♡
MA'AM? IS SOME-THING WRONG?
IT'S JUST THE STARS. I SENSE A DISTURBANCE.
THEY'RE TELLING ME THIS CASE IS FAR FROM OVER.
HUH ...?
C'MON YOUNG BOYS!
DON'T DAWDLE OR WE'LL LEAVE YOU BEHIND!
...
OH ...
OH, BUT MY FORTUNE-TELLING IS OFTEN WRONG, DEAR.

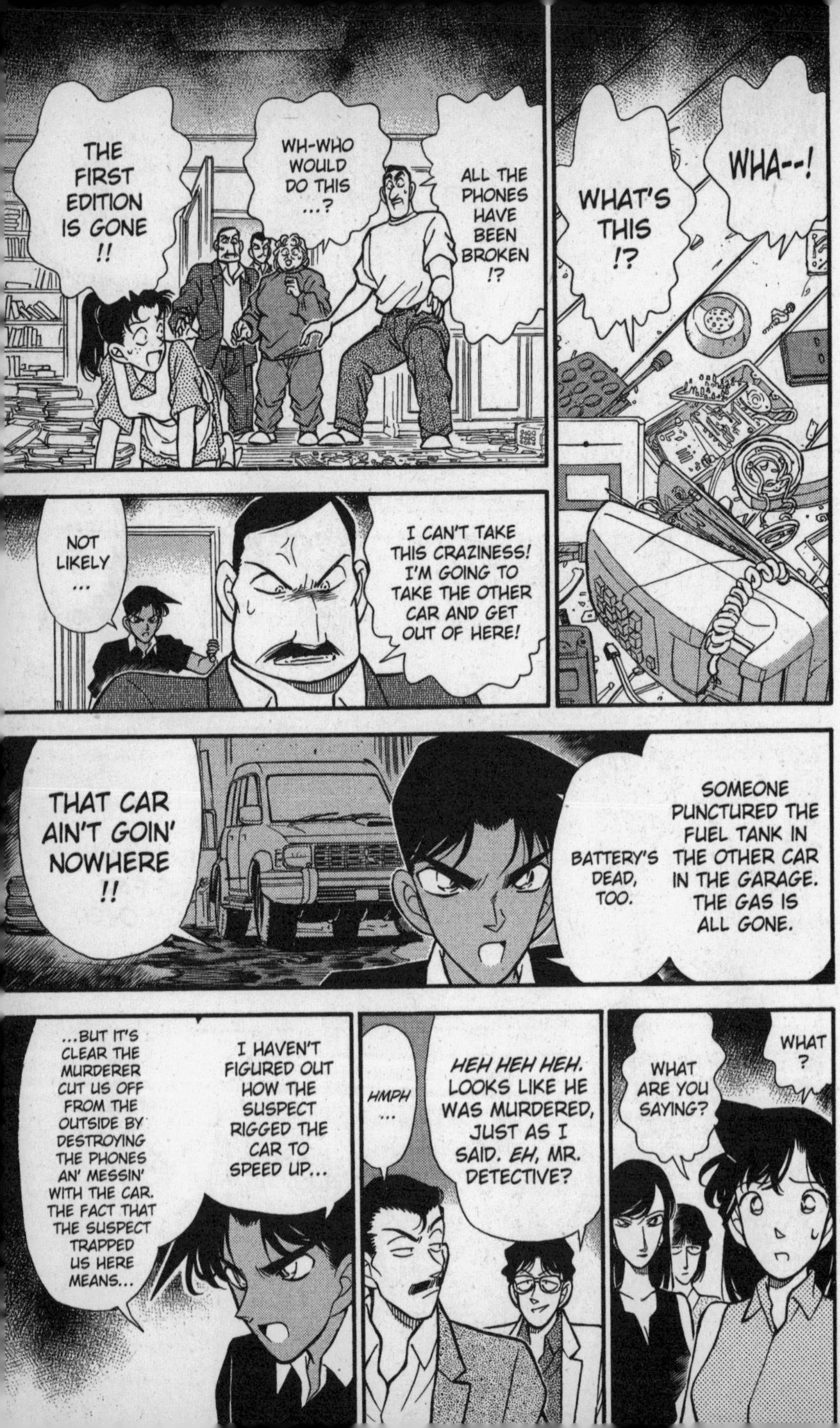
WHA--!
WHAT'S THIS !?
ALL THE PHONES HAVE BEEN BROKEN !?
WH-WHO WOULD DO THIS ...?
THE FIRST EDITION IS GONE !!
I CAN'T TAKE THIS CRAZINESS! I'M GOING TO TAKE THE OTHER CAR AND GET OUT OF HERE!
NOT LIKELY ...
SOMEONE PUNCTURED THE FUEL TANK IN THE OTHER CAR IN THE GARAGE. THE GAS IS ALL GONE.
BATTERY'S DEAD, TOO.
THAT CAR AIN'T GOIN' NOWHERE !!
WHAT ?
WHAT ARE YOU SAYING?
HEH HEH HEH. LOOKS LIKE HE WAS MURDERED, JUST AS I SAID. *EH,* MR. DETECTIVE?
HMPH ...
I HAVEN'T FIGURED OUT HOW THE SUSPECT RIGGED THE CAR TO SPEED UP...
...BUT IT'S CLEAR THE MURDERER CUT US OFF FROM THE OUTSIDE BY DESTROYING THE PHONES AN' MESSIN' WITH THE CAR. THE FACT THAT THE SUSPECT TRAPPED US HERE MEANS...

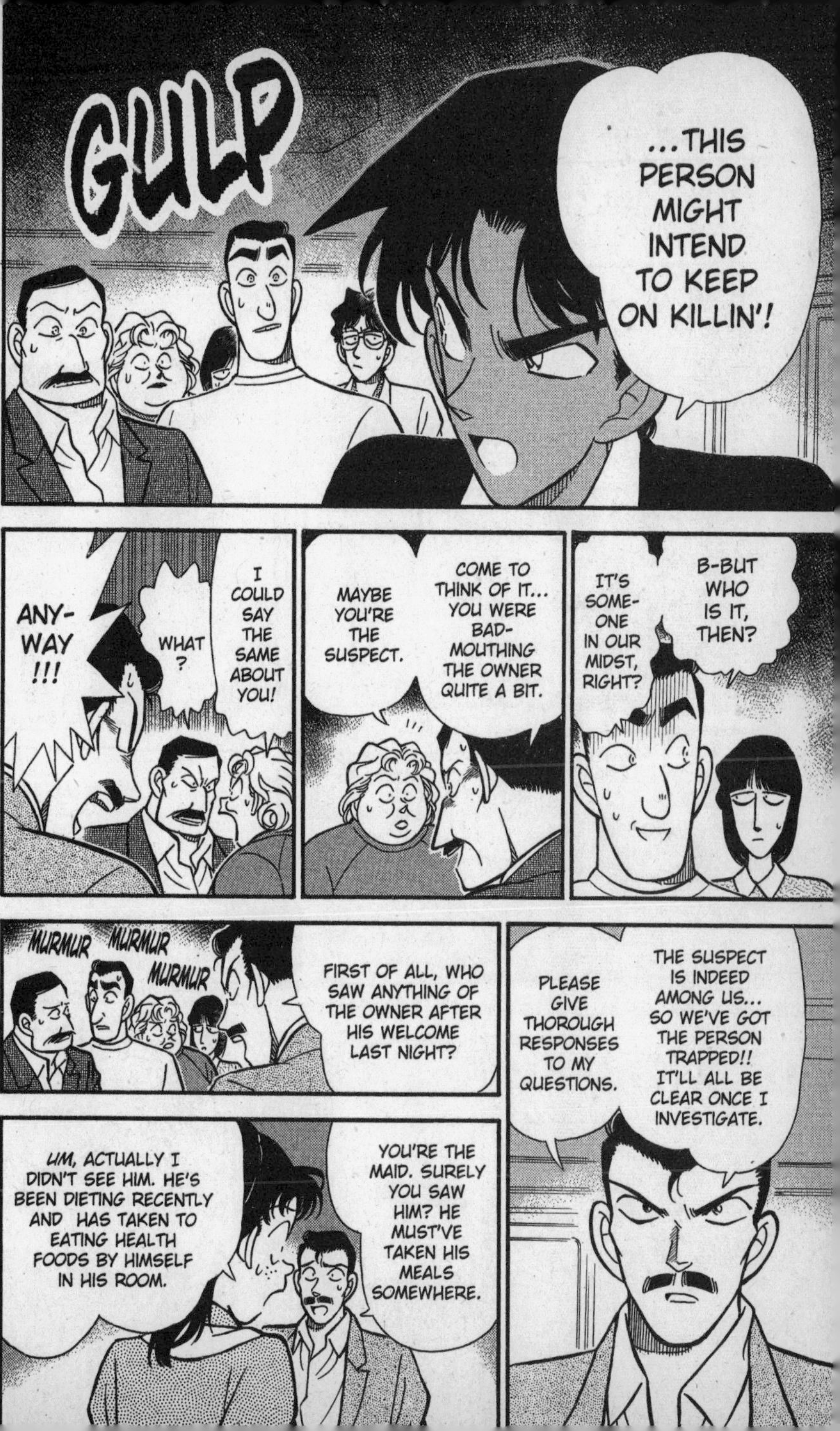
...THIS PERSON MIGHT INTEND TO KEEP ON KILLIN'!
GULP
B-BUT WHO IS IT, THEN?
IT'S SOMEONE IN OUR MIDST, RIGHT?
COME TO THINK OF IT... YOU WERE BAD-MOUTHING THE OWNER QUITE A BIT.
MAYBE YOU'RE THE SUSPECT.
I COULD SAY THE SAME ABOUT YOU!
WHAT?
ANYWAY!!!
THE SUSPECT IS INDEED AMONG US... SO WE'VE GOT THE PERSON TRAPPED!! IT'LL ALL BE CLEAR ONCE I INVESTIGATE.
PLEASE GIVE THOROUGH RESPONSES TO MY QUESTIONS.
FIRST OF ALL, WHO SAW ANYTHING OF THE OWNER AFTER HIS WELCOME LAST NIGHT?
MURMUR
MURMUR
MURMUR
YOU'RE THE MAID. SURELY YOU SAW HIM? HE MUST'VE TAKEN HIS MEALS SOMEWHERE.
UM, ACTUALLY I DIDN'T SEE HIM. HE'S BEEN DIETING RECENTLY AND HAS TAKEN TO EATING HEALTH FOODS BY HIMSELF IN HIS ROOM.

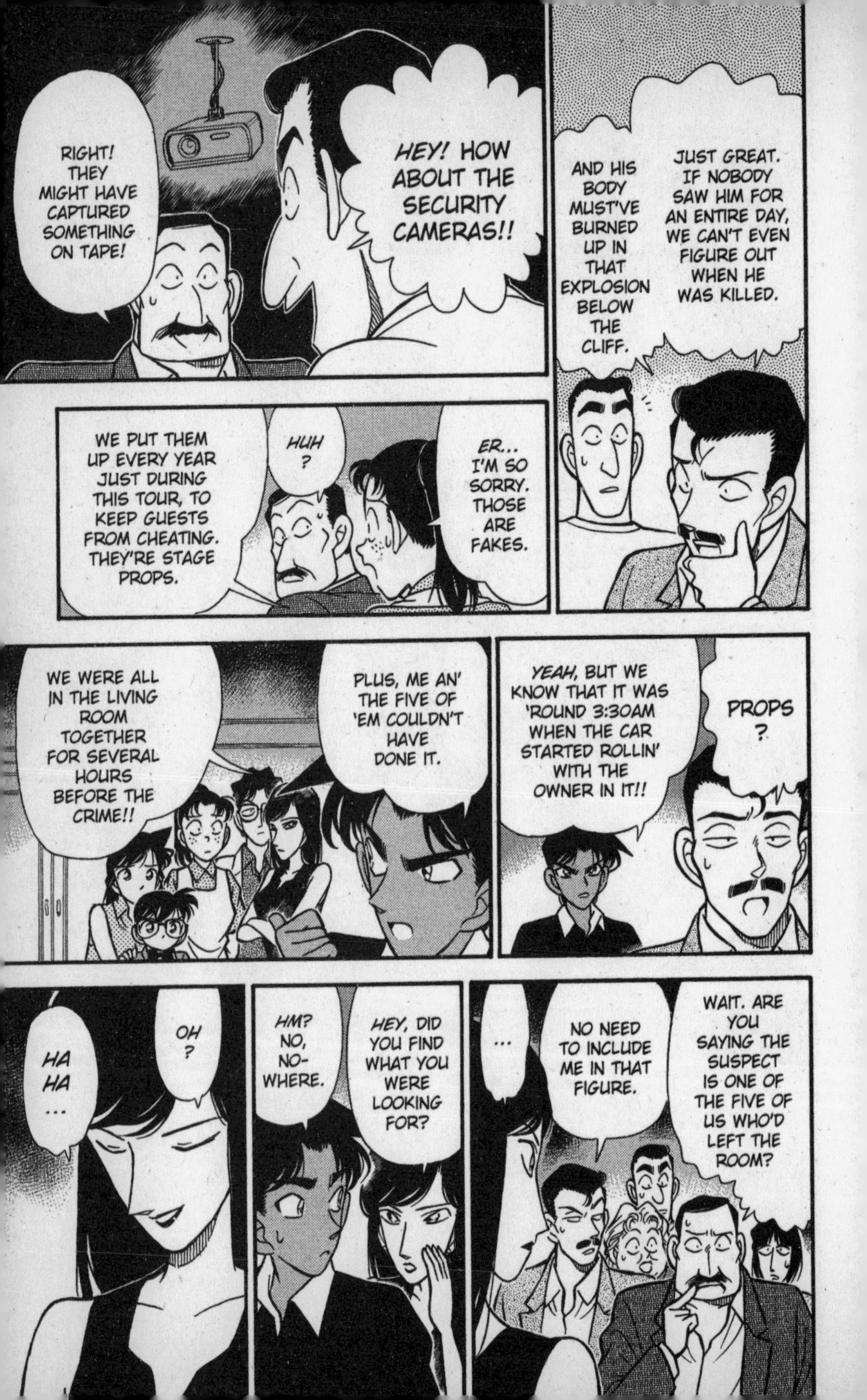
JUST GREAT. IF NOBODY SAW HIM FOR AN ENTIRE DAY, WE CAN'T EVEN FIGURE OUT WHEN HE WAS KILLED.
AND HIS BODY MUST'VE BURNED UP IN THAT EXPLOSION BELOW THE CLIFF.
HEY! HOW ABOUT THE SECURITY CAMERAS!!
RIGHT! THEY MIGHT HAVE CAPTURED SOMETHING ON TAPE!
ER... I'M SO SORRY. THOSE ARE FAKES.
HUH?
WE PUT THEM UP EVERY YEAR JUST DURING THIS TOUR, TO KEEP GUESTS FROM CHEATING. THEY'RE STAGE PROPS.
PROPS?
YEAH, BUT WE KNOW THAT IT WAS 'ROUND 3:30AM WHEN THE CAR STARTED ROLLIN' WITH THE OWNER IN IT!!
PLUS, ME AN' THE FIVE OF 'EM COULDN'T HAVE DONE IT.
WE WERE ALL IN THE LIVING ROOM TOGETHER FOR SEVERAL HOURS BEFORE THE CRIME!!
WAIT. ARE YOU SAYING THE SUSPECT IS ONE OF THE FIVE OF US WHO'D LEFT THE ROOM?
NO NEED TO INCLUDE ME IN THAT FIGURE.
...
HEY, DID YOU FIND WHAT YOU WERE LOOKING FOR?
HM? NO, NO-WHERE.
OH?
HA HA ...

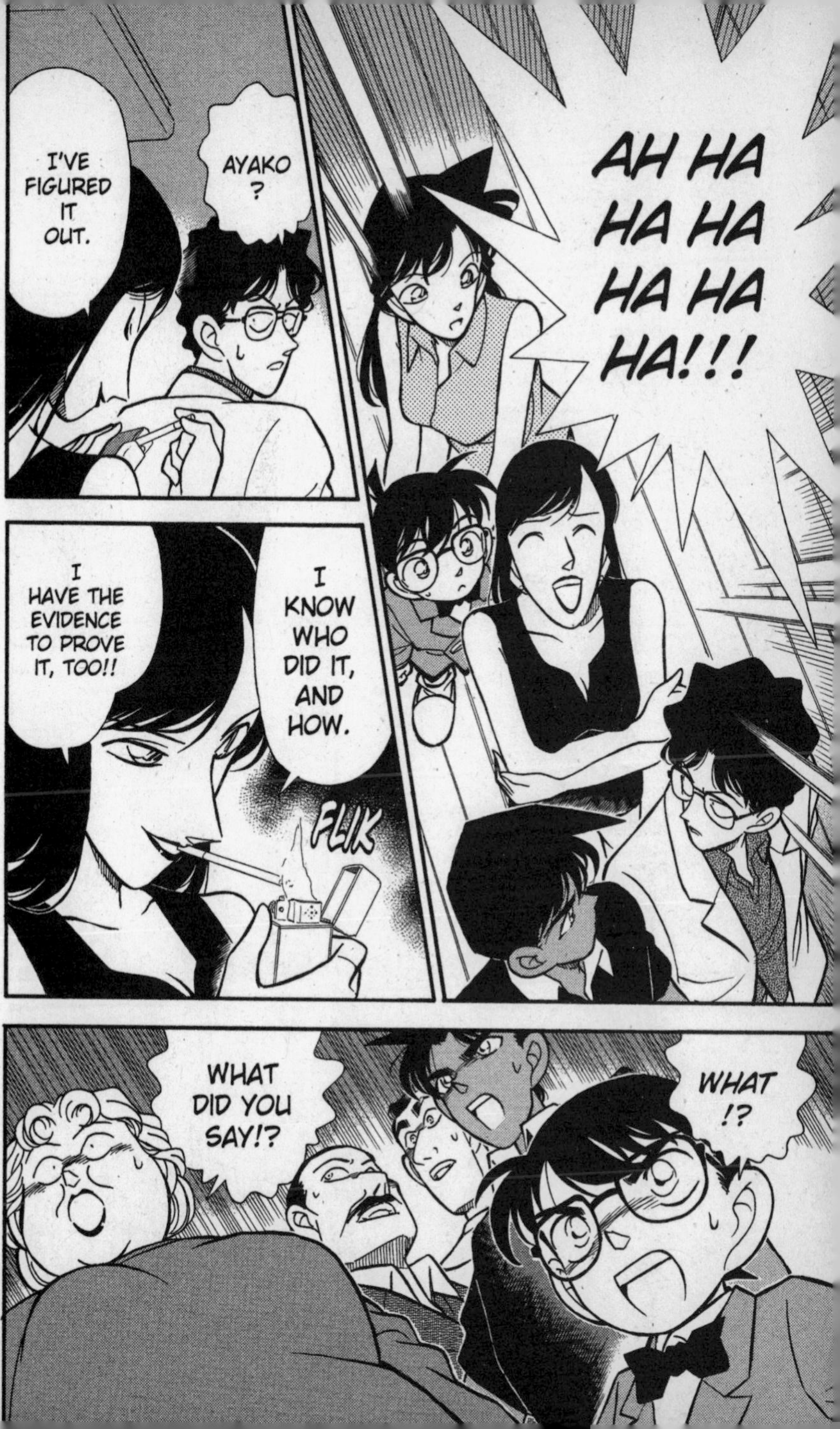
I'VE FIGURED IT OUT.
AYAKO?
AH HA HA HA HA HA HA!!!
I KNOW WHO DID IT, AND HOW.
I HAVE THE EVIDENCE TO PROVE IT, TOO!!
FLIK
WHAT DID YOU SAY!?
WHAT!?

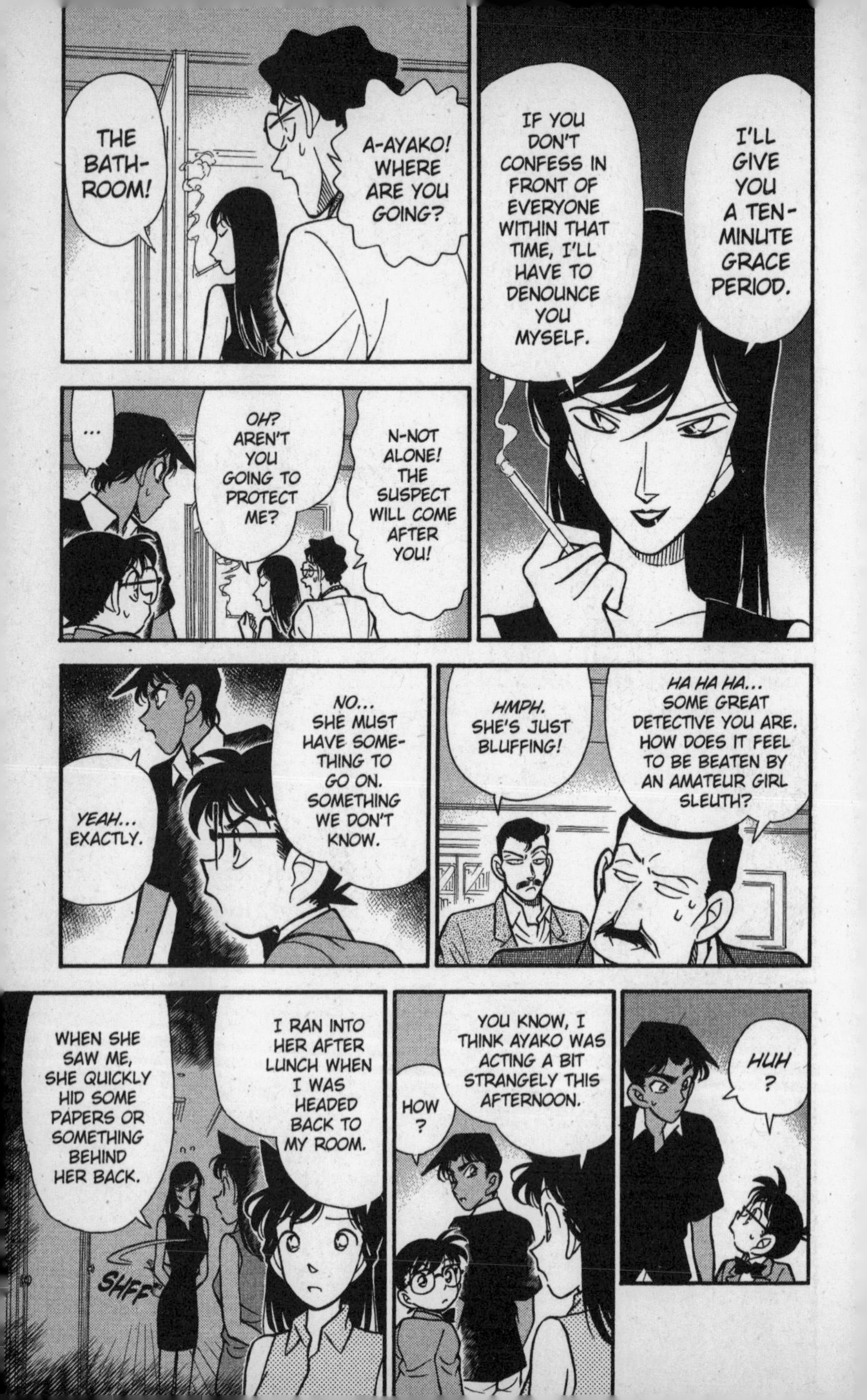
I'LL GIVE YOU A TEN-MINUTE GRACE PERIOD.
IF YOU DON'T CONFESS IN FRONT OF EVERYONE WITHIN THAT TIME, I'LL HAVE TO DENOUNCE YOU MYSELF.
A-AYAKO! WHERE ARE YOU GOING?
THE BATH-ROOM!
N-NOT ALONE! THE SUSPECT WILL COME AFTER YOU!
OH? AREN'T YOU GOING TO PROTECT ME?
...
HA HA HA... SOME GREAT DETECTIVE YOU ARE. HOW DOES IT FEEL TO BE BEATEN BY AN AMATEUR GIRL SLEUTH?
HMPH. SHE'S JUST BLUFFING!
NO... SHE MUST HAVE SOME-THING TO GO ON. SOMETHING WE DON'T KNOW.
YEAH... EXACTLY.
HUH?
YOU KNOW, I THINK AYAKO WAS ACTING A BIT STRANGELY THIS AFTERNOON.
HOW?
I RAN INTO HER AFTER LUNCH WHEN I WAS HEADED BACK TO MY ROOM.
WHEN SHE SAW ME, SHE QUICKLY HID SOME PAPERS OR SOMETHING BEHIND HER BACK.
SHFF

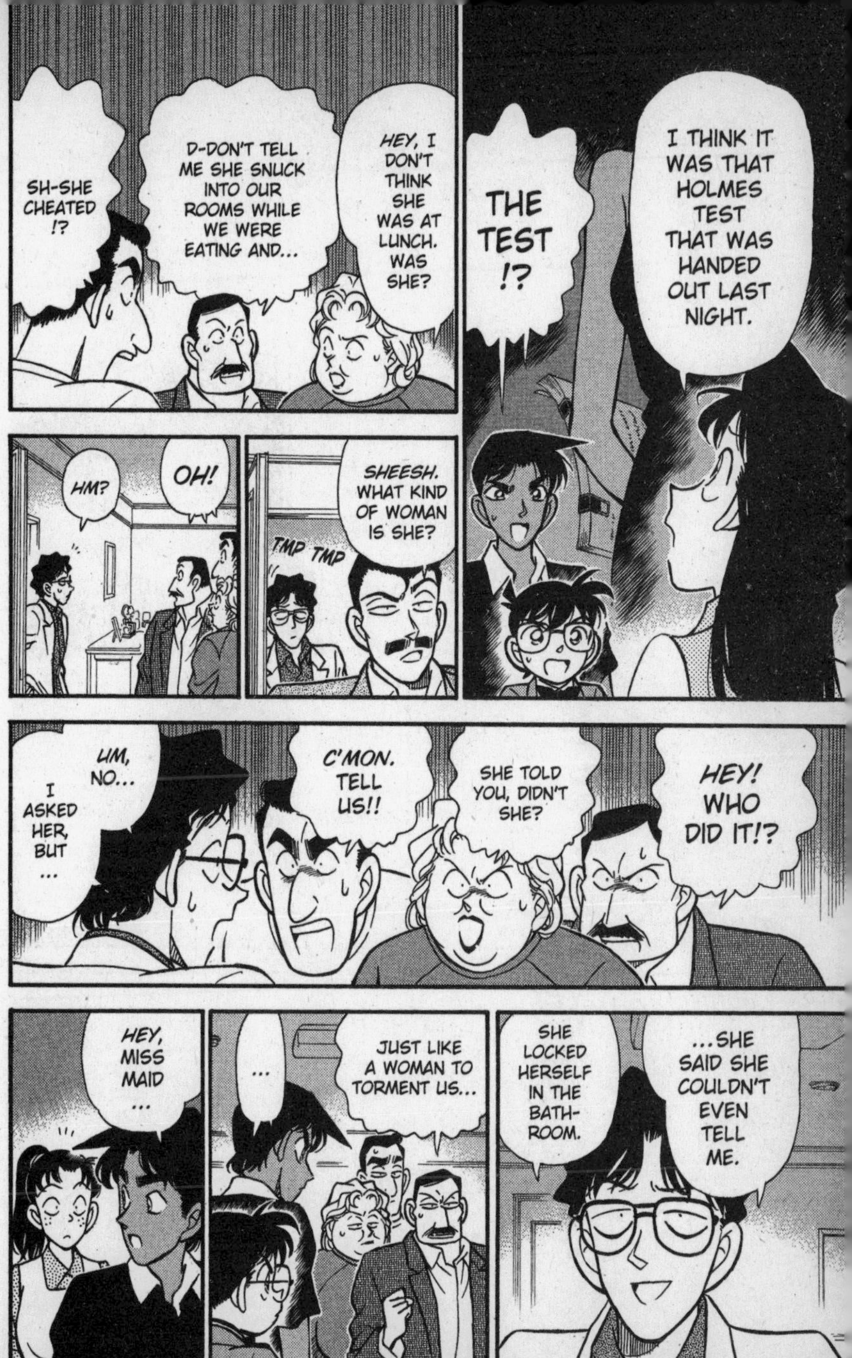
I THINK IT WAS THAT HOLMES TEST THAT WAS HANDED OUT LAST NIGHT.
THE TEST !?
HEY, I DON'T THINK SHE WAS AT LUNCH. WAS SHE?
D-DON'T TELL ME SHE SNUCK INTO OUR ROOMS WHILE WE WERE EATING AND...
SH-SHE CHEATED !?
SHEESH. WHAT KIND OF WOMAN IS SHE?
TMP TMP
OH!
HM?
HEY! WHO DID IT!?
SHE TOLD YOU, DIDN'T SHE?
C'MON. TELL US!!
UM, NO...
I ASKED HER, BUT ...
...SHE SAID SHE COULDN'T EVEN TELL ME.
SHE LOCKED HERSELF IN THE BATH-ROOM.
JUST LIKE A WOMAN TO TORMENT US...
...
HEY, MISS MAID ...

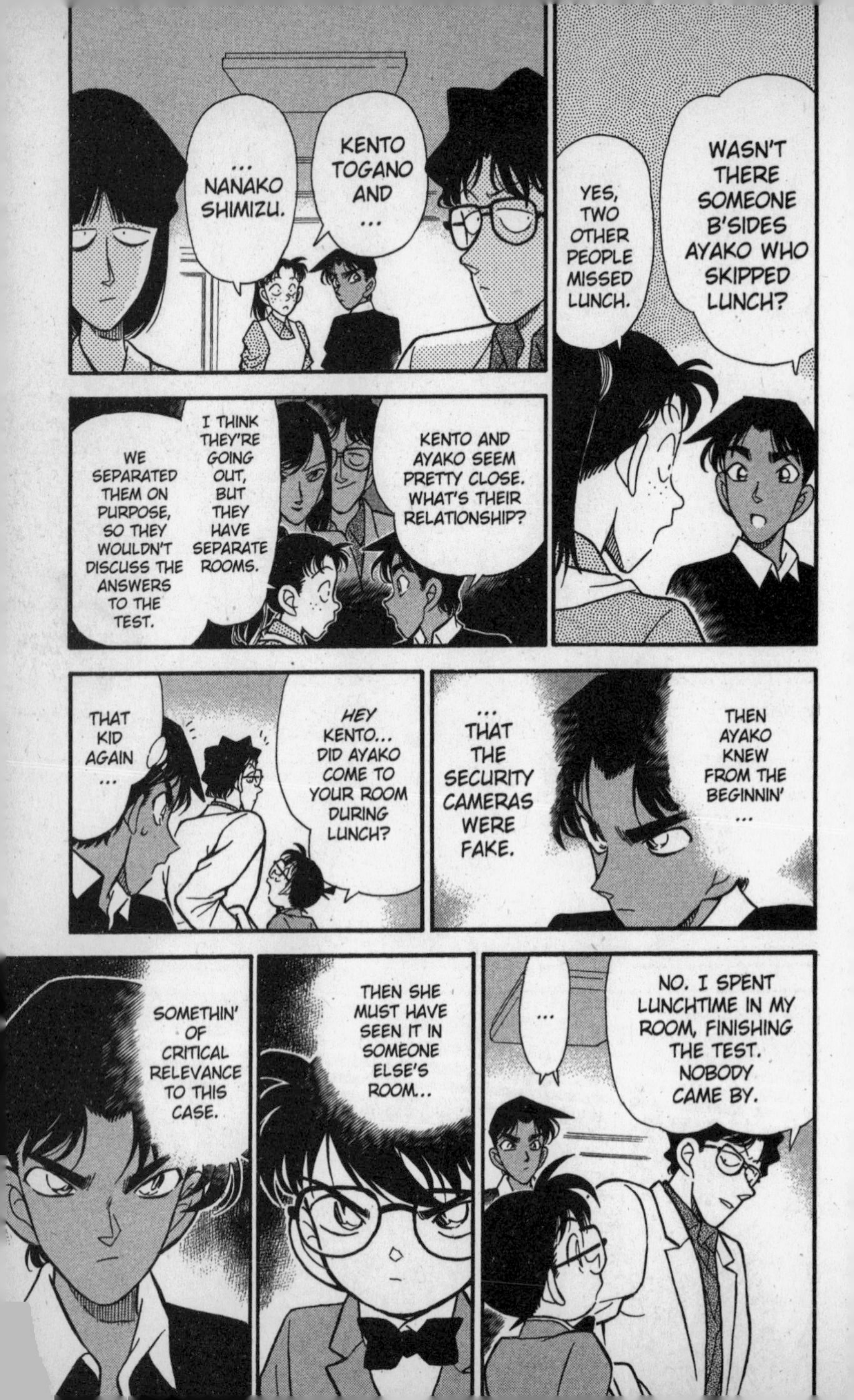
WASN'T THERE SOMEONE B'SIDES AYAKO WHO SKIPPED LUNCH?
YES, TWO OTHER PEOPLE MISSED LUNCH.
KENTO TOGANO AND ...
... NANAKO SHIMIZU.
KENTO AND AYAKO SEEM PRETTY CLOSE. WHAT'S THEIR RELATIONSHIP?
I THINK THEY'RE GOING OUT, BUT THEY HAVE SEPARATE ROOMS.
WE SEPARATED THEM ON PURPOSE, SO THEY WOULDN'T DISCUSS THE ANSWERS TO THE TEST.
THEN AYAKO KNEW FROM THE BEGINNIN' ...
... THAT THE SECURITY CAMERAS WERE FAKE.
HEY KENTO... DID AYAKO COME TO YOUR ROOM DURING LUNCH?
THAT KID AGAIN ...
NO. I SPENT LUNCHTIME IN MY ROOM, FINISHING THE TEST. NOBODY CAME BY.
...
THEN SHE MUST HAVE SEEN IT IN SOMEONE ELSE'S ROOM...
SOMETHIN' OF CRITICAL RELEVANCE TO THIS CASE.

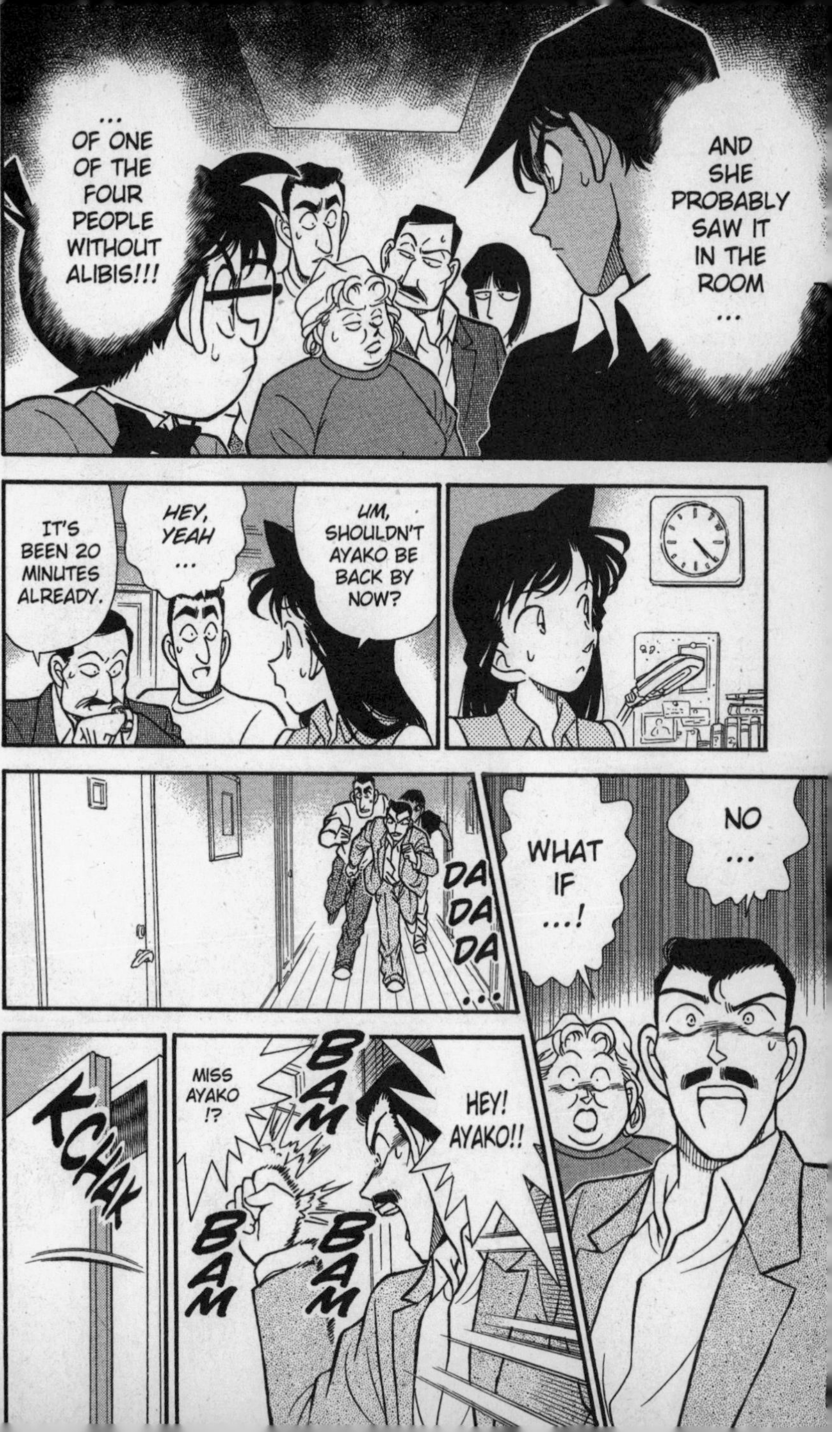
AND SHE PROBABLY SAW IT IN THE ROOM ...
... OF ONE OF THE FOUR PEOPLE WITHOUT ALIBIS!!!
UM, SHOULDN'T AYAKO BE BACK BY NOW?
HEY, YEAH ...
IT'S BEEN 20 MINUTES ALREADY.
NO ...
WHAT IF ...!
DA DA DA ...
HEY! AYAKO!!
BAM
BAM
BAM
MISS AYAKO !?
KCHAK

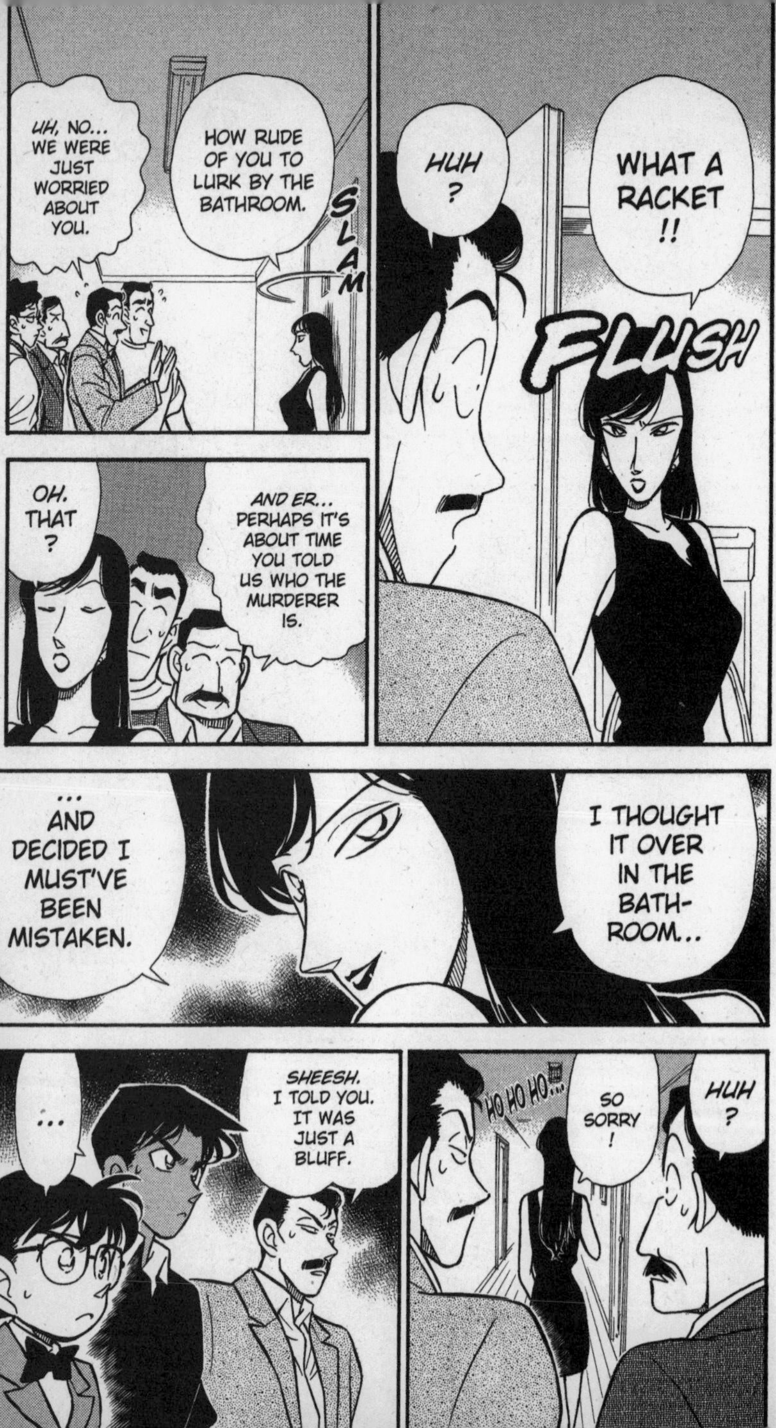
WHAT A RACKET !!
FLUSH
HUH ?
SLAM
HOW RUDE OF YOU TO LURK BY THE BATHROOM.
UH, NO... WE WERE JUST WORRIED ABOUT YOU.
AND ER... PERHAPS IT'S ABOUT TIME YOU TOLD US WHO THE MURDERER IS.
OH. THAT ?
I THOUGHT IT OVER IN THE BATH- ROOM...
... AND DECIDED I MUST'VE BEEN MISTAKEN.
HUH ?
SO SORRY !
HO HO HO...
SHEESH. I TOLD YOU. IT WAS JUST A BLUFF.
...

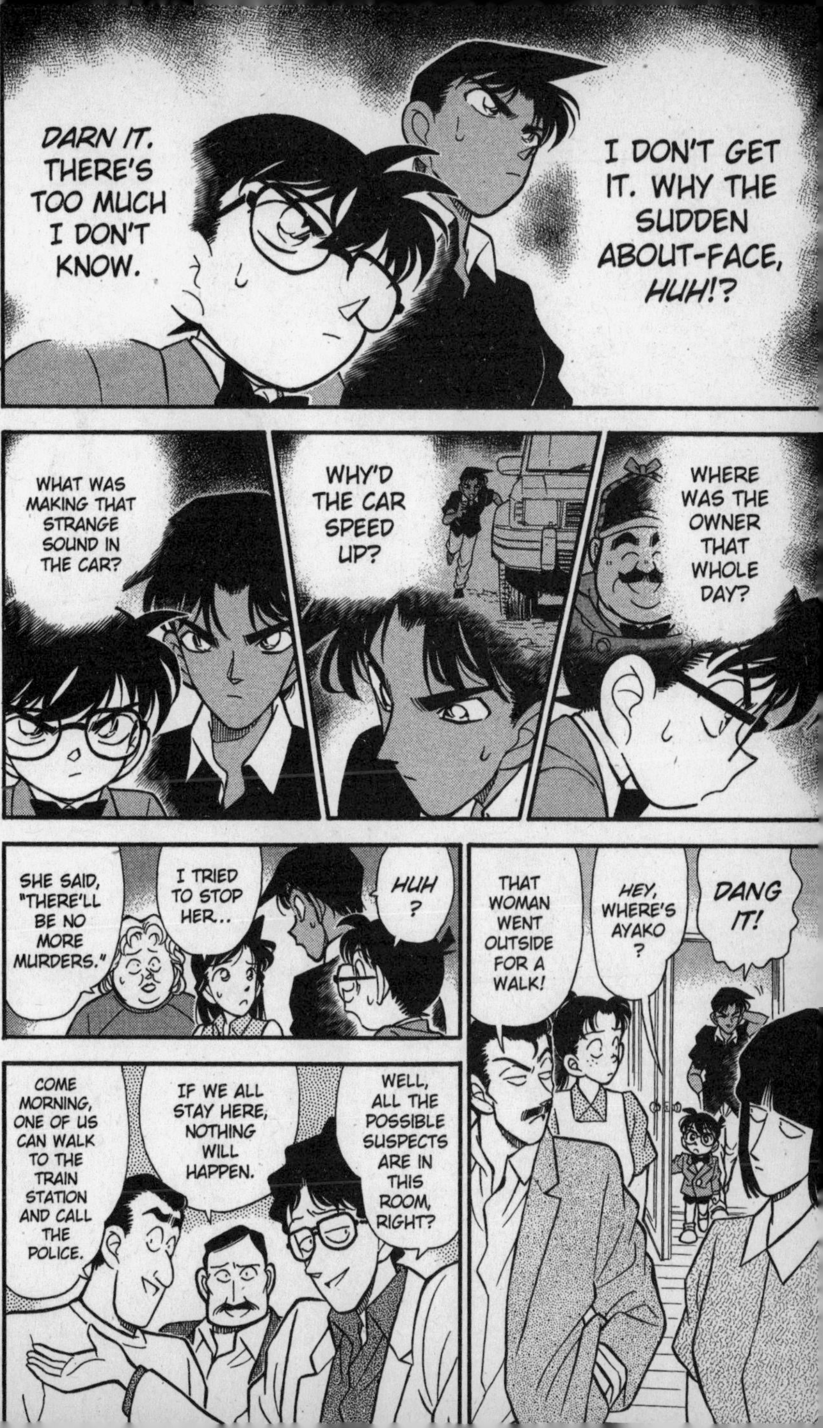
I DON'T GET IT. WHY THE SUDDEN ABOUT-FACE, HUH!?
DARN IT. THERE'S TOO MUCH I DON'T KNOW.
WHERE WAS THE OWNER THAT WHOLE DAY?
WHY'D THE CAR SPEED UP?
WHAT WAS MAKING THAT STRANGE SOUND IN THE CAR?
DANG IT!
HEY, WHERE'S AYAKO?
THAT WOMAN WENT OUTSIDE FOR A WALK!
HUH?
I TRIED TO STOP HER...
SHE SAID, "THERE'LL BE NO MORE MURDERS."
WELL, ALL THE POSSIBLE SUSPECTS ARE IN THIS ROOM, RIGHT?
IF WE ALL STAY HERE, NOTHING WILL HAPPEN.
COME MORNING, ONE OF US CAN WALK TO THE TRAIN STATION AND CALL THE POLICE.

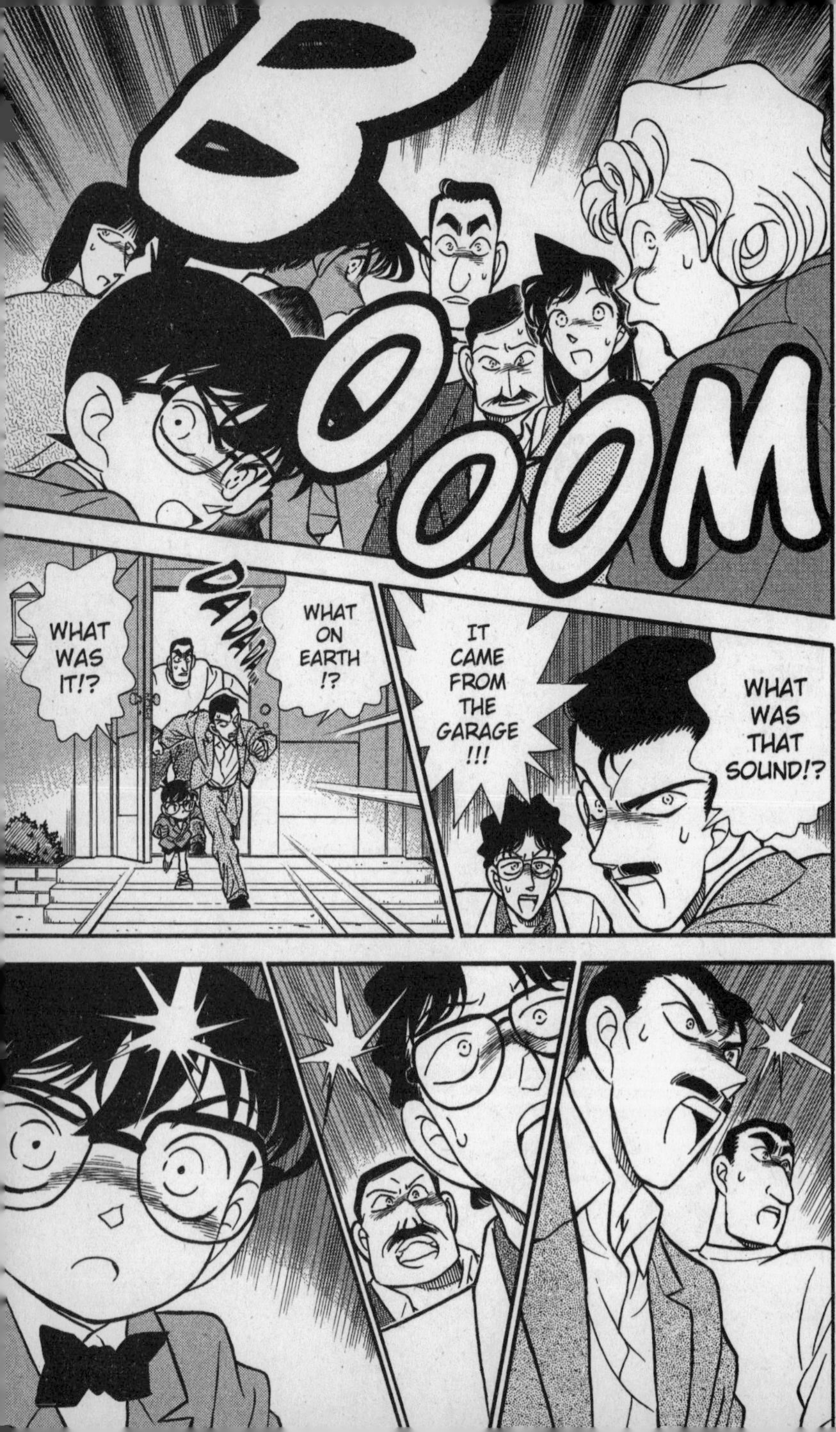
BOOOOM
WHAT WAS THAT SOUND!?
IT CAME FROM THE GARAGE!!!
DADADA
WHAT ON EARTH!?
WHAT WAS IT!?

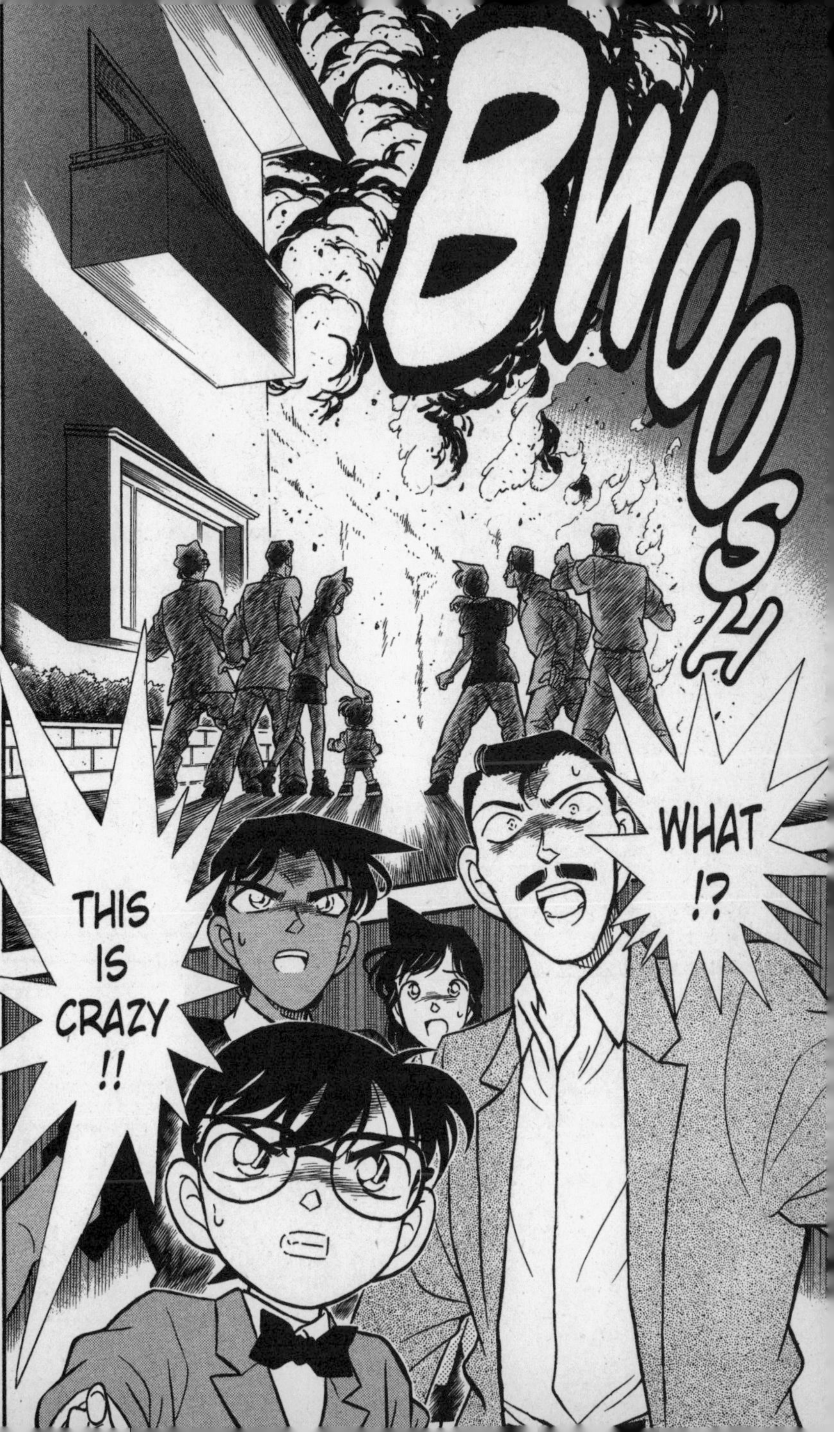
BWOOOSH
WHAT !?
THIS IS CRAZY !!

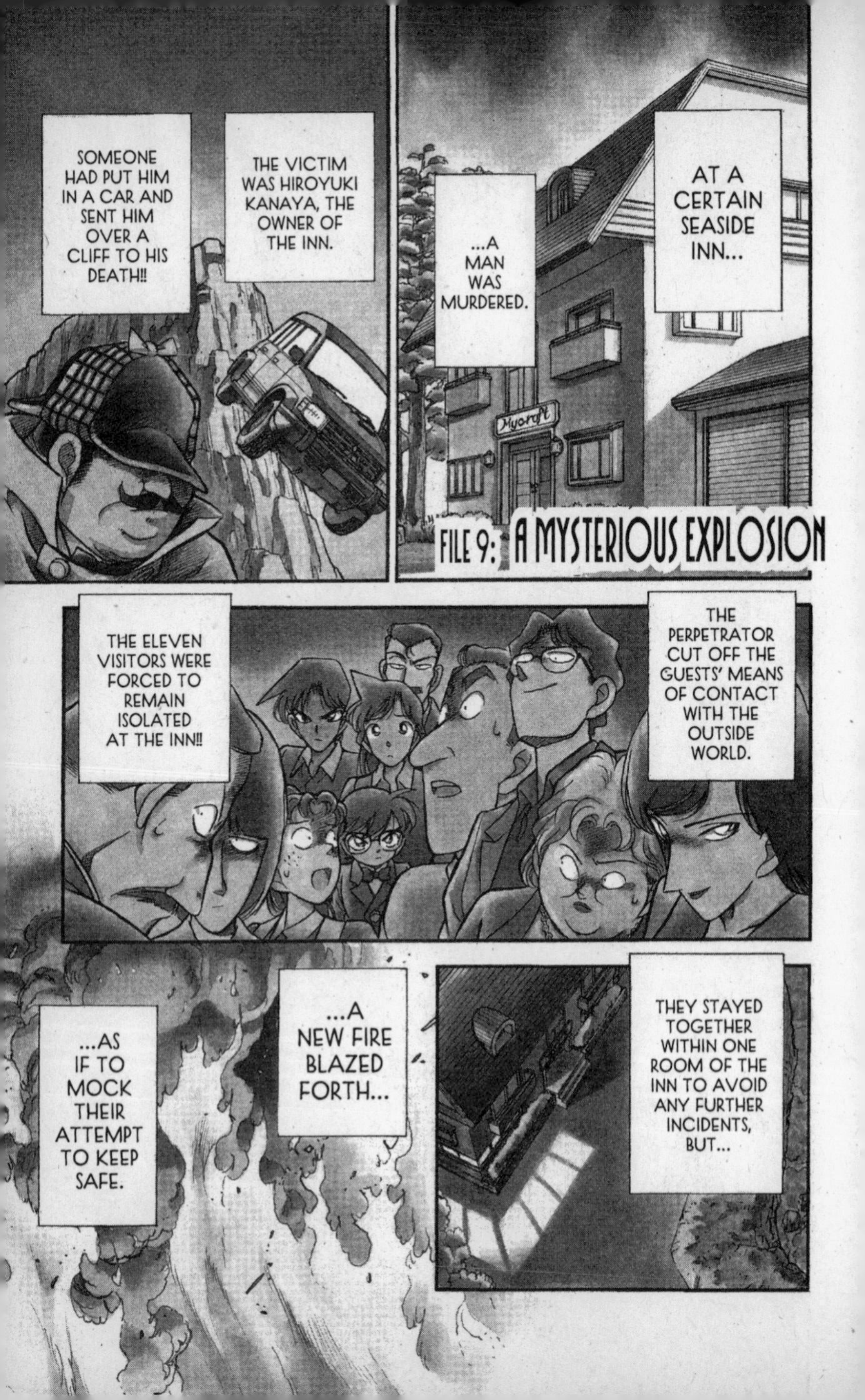

AT A CERTAIN SEASIDE INN...
...A MAN WAS MURDERED.
Myoraft
FILE 9: A MYSTERIOUS EXPLOSION
THE VICTIM WAS HIROYUKI KANAYA, THE OWNER OF THE INN.
SOMEONE HAD PUT HIM IN A CAR AND SENT HIM OVER A CLIFF TO HIS DEATH!!
THE PERPETRATOR CUT OFF THE GUESTS' MEANS OF CONTACT WITH THE OUTSIDE WORLD.
THE ELEVEN VISITORS WERE FORCED TO REMAIN ISOLATED AT THE INN!!
THEY STAYED TOGETHER WITHIN ONE ROOM OF THE INN TO AVOID ANY FURTHER INCIDENTS, BUT...
...A NEW FIRE BLAZED FORTH...
...AS IF TO MOCK THEIR ATTEMPT TO KEEP SAFE.

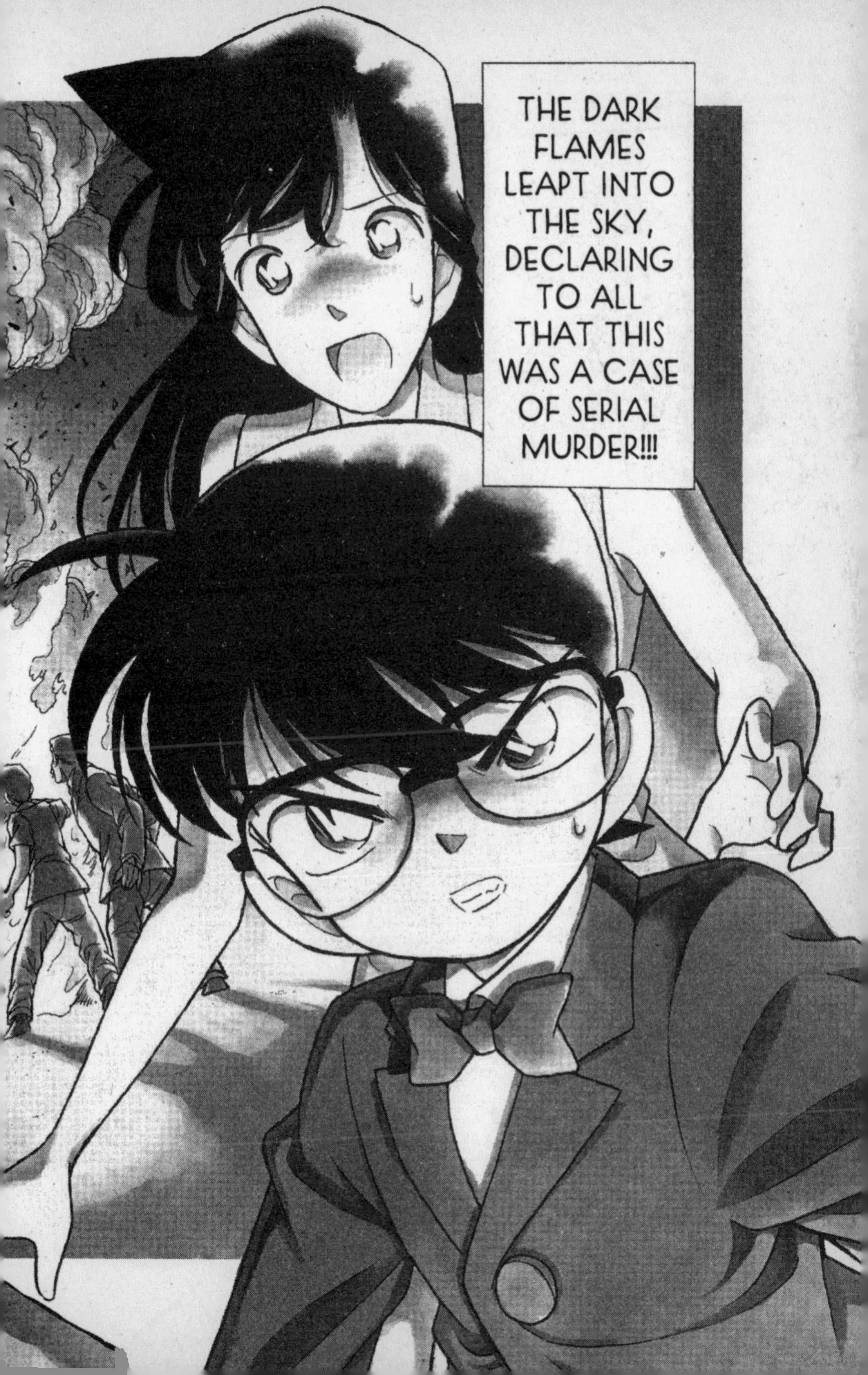
THE DARK FLAMES LEAPT INTO THE SKY, DECLARING TO ALL THAT THIS WAS A CASE OF SERIAL MURDER!!!

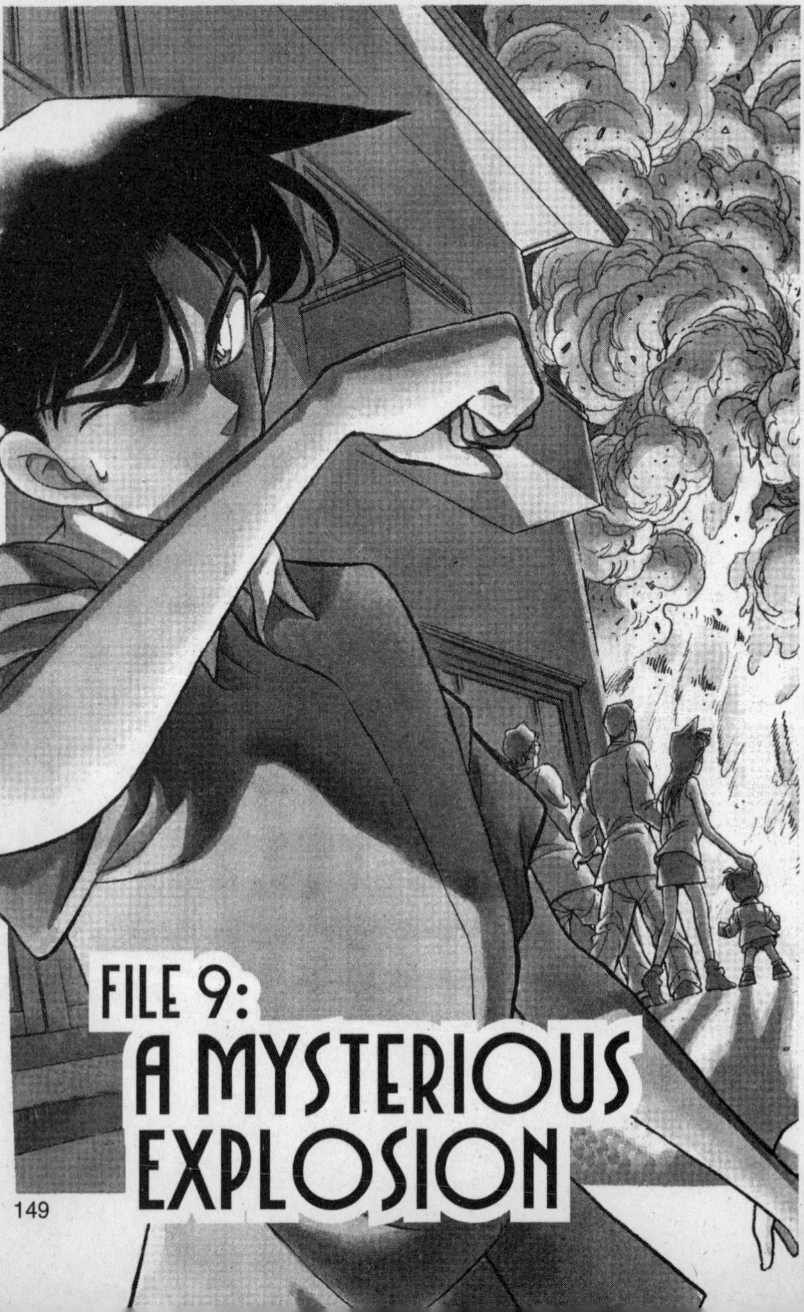
FILE 9:
A MYSTERIOUS EXPLOSION

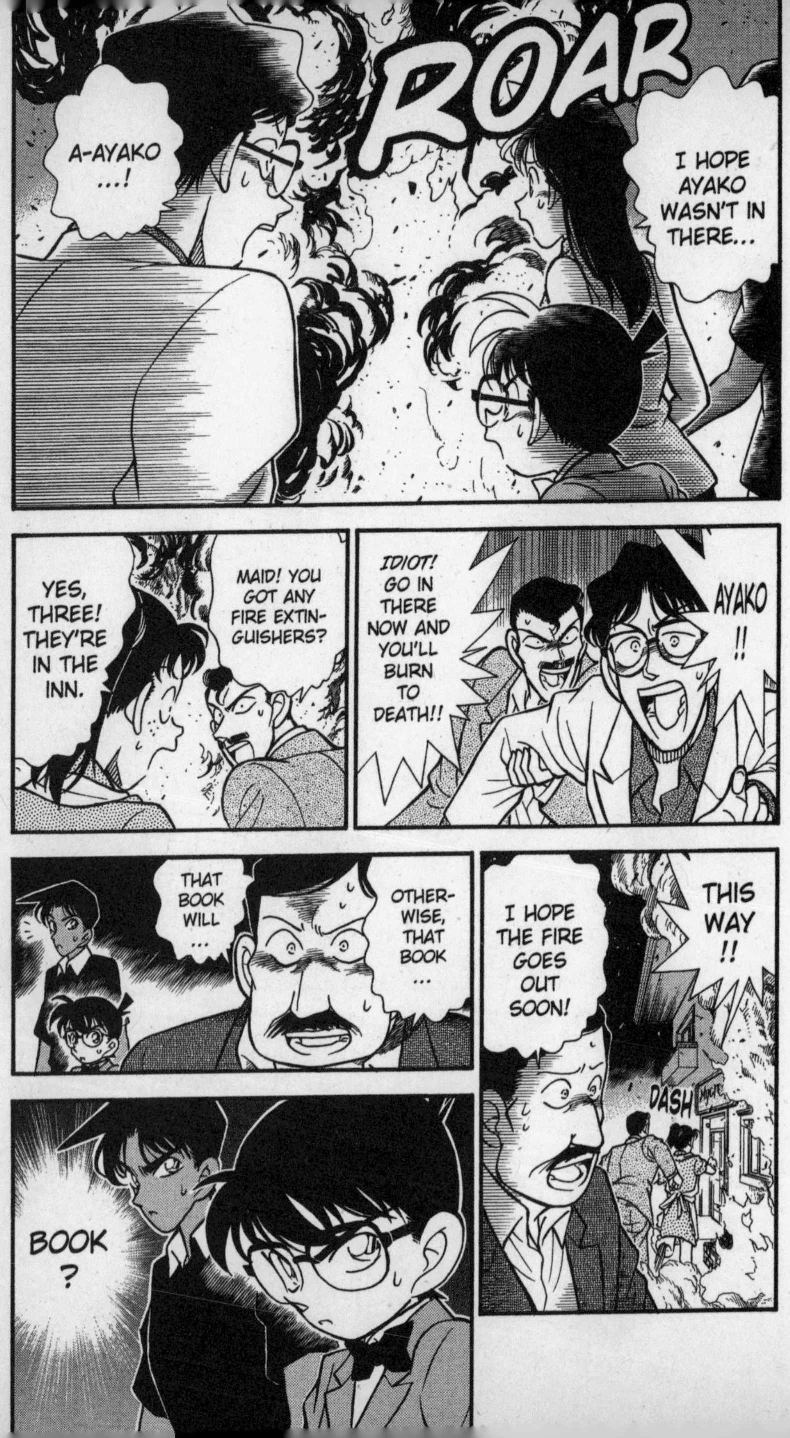
ROAR
I HOPE AYAKO WASN'T IN THERE...
A-AYAKO ...!
AYAKO !!
IDIOT! GO IN THERE NOW AND YOU'LL BURN TO DEATH!!
MAID! YOU GOT ANY FIRE EXTIN-GUISHERS?
YES, THREE! THEY'RE IN THE INN.
THIS WAY !!
DASH
I HOPE THE FIRE GOES OUT SOON!
OTHER-WISE, THAT BOOK ...
THAT BOOK WILL ...
BOOK ?

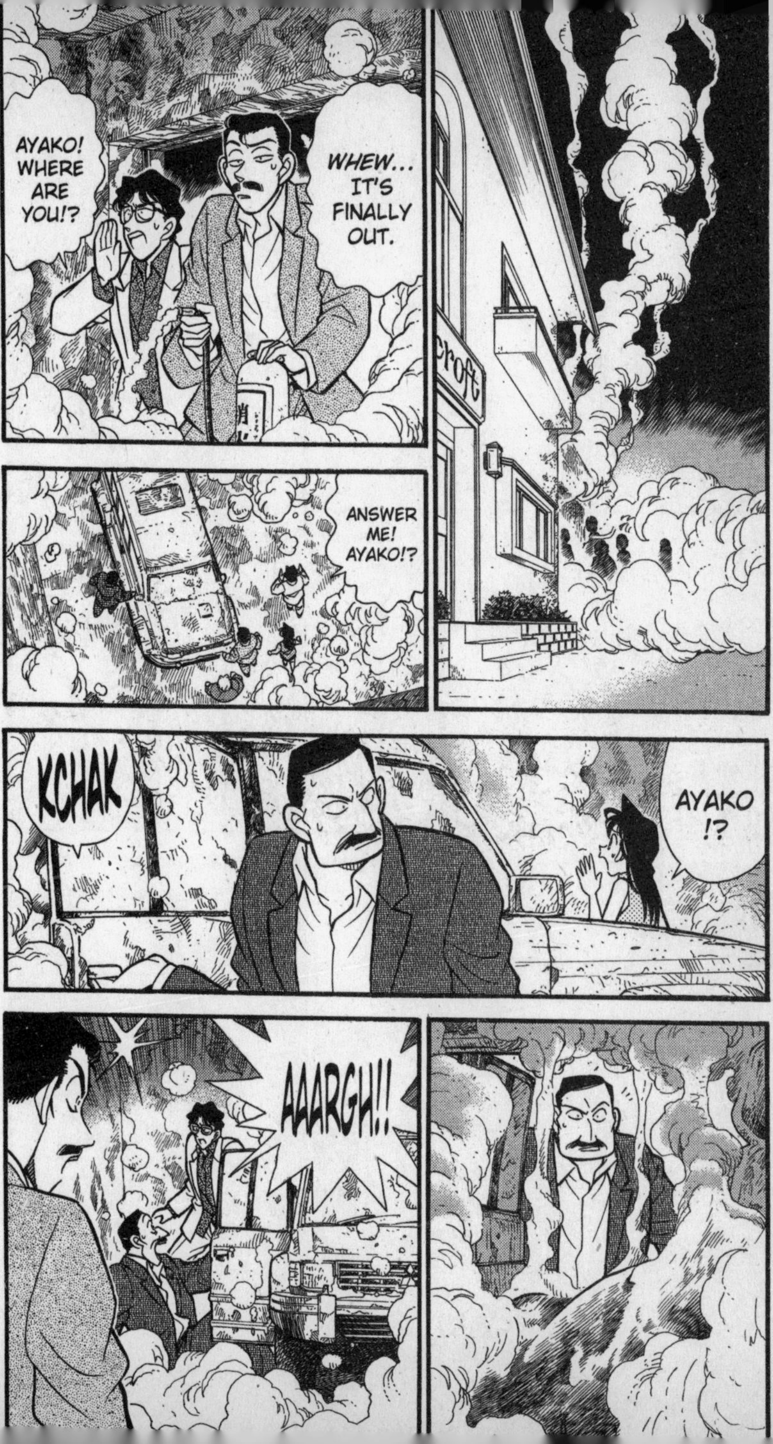
WHEW... IT'S FINALLY OUT.
AYAKO! WHERE ARE YOU!?
ANSWER ME! AYAKO!?
AYAKO !?
KCHAK
AAARGH!!

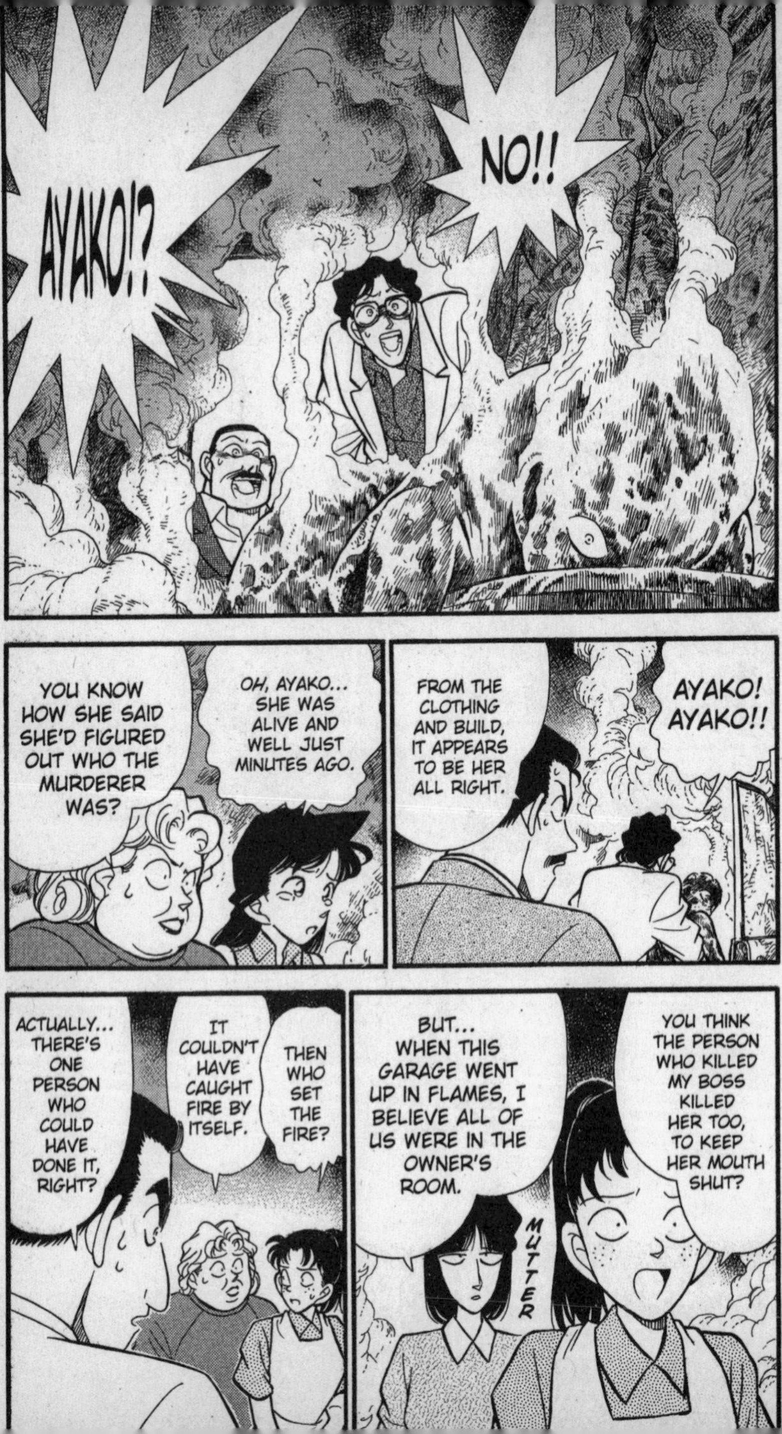
NO!!
AYAKO!?
AYAKO! AYAKO!!
FROM THE CLOTHING AND BUILD, IT APPEARS TO BE HER ALL RIGHT.
OH, AYAKO... SHE WAS ALIVE AND WELL JUST MINUTES AGO.
YOU KNOW HOW SHE SAID SHE'D FIGURED OUT WHO THE MURDERER WAS?
YOU THINK THE PERSON WHO KILLED MY BOSS KILLED HER TOO, TO KEEP HER MOUTH SHUT?
MUTTER
BUT... WHEN THIS GARAGE WENT UP IN FLAMES, I BELIEVE ALL OF US WERE IN THE OWNER'S ROOM.
THEN WHO SET THE FIRE?
IT COULDN'T HAVE CAUGHT FIRE BY ITSELF.
ACTUALLY... THERE'S ONE PERSON WHO COULD HAVE DONE IT, RIGHT?

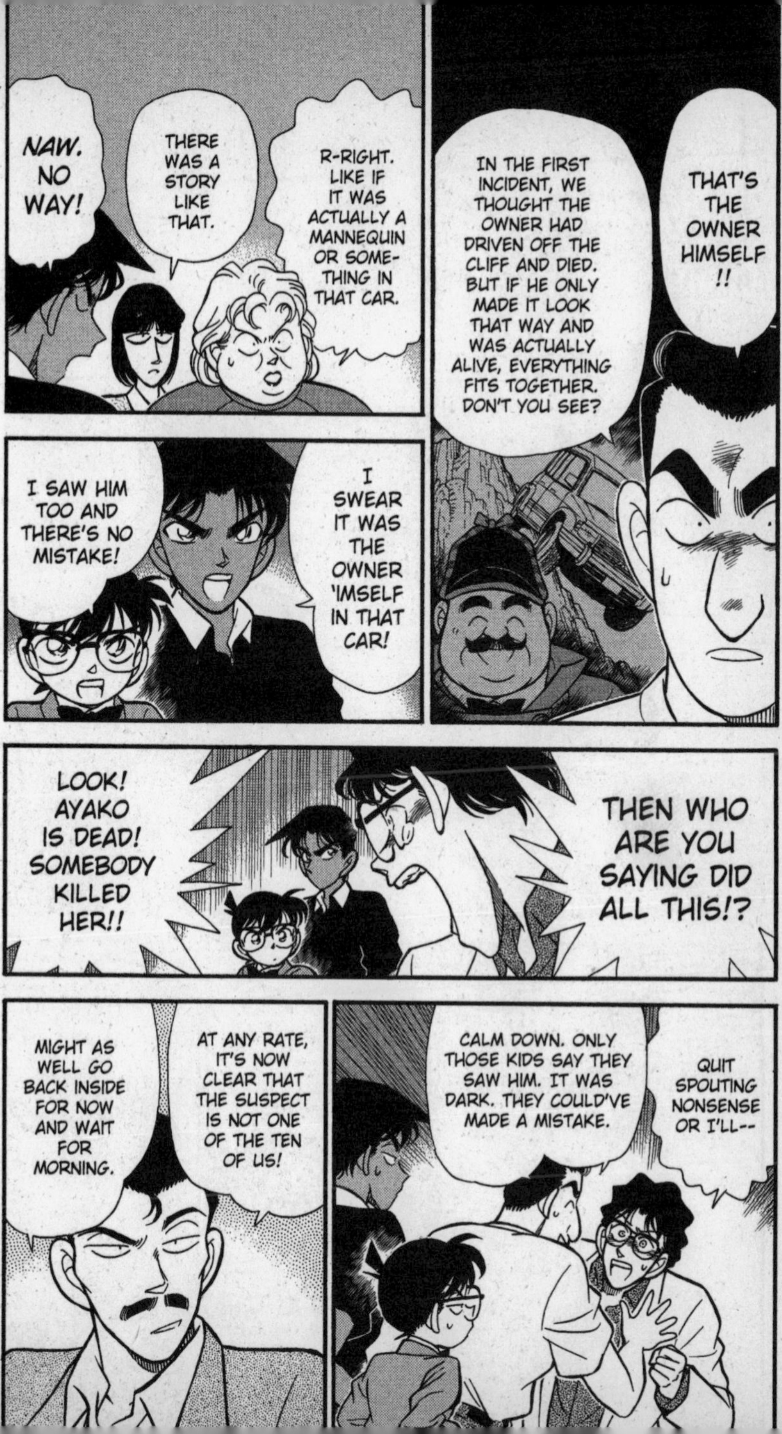
NAW. NO WAY!
THERE WAS A STORY LIKE THAT.
R-RIGHT. LIKE IF IT WAS ACTUALLY A MANNEQUIN OR SOME-THING IN THAT CAR.
IN THE FIRST INCIDENT, WE THOUGHT THE OWNER HAD DRIVEN OFF THE CLIFF AND DIED. BUT IF HE ONLY MADE IT LOOK THAT WAY AND WAS ACTUALLY ALIVE, EVERYTHING FITS TOGETHER. DON'T YOU SEE?
THAT'S THE OWNER HIMSELF!!
I SAW HIM TOO AND THERE'S NO MISTAKE!
I SWEAR IT WAS THE OWNER 'IMSELF IN THAT CAR!
LOOK! AYAKO IS DEAD! SOMEBODY KILLED HER!!
THEN WHO ARE YOU SAYING DID ALL THIS!?
MIGHT AS WELL GO BACK INSIDE FOR NOW AND WAIT FOR MORNING.
AT ANY RATE, IT'S NOW CLEAR THAT THE SUSPECT IS NOT ONE OF THE TEN OF US!
CALM DOWN. ONLY THOSE KIDS SAY THEY SAW HIM. IT WAS DARK. THEY COULD'VE MADE A MISTAKE.
QUIT SPOUTING NONSENSE OR I'LL--

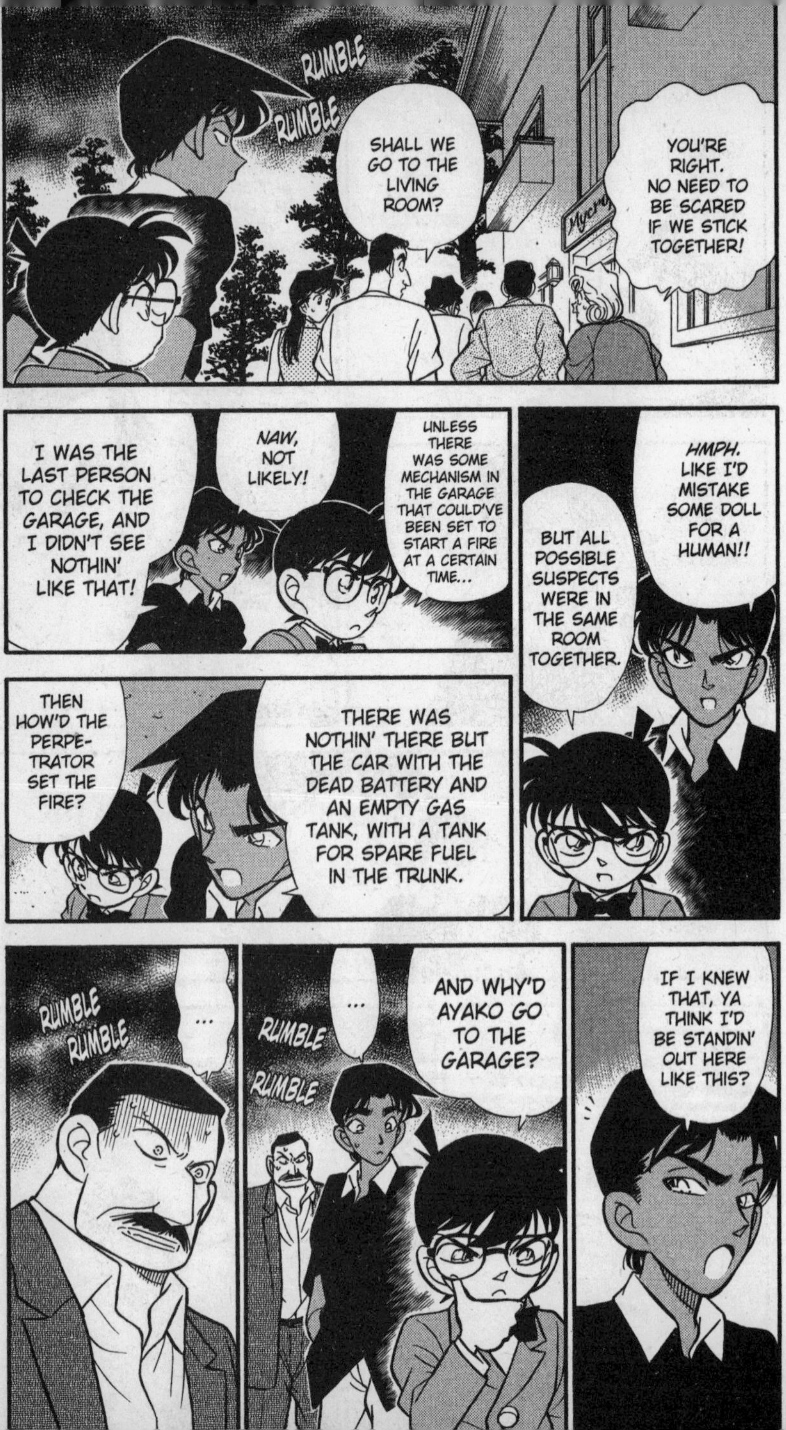
RUMBLE
RUMBLE
SHALL WE GO TO THE LIVING ROOM?
YOU'RE RIGHT. NO NEED TO BE SCARED IF WE STICK TOGETHER!
UNLESS THERE WAS SOME MECHANISM IN THE GARAGE THAT COULD'VE BEEN SET TO START A FIRE AT A CERTAIN TIME...
NAW, NOT LIKELY!
I WAS THE LAST PERSON TO CHECK THE GARAGE, AND I DIDN'T SEE NOTHIN' LIKE THAT!
HMPH. LIKE I'D MISTAKE SOME DOLL FOR A HUMAN!!
BUT ALL POSSIBLE SUSPECTS WERE IN THE SAME ROOM TOGETHER.
THERE WAS NOTHIN' THERE BUT THE CAR WITH THE DEAD BATTERY AND AN EMPTY GAS TANK, WITH A TANK FOR SPARE FUEL IN THE TRUNK.
THEN HOW'D THE PERPE-TRATOR SET THE FIRE?
...
RUMBLE
RUMBLE
...
...
RUMBLE
RUMBLE
AND WHY'D AYAKO GO TO THE GARAGE?
IF I KNEW THAT, YA THINK I'D BE STANDIN' OUT HERE LIKE THIS?

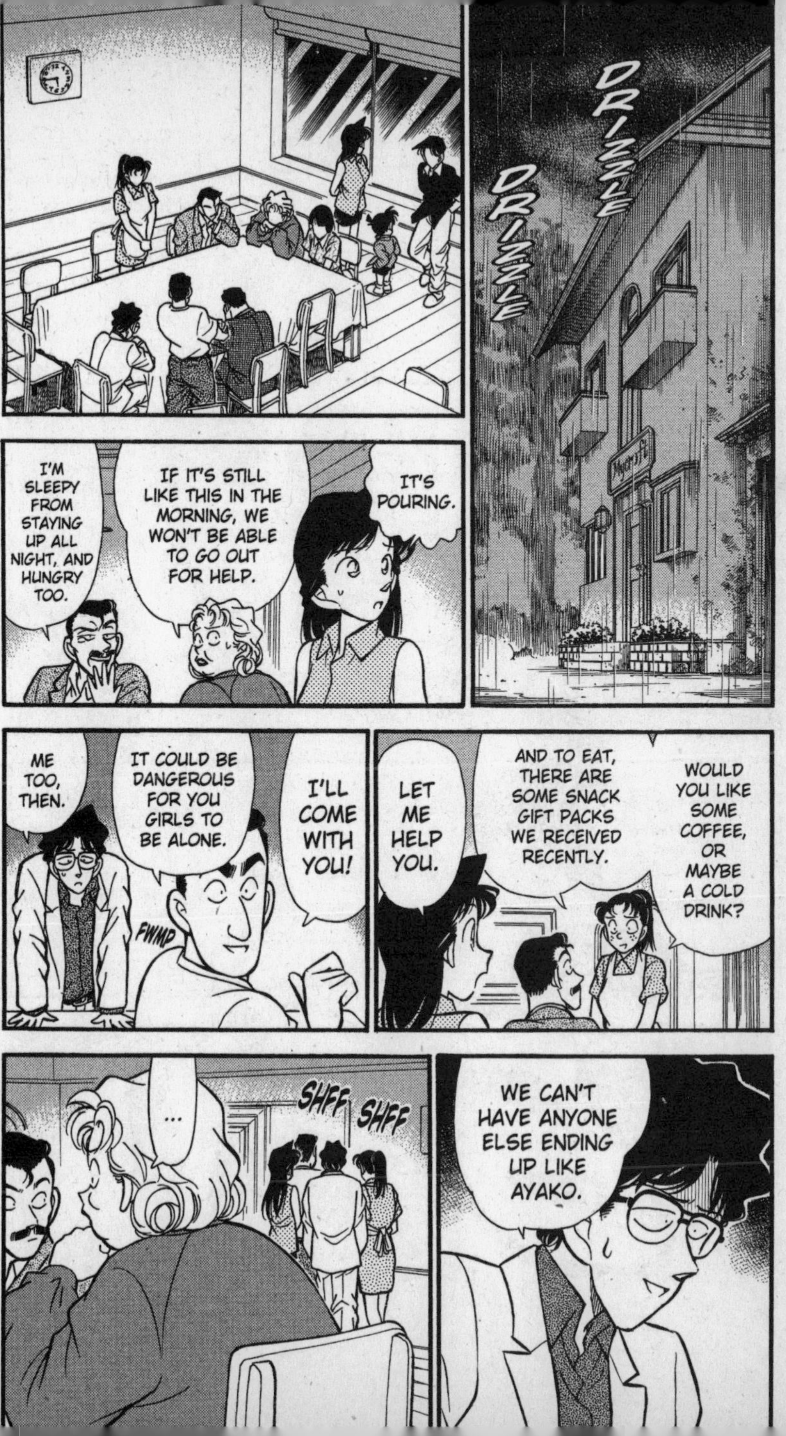

DRIZZLE
DRIZZLE
IT'S POURING.
IF IT'S STILL LIKE THIS IN THE MORNING, WE WON'T BE ABLE TO GO OUT FOR HELP.
I'M SLEEPY FROM STAYING UP ALL NIGHT, AND HUNGRY TOO.
WOULD YOU LIKE SOME COFFEE, OR MAYBE A COLD DRINK?
AND TO EAT, THERE ARE SOME SNACK GIFT PACKS WE RECEIVED RECENTLY.
LET ME HELP YOU.
I'LL COME WITH YOU!
IT COULD BE DANGEROUS FOR YOU GIRLS TO BE ALONE.
ME TOO, THEN.
FWMP
WE CAN'T HAVE ANYONE ELSE ENDING UP LIKE AYAKO.
SHFF
SHFF
...

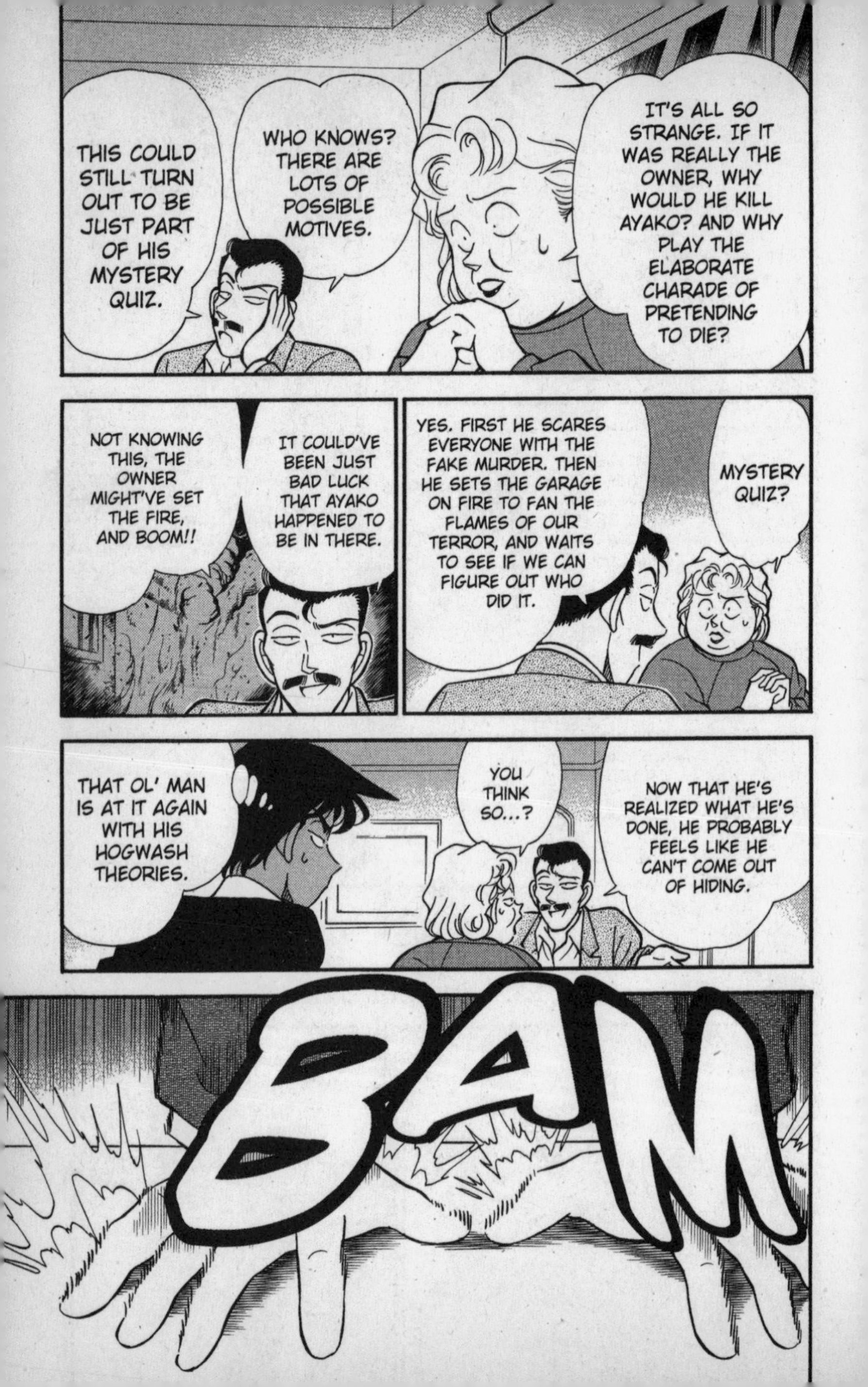

IT'S ALL SO STRANGE. IF IT WAS REALLY THE OWNER, WHY WOULD HE KILL AYAKO? AND WHY PLAY THE ELABORATE CHARADE OF PRETENDING TO DIE?
WHO KNOWS? THERE ARE LOTS OF POSSIBLE MOTIVES.
THIS COULD STILL TURN OUT TO BE JUST PART OF HIS MYSTERY QUIZ.
MYSTERY QUIZ?
YES. FIRST HE SCARES EVERYONE WITH THE FAKE MURDER. THEN HE SETS THE GARAGE ON FIRE TO FAN THE FLAMES OF OUR TERROR, AND WAITS TO SEE IF WE CAN FIGURE OUT WHO DID IT.
IT COULD'VE BEEN JUST BAD LUCK THAT AYAKO HAPPENED TO BE IN THERE.
NOT KNOWING THIS, THE OWNER MIGHT'VE SET THE FIRE, AND BOOM!!
NOW THAT HE'S REALIZED WHAT HE'S DONE, HE PROBABLY FEELS LIKE HE CAN'T COME OUT OF HIDING.
YOU THINK SO...?
THAT OL' MAN IS AT IT AGAIN WITH HIS HOGWASH THEORIES.
BAM

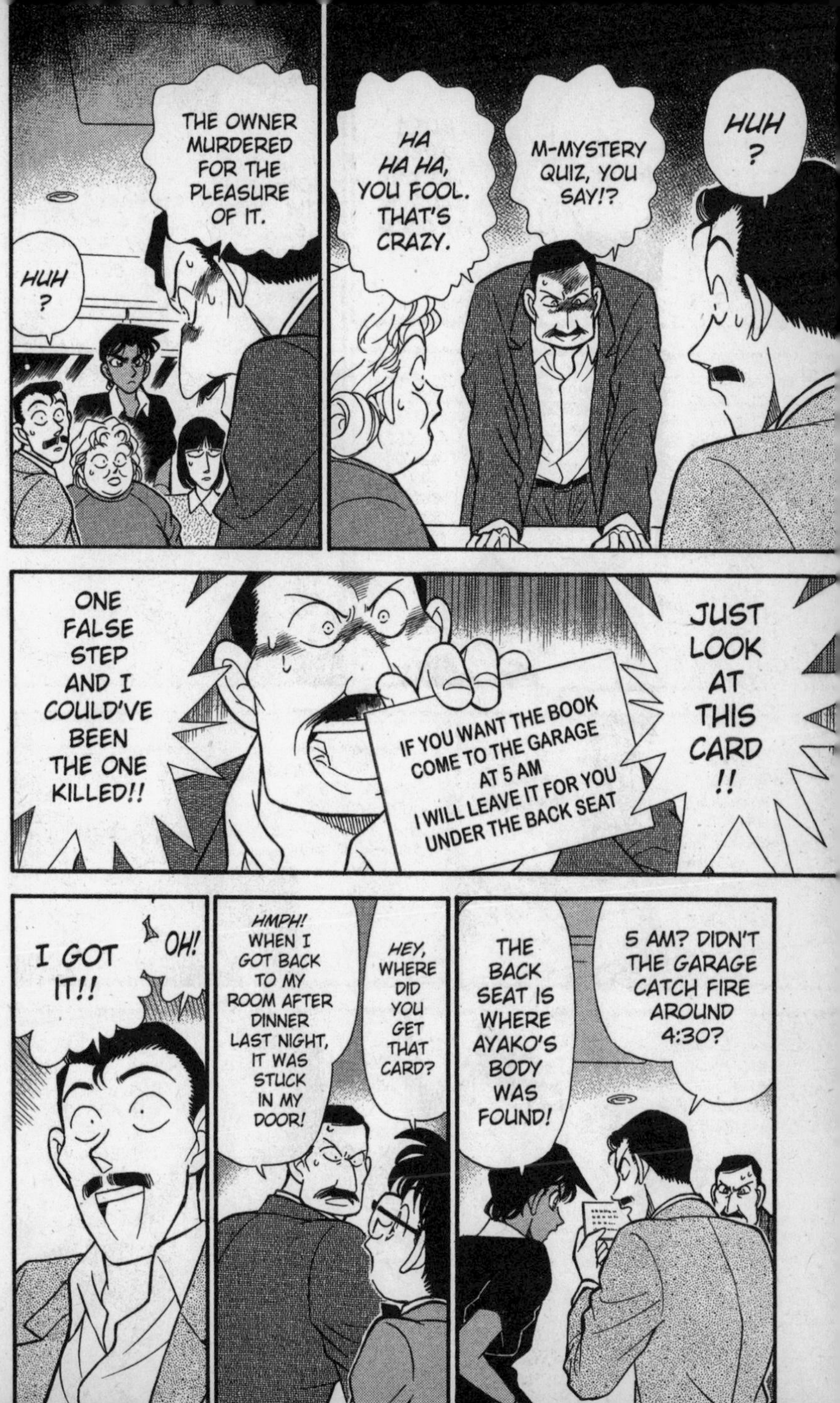
THE OWNER MURDERED FOR THE PLEASURE OF IT.
HUH ?
HA HA HA, YOU FOOL. THAT'S CRAZY.
M-MYSTERY QUIZ, YOU SAY!?
HUH ?
ONE FALSE STEP AND I COULD'VE BEEN THE ONE KILLED!!
IF YOU WANT THE BOOK COME TO THE GARAGE AT 5 AM I WILL LEAVE IT FOR YOU UNDER THE BACK SEAT
JUST LOOK AT THIS CARD!!
I GOT IT!!
OH!
HMPH! WHEN I GOT BACK TO MY ROOM AFTER DINNER LAST NIGHT, IT WAS STUCK IN MY DOOR!
HEY, WHERE DID YOU GET THAT CARD?
THE BACK SEAT IS WHERE AYAKO'S BODY WAS FOUND!
5 AM? DIDN'T THE GARAGE CATCH FIRE AROUND 4:30?

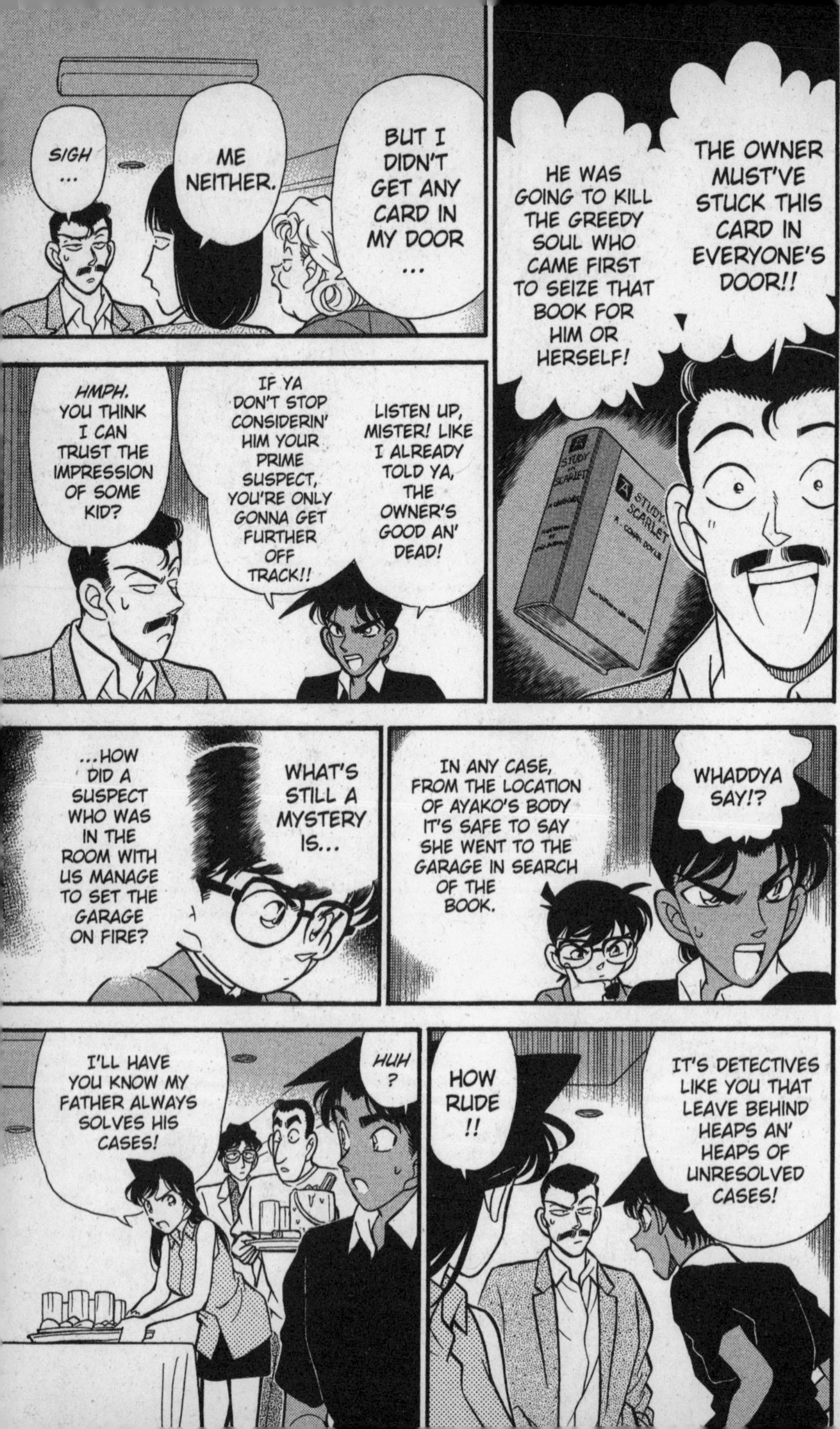
THE OWNER MUST'VE STUCK THIS CARD IN EVERYONE'S DOOR!!
HE WAS GOING TO KILL THE GREEDY SOUL WHO CAME FIRST TO SEIZE THAT BOOK FOR HIM OR HERSELF!
BUT I DIDN'T GET ANY CARD IN MY DOOR ...
ME NEITHER.
SIGH ...
LISTEN UP, MISTER! LIKE I ALREADY TOLD YA, THE OWNER'S GOOD AN' DEAD!
IF YA DON'T STOP CONSIDERIN' HIM YOUR PRIME SUSPECT, YOU'RE ONLY GONNA GET FURTHER OFF TRACK!!
HMPH. YOU THINK I CAN TRUST THE IMPRESSION OF SOME KID?
WHADDYA SAY!?
IN ANY CASE, FROM THE LOCATION OF AYAKO'S BODY IT'S SAFE TO SAY SHE WENT TO THE GARAGE IN SEARCH OF THE BOOK.
WHAT'S STILL A MYSTERY IS...
...HOW DID A SUSPECT WHO WAS IN THE ROOM WITH US MANAGE TO SET THE GARAGE ON FIRE?
IT'S DETECTIVES LIKE YOU THAT LEAVE BEHIND HEAPS AN' HEAPS OF UNRESOLVED CASES!
HOW RUDE !!
HUH ?
I'LL HAVE YOU KNOW MY FATHER ALWAYS SOLVES HIS CASES!

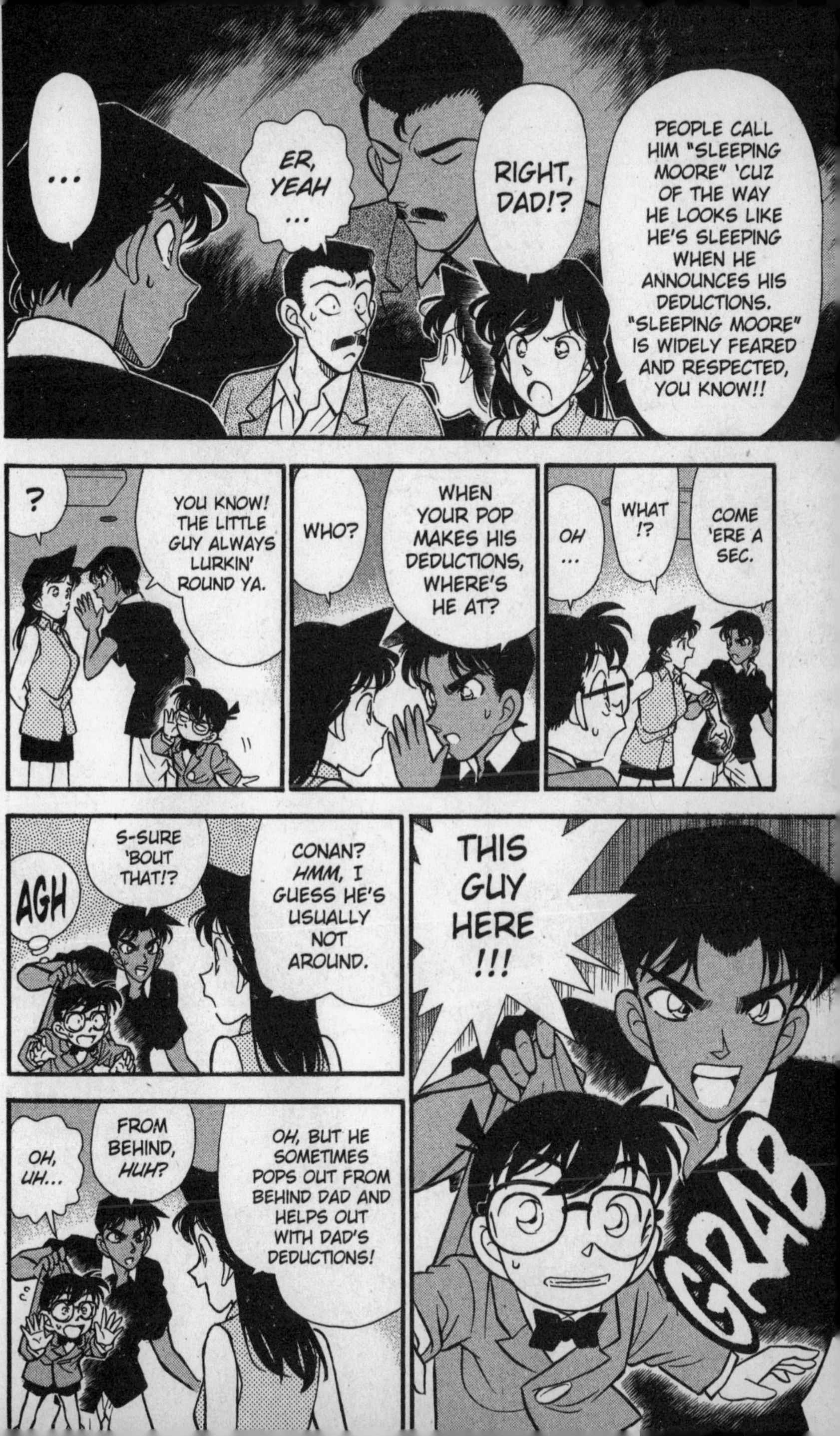
PEOPLE CALL HIM "SLEEPING MOORE" 'CUZ OF THE WAY HE LOOKS LIKE HE'S SLEEPING WHEN HE ANNOUNCES HIS DEDUCTIONS. "SLEEPING MOORE" IS WIDELY FEARED AND RESPECTED, YOU KNOW!!
RIGHT, DAD!?
ER, YEAH ...
...
COME 'ERE A SEC.
WHAT !?
OH ...
WHEN YOUR POP MAKES HIS DEDUCTIONS, WHERE'S HE AT?
WHO?
?
YOU KNOW! THE LITTLE GUY ALWAYS LURKIN' ROUND YA.
THIS GUY HERE !!!
GRAB
CONAN? HMM, I GUESS HE'S USUALLY NOT AROUND.
S-SURE 'BOUT THAT!?
AGH
OH, BUT HE SOMETIMES POPS OUT FROM BEHIND DAD AND HELPS OUT WITH DAD'S DEDUCTIONS!
FROM BEHIND, HUH?
OH, UH...

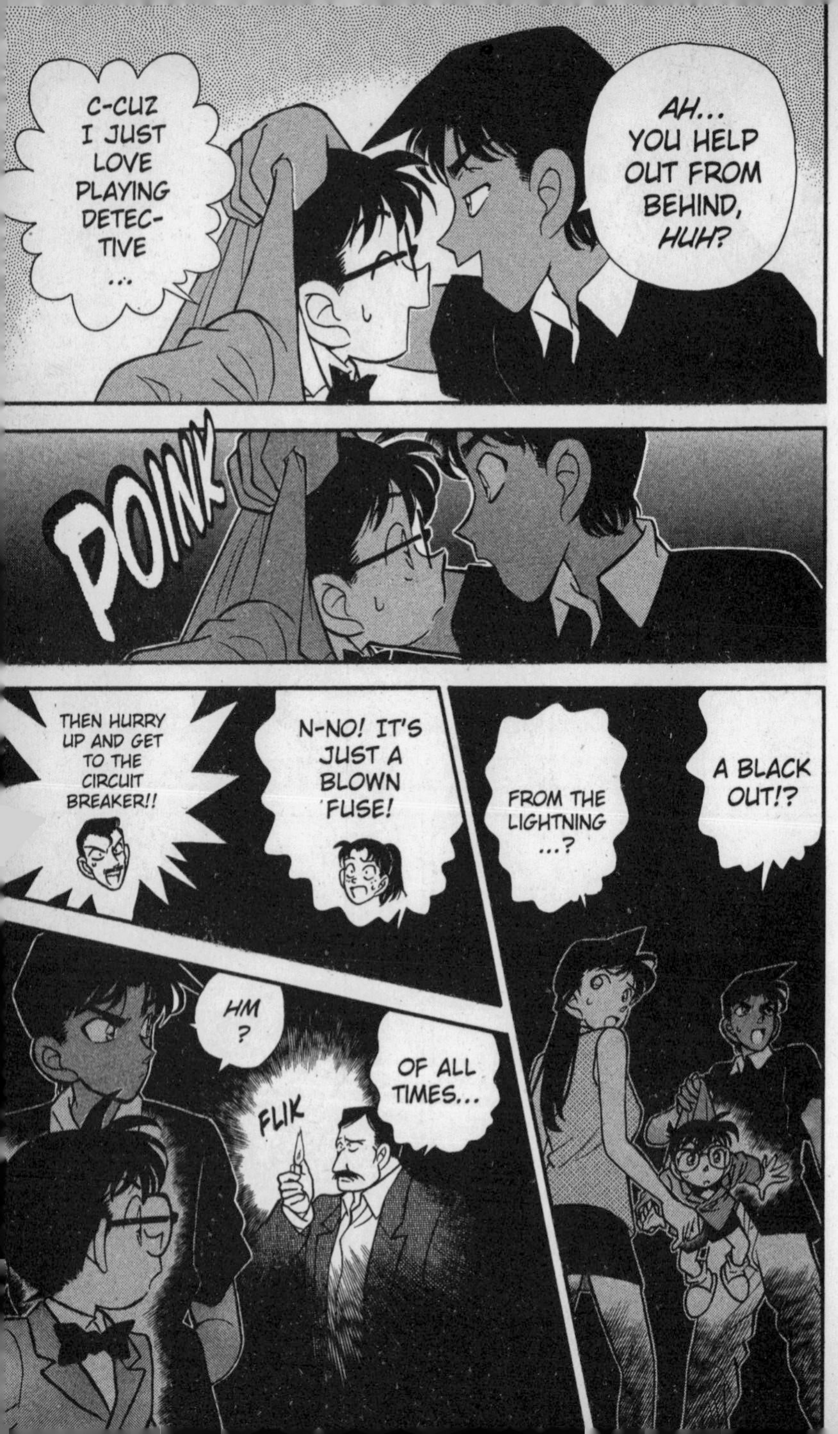

AH... YOU HELP OUT FROM BEHIND, HUH?
C-CUZ I JUST LOVE PLAYING DETECTIVE ...
POINK
A BLACK OUT!?
FROM THE LIGHTNING ...?
N-NO! IT'S JUST A BLOWN FUSE!
THEN HURRY UP AND GET TO THE CIRCUIT BREAKER!!
FLIK
OF ALL TIMES...
HM ?

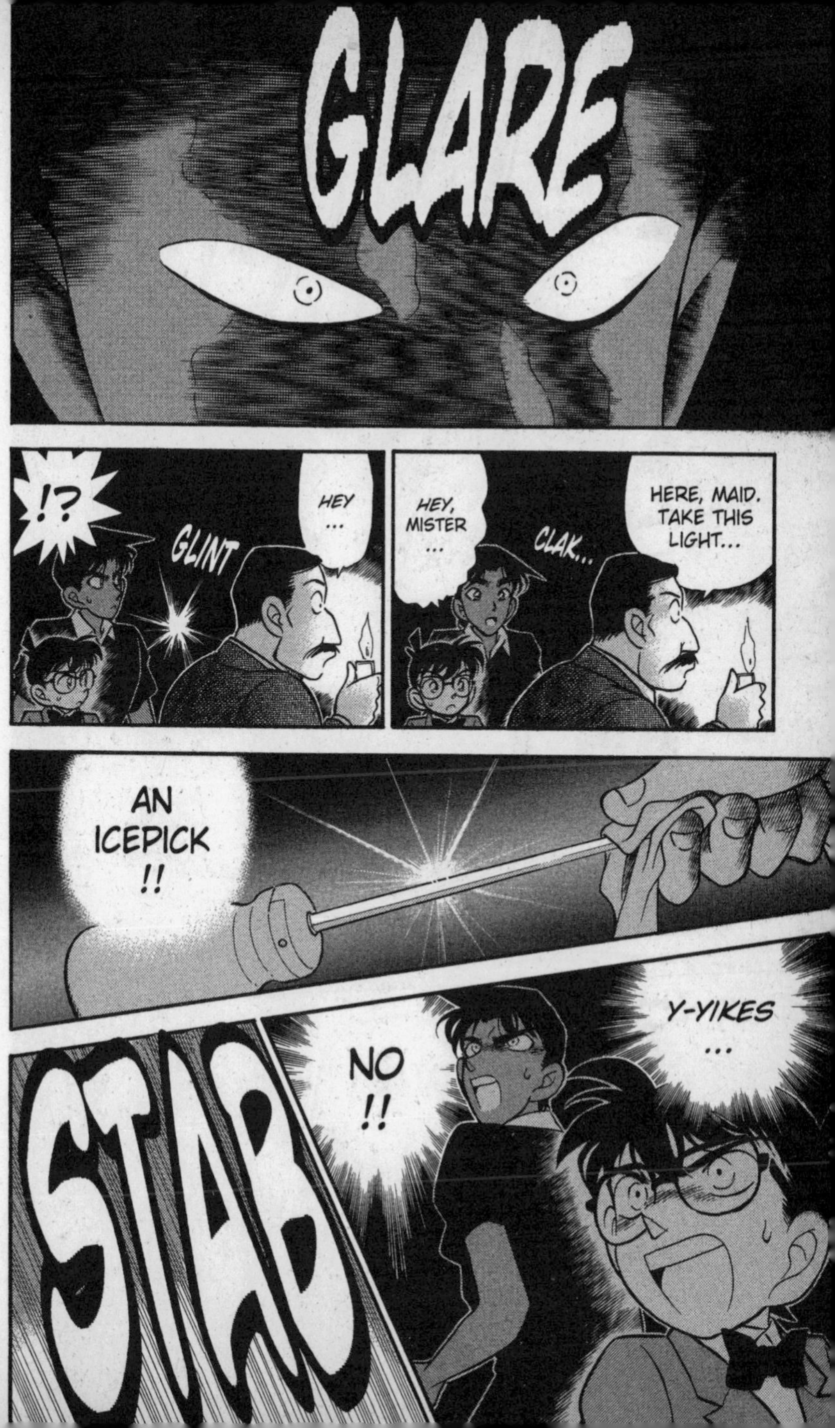
GLARE
HERE, MAID. TAKE THIS LIGHT...
CLAK...
HEY, MISTER ...
HEY ...
GLINT
!?
AN ICEPICK !!
Y-YIKES ...
NO !!
STAB

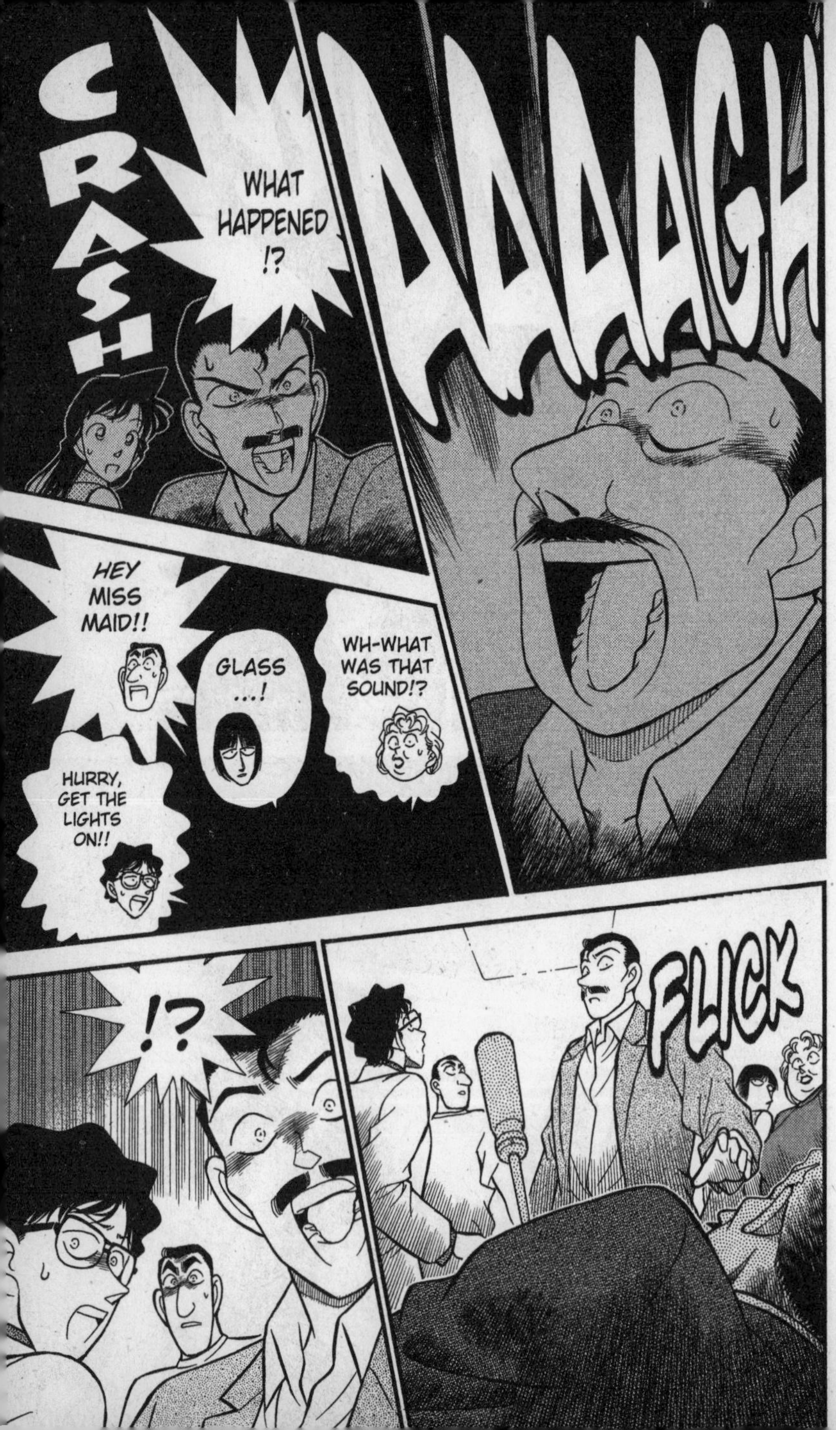
AAAAGH
CRASH
WHAT HAPPENED !?
WH-WHAT WAS THAT SOUND!?
GLASS ...!
HEY MISS MAID!!
HURRY, GET THE LIGHTS ON!!
FLICK
!?

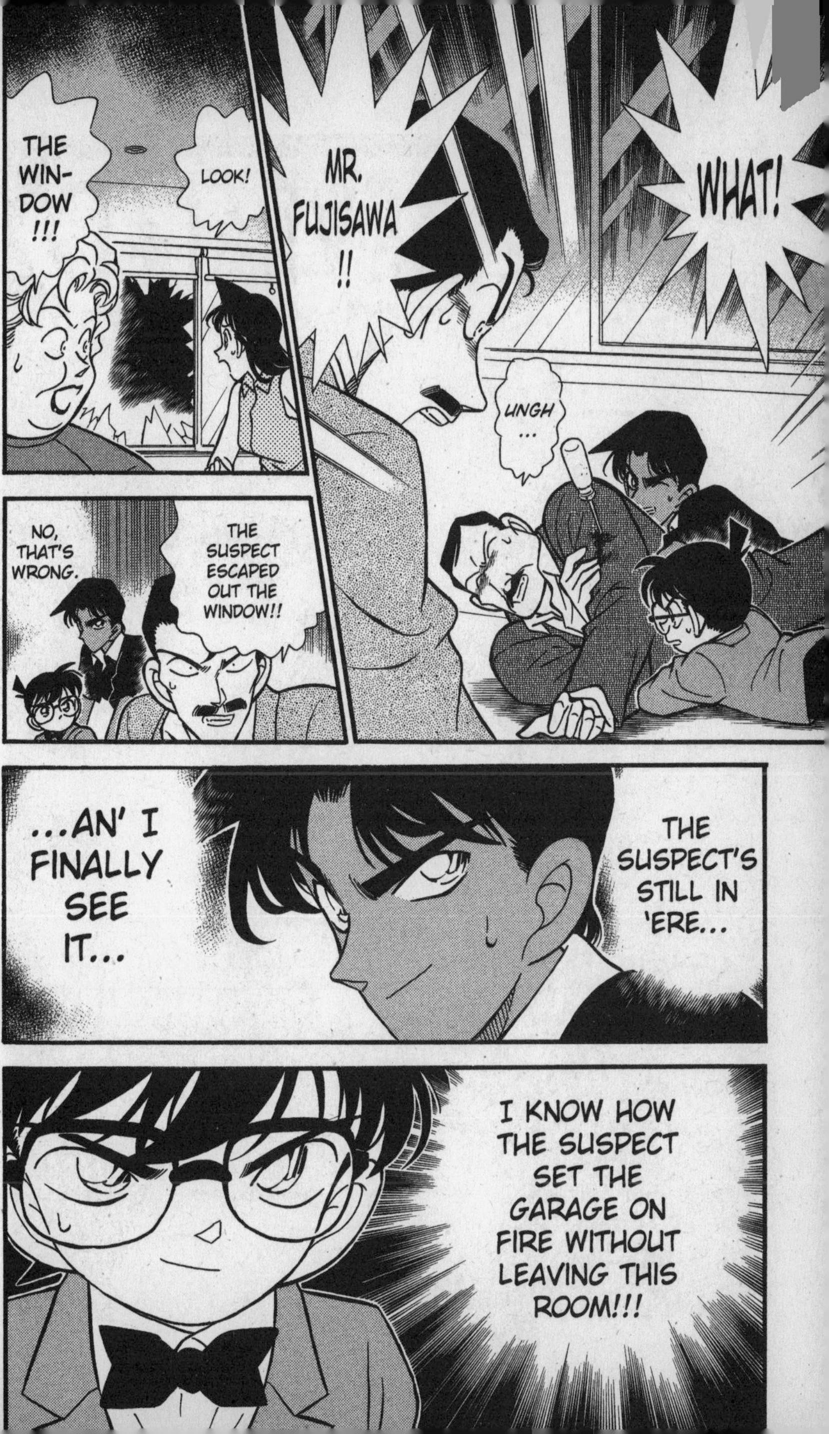
WHAT!
MR. FUJISAWA !!
UNGH ...
LOOK!
THE WIN-DOW !!!
THE SUSPECT ESCAPED OUT THE WINDOW!!
NO, THAT'S WRONG.
THE SUSPECT'S STILL IN 'ERE...
...AN' I FINALLY SEE IT...
I KNOW HOW THE SUSPECT SET THE GARAGE ON FIRE WITHOUT LEAVING THIS ROOM!!!

FILE 10: A LIE REVEALED

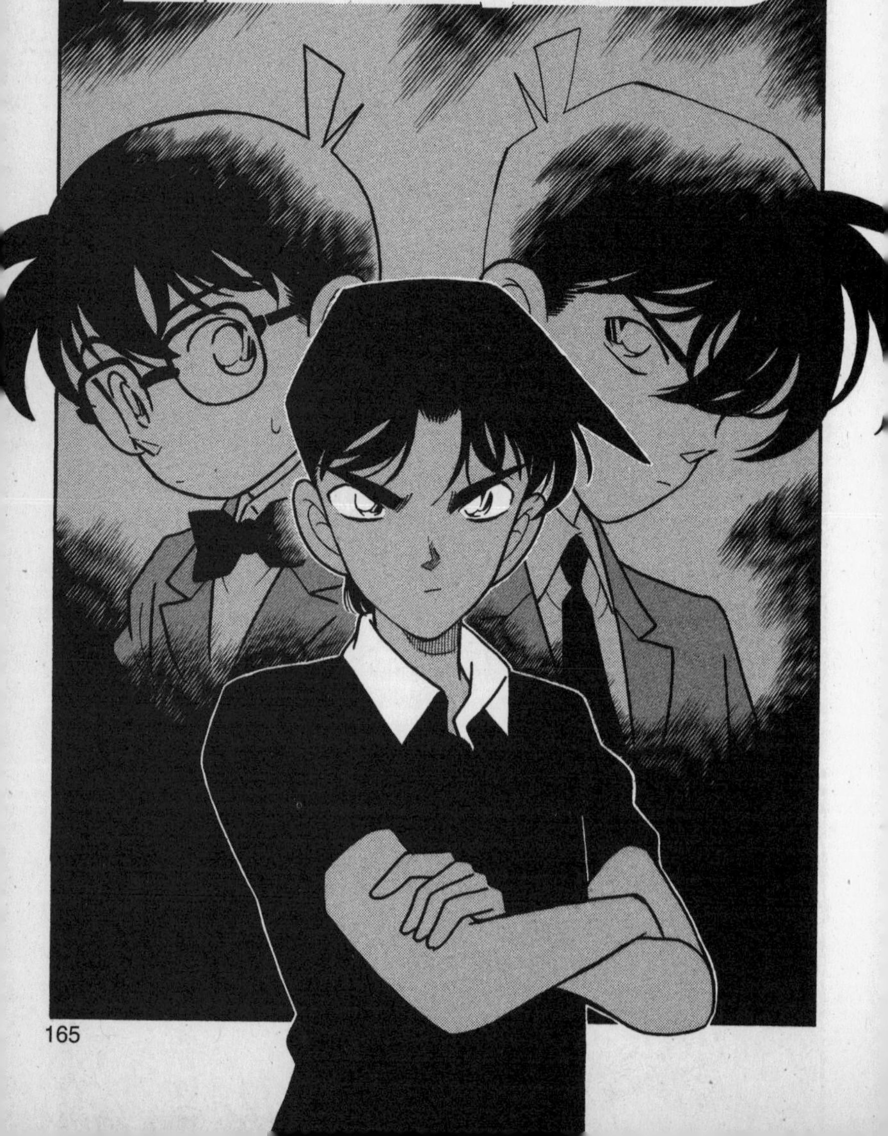

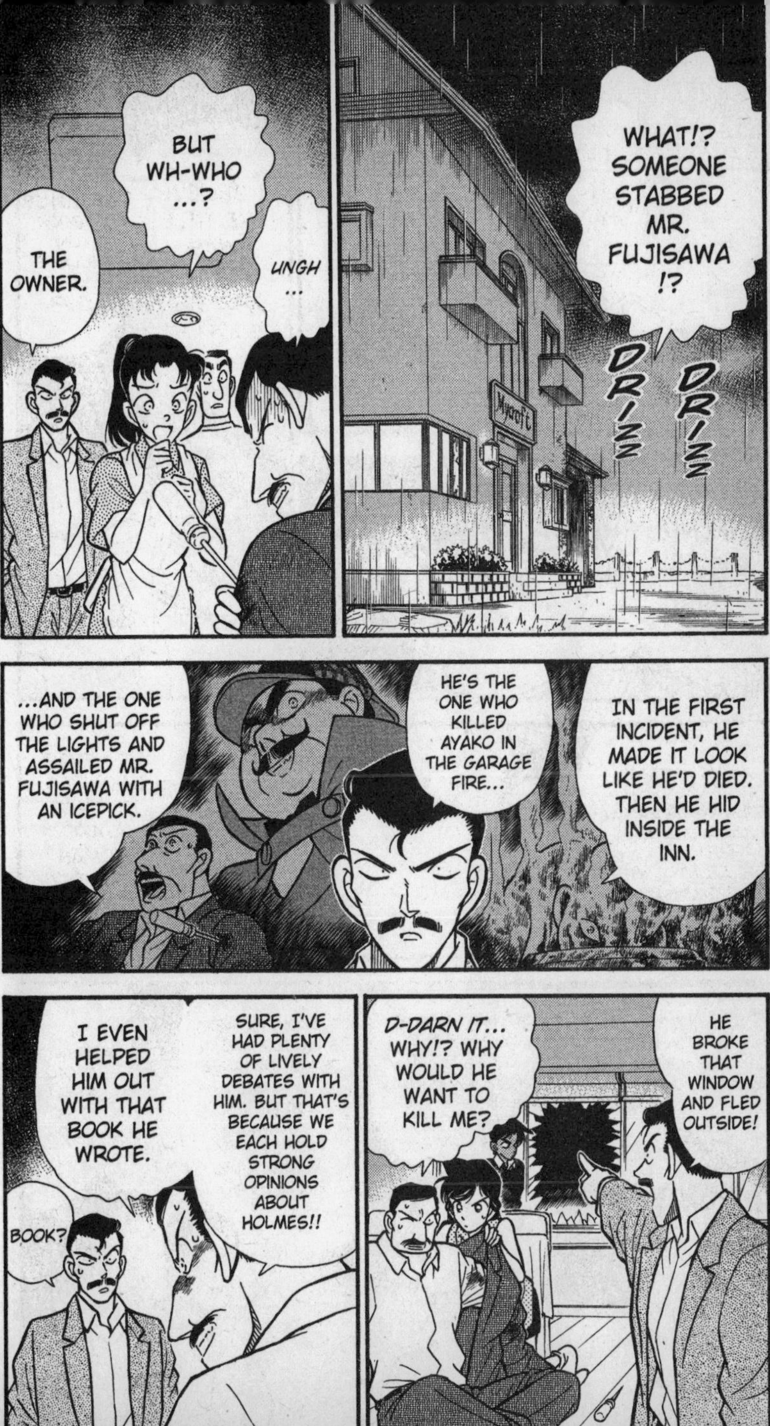
WHAT!? SOMEONE STABBED MR. FUJISAWA !?
DRIZZ
DRIZZ
UNGH ...
BUT WH-WHO ...?
THE OWNER.
IN THE FIRST INCIDENT, HE MADE IT LOOK LIKE HE'D DIED. THEN HE HID INSIDE THE INN.
HE'S THE ONE WHO KILLED AYAKO IN THE GARAGE FIRE...
...AND THE ONE WHO SHUT OFF THE LIGHTS AND ASSAILED MR. FUJISAWA WITH AN ICEPICK.
HE BROKE THAT WINDOW AND FLED OUTSIDE!
D-DARN IT... WHY!? WHY WOULD HE WANT TO KILL ME?
SURE, I'VE HAD PLENTY OF LIVELY DEBATES WITH HIM. BUT THAT'S BECAUSE WE EACH HOLD STRONG OPINIONS ABOUT HOLMES!!
I EVEN HELPED HIM OUT WITH THAT BOOK HE WROTE.
BOOK?

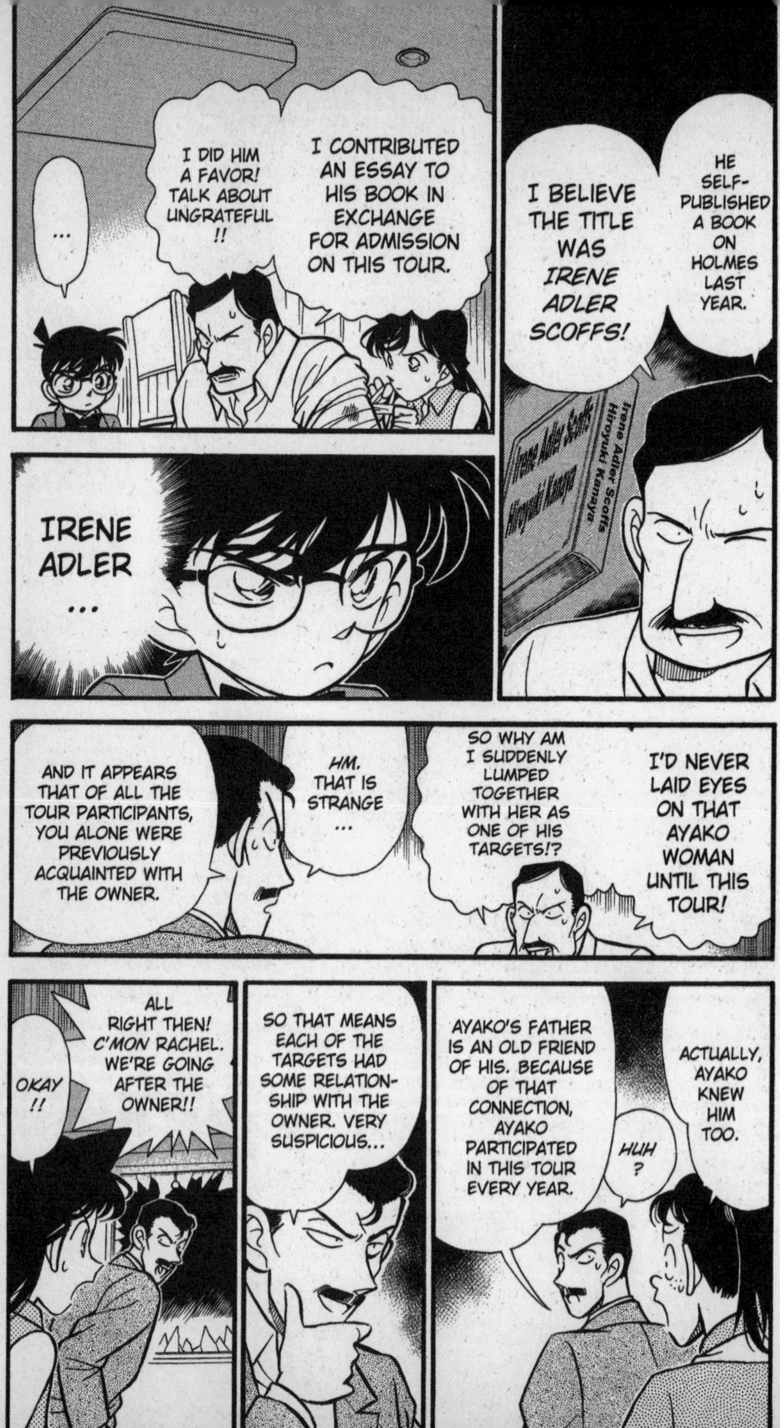
HE SELF-PUBLISHED A BOOK ON HOLMES LAST YEAR.
I BELIEVE THE TITLE WAS IRENE ADLER SCOFFS!
Irene Adler Scoffs
Hiroyuki Kanaya
I CONTRIBUTED AN ESSAY TO HIS BOOK IN EXCHANGE FOR ADMISSION ON THIS TOUR.
I DID HIM A FAVOR! TALK ABOUT UNGRATEFUL !!
...
IRENE ADLER ...
I'D NEVER LAID EYES ON THAT AYAKO WOMAN UNTIL THIS TOUR!
SO WHY AM I SUDDENLY LUMPED TOGETHER WITH HER AS ONE OF HIS TARGETS!?
HM. THAT IS STRANGE ...
AND IT APPEARS THAT OF ALL THE TOUR PARTICIPANTS, YOU ALONE WERE PREVIOUSLY ACQUAINTED WITH THE OWNER.
ACTUALLY, AYAKO KNEW HIM TOO.
HUH ?
AYAKO'S FATHER IS AN OLD FRIEND OF HIS. BECAUSE OF THAT CONNECTION, AYAKO PARTICIPATED IN THIS TOUR EVERY YEAR.
SO THAT MEANS EACH OF THE TARGETS HAD SOME RELATIONSHIP WITH THE OWNER. VERY SUSPICIOUS...
ALL RIGHT THEN! C'MON RACHEL. WE'RE GOING AFTER THE OWNER!!
OKAY !!

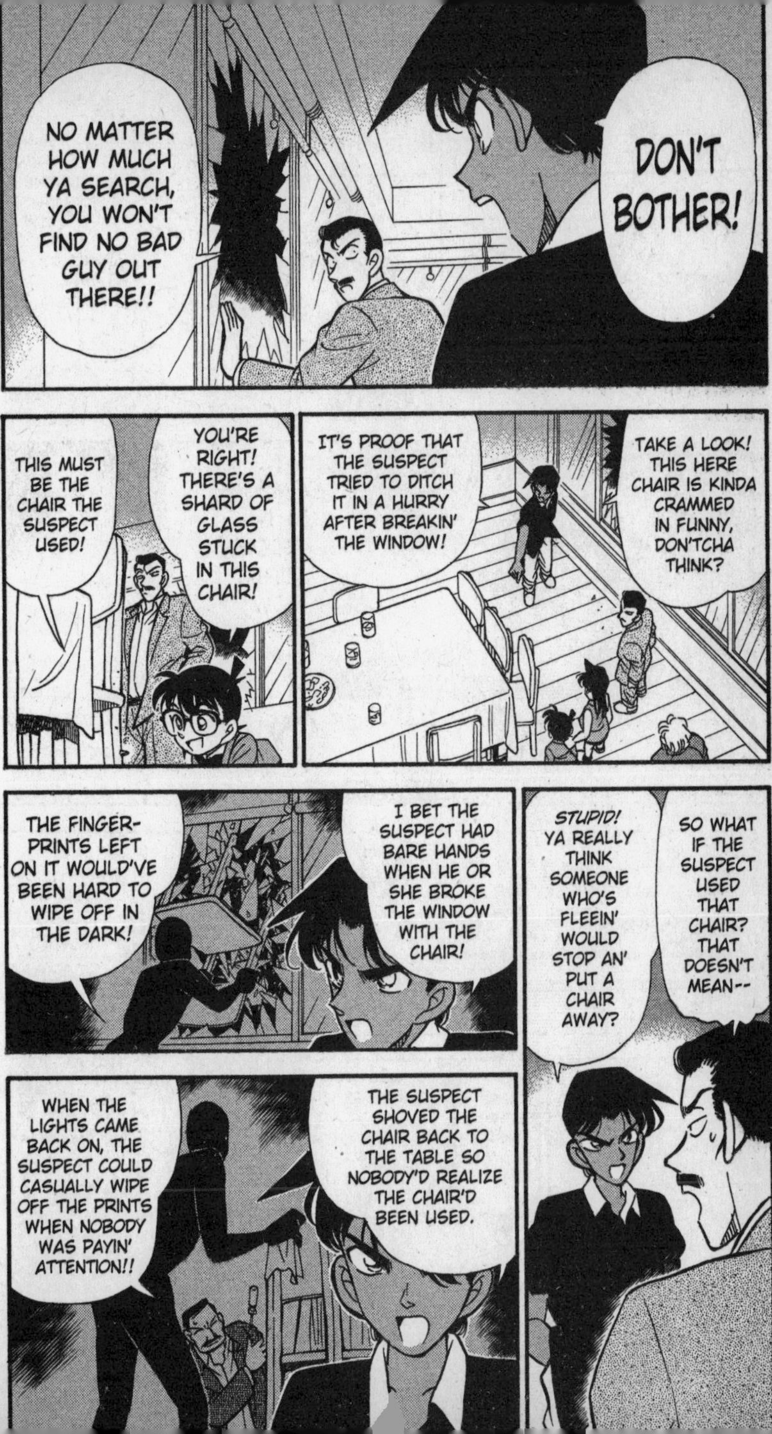
DON'T BOTHER!
NO MATTER HOW MUCH YA SEARCH, YOU WON'T FIND NO BAD GUY OUT THERE!!
TAKE A LOOK! THIS HERE CHAIR IS KINDA CRAMMED IN FUNNY, DON'TCHA THINK?
IT'S PROOF THAT THE SUSPECT TRIED TO DITCH IT IN A HURRY AFTER BREAKIN' THE WINDOW!
YOU'RE RIGHT! THERE'S A SHARD OF GLASS STUCK IN THIS CHAIR!
THIS MUST BE THE CHAIR THE SUSPECT USED!
SO WHAT IF THE SUSPECT USED THAT CHAIR? THAT DOESN'T MEAN--
STUPID! YA REALLY THINK SOMEONE WHO'S FLEEIN' WOULD STOP AN' PUT A CHAIR AWAY?
I BET THE SUSPECT HAD BARE HANDS WHEN HE OR SHE BROKE THE WINDOW WITH THE CHAIR!
THE FINGER-PRINTS LEFT ON IT WOULD'VE BEEN HARD TO WIPE OFF IN THE DARK!
THE SUSPECT SHOVED THE CHAIR BACK TO THE TABLE SO NOBODY'D REALIZE THE CHAIR'D BEEN USED.
WHEN THE LIGHTS CAME BACK ON, THE SUSPECT COULD CASUALLY WIPE OFF THE PRINTS WHEN NOBODY WAS PAYIN' ATTENTION!!

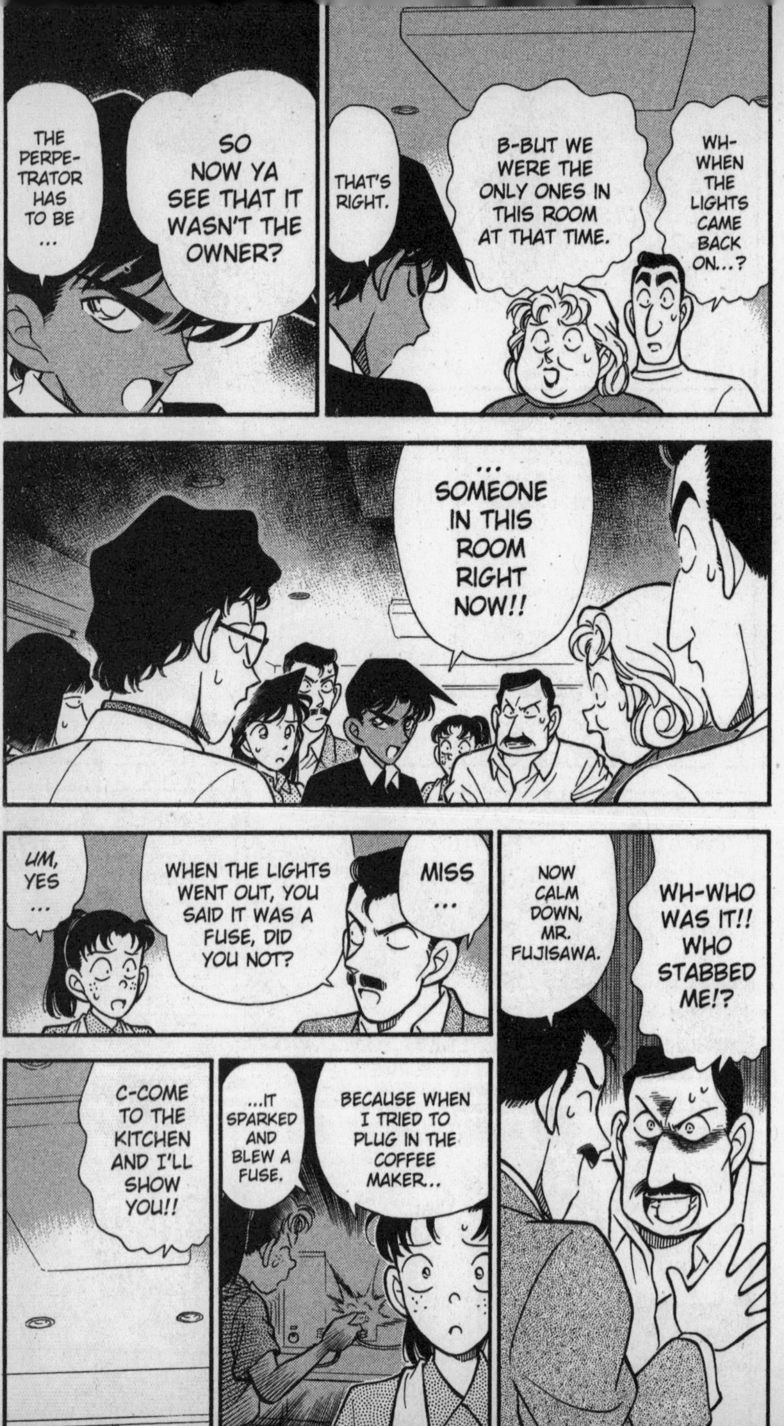
WH-WHEN THE LIGHTS CAME BACK ON...?
B-BUT WE WERE THE ONLY ONES IN THIS ROOM AT THAT TIME.
THAT'S RIGHT.
SO NOW YA SEE THAT IT WASN'T THE OWNER?
THE PERPETRATOR HAS TO BE ...
... SOMEONE IN THIS ROOM RIGHT NOW!!
WH-WHO WAS IT!! WHO STABBED ME!?
NOW CALM DOWN, MR. FUJISAWA.
MISS ...
WHEN THE LIGHTS WENT OUT, YOU SAID IT WAS A FUSE, DID YOU NOT?
UM, YES ...
BECAUSE WHEN I TRIED TO PLUG IN THE COFFEE MAKER...
...IT SPARKED AND BLEW A FUSE.
C-COME TO THE KITCHEN AND I'LL SHOW YOU!!

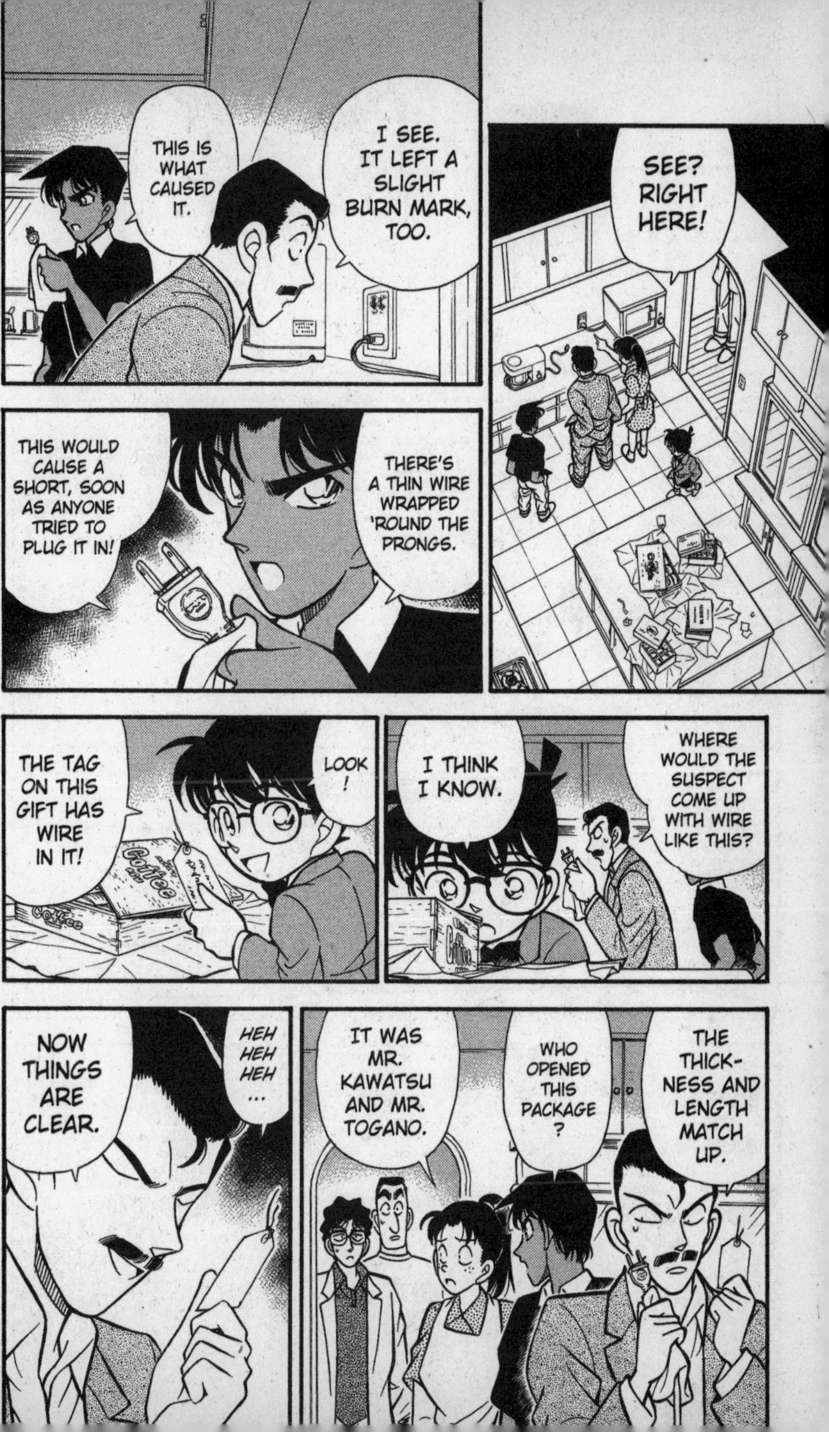
THIS IS WHAT CAUSED IT.
SEE? RIGHT HERE!
I SEE. IT LEFT A SLIGHT BURN MARK, TOO.
THERE'S A THIN WIRE WRAPPED 'ROUND THE PRONGS.
THIS WOULD CAUSE A SHORT, SOON AS ANYONE TRIED TO PLUG IT IN!
WHERE WOULD THE SUSPECT COME UP WITH WIRE LIKE THIS?
I THINK I KNOW.
LOOK!
THE TAG ON THIS GIFT HAS WIRE IN IT!
THE THICK-NESS AND LENGTH MATCH UP.
WHO OPENED THIS PACKAGE?
IT WAS MR. KAWATSU AND MR. TOGANO.
HEH HEH HEH ...
NOW THINGS ARE CLEAR.

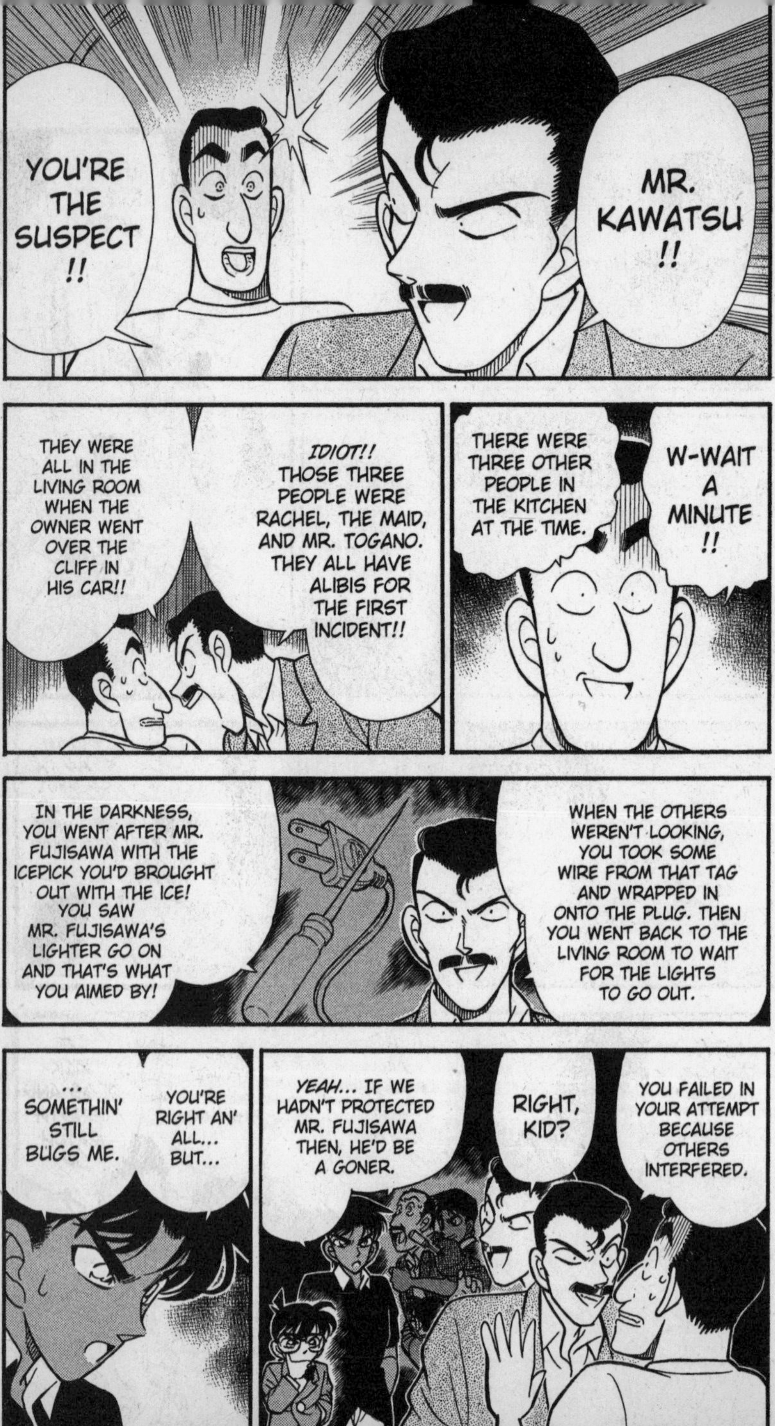
MR. KAWATSU !!
YOU'RE THE SUSPECT !!
W-WAIT A MINUTE !!
THERE WERE THREE OTHER PEOPLE IN THE KITCHEN AT THE TIME.
IDIOT!! THOSE THREE PEOPLE WERE RACHEL, THE MAID, AND MR. TOGANO. THEY ALL HAVE ALIBIS FOR THE FIRST INCIDENT!!
THEY WERE ALL IN THE LIVING ROOM WHEN THE OWNER WENT OVER THE CLIFF IN HIS CAR!!
WHEN THE OTHERS WEREN'T LOOKING, YOU TOOK SOME WIRE FROM THAT TAG AND WRAPPED IN ONTO THE PLUG. THEN YOU WENT BACK TO THE LIVING ROOM TO WAIT FOR THE LIGHTS TO GO OUT.
IN THE DARKNESS, YOU WENT AFTER MR. FUJISAWA WITH THE ICEPICK YOU'D BROUGHT OUT WITH THE ICE! YOU SAW MR. FUJISAWA'S LIGHTER GO ON AND THAT'S WHAT YOU AIMED BY!
YOU FAILED IN YOUR ATTEMPT BECAUSE OTHERS INTERFERED.
RIGHT, KID?
YEAH... IF WE HADN'T PROTECTED MR. FUJISAWA THEN, HE'D BE A GONER.
YOU'RE RIGHT AN' ALL... BUT...
... SOMETHIN' STILL BUGS ME.

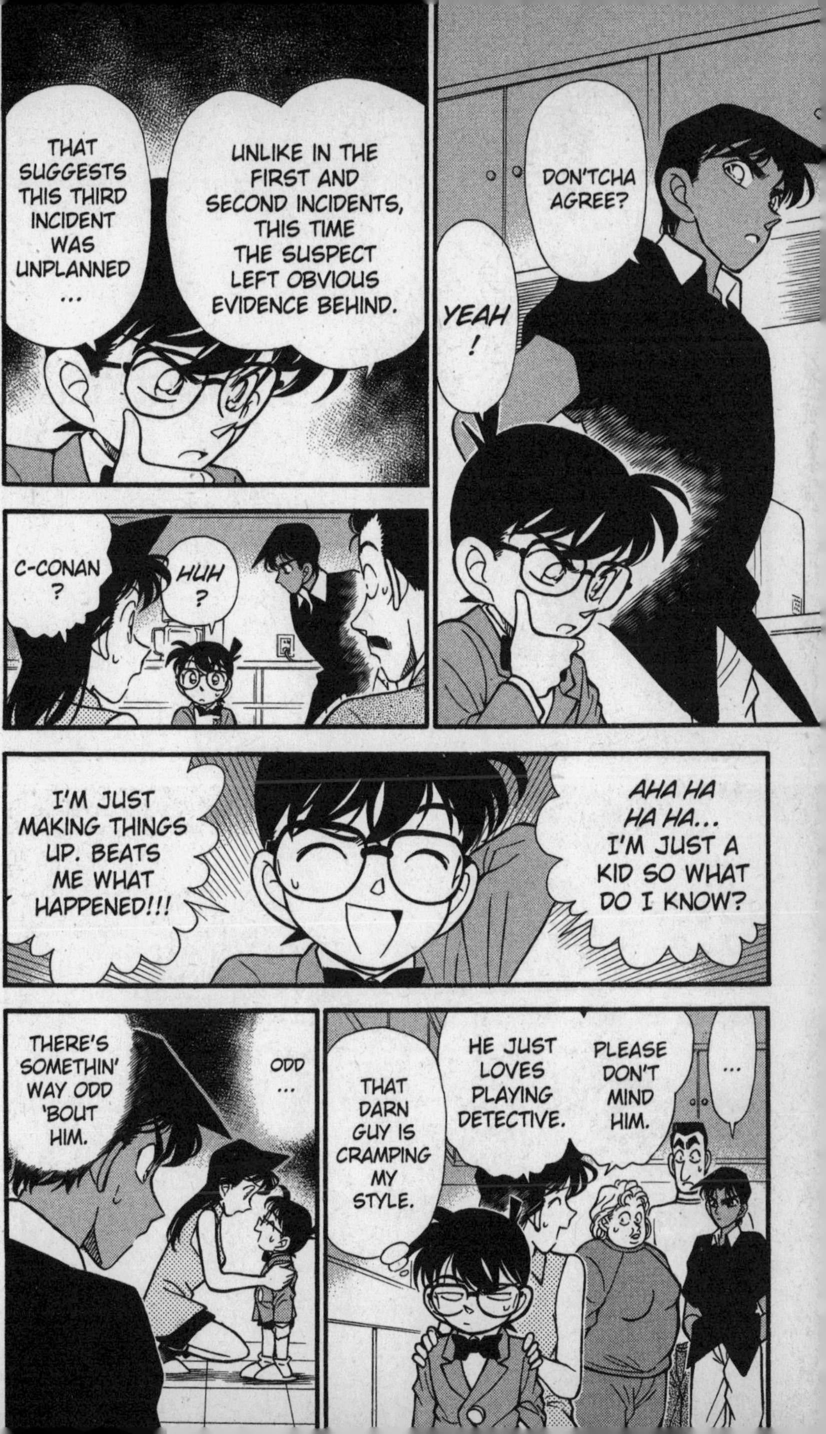
UNLIKE IN THE FIRST AND SECOND INCIDENTS, THIS TIME THE SUSPECT LEFT OBVIOUS EVIDENCE BEHIND.
THAT SUGGESTS THIS THIRD INCIDENT WAS UNPLANNED ...
DON'TCHA AGREE?
YEAH!
HUH?
C-CONAN?
AHA HA HA HA... I'M JUST A KID SO WHAT DO I KNOW?
I'M JUST MAKING THINGS UP. BEATS ME WHAT HAPPENED!!!
...
PLEASE DON'T MIND HIM.
HE JUST LOVES PLAYING DETECTIVE.
THAT DARN GUY IS CRAMPING MY STYLE.
ODD ...
THERE'S SOMETHIN' WAY ODD 'BOUT HIM.

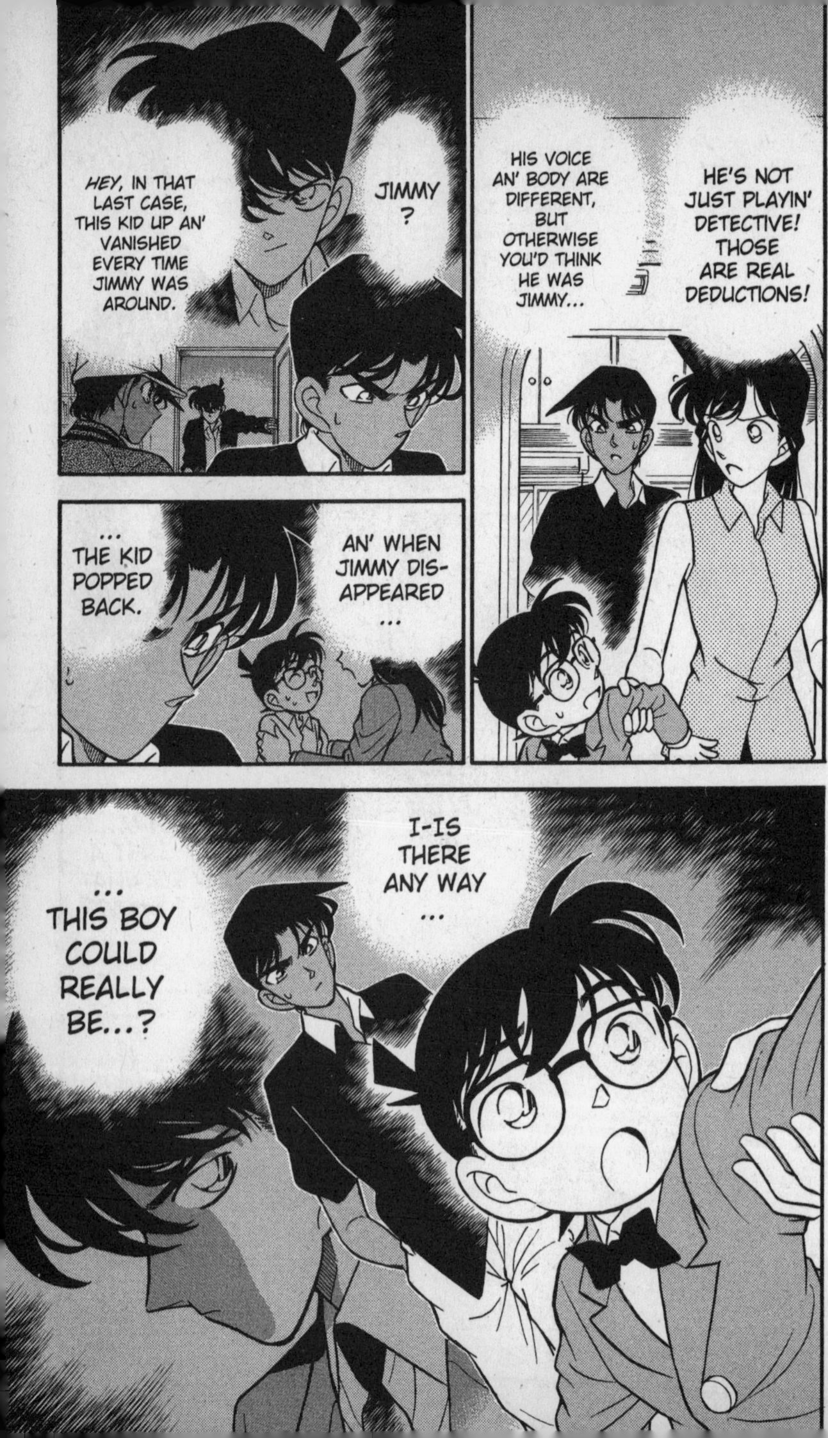
JIMMY ?
HEY, IN THAT LAST CASE, THIS KID UP AN' VANISHED EVERY TIME JIMMY WAS AROUND.
AN' WHEN JIMMY DIS-APPEARED ...
... THE KID POPPED BACK.
HE'S NOT JUST PLAYIN' DETECTIVE! THOSE ARE REAL DEDUCTIONS!
HIS VOICE AN' BODY ARE DIFFERENT, BUT OTHERWISE YOU'D THINK HE WAS JIMMY...
I-IS THERE ANY WAY ...
... THIS BOY COULD REALLY BE...?

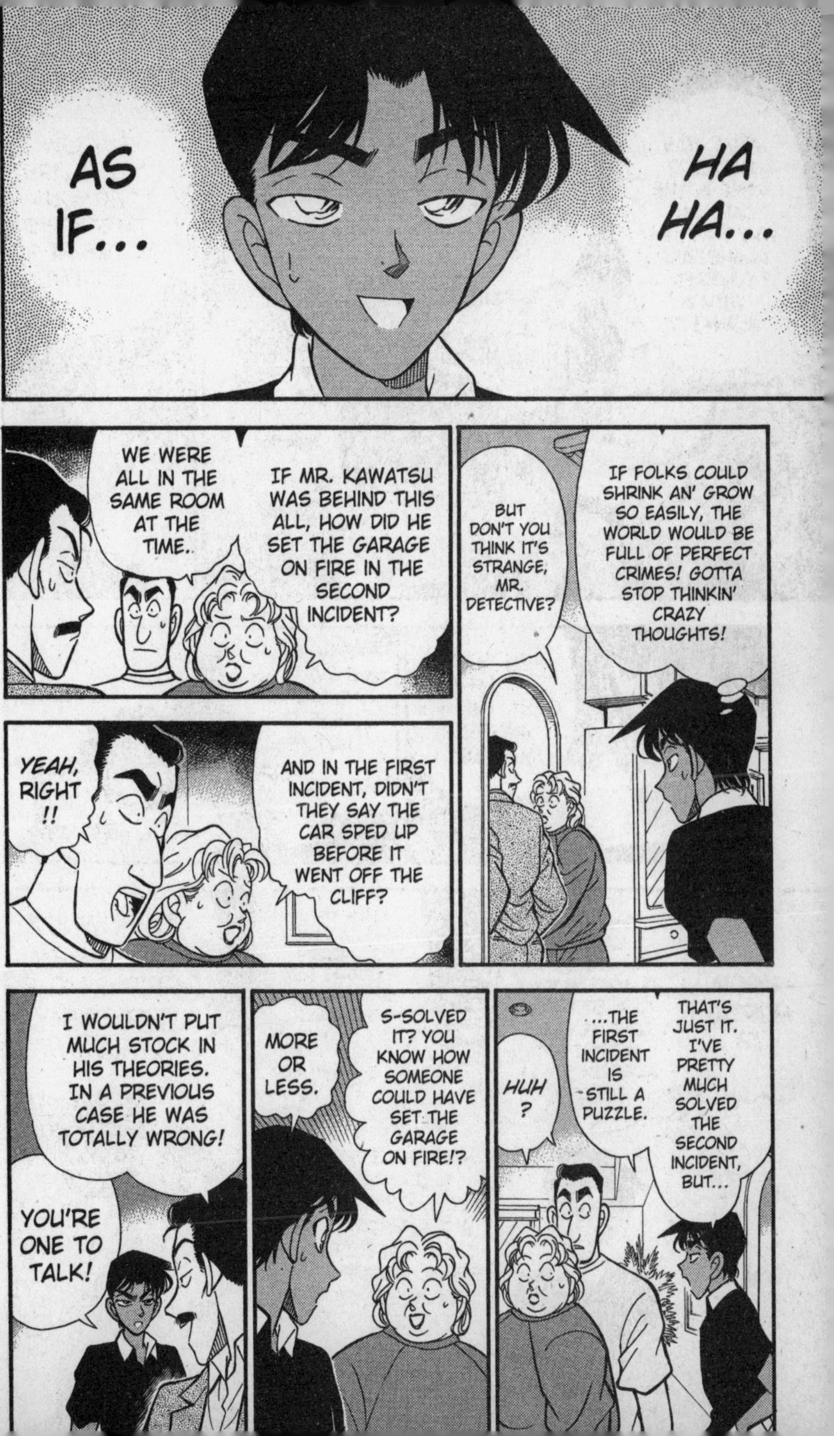
HA HA...
AS IF...
IF FOLKS COULD SHRINK AN' GROW SO EASILY, THE WORLD WOULD BE FULL OF PERFECT CRIMES! GOTTA STOP THINKIN' CRAZY THOUGHTS!
BUT DON'T YOU THINK IT'S STRANGE, MR. DETECTIVE?
IF MR. KAWATSU WAS BEHIND THIS ALL, HOW DID HE SET THE GARAGE ON FIRE IN THE SECOND INCIDENT?
WE WERE ALL IN THE SAME ROOM AT THE TIME..
AND IN THE FIRST INCIDENT, DIDN'T THEY SAY THE CAR SPED UP BEFORE IT WENT OFF THE CLIFF?
YEAH, RIGHT!!
THAT'S JUST IT. I'VE PRETTY MUCH SOLVED THE SECOND INCIDENT, BUT...
...THE FIRST INCIDENT IS STILL A PUZZLE.
HUH?
S-SOLVED IT? YOU KNOW HOW SOMEONE COULD HAVE SET THE GARAGE ON FIRE!?
MORE OR LESS.
I WOULDN'T PUT MUCH STOCK IN HIS THEORIES. IN A PREVIOUS CASE HE WAS TOTALLY WRONG!
YOU'RE ONE TO TALK!

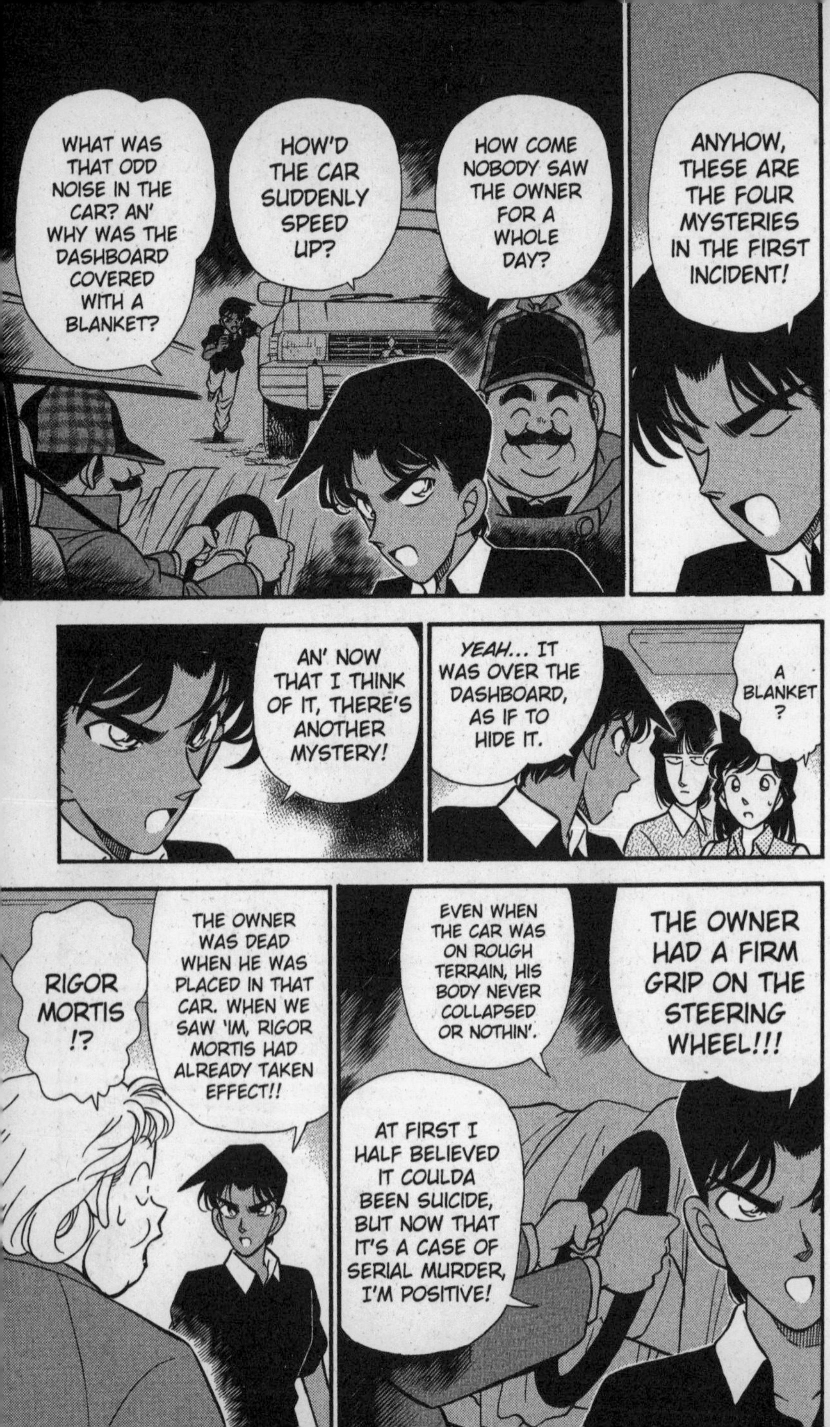
WHAT WAS THAT ODD NOISE IN THE CAR? AN' WHY WAS THE DASHBOARD COVERED WITH A BLANKET?
HOW'D THE CAR SUDDENLY SPEED UP?
HOW COME NOBODY SAW THE OWNER FOR A WHOLE DAY?
ANYHOW, THESE ARE THE FOUR MYSTERIES IN THE FIRST INCIDENT!
AN' NOW THAT I THINK OF IT, THERE'S ANOTHER MYSTERY!
A BLANKET?
YEAH... IT WAS OVER THE DASHBOARD, AS IF TO HIDE IT.
THE OWNER HAD A FIRM GRIP ON THE STEERING WHEEL!!!
EVEN WHEN THE CAR WAS ON ROUGH TERRAIN, HIS BODY NEVER COLLAPSED OR NOTHIN'.
AT FIRST I HALF BELIEVED IT COULDA BEEN SUICIDE, BUT NOW THAT IT'S A CASE OF SERIAL MURDER, I'M POSITIVE!
THE OWNER WAS DEAD WHEN HE WAS PLACED IN THAT CAR. WHEN WE SAW 'IM, RIGOR MORTIS HAD ALREADY TAKEN EFFECT!!
RIGOR MORTIS!?

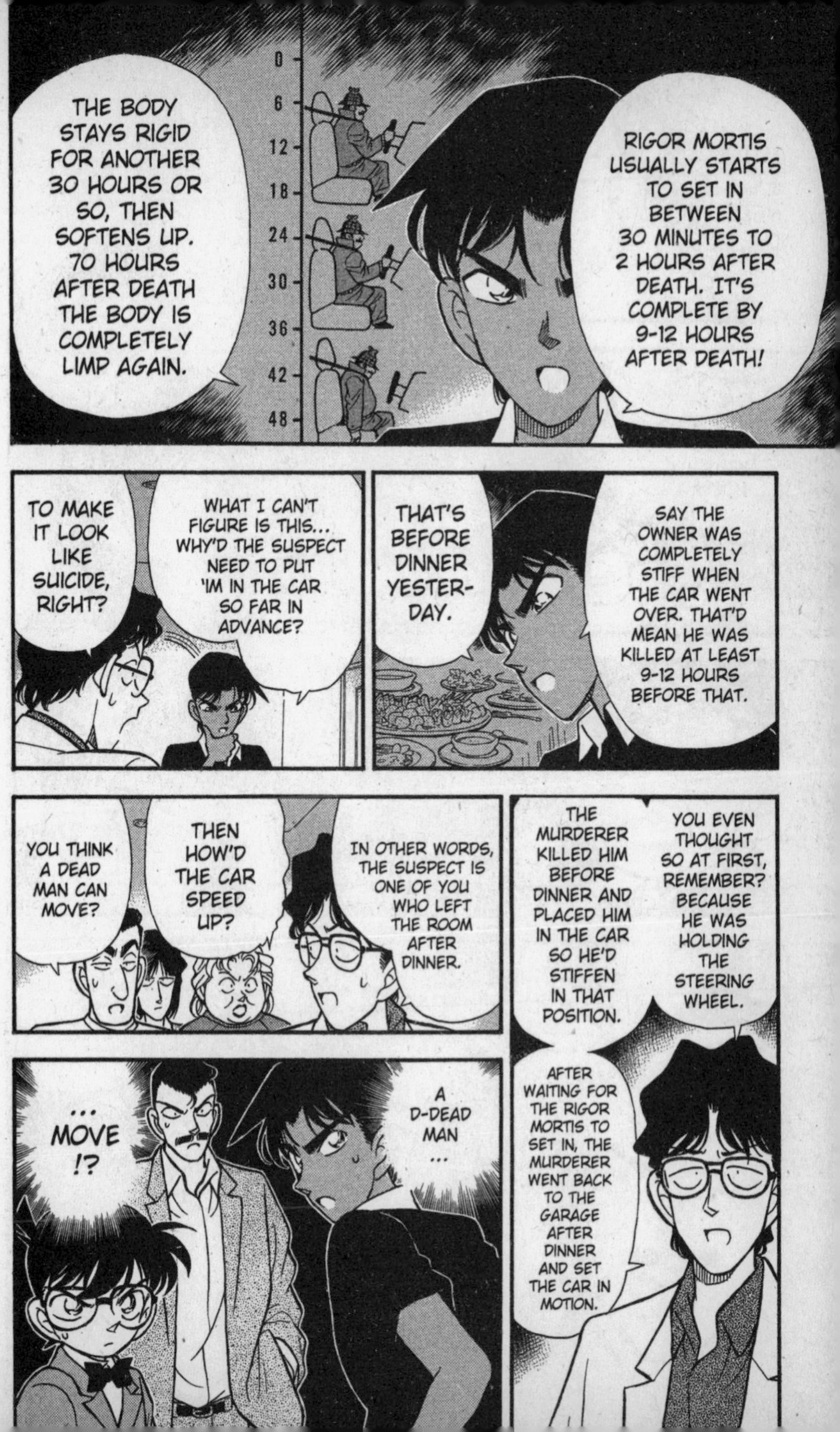
RIGOR MORTIS USUALLY STARTS TO SET IN BETWEEN 30 MINUTES TO 2 HOURS AFTER DEATH. IT'S COMPLETE BY 9-12 HOURS AFTER DEATH!
0
6
12
18
24
30
36
42
48
THE BODY STAYS RIGID FOR ANOTHER 30 HOURS OR SO, THEN SOFTENS UP. 70 HOURS AFTER DEATH THE BODY IS COMPLETELY LIMP AGAIN.
SAY THE OWNER WAS COMPLETELY STIFF WHEN THE CAR WENT OVER. THAT'D MEAN HE WAS KILLED AT LEAST 9-12 HOURS BEFORE THAT.
THAT'S BEFORE DINNER YESTER-DAY.
WHAT I CAN'T FIGURE IS THIS... WHY'D THE SUSPECT NEED TO PUT 'IM IN THE CAR SO FAR IN ADVANCE?
TO MAKE IT LOOK LIKE SUICIDE, RIGHT?
YOU EVEN THOUGHT SO AT FIRST, REMEMBER? BECAUSE HE WAS HOLDING THE STEERING WHEEL.
THE MURDERER KILLED HIM BEFORE DINNER AND PLACED HIM IN THE CAR SO HE'D STIFFEN IN THAT POSITION.
IN OTHER WORDS, THE SUSPECT IS ONE OF YOU WHO LEFT THE ROOM AFTER DINNER.
THEN HOW'D THE CAR SPEED UP?
YOU THINK A DEAD MAN CAN MOVE?
AFTER WAITING FOR THE RIGOR MORTIS TO SET IN, THE MURDERER WENT BACK TO THE GARAGE AFTER DINNER AND SET THE CAR IN MOTION.
A D-DEAD MAN...
...MOVE!?

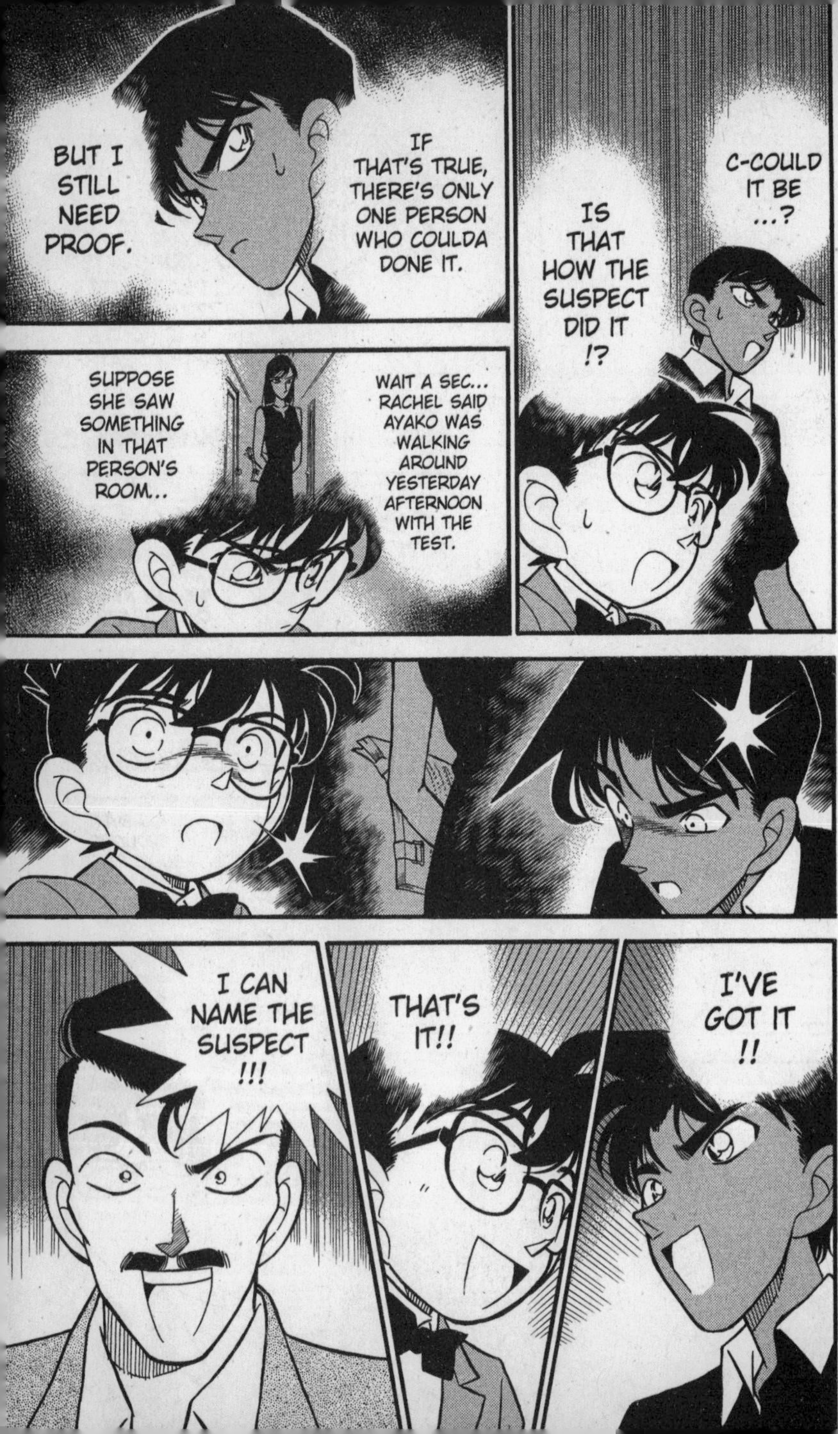

C-COULD IT BE ...?
IS THAT HOW THE SUSPECT DID IT !?
IF THAT'S TRUE, THERE'S ONLY ONE PERSON WHO COULDA DONE IT.
BUT I STILL NEED PROOF.
WAIT A SEC... RACHEL SAID AYAKO WAS WALKING AROUND YESTERDAY AFTERNOON WITH THE TEST.
SUPPOSE SHE SAW SOMETHING IN THAT PERSON'S ROOM...
I'VE GOT IT !!
THAT'S IT!!
I CAN NAME THE SUSPECT !!!

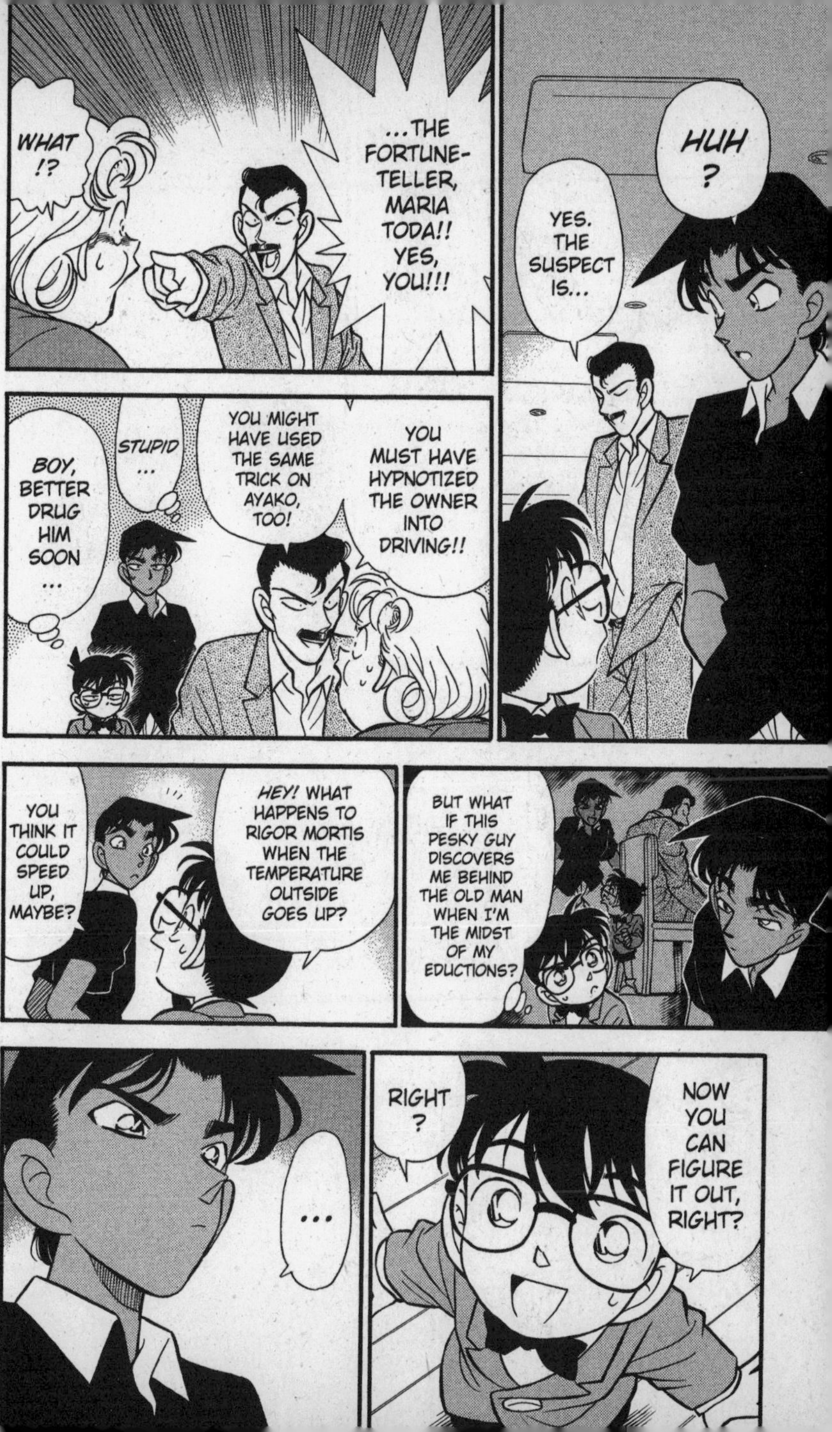

HUH ?
YES. THE SUSPECT IS...
...THE FORTUNE-TELLER, MARIA TODA!! YES, YOU!!!
WHAT !?
YOU MUST HAVE HYPNOTIZED THE OWNER INTO DRIVING!!
YOU MIGHT HAVE USED THE SAME TRICK ON AYAKO, TOO!
STUPID ...
BOY, BETTER DRUG HIM SOON ...
BUT WHAT IF THIS PESKY GUY DISCOVERS ME BEHIND THE OLD MAN WHEN I'M THE MIDST OF MY EDUCTIONS?
HEY! WHAT HAPPENS TO RIGOR MORTIS WHEN THE TEMPERATURE OUTSIDE GOES UP?
YOU THINK IT COULD SPEED UP, MAYBE?
NOW YOU CAN FIGURE IT OUT, RIGHT?
RIGHT ?
...

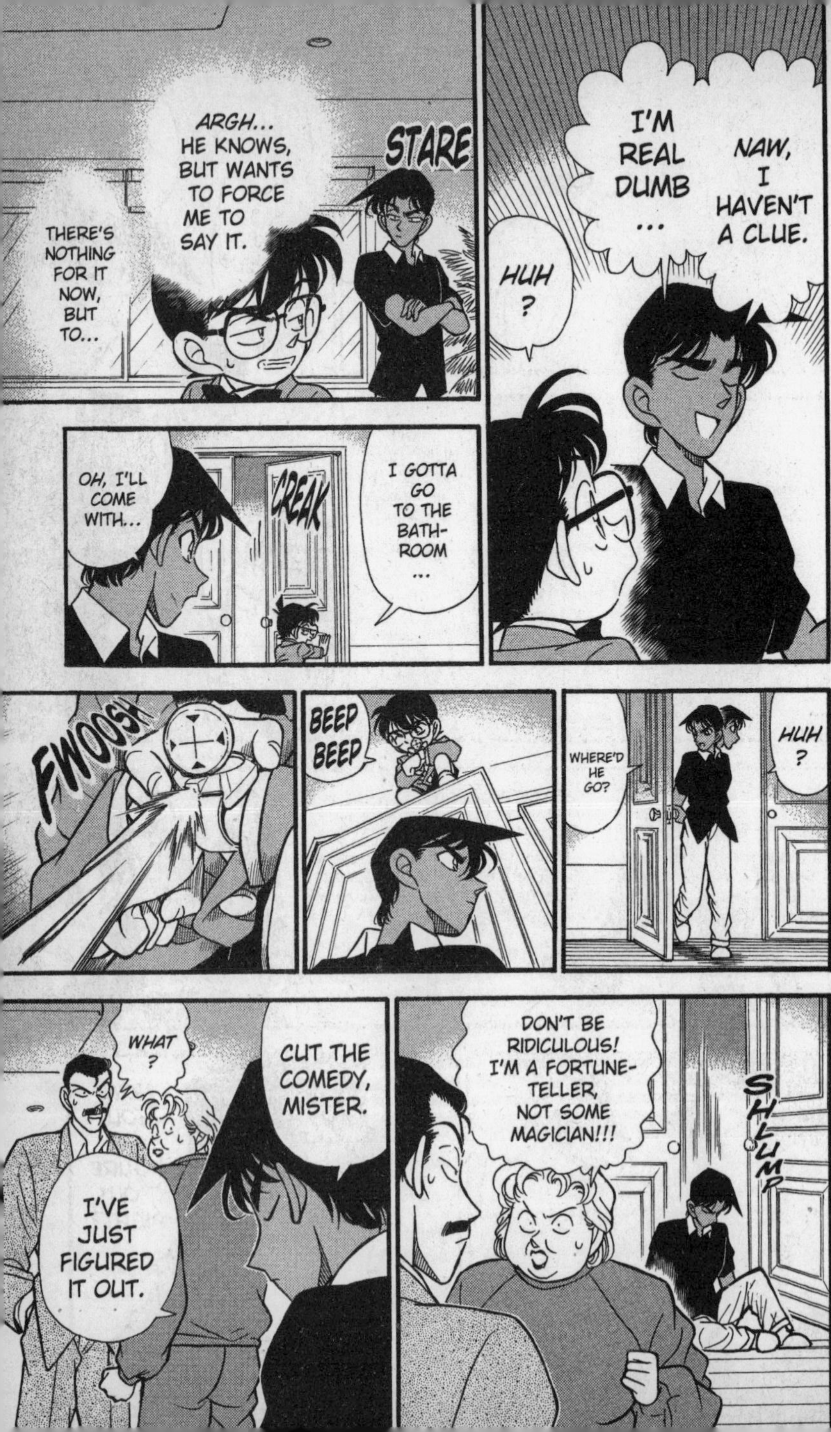

I'M REAL DUMB ...
NAW, I HAVEN'T A CLUE.
HUH ?
STARE
ARGH... HE KNOWS, BUT WANTS TO FORCE ME TO SAY IT.
THERE'S NOTHING FOR IT NOW, BUT TO...
I GOTTA GO TO THE BATH-ROOM ...
CREAK
OH, I'LL COME WITH...
HUH ?
WHERE'D HE GO?
BEEP BEEP
FWOOSH
SHLUMP
DON'T BE RIDICULOUS! I'M A FORTUNE-TELLER, NOT SOME MAGICIAN!!!
CUT THE COMEDY, MISTER.
WHAT ?
I'VE JUST FIGURED IT OUT.

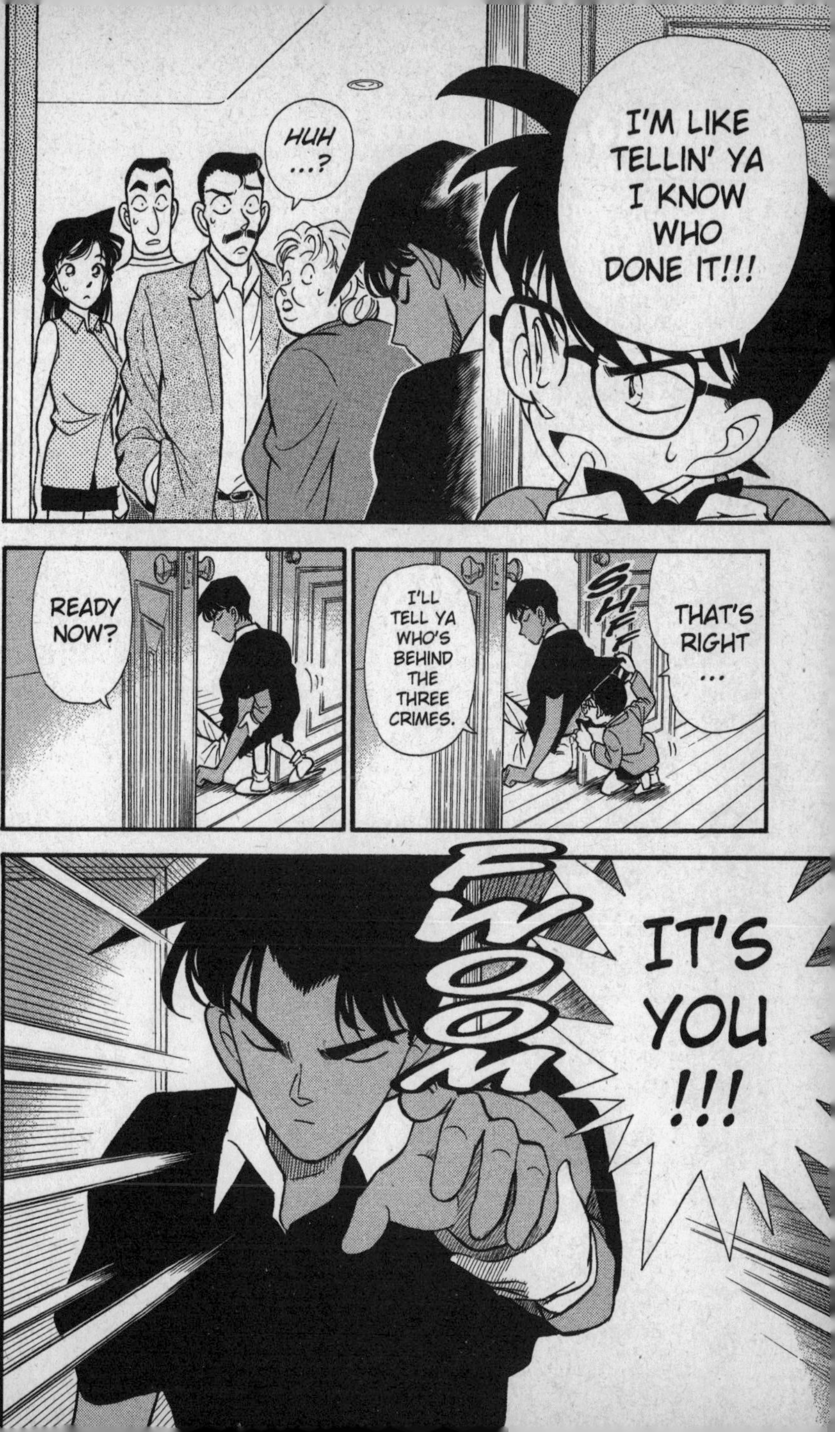
I'M LIKE TELLIN' YA I KNOW WHO DONE IT!!!
HUH ...?
THAT'S RIGHT ...
SHFF
I'LL TELL YA WHO'S BEHIND THE THREE CRIMES.
READY NOW?
IT'S YOU !!!
FWOOM

Hello, Aoyama here.

You can see fireworks from my house so some anime voice actors, directors, and friends came over and we spent a fun summer night together drinking and enjoying the fireworks.

Sigh... If only there were fireworks every day...

That's the kind of stupid stuff I think about as I scribble away at work....(*yawn.*)

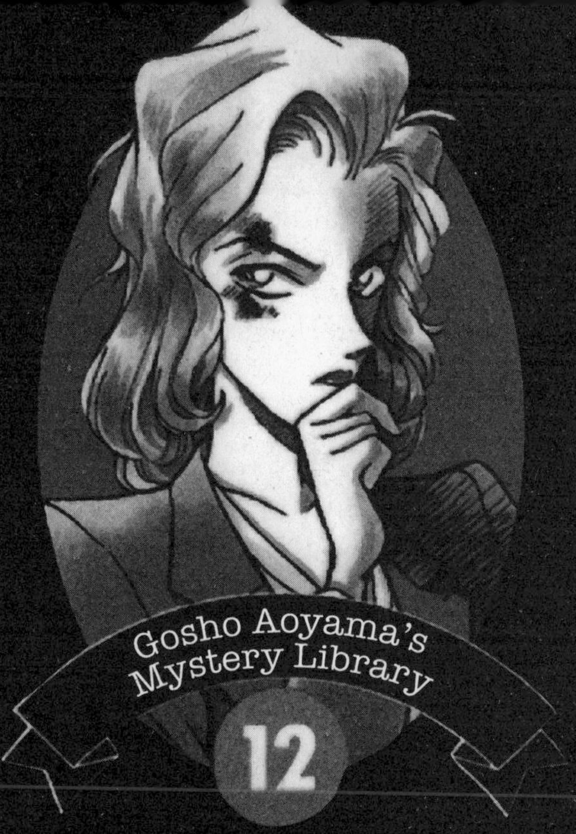
Gosho Aoyama's
Mystery Library
12

V. I. WARSHAWSKI

er name is V. I. Warshawski. She's the tough, hard-boiled, beautiful
male private eye created by author Sara Paretsky. She had a career
; an attorney before opening her own detective agency in Chicago. To
void being treated as a woman, she goes by V.I. instead of her real
ame, Victoria. Once she takes on a case she's the type that has to go
; it full throttle, ending up causing a lot of trouble wherever she goes.
he's an expert in karate, too, which often just makes the situation
ven worse. She's regularly knocked unconscious and has to be car-
ed home with bruises on her face. Thanks to her late father, a cop,
ne's no slouch with a pistol, either. But she's hopeless at keeping her
ome clean and her room is always a big mess. Given how she is, it's
ot likely she'll ever find a boyfriend...but if I said that I'd probably get
hopped by her iron fist. (I recommend *Deadlock.*)

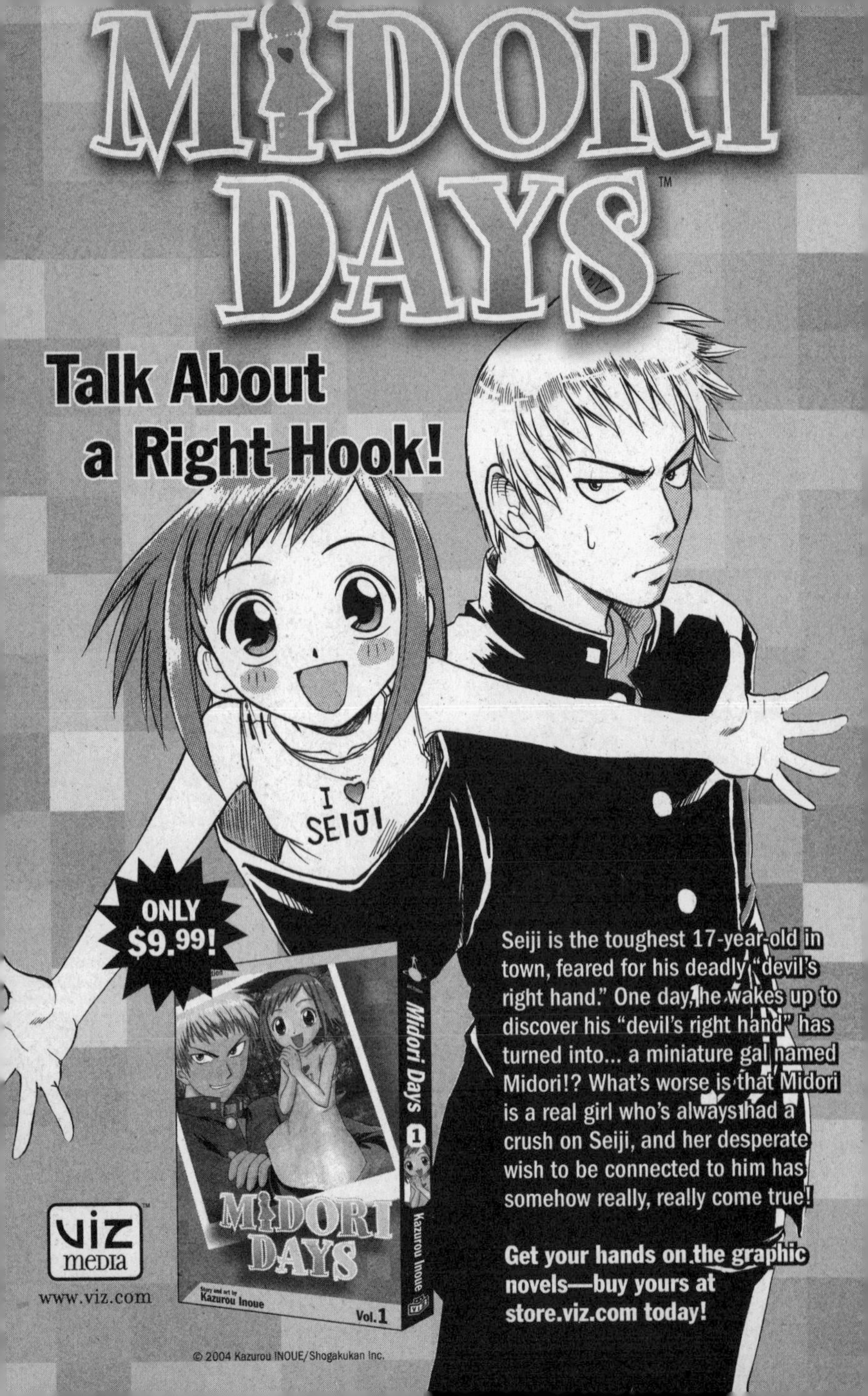

MIDORI DAYS™
Talk About a Right Hook!
I ♥ SEIJI
ONLY $9.99!
Midori Days 1
MIDORI DAYS
Story and art by Kazurou Inoue
Kazurou Inoue
Vol. 1
Seiji is the toughest 17-year-old in town, feared for his deadly "devil's right hand." One day, he wakes up to discover his "devil's right hand" has turned into... a miniature gal named Midori!? What's worse is that Midori is a real girl who's always had a crush on Seiji, and her desperate wish to be connected to him has somehow really, really come true!
Get your hands on the graphic novels—buy yours at store.viz.com today!
viz media
www.viz.com
© 2004 Kazurou INOUE/Shogakukan Inc.

LOVE MANGA?
LET US KNOW WHAT YOU THINK!

OUR MANGA SURVEY IS NOW AVAILABLE ONLINE. PLEASE VISIT: VIZ.COM/MANGASURVEY

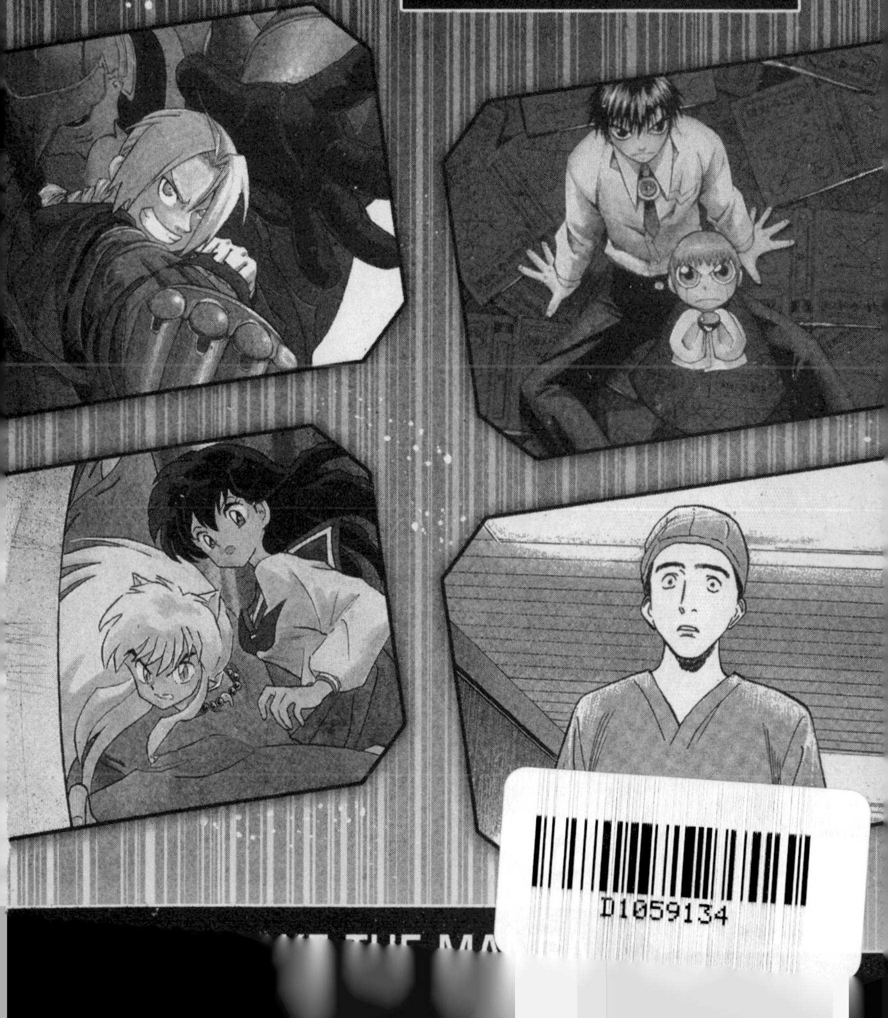